Sociological Theory Beyond the Canon

Syed Farid Alatas • Vineeta Sinha

Sociological Theory Beyond the Canon

palgrave
macmillan

Syed Farid Alatas
Sociology
National University of Singapore
Singapore, Singapore

Vineeta Sinha
Sociology
National University of Singapore
Singapore, Singapore

ISBN 978-1-137-41133-4   ISBN 978-1-137-41134-1 (eBook)
DOI 10.1057/978-1-137-41134-1

Library of Congress Control Number: 2017934880

Cover design and illustration by Oscar Spigolon

Printed on acid-free paper

This Palgrave Macmillan imprint is published by Springer Nature
The registered company is Macmillan Publishers Ltd.
The registered company address is: The Campus, 4 Crinan Street, London, N1 9XW, United Kingdom

To the memories of our late fathers,
Panday Rewati Raman Sinha
&
Syed Hussein Alatas,
whose working, providing and mentoring made us

Acknowledgments

This book has long been in the making. The germ of this idea surfaced in 1998 in the course of our co-teaching an undergraduate module on classical sociological theory, Social Thought and Social Theory, at the Department of Sociology at the National University of Singapore. For many years since then this teaching opportunity provided the testing ground for the ideas and content reflected in the book that has materialized. During the many semesters that we co-taught this course we appreciated and learnt a great deal from the many conversations, disagreements and debates we had had about rethinking social theory and its teaching. One of the results of those discussions was the decision to write a book together that would feature social theory the way we felt it should be presented to students and others interested in social thought. We have been intellectual allies and companions in the journey that led to the writing of this book. Not to be forgotten, of course, are the many cohorts of students whom we have encountered in this module have played a key role as well. Their provocations and interventions have made a crucial difference to the ways in which we have thought about the book. The staunch support from like-minded colleagues as well as from detractors and critics has been very welcome.

Vineeta would like to thank Mamta Sachan Kumar and Shivani Gupta for their help with some of the background research for the chapters she has written and Ravinran Kumaran for his careful proof-reading and editing.

Our families and friends have, as always, provided that peaceful and tranquil atmosphere so needed for the peace of mind to engage in intellectual work. Their enormous and unconditional support continues to sustain us in all our endeavors.

Contents

Introduction: Eurocentrism, Androcentrism and Sociological Theory

Syed Farid Alatas and Vineeta Sinha

The need for another text on social thought and theory must be justified in view of the existing works that have been published and used in sociological theory courses throughout the world. Although many of these texts are well written and useful for students and others desiring initiation to the field of sociological theory, they generally suffer from two important biases that continue to define not just theory but the entire field of sociology. These are the biases of Eurocentrism and Androcentrism. We specifically refer here to the neglect of non-Western sources and female voices in accounts in the formative period of the development of sociological theory. The dominant account of the development of sociological theory would have us believe that it was only Western European and later North American white males in the nineteenth and early twentieth century who thought in a creative and systematic manner about the origins and nature of the emerging modernity of their time.

It should be stressed, however, that it is not our contention that the recognition of these biases requires that Western sociological theory be deleted from sociology curricula in non-Western universities. Rather, we argue from experience, for a fresh approach to teaching classical

© The Author(s) 2017
S.F. Alatas, V. Sinha, *Sociological Theory Beyond the Canon*,
DOI 10.1057/978-1-137-41134-1_1

sociological theory that attunes students in more meaningful and critical ways to the works of Marx, Weber, Durkheim and other representatives of the canon. Ironically, such an approach constitutes a new form of legitimating the classics by revealing their timeless qualities, notwithstanding their various conceptual, methodological and ideological limitations.

This book self-consciously seeks to offer an atypical teaching resource to students of classical sociological theory. Apart from highlighting the biases of Eurocentrism and Androcentrism *and* offering much-needed correctives to them (through highlighting a list of neglected non-Western and women social thinkers), this book also provides an alternative conceptualization of the introductory, historical 'first chapter' in theory textbooks. This typically narrates the origins and history of the discipline's foundations and highlights the various social, political and intellectual forces that led to the rise of sociological thought and theory. Again typically, students are directed to the Enlightenment, the Industrial and French Revolutions, as the backdrop against which a body of social thought emerged. Thus the rise of sociological thought and theory is explained as the cumulative effect of these various social, economic and political forces. Specific historical events and processes that are important in the experience of European modernity are highlighted as being critical to the shaping of sociological theory. The introductory chapter we would write would certainly attend to these same forces but would also ask how these were perceived and experienced outside of a European context. Additionally, it would devote space to a discussion of historical events and processes that are missing in mainstream theory texts, namely the experience of colonization and decolonization. We argue for example that a comprehensive discussion of industrial capitalism in Europe is incomplete without due attention to the phenomenon of colonial capitalism. The proposed text would plug gaps like these and look at the ways in which the industrial revolution in Europe was global and inevitably and inextricably entangled with the colonization of non-Europe. A related dimension would be to detail the broader intellectual milieu within non-European contexts in the eighteenth and nineteenth centuries, periods which are recognized as formative for the rise of sociological thought.

Another critical feature of this book relates to the specific treatment of the 'founding fathers' of sociological theory. We are not arguing that Marx, Weber and Durkheim should not be included in the teaching of classical sociological thought and theorizing. Rather, we are suggesting that there is a need to read their works far more critically and highlight aspects of their writings that have thus far been eclipsed. Thus in reading Marx, we would highlight his views on the Asiatic mode of production alongside his analysis and critique of industrial capitalism just as the Eurocentrism of Weber's writings on comparative sociology of religion would be included alongside his arguments in *The Protestant Ethic*.

Rethinking Social Theory: Critiquing Eurocentrism

No doubt all students of sociology have at some point encountered Marx, Weber and Durkheim as the 'founding fathers' of their discipline. An essential component of sociological training in most universities is the teaching of sociological theory. The latter is seen as the basic grounding for the making of a sociologist. What constitutes sociological theory is generally defined as the particular writings of a set of European scholars, names with which most social scientists are familiar. Starting from a rather large pool, some central figures have emerged and are consistently viewed as forefathers of sociology. There is further a 'universal' acceptance that anyone, anywhere who wants to study sociology must 'know' the writings of Marx, Weber and Durkheim. Courses in sociological theory and social thought throughout the world tend to restrict themselves to discussions and expositions of their works and of some other Western scholars. Furthermore, in mainstream discourse, the social sciences are defined and accepted as being of 'Western' origin. This is institutionalized as common wisdom not just in Western academic circles but also in the non-West. This is not to say that there are no scholars who problematize the taken-for-granted definition of the social sciences as 'Western' disciplines.[1]

---

[1] See Alatas 2006 and Sinha 1997.

It is rather surprising that classical sociological theory courses have been taught in a number of Asian countries without due recognition of the historical context and cultural practices of the students who enrol in these courses. What is often discussed is the context of the rise of sociological theories in Europe, dealing with issues that may bear little historical relevance or cultural meaning to the students. Sociological theory is said to have emerged as a result of communities of thinkers reflecting upon various social forces and problems, such as political revolutions, the industrial revolution and the rise of capitalism, urbanization and the growth of science (Ritzer 1983: 6–8). A glance at the course outlines of undergraduate sociological theory courses in a number of universities in Asia and Africa would show that theory is taught in much the same way as it is offered in British or North American universities. In general, we discern two fundamental problems with such syllabi.

One is that non-Western founders or precursors of social thought and social theory are generally left out of the course outlines. The other is that classical sociological theory is not contextualized in a manner that establishes a relevant reference point for the students. While it is true that the European Enlightenment, the transition from feudalism to capitalism, and democratization in Europe and so on, form the relevant context within which the emergence of sociological theory can be understood, the context of European colonial expansion and Eurocentrism is equally relevant to both Euroamerican and Asian or African. Bringing in colonialism is an example of how classical sociological theory can be further contextualized to accord with the historical background of students.

What we view as a crucial, additional context for the rise of sociological theory, that is the historical fact of European political and cultural domination from the fifteenth century onwards, is seldom given any space, let alone equal weight in conventional teaching of classical theory. Furthermore, such a context suggests topics and readings from the classics that are not normally assigned in a course on classical sociological theory. As is well known, this domination resulted, among other things, in the implantation of European social sciences in non-European societies, whether these societies were colonized by the

Europeans or not (Dube 1984; Karim 1984; Kyi 1984; Rana 1984). Furthermore and more importantly, it was in the period of European colonial domination that the European classical theorists wrote not only about their own societies but the 'Orient' as well. Often, their analysis and reflections on non-Western societies were as much statements on the 'Occident' as they were on the 'Orient'. For example, Marx's discourse on India served to confirm the uniqueness of Europe as far as its propensity for capitalist development was concerned.

This book formulates an alternative way of teaching sociological theory, dealing with biases that must be corrected in any context. It is important to emphasize that this alternative conceptualization was not designed to replace Marx, Weber and Durkheim. Using these scholars as our starting point, we aim to offer a way of teaching the sociological canon that incorporates our theoretical concerns with Eurocentrism.

Bearing in mind the 'Western' origins of writings that are seen to constitute the corpus of sociological theory, this book begins with the theme of Eurocentrism as it is felt that it provides a crucial point of orientation. A cautionary word on our usage of the term 'Eurocentrism' is necessary. As we understand the term, it signifies far more than its literal and common-place meaning 'Europe-centredness'. We hold that Eurocentrism connotes a particular position, a perspective, a way of seeing *and* not-seeing that is rooted in a number of problematic claims and assumptions. We also did not want to essentialize ourselves by assigning to the three theorists the same, generalized usage of the label 'Eurocentrism'. In fact, we quite consciously strived to establish the specific and different ways in which aspects of the theories under consideration might be Eurocentric or not. We are further aware that the recognition of Eurocentrism in the writings of Marx, Weber and Durkheim is neither a surprise nor a recent discovery. Yet despite the datedness of this theme in the social sciences, the critique of Eurocentrism has not meaningfully reshaped or restructured the ways in which we theorize the emergence of the classical sociological canon. So despite 'knowing' that some aspects of Marx's, Weber's and Durkheim's writings are 'Eurocentric' and expectedly so, the issue of how this impacts our contemporary reading of their works remains largely unaddressed and untheorized.

This book adopts the view that a creative approach to sociological theory would be one which incorporates the following three inter-related objectives: (a) to generate consciousness of 'Eurocentrism' as a theme and context that informs classical sociological theory; (b) to separate out the Eurocentric from the universalistic aspects of classical theory; and (c) to introduce non-Western social thinkers with the aim of universalizing the canon. The need to reorient the teaching of sociological theory is held to be all the more important because we note that Eurocentrism is not only found in European scholarship, but has affected the development of the social sciences in non-Western societies in a number of ways:

(i) The lack of knowledge of our own histories as evidenced in textbooks. In textbooks used in Asia and Africa, there tends to be less information on these parts of the world because the textbooks are invariably written in the United States or the United Kingdom. For example, we know more about the daily life of the European premodern family than that of our own. This is because sociology arose in the context of the transition from feudalism to capitalism and, therefore, the European historical context is the defining one. Normal development is defined as a move from feudalism to capitalism, therefore, that is the normal thing to study. The object of study is defined by this bias of normal development. In our own societies, while the priority is to study modern capitalist societies as well, the problem is that we begin with European precapitalist societies and draw attention to our own precapitalist societies in order to show that they constituted obstacles to modernization.

(ii) Through Eurocentrism, images of our society are constructed which we come to regard as real until Eurocentric scholarship yields alternative images which may be equally Eurocentric.

(iii) The lack of original theorizing. Because of the deluge of works on theory, methodology and empirical research arising mainly from North America and Europe, there has been much consumption of imported theories, techniques and research agendas.

To the extent that this book is concerned with the Western canon, its objective is to ask how we should read theorists such as Marx, Weber or Durkheim given the Eurocentrism of the 'Western' social sciences.

Thus, the rethinking of sociological theory entails emphasizing those aspects of their works that demonstrate their Eurocentrism. Examples would be Marx's theory of the Asiatic mode of production or Weber's writings on capitalism in the context of non-Western religions.

Introducing Non-Western Social Thought

A course on social theory that corrects the Eurocentric bias should not only critically deal with Western thinkers that make up the canon. It should also provide a focus on non-Western thinkers. A glance at the sociological curriculum of many universities would certainly expose the Eurocentrism that characterizes the way the history of social thought and sociological theory are taught. Such courses usually discuss theorists such as Montesquieu, Vico, Comte, Spencer, Marx, Weber, Durkheim, Simmel, Toennies, Sombart, Mannheim, Pareto, Sumner, Ward, Small and others. The traits of Eurocentrism that underlie such courses include the subject/object dichotomy, the dominance of European categories and concepts and the representation of Europeans as the sole originators of ideas. Much of the thinking on sociological theory or history of social thought and theory is informed by the subject/object dichotomy. It can be seen to be a dominant, if unarticulated principle that determines which authors are treated. In most sociological theory textbook or works on the history of social thought, Europeans are the knowing subjects, that is those who do the thinking and writing. Invariably, non-Europeans do appear in these writings, but usually as the subject matter, as objects of study of the European knowing subjects. It is extremely rare to find a non-Western thinker featured as a source of sociological theories and concepts. Indeed, the impression that is given is that there were no thinkers in Asia and Africa contemporaneous with Europeans such as Marx, Weber and Durkheim who thought systematically about the process of development and modernization that took place in their societies.

The failure to mention non-European scholars is particularly scandalous when it is noted that there were instances when such thinkers had an impact on the development of sociology. For example, Ibn Khaldun is sometimes referred to in histories of sociology but is rarely discussed as a source of relevant sociological theories and ideas, although he is said to have influenced some nineteenth- and early twentieth-century European thinkers. A major objective of this book, therefore, is to introduce to the sociological canon what we consider to be non-Western founders of social thought and theory such as José Rizal (Philippines, 1861–1896), Benoy Kumar Sarkar (India, 1887–1949) and others.

Rethinking Sociological Theory: Critiquing Androcentrism

The recorded history of Sociology and sociological theory is steeped in Androcentrism such that it remembers, lists, records and reproduces contributions by male scholars.[2] Harriet Martineau, Florence Nightingale Harriet Taylor Mill and Pandita Ramabai are but some names absent from a long list of pioneering women social thinkers. They were present before the birth of the formalized discipline of Sociology and instrumental in contributing to the emergence of a new science of society. We know that this list is a long one, by now having been provided firm evidence of numerous women thinkers and theorists (Western and non-Western) who have been routinely left out, remain unmentioned and marginalized in standard narratives of Sociology's history.[3] This non-presence and non-recognition of women in the discipline's archives has been received with vivid, memorable and blunt imagery from critics. A. March speaks of this as 'female invisibility', D. E. Smith evokes the notion of 'eclipsing' to signal the marginalization of women and female perspectives, while L. McDonald sees these female social thinkers and methodologists as 'missing persons' in the historiography of the social sciences.

Collectively, this scholarship has highlighted what we denote as the 'first wave of forgetting,' that is the omission of women social thinkers,

---

[2] Deegan 1991, Hoecker-Drysdale 1992, Hill 1989, March 1982, McDonald 1993.
[3] Deegan 1991, McDonald 1993.

theorists and methodologists from characteristic accounts of Sociology and its origins, particularly as reflected in surveys of the discipline's founders and pioneers, carried in introductory and advanced sociology textbooks, encyclopaedias, manuals and anthologies. This roughly spans the decades of the 1970s and into the early 1980s, evident in the standard commentaries in Sociology textbooks and in course curricula pertaining to the beginnings of Sociology, in introductory courses as well as the more advanced courses on social thought and social theory. Both the reasons for such neglect as well as its attendant consequences are numerous and well documented by now. The founders and pioneers of Sociology are presented to students as 'great men of ideas,' 'founding fathers' and 'the great masters', producing a gendered and male-d accounts of Sociology's history and its establishment. The singular notice of male contributions conveys a limited, selective and distorted picture, and does not acknowledge the variety of actors (including the men and women thinkers and theorists) and the roles they played in the formulation and founding of Sociology.

Irving Zeitlin's *Ideology and the Development of Sociological Theory* (1997, 6th ed.) carries a chapter on Harriet Martineau, Mary Wollstonecraft and Harriet Taylor Mill. Osborne and Van Loon's *Sociology for Beginners* (1996) mentions Martineau thus: 'Anticipating much later feminist critique of sociology's masculine bias and approach, Harriet Martineau (1802–1876) published a work that had little impact at the time but became recognised as an interesting comparative analysis of social structure.' Referring to the book *How to Observe Morals and Manners*, he adds, 'It was an early instance of what we might now call cultural studies, an important branch of sociology' (ibid. 29). In Ritzer and Goodman's *Sociological Theory* (2003),[4] an authoritative and popular book with Sociology students, Harriet Martineau is mentioned three times in the entire book, twice in relation to the 'work of a number of women in or associated with the field'[5] and once in relation to Comte's work, 'part of which had been translated into English in the

---

[4] Ritzer and Goodman 2003.
[5] Ritzer and Goodman 2003, 9.

1850s by Harriet Martineau'.[6] The fourth edition of Ritzer and Goodman's *Classical Sociological Theory* (2004)[7] fares better in including an entire chapter on 'Early women sociologists and classical theory: 1830–1930', contributed by P. M. Lengermann and J. Niebrugge-Brantley Hill.[8] Ritzer and Goodman do acknowledge and list a number of women who had an 'impact on the development of sociology'[9] and admit further the hand of gender discrimination, gender politics and patriarchal forms of domination in the subsequent marginalization of women's contributions to the field of sociological studies thus, '[t]heir creations were over time, pushed to the periphery of the profession, annexed or discounted or written out of sociology's public record by the men who were organizing sociology as a professional power base'.[10]

While women like Harriet Martineau and Harriet Taylor Mill are somewhat visible in Sociology textbooks, the contributions of male and female thinkers continue to be presented here in separate and parallel streams. For example, in texts by Zeitlin and Ritzer & Goodman, separate chapters are devoted to Martineau, Comte and Durkheim, with little attempt to demonstrate intellectual interaction, influence and contact amongst the different players. Sections that discuss Comte's *The Positive Philosophy* make little or no reference to the role played by Martineau in translating, and thus introducing, Comte's ideas to English reading sociologists. Durkheim's pioneering contribution is noted with the description of his *The Rules of Sociological Method* as sociology's 'first' methodological classic, without acknowledging that Martineau's text on methodology predates Durkheim's book by some six decades. A rare recent example is, however, found in the Reader's Guide to the Social Sciences,[11] edited by Jonathan Michie, who

---

[6] Ritzer and Goodman 2004, 33.

[7] George Ritzer and Douglas J. Goodman, *Classical Sociological Theory* (New York: McGraw-Hill, 2004).

[8] Hill 1998.

[9] George Ritzer and Douglas J. Goodman, *Sociological Theory*, 2003, 9.

[10] Ritzer and Goodman, *Sociological Theory*, 2003, 9.

[11] Jonathan Michie, *The Reader's Guide to the Social Sciences*, 1 (London: New York: Routledge, 2001).

articulates Comte and Martineau's intellectual encounter and its historical significance for sociologists thus:

> Comte's writings would have reached an English-speaking audience far later if it had not been for the labours of Harriet Martineau. She was the first person to translate and condense *The Positive Philosophy* into English. Although there have been recent efforts to re-establish her role as a premier 'Comtean' of the 19th century, feminists have claimed that her contribution to the development of sociology has been underestimated, especially in the English-speaking world.[12]

A related problem is that when mentioned, they are not typically invoked in an independent capacity, but comparatively and with reference[13] to other thinkers. This is certainly true of Martineau's comparisons with Tocqueville and Emile Durkheim.[14] Teaching Martineau, Nightingale and Ramabai alongside recognized classical sociological thinkers will no doubt be productive in demonstrating the alignments, parallels, divergences and cross-conversations between their respective theories. While such contrasts are illuminating, we agree with James Terry that 'women like Martineau should be approached independently'.[15] We argue for an *integrated* account of these various endeavours, which collectively culminated in the formalized discipline of Sociology.

Introducing Women Thinkers

Just as a course on social theory that corrects the Eurocentric bias should not only critically deal with Western thinkers that make up the canon but also discuss non-Western thinkers, so should the critique of

---

[12] Michie, *The Reader's Guide*, 76.

[13] This point is made by Hill 2002, Kandal. Terry. *The woman question in classical sociological theory*. Miami: Florida University Press. 1988., Nisbet 1988.

[14] Lengermann and Niebrugge-Brantley 2002 and Reinharz 1989.

[15] Terry 1983.

Androcentrism introduce female founders of sociology to students of sociology. In 1994, Lynn McDonald notes with appreciation the redis-covery and restoration of women's contributions in the social sciences but poses this disturbing question, 'Welcome as the recovery of this lost or ignored material is, the question naturally arises as to whether or not it will all again disappear.'[16] While the neglect of pioneering women thinkers in the story of sociology's founding has been an important issue to highlight and critique, it is also timely to shift the contours of the discourse beyond this notice.

We suggest several concrete strategies for achieving this in practice. In this regard, a primary objective of this book is to introduce the social thought and method of inquiry of three women thinkers – Harriet Martineau (1802–1876), Florence Nightingale (1820–1910), and Pandita Ramabai Saraswati (1858–1922). It is noteworthy that while these women remained outside and/or on the margins of the formal academia, they articulated and practiced their views on the possibility of 'Sociology,' 'moral sciences' and the 'social sciences'. A second crucial strategy is to engage substantively and theoretically with the primary writings of women thinkers (non-Western and Western) as researchers and educators. Thirdly, it is important to demonstrate and abstract sociological insight and evidence of theorizing in their corpus of writings.

The failure to notice the contributions of women thinkers is possible because not only are they absent from the historiography of the disci-pline, they also do not feature in too many under-graduate or post-graduate sociology course syllabi and curricula. There is a crucial gap between research on women thinkers and the teaching of sociology's pioneering figures in mainstream undergraduate curriculum. By now there is a wealth of published and on-going research about women thinkers from different socio-cultural contexts. However, this material has not entered mainstream sociological discourse and practice in insti-tutional settings. Hence the continued location of women thinkers on the periphery, if not outside the discipline. This is not just a function of

---

[16] McDonald 1994, 239.

marginalizing women thinkers but also the vast scholarship *about them* that is currently available.

Social Thought and Social Theory

Social thought differs from social theory in the sense that it is less formal and less systematically expressed. It also contains a great deal of reflection on experiences, opinions, assessments, valuations and so on. In other words, it includes elements that are not couched in terms of formal definitions, concepts and theories. This does not make social thought less important than social theory. In fact, social thought may be the basis of a more formal and systematic construction, that is, social theory. The distinction between social thought and social theory is important in view of the selection of thinkers presented in this volume. Thinkers like Ibn Khaldun, Marx, Weber, Abd Durkheim are clearly theorists. The same may not be said for Ramabai, Nightingale and Rizal. While these thinkers did write about broad ranging social issues, they were far less systematic in their approach than the theorists. Nevertheless, they are deemed important for having provided original contributions to our understanding of modern society. Furthermore, it can also be said that their works provide the basis of more systematic theorizing for those who have the inclination to engage in concept formation and theory building.

One important point to note about the ideas of the thinkers discussed in this volume is the common theme of freedom that underlies their work, regardless of whether their writings are thorough-going social theory or the less systematic social thought. The Western tradition of classical sociological theory addressed the issue of the human condition under the conditions of modernity. The works of many social theorists, along with psychologists, philosophers, poets and novelists and other artists were informed by the recognition of the failure of the Enlightenment to make good on its promise to deliver freedom through the application of reason and scientific inquiry. Much of classical social theory dealt with the negative side of modern civilization and emphasized the enslavement of humans or the loss of freedom.

This was seen by each theorist to have taken different forms. For Marx it was alienation, the lack of freedom to develop human potential. For Weber, it was enslavement in the iron cage of rationality, while for Durkheim anomie or the enslavement to desire. In the case of Rizal, the theme of enslavement was related to colonialism as that was the context in which he wrote. Martineau valued the freedom to think and act autonomously, the right to work, political emancipation and empowerment and the capacity to challenge received, customary wisdom. Ramabai was a social thinker and reformer who advocated freedom of thought and action so that equality and progress could be achieved for Hindu women. Her ideas reveal a conception of 'freedom' as the desire to achieve self-reliance, self-determination, independence and autonomy through knowledge, industry and dedication and, above all, exercising reason. Nightingale wanted women to exercise freedom of thought, and be self-determined actors, have the right to be educated and expand their horizons beyond the narrow confines of domesticity and the socially acceptable roles of wives, daughters and mothers. Sarkar's political and sociological theorizing were embedded in a conception of rugged individualism, human agency and activism. Like Marx, Sarkar too conceived of individuals as history-making agents. In this context, positioning Marx's theory of human nature alongside Sarkar's view of individuals as creative, inventive, moral and rational beings who desired to be self-autonomous and self-determining is illuminating. Ibn Khaldun, on the other hand, lived in the premodern period centuries before Martineau, Marx and the others. Yet, we may also identify in his work the theme of enslavement the absence of freedom or enslavement as well. For Ibn Khaldun, this is related to the role of luxury in state formation. That it is possible to identify a common theme underlying the works of all out theorists, whether male or female, Western or Asian, modern or premodern, is testimony to the universality of social theory, whatever its civilizational source may be.

Looking at sociological theory through the lens of Eurocentrism and Androcentrism allows us to make larger points. In drawing attention to neglected thinkers – male and female, Western and non-Western – we argue that the tapestry of contributions to social thought and theorizing is multifaceted; a pulsating, synergized and complex history of the discipline would emerge in the recognition of diverse inputs by thinkers from different cultural contexts. The aim is to expand the playing field rather than restrict it. Thus we stand with Hill when he says that: 'Our discipline grows stronger from inclusion and dialogue, not from exclusion and silence.'[17] Furthermore, we do have reservations about generating yet another 'must read' list of thinkers. The objective is more about opening the door to a serious consideration of a larger pool of potential contributors to sociological theorizing *in addition* to existing names. There are no doubt numerous others, men and women, located in different societal contexts – European and non-European – across timeframes whose contributions and insights for sociological theorizing have for too long gone unnoticed in narrating a history of sociological theory. It is time this lack of attention was problematized and *acted upon* by its practitioners.

References

Alatas, Syed Farid. *Alternative Discourses in Asian Social Science: Responses to Eurocentrism*. New Delhi: Sage Publications, 2006.

Deegan, Mary Jo. *Women in Sociology: A Bio-Bibliographical Sourcebook*. New York: Greenwood, 1991.

Dube, S.C. 'India'. In *Social Sciences in Asia and the Pacific*, 229–248. Paris: UNESCO, 1984.

Hill, Michael R. 'Empiricism and Reason in Harriet Martineau's Sociology'. Vols. xv–lx, in *How to Observe Morals and Manners*, edited by Harriet Martineau, News Brunswick, New Jersey: Transaction Books, 1989.

Hill, Michael R. 'Martineau in Current Introductory Textbooks: An Empirical Survey'. *The Harriet Martineau Sociological Society Newsletter*, no. 4 (Spring 1998): 4–5.

Hill, Michael R. 'Empiricism and Reason in Harriet Martineau's Sociology'. In *Martineau, How to Observe Morals and Manners*, xv–lx. New Brunswick: Rutgers University Press, 2002.

---

[17] Hill 2002, 191.

Hoecker-Drysdale, Susan. *Harriet Martineau: First Woman Sociologist*. Oxford: Berg, 1992.

Karim, A.K. Nazmul. 'Bangladesh'. In *Social Sciences in Asia and the Pacific*, edited by UNESCO, 79–92. Paris: UNESCO, 1984.

Kyi, Khin Maung. 'Burma'. In *Social Sciences in Asia and the Pacific*, edited by UNESCO, 93–141. Paris: UNESCO, 1984.

March, Artemis. 'Female Invisibility and in Androcentric Sociological Theory'. *Insurgent Sociologist* IX, no. 2 (1982): 99–107.

McDonald, Lynn. *The Early Origins of the Social Sciences*. Montreal; Buffalo: McGill-Queen's University Press, 1993.

McDonald, Lynn. *The Women Founders of the Social Sciences*. Ottawa, Canada: Carleton University Press, 1994.

Niebrugge-Brantley, Jill, and Patricia Lengermann. 'Back to the Future: Settlement Sociology'. *The American Sociologist* 33, no. 3 (2002): 5–20.

Nisbet, Robert. 'Tocquville's Ideal Types'. In *Reconsidering Tocquvelli's Democracy in America*, edited by S. Abraham Eisentadt, New Brunswick, NJ: Rutgers University Press, 1988.

Osborne, Richard and Borin Van Loon. *Sociology for Beginners*. Cambridge: Icon, 1996.

Rana, Ratna S.J.B. 'Nepal'. In *Social Sciences in Asia and the Pacific*, edited by UNESCO, 354–373. Paris: UNESCO, 1984.

Reinharz, Shulamit. 'Teaching the History of Women in Sociology: Or Dorothy Swaine Thomas, Wasn't She the Woman Married to William I?' *The American Sociologist* 20, no. 1 (1989): 87–94.

Ritzer, George. *Sociological Theory*. New York: Alfred A Knopf, 1983.

Ritzer, George, and Douglas J. Goodman. *Sociological Theory* (Sixth edn.). McGraw-Hill, 2003.

Ritzer, George, and Douglas J Goodman, eds. *Sociological Theory*. Boston: McGraw-Hill, 2004.

Sinha, Vineeta. 'Reconceptualising the Social Sciences in Non-Western Settings: Challenges and Dilemmas'. *Southeast Asian Journal of Social Science* 25, no. 1 (1997): 167–182.

Terry, James L. 'Bringing Women…A Modest Proposal.' *Teaching Sociology* 10, no. 2 (1983): 251–261.

Zeitlin, I.M. *Ideology and Development of Sociological Theory* (Sixth edn.). New Jersey: Prentice Hall, 1997.

Ibn Khaldun (1332–1406)

Syed Farid Alatas

The Life and Times of Ibn Khaldun

Wal al-Dn 'Abd al-Rahman Ibn Muhammad Ibn Khaldun al-Tunisi al-Hadhrami (732–808 A.H./1332–1406 A.D.) is highly recognized by scholars, Muslims and non-Muslims alike, as a progenitor of sociology. He is arguably the most renowned among Muslims scholars, in both the Islamic and Western world in the field of social sciences.

Ibn Khaldun's most distinguished work, and the one that is relevant to the modern discipline of sociology, the *Muqaddimah*, constitutes a part of his grand study, the *Kitab al-'Ibar wa Diwan al-Mubtada' wa l-Khabar fi Ayyam al-'Arab wa l-'Ajam wa l-Barbar* (*Book of Examples and the Collection of Origins of the History of the Arabs and Berbers*), a voluminous empirical study on the history of the Arabs and Berbers. The *Muqaddimah* or *Prolegomenon* was authored as the introduction to the *Kitab al-'Ibar*. Ibn Khaldun understood the *Muqaddimah* to be the exposition of the elemental causes and inner meaning of that history, while the *Kitab al-'Ibar* was the descriptive part of his history. It is the study of the causes and inner meaning of history that Ibn Khaldun referred to as *'ilm al-ijtima' al-insani* (the science of human society). The

© The Author(s) 2017
S.F. Alatas, V. Sinha, *Sociological Theory Beyond the Canon*,
DOI 10.1057/978-1-137-41134-1_2

Kitab al-'Ibar consists of three books, the *Muqaddimah* or *Prolegomenon* comprising Book One.

An Outline of Ibn Khaldun's Sociological Theory

It was probably his term in politics, his first-hand experience of the uncertainties and inconsistent nature of political life and his perceptions of the dubious relationship between rulers and tribes that led Ibn Khaldun to probe into the causes of historical events. The political economic conundrums of Ibn Khaldun's century, which he thought was of critical proportions, was stated by him as requiring methodical treatment.[1] This methodical treatment, however, required an understanding of not just political issues but, rather, the fundamental structure of historical change. Such an understanding of history, however, was not provided for an existing scholarship. Ibn Khaldun states in the foreword to the *Muqaddimah* that the field of history merely deals with the surface phenomena (*zahir*) of history, if all it does is to provide information about political events and facts about dynasties. This should be distinguished from the inner meaning (*batin*) of history which is arrived at through 'speculation and an attempt to get at the truth, subtle explanation of the causes and origins of existing things, and deep knowledge of the how and why of events'.[2] Ibn Khaldun raised the problem of truth and the need to arrive at the 'subtle explanation of the causes and origins of existing things, and deep knowledge of the how and why of events' because of what he perceived to be the problems of existing historical works.

For Ibn Khaldun, existing historical reports were inflicted with stories of the absurd. These could only be corrected by applying knowledge of the nature of society to such reports. In other words, faulty historical reports could only be rectified by a science that distinguishes fact from

---

[1] Ibn Khaldûn, *Ibn Khaldun: The Muqadimmah*, vol. 1, 64.
[2] Ibn Khaldûn, *Ibn Khaldun: The Muqadimmah*, vol. 1, 6.

error or truth from falsehood on the grounds of their possibility (*imkan*) or absurdity (*istihalah*). This is the science of human society.

> We must distinguish the conditions that attach themselves to the essence of civilization as required by its very nature; the things that are accidental (to civilization) and cannot be counted on; and the things that cannot possibly attach themselves to it. If we do that, we shall have a normative method for distinguishing right from wrong and truth from falsehood in historical information by means of a logical demonstration that admits of no doubts. Then whenever we hear about certain conditions occurring in civilization, we shall know what to accept and what to declare spurious. We shall have a sound yardstick with the help of which historians may find the path of truth and correctness where their reports are concerned.[3]

What Ibn Khaldun is stating here is that the scholar had to test for the probity of report itself, he had to ascertain if it was possible that the reported event could have actually happened. His new science established a theory of society that enabled the scholar to test a report for its probity. Ibn Khaldun gave the example of discussions in historical works concerning the Alid descent of Idris bin Idris. It was suggested that Idris was a product of an adulterous relationship between his mother and one Rashid. For Ibn Khaldun, the fact that Idris' parents lived among the Berber nomads made it practically impossible for illicit relations to take place without people knowing about them. Knowledge of the nature of desert society would lead to the conclusion that it was highly unlikely that Idris bin Idris could have hidden his true parentage from society. The nature of desert society was such that it was unlikely that an adulterous relationship could take place without the community coming to know about it.[4]

What was needed to correct the errors of history was an approach that examined the probity of historical report, the theories and concepts of which form the basis of a new science of society. Only knowledge of the nature of society can result in a proper approach to history as it was only

---

[3] Ibn Khaldûn, *Ibn Khaldun: The Muqadimmah*, vol. 1, 77.
[4] Ibn Khaldûn, *Ibn Khaldun: The Muqadimmah*, vol. 1, 47–8.

such knowledge that would enable the scholar to reject the impossible and absurd and, thereby, distinguish truth from falsehood. Ibn Khaldun believed that such knowledge constituted an original science.

> In fact, I have not come across a discussion along these lines by anyone. I do not know if this is because people have been unaware of it, but there is no reason to suspect them (of having been unaware of it). Perhaps they have written exhaustively on this topic, and their work did not reach us. There are many sciences. There have been numerous sages among the nations of mankind. The knowledge that has not come down to us is larger than the knowledge that has. Where are the sciences of the Persians that 'Umar ordered wiped out at the time of the conquest! Where are the sciences of the Chaldaeans, the Syrians, and the Babylonians, and the scholarly products and results that were theirs! Where are the sciences of the Copts, their predecessors! The sciences of only one nation, the Greek, have come down to us, because they were translated through al-Ma'mun's efforts'.[5]

The *Muqaddimah* presented this new science and elaborated on the various factors of human society that affect the way in which human society is organized. The main factors discussed by Ibn Khaldun are the modes of making a living or occupation, social cohesion, authority and the state, and the sciences and crafts. In Ibn Khaldun's time and environment, two types of societies were known, that is nomadic society (*'umran badawi*) and sedentary society (*'umran hadhrari*). The former is found in outlying regions and mountains, in pastureland, in wasteland regions and on the fringes of deserts, while the latter refers to cities, towns, villages and small communities.[6] It is these factors of society that constitute Ibn Khaldun's new science.

The *Muqaddimah* attempts to yield explanations of the causes and origins of those facts. It attempts to theorize the surface aspects (*zahir*) of history, yielding knowledge of the inner dimensions (*batin*) of history. The *Muqaddimah* is the first book of the *Kitab al-'Ibar*, which comprises

---

[5] Ibn Khaldûn, *Ibn Khaldun: The Muqadimmah*, vol. 1, 78.
[6] Ibn Khaldûn, *Ibn Khaldun: The Muqadimmah*, vol. 1, 84–5.

three books. Books Two and Three discuss selected aspects of the history of the Arabs, Israelites, Persians, Greeks, Byzantines, Turks and Berbers. Meticulously dealing with such empirical topics as covered in the Books Two and Three, however, requires what El-Azmeh calls a master science,[7] or what Ibn Khaldun called the science of human society.

Ibn Khaldun's perspective was a positive and not normative one, concerned with what is rather than what should be.[8] In this respect, he moved beyond the prevailing writings on the state and society that preceded him. The traditional method of distinguishing between right and wrong in historical studies, which depended on appraising the credibility of sources, the character of transmitters of information and so on, was deemed by Ibn Khaldun as inadequate. Instead, he regarded it necessary to assess the innate possibility or incongruity of reported historical facts and events by examining the nature of human society.

The *Muqaddimah*, therefore, was written in order to introduce a better method for the study of history, that is the method that would enable scholars to eschew producing false narratives that contained manifold errors and were informed by baseless assumptions. At the empirical and substantive levels, Ibn Khaldun's concerns were with the macro issue of the rise and decline of dynasties and states, but he suggested that dealing with this sufficiently necessitated an understanding of the nature of society. His approach was to study the fundamental elements of society such as economic and urban institutions, the state and solidarity (*'asabiyyah*). These are the integral elements of Ibn Khaldun's general sociology, in that it is relevant and applicable to all types of societies, nomadic or sedentary, feudal or prebendal, Muslim or non-Muslim.

Ibn Khaldun's sociology consists of the following areas: (i) society (*'umran*) in general and its divisions, (ii) Bedouin society (*al-'umran al-badawi*), tribal societies (*qaba'il*) and primitive peoples (*al-wahshiyyah*), (iii) the state (*al-dawlah*), royal (*mulk*) and caliphate (*khilafah*) authority,

---

[7] Aziz El-Azmeh, 'The Muqaddima and Kitab Al'Ibar: Perspectives from a Common Formula' *The Maghreb Review* 4, 1 (1979), 17.

[8] Ibn Khaldûn, *Ibn Khaldun: The Muqadimmah*, vol. 1, 11.

(iv) sedentary society (*al-'umran al-hadhari*), cities and (v) the crafts, ways of making a living, occupations.[9]

Most of the *Muqaddimah* is dedicated to elaborating a theory of state formation and decline. This is presented in the course of three major sections, that is Sections 2 to 4. Section Two deals with the nature of nomadic society, the dominance of tribal social solidarity (*'asabiyyah*) or group feeling, the role of kinship and blood ties in group feeling and the natural aptitude of nomadic society to accomplish royal authority (*mulk*) in founding a dynasty. Section Three focuses on the development and decline of royal authority, the role of religion in this, the various groups and forces that play a part in dynastic decline and the mode of origin and disintegration of dynasties. Section Four elucidates a number of aspects of the nature of sedentary civilization.

For Ibn Khaldun the key to understanding the rise and decline of North African states was to be found in the fundamental differences in social organization between pastoral nomadic and sedentary societies. A central concept vital for the understanding of these differences is *'asabiyyah*, referring to a type of group feeling or social cohesion. In Ibn Khaldun's theory of state formation, social groups with strong *'asabiyyah* could dominate and assert rule over those with weak *'asabiyyah*.[10]

'Asabiyyah was inclined to be stronger among the pastoral nomadic peoples. Nomadic society matured into sedentary society in the sense that 'sedentary culture is the goal of bedouin life' and that 'the goal of civilization is sedentary culture and luxury'.[11] *'Asabiyyah* here refers to the feeling of unity among the members of a group that is acquired from the knowledge that they share a common descent. The Bedouin or nomadic groups had a greater degree of *'asabiyyah* and therefore could subjugate sedentary people in urban areas and form their own dynasties. In doing so, they themselves progressively became urbanized and experienced a weakening in their *'asabiyyah*. This in turn ensued in the waning of their military strength, leaving them very prone to attack by another

[9] Ibn Khaldûn, *Ibn Khaldun: The Muqadimmah*, vol. 1, 85.
[10] Ibn Khaldûn, *Ibn Khaldun: The Muqadimmah*, vol. 1, 282–313.
[11] Ibn Khaldûn, *Ibn Khaldun: The Muqadimmah*, vol. 1, 285.

group of nomads with superior *'asabiyyah*. The change is repeated and tribal elites are circulated. While the tribes establish rule, they in turn are reliant on the city for some of the basic necessities of life.[12]

The Method of the New Science

Before moving on to a discussion of Ibn Khaldun's social theory, it would be useful to look at the methods of the science that he proposed.

We have noted that Ibn Khaldun saw the traditional method of assessing historical accounts for their veracity as questionable because of what he would have deemed a preoccupation with the reliability of sources and the personalities of the transmitters of information. It was crucial to focus on the possibility or absurdity of reported events which in turn necessitated knowledge of the nature of human society. The authenticity and reliability of reported facts and events can be logically demonstrated from what is known about the nature of society. It is therefore the method of demonstration (*burhan*) that is given the greatest significance in Ibn Khaldun's theory of society. It is also stated here that we can locate him objectively within the classical Islamic tradition, which rendered the method of demonstration the most reliable in terms of producing certain knowledge. Ibn Khaldun did not present a new method in his scholarship. He inherited the tradition of the philosophers of Islam who learned and enhanced the Greek methods of argumentation. What was original was the application of the method of the philosophers to the study of history.

In the classical Islamic tradition, method (*mantiq*) had to do with the rules that enable one to differentiate right from wrong. The ability to make this distinction is determined by the skills with which definitions (*hudud*) that provide the essence (*mahiyat*) of things are yielded and arguments that lead to judgement or apperception (*tasdiqat*) are made.[13] While both animals and humans have the five senses, humans have the

---

[12] Ibn Khaldûn, *Ibn Khaldun: The Muqadimmah*, vol. 1, 296–99.
[13] Ibn Khaldûn, *Al-Muqaddimah*, III, 91 [III, 137].

ability to abstract universals (*kulliyat*) from the *sensibilia*. Knowledge consists of either conception (*tasawwur*), that is the perception of the essence of things, or it is apperception (*tasdiq*). Unlike conception, apperception entails judgement or assent in order to create the correspondence between the concept and the object to which the concept refers. The purpose of apperception is knowledge of the realities of things (*haqa'iq al-ashya*).[14] In other words, knowledge as concept or perception refers to the knowledge of universals of which there are five. These are genus (*jins*), difference (*fasl*), species (*nu'*), property (*khasah*) and general accident (*'ardh al-'am*).[15] Ibn Khaldun says:

> Every event (or phenomenon), whether (it comes into being in connection with some) essence or (as the result of an) action, must inevitably possess a nature peculiar to its essence as well as to the accidental conditions that may attach themselves to it. If the student knows the nature of events and the circumstances and requirements in the world of existence, it will help him to distinguish truth from untruth in investigating the historical information critically. This is more effective in critical investigation than any other aspect that may be brought up in connection with it.[16]

According to the philosophical tradition, which Ibn Khaldun was a part of, knowledge is attributed to knowing the essence (*dhat*) as well as accidents (*'awaridh*, sing. *'ardh*) of phenomena. Knowing something about a phenomenon means being able to distinguish between its essence, on the one hand, and its accidental properties, on the other. Essences of things are understood in terms of genus, species and difference. When this rule is applied to history, it makes necessary for the historian to differentiate between what is essential and natural from what is accidental to events and conditions.

Understanding a phenomenon in terms of their essences and accidental properties requires the process of abstraction. The process of abstraction continues until the highest universal is attained. For example, the

---

[14] Ibn Khaldûn, *Al-Muqaddimah*, III, 92 [III, 138–139].
[15] Ibn Khaldûn, *Al-Muqaddimah*, III, 94 [III, 142].
[16] Ibn Khaldûn, *Al-Muqaddimah*, I, 53 [I, 72–73].

perception of 'human' results in the abstraction of the species (*nu'*) to which 'human' belongs. At another level, the comparison between 'human' and 'animal' is made resulting in the abstraction of the genus (*jins*) to which both belong. The comparisons continue in this way until the highest genus is attained, that is substance (*jawhar*). After this point, no further abstractions can be done. This process of abstraction may take place in the right way or not. For this reason, the field of logic was developed so that the methods of logic could be understood and presented in a systematic manner to complement the process of analogical reasoning (*qiyas*). The Muslims, including Ibn Khaldun, followed Aristotle in observing five kinds of analogical reasoning.[17]

1. Demonstration (*burhan*). This refers to a type of analogical reasoning, the syllogism, that yields certain knowledge;
2. Dialectics (*jadal*) or disputation. This refers to analogical reasoning that has the goal of winning an argument with an opponent. It does not produce certain knowledge but probable knowledge as its premises are not certain ones. It may involve deductive, inductive or other forms of arguments;
3. Rhetoric (*khitabah*). This refers to reasoning that instructs how to influence or persuade people. It is less inclined towards instruction.
4. Poetics (*shi'ir*). This is reasoning that teaches the invention and use of parable (*tamthil*) and similes (*tashbih*) with the aim of rousing the imagination and inspiring people;
5. Sophistry (*safsatah*) is a form of reasoning that teaches the opposite of truth and seeks to confuse and deceive an opponent.

Ibn Khaldun was part of a tradition that viewed demonstrative methods as the best for establishing the truth. The arguments in demonstration derive from premises that are certain and they yield certain knowledge. This was the method Ibn Khaldun used in the *Muqaddimah*. Ibn Khaldun's science of society is founded on six premises or *muqaddimat*. These are assertions whose demonstration is

---

17 Ibn Khaldûn, *Al-Muqaddimah*, III, 93–94 [III, 140–141].

not situated within the scope of the new science. We will refer to these in the next section.

Ibn Khaldun questioned the tendency among certain scholars to reduce logic to a discipline in its own right rather than rendering it as a tool for the other sciences. For Ibn Khaldun's own work, methods of demonstration and dialectics were tools that he utilized for the critique of the existing historical scholarship up to his time and the advancement of his new science of human society.

The Theory of State Formation and Decline

Ibn Khaldun's world of fourteenth-century North Africa was very different from the centuries before it. He seemed to be cognizant of the fact that he lived in a time of cultural inertia and political disintegration. Long before Ibn Khaldun's time, the political economy of the region was defined by a high level of monetization and a relatively lesser propensity for the development of large-scale landed property. The ruling aristocracy was tribal-based and the expropriation of the economic surplus was mainly from trade, especially the trans-Saharan trade in Sudanese gold. Centuries before Ibn Khaldun, the growth of merchant capitalism, especially in relation to the gold trade, led to the growth of cities, petty commodity production and the advancement of bureaucracy.[18] Accompanying these developments was a flourishing scientific, literary and artistic culture. By the time of Ibn Khaldun's birth, however, North Africa had fragmented into three dynasties: the Marinids, the Abd al-Wadids and the Hafsids. The relative unity that constituted the Maghreb under the previous successive dynasties, such as the Almoravids and the Almohads, had been dissolved during Ibn Khaldun's time. Agriculture and urban life were continuously under threat from nomadic invasions and pilfering. Territories within a state

---

[18] Yves Lacoste, *Ibn Khaldun: The Birth of History and the Past of the Third World* (London: Verso, 1984), 20; Heinrich Simon, *Ibn Khaldun's Science of Human Culture* (Lahore, SH. Muhammad Ashraf, 1978), 15.

were distinguished from each other in terms of regions under government control that paid taxes (*bilad al-maghzan*) and those outlying areas
that were able to avoid such requirements (*bilad al-siba*).[19] The tribes
assigned to collect taxes by the ruler in the *maghzan* areas regularly
conducted raids on the peasantry, largely ensuing in economic insecurity
and a sense of helplessness. This was aggravated by wars between the
rulers of the three states, tribal wars and internal rebellions.

Following the deductive method, as called for by demonstration, Ibn
Khaldun starts the *Muqaddimah* with a discussion of premises or
muqaddimat, that is assertions whose proof do not fall within the
breadth of the new science. Six *muqaddimat* are listed but can be
subsumed under three. The first is that human society is imperative
and necessary, the second that humans are influenced physically, mentally and socially by the physical environment and the third that humans
are influenced physically, mentally and socially by the physical environment.[20] The most important premise in terms of being more directly
linked to the problematique of the *Muqaddimah* is that human society is
imperative. To contend that human society is imperative is also to
contend that humans are inherently political and that they cannot
function without the kind of social organization that the philosophers
term *polis* (*madinah*). This is the meaning of social organization
(*'umran*). Although human beings are equipped with the means to
obtain sustenance, they are not able to meet these needs on an individual
basis. They are compelled to cooperate with fellow human beings, for it
is through the cooperation of a few that the needs of many can be
satisfied.[21] The idea of the indispensability of human society is taken by
Ibn Khaldun as a premise, as a given.

When humans reach a certain level of the social organization of
society, there is a need for a circumscribing influence as violence and
transgressions are part of human nature. Reaching this certain level
necessitates the supremacy of a power and a type of authority that Ibn

[19] Lacoste, *Ibn Khaldun*, 35.
[20] Ibn Khaldûn, *Ibn Khaldun: The Muqadimmah*, vol. 1, 89, 94, 167, 174, 177, 184.
[21] Ibn Khaldûn, *Ibn Khaldun: The Muqadimmah*, vol. 1, 89.

Khaldun refers to as kingship (*mulk*). Kingship is indispensable to humans and is a natural property. Given that society is vital and that kingship is a natural property of humans, what are the factors that explain the transition from nomadic to sedentary societies and the concurrent rise and decline of dynasties? The answer necessitates an illustration of the nature of nomadic and sedentary societies. The rest of the *Muqaddimah* devotes attention to these matters. Ibn Khaldun's analysis of nomadic society, dynasties and authority, sedentary society and the modes of making a living form the basis of a theory of the rise and decline of states. The essential elements of this theory are the nature and characteristics of nomadic and sedentary societies, the function of the interaction between these types of societies in the rise of states and the conditions of both that cause the rise, decline and disintegration of states.

Nomadic people, like sedentary people, comprise of a natural group. It is the mode of making a living (*al-ma'ash*) that explains the different conditions of a people. Those people who live from agriculture or animal husbandry are situated in desert areas. Their social organization is of a nature that does not enable much more than a subsistence-level life. If there is an increase in their economic well-being and they begin to live beyond subsistence level, they may settle in towns and cities and start to appreciate good cuisine, the fine arts, refined architecture and greater well-being and pleasure. Their mode of making a living reflects their wealth.[22] Those who make their living from animals include nomads who raise sheep and cattle and encircle the desert in search of water and pasture. They are shepherds who do not travel far into the desert where good pastures are absent. Those who rely on camels go venture further into the desert where camels can find subsistence.

Nomadic society is the harbinger and foundation of sedentary society. The proof for this is that a majority of the dwellers of cities originate from Bedouins. Ibn Khaldun makes a point regarding the difference between nomadic and sedentary life that is important in the development of his theory:

---

[22] Ibn Khaldûn, *Ibn Khaldun: The Muqadimmah*, vol. 1, 249–50.

It has thus become clear that the existence of Bedouins is prior to, and the basis of, the existence of towns and cities. Likewise, the existence of towns and cities results from luxury customs pertaining to luxury and ease, which are posterior to the customs that go with the bare necessities of life.[23]

Nomadic people are also more tenacious than sedentary people. The lifestyle of sedentary people makes them more accustomed to laziness and comfort. They rely on the leadership for their protection, do not possess military equipment and do not need to hunt for sustenance. The Bedouins lack the resources available to sedentary people. They are compelled to hunt and carry weapons for their self-protection. Ibn Khaldun said of them:

> They watch carefully all sides of the road. They take hurried naps only when they are together in company or when they are in the saddle. They pay attention to every faint barking and noise. They go alone into the desert, guided by their fortitude, putting their trust in themselves. Fortitude has become a character quality of theirs, and courage their nature. They use it whenever they are called upon or an alarm stirs them. When sedentary people mix with them in the desert or associate with them on a journey, they depend on them. They cannot do anything for themselves without them. This is an observed fact. (Their dependence extends) even to knowledge of the country, the (right) directions, watering places, and crossroads.[24]

It is not only the positive qualities of tenacity and endurance that enable the Bedouin to live in the desert. These qualities are inadequate if the Bedouin do not possess a high degree of solidarity or group feeling ('asabiyyah). 'Asabiyyah is a key concept in Ibn Khaldun's science of society. It refers to a form of solidarity of group that is premised on the knowledge of its members that they share a common ancestry. Ibn Khaldun believed that the form of group feeling or solidarity based on

---

[23] Ibn Khaldûn, *Ibn Khaldun: The Muqadimmah*, vol. 1, 253.
[24] Ibn Khaldûn, *Ibn Khaldun: The Muqadimmah*, vol. 1, 258.

'*asabiyyah* was far more influential than other forms of solidarity. The stronger the '*asabiyyah*, the tighter the group and the greater the degree of mutual support and assistance. The '*asabiyyah* of the Bedouin was more stable than that of the townspeople. This enabled them a greater degree of mutual cooperation and courage. However, '*asabiyyah* tends to decrease over time owing to certain policies employed by a leader as well as the characteristics of settled, urban life. The relatively more opulent nature of urban life has the effect of reducing '*asabiyyah* to the point that it separates the rich from the poor. Other than that, as time goes by the leader seeks to distance himself from his kinsmen, whom he regards as possible supplanters of his power, by introducing outsiders or non-kinsmen into his circle. This leads to the reduction of '*asabiyyah*. The relative military supremacy of the Bedouin is attributed to their greater '*asabiyyah*, dependent on them being a close-knit group of common descent.

The circumscribing influence among Bedouin tribes is derived from their leaders. It results from the great respect and admiration they generally enjoy among the people. The communities of the Bedouins are protected from enemies by a tribal militia comprising of youths of the tribe renowned for their bravery. Their defence and protection are effectual so long as they are a close-knit group of common descent. Compassion and affection for one's blood ties and relatives makes for mutual support and assistance, and raises the fear felt by the enemy.[25]

By '*asabiyyah* Ibn Khaldun meant a sense of togetherness and loyalty to a group that is founded largely on blood ties. Three types of relationships form '*asabiyyah*. These are blood ties (*silat al-rahim*), clientship (*wala*') and alliance (*hilf*).[26] The type of '*asabiyyah* is dependent on the predominance of each element. '*Asabiyyah* that springs solely from close blood ties is most influential and reliable and establishes the strongest feelings of solidarity. However, as the kinship element weakens, affiliation and clientship may assume the dominant elements in group relations, resulting in weaker forms of '*asabiyyah*.

---

[25] Ibn Khaldûn, *Ibn Khaldun: The Muqadimmah*, vol. 1, 262–3.
[26] Ibn Khaldûn, *Ibn Khaldun: The Muqadimmah*, vol. 1, 264.

Social cohesion or 'asabiyyah is not wholly derived from patrilineal ties in tribal social organizations. While it is true that all tribal groups have stronger or weaker 'asabiyyahs based on kinship, religion can additionally serve to form a high degree of social cohesion. This was the case with the Arabs who developed a strong 'asabiyyah as a result of being united under the bulwark of Islam (151 [120]). In advocating this idea, Ibn Khaldun quotes the hadith of the Prophet, 'God sent no prophet who did not enjoy the protection of his people'.[27]

Furthermore, the understanding of 'asabiyyah, however, is not to be restricted to its psychological or cultural dimensions. Its material man-ifestations also exist. A tribal chieftain has authority over the tribesmen because of 'asabiyyah. This is a prerequisite for achieving royal authority. However, it is not merely the psychological feeling of cohesion that makes royal authority achievable. What contributes to 'asabiyyah and the authority exerted by the chieftain is his economic standing he achieves from surpluses he expropriates from trade, plunder and pillage (Lacoste 1984: 107). 'Asabiyyah, then, refers to (1) kinship ties, (2) a socially cohesive religion such as Islam that enables a common ideology that serves to legitimize the chieftain's ambitions for mulk, and (3) the strength of the chieftain through trade, booty, pillage and conquest.

Having a house (al-bayt) and nobility (al-sharaf) is only possible among people who are united by a group feeling. One is said to have a house when he is able to include noble and famous people among his ancestry. The benefit of common descent is that it establishes a strong group feeling that promotes mutual assistance and affection. Having noble ancestors and the esteem that they bring solidifies a group. Sedentary life weakens group feeling as tribal affiliations weaken. Nobility disappears along with the weakening of group feeling.[28] Clients, followers and slaves of a people belonging to a noble house experience the group feeling of that house while experiencing a decrease in their own group feeling, owing to their being attached to a superior group. If the client attains nobility and house, they are attributed to the

---

[27] Ibn Khaldûn, Ibn Khaldun: The Muqadimmah, vol. 1, 322.
[28] Ibn Khaldûn, Ibn Khaldun: The Muqadimmah, vol. 1, 273–4.

nobility and house of his masters. This happened to the Barmecides. They belonged to a Persian house but subsequently became clients of the Abbasids. Their descent was not a factor, and their subsequent nobility was a result of their position as followers of the Abbasids.[29]

The prestige (al-ḥasb) of a house lasts for a maximum of four generations. The one who establishes the glory of the house preserves the qualities that established the glory. This is continued by the son who had contact with his father and imbibed those qualities. He is, however, deficient compared to his father in the sense that what he has learnt from his father is through study rather than from applied experience. The third generation adheres to the tradition and is lower than the second generation in that it depends on imitation rather than perception. The fourth generation is the most inferior in that its members no longer possess the qualities of the first generation that established the glory. A fourth generation descendent supposes that the glory of the house merely originates from noble descent rather than the qualities and endeavours of earlier generations. He is deceived by the respect that people confer on him, thinking that it is due solely to his descent. He distances himself from those who share in his group feeling, thinking that they will follow him owing to his descent. His upbringing was such that he assumes their obedience as a given. He lacks respect for them, and they in turn come to resent him. They eventually rebel and transfer their loyalties to another branch of his tribe. The family of the new leader then expands, while the house of the original leader declines and collapses. This is the outcome of kingship as well as the houses of tribes, emirs and all who experience a ruler's group feeling. When one house weakens, another from among the same descent arises.[30]

Ibn Khaldun had already pointed out that nomadic groups are more courageous and superior to sedentary people in terms of their determination and group feeling. Group feeling encourages mutual defence and social life. At the same time, every social organization requires a power to assert control over the group. The superior one is the one with the

[29] Ibn Khaldûn, *Ibn Khaldun: The Muqadimmah*, vol. 1, 277–8.
[30] Ibn Khaldûn, *Ibn Khaldun: The Muqadimmah*, vol. 1, 278–80.

greater degree of group feeling such that he can command the conformity of others. Such superiority is kingship. If a tribe has a multiplicity
of houses and group feelings, it is the superior or stronger of group
feelings that rules.[31] Once a particular group feeling has affirmed its
superiority over the people who share in that group feeling, it then
establishes its supremacy over other group feelings. If it is able to over-
power another group, the two group feelings come into close contact
with the superior group feeling and grow in strength. As the ruling
dynasty becomes weaker, and if there is no one from among those who
share in its group feeling to defend it, the new group feeling assumes rule
and attains kingship.[32]

The goal of group feeling is the acquisition of kingship. The tribe
symbolizing the superior group feeling obtains kingship either by acquiring actual control of the state or providing aid to the ruling dynasty. If
people are able to preserve their group feeling, kingship that disappears
in one branch will be given to another branch of the same people. When
the group feeling of the ruling group weakens and its kingship is
disputed, there is an opportunity for another strong group feeling
from within the same nation (ummah) to attain kingship. They are
then bound to the same process of decline that their predecessors
experienced. Kingship in any nation lasts until the group feeling of the
entire nation weakens.[33]

When a dynasty declines, its power is passed on to those who have a
share in the group feeling of that dynasty. The same group feeling exists
among those who are related to members of the dynasty in decline
because the strength of the group feeling is correlated to the closeness
of the relationship. The cycle repeats itself until a major change in
conditions transpires, such as a transformation by a religion or the fall
of a civilization, when kingship is then transferred to a wholly new
nation.[34]

[31] Ibn Khaldûn, *Ibn Khaldun: The Muqadimmah*, vol. 1, 284.
[32] Ibn Khaldûn, *Ibn Khaldun: The Muqadimmah*, vol. 1, 285.
[33] Ibn Khaldûn, *Ibn Khaldun: The Muqadimmah*, vol. 1, 296–7.
[34] Ibn Khaldûn, *Ibn Khaldun: The Muqadimmah*, vol. 1, 298–9.

Once a dynasty is in power, it is able to forgo the very group feeling that enabled it to be created. Once kingship authority is exercised and inherited over several generations and dynasties, the leaders are respected for their own qualities rather than for reasons of group feeling. The rulers then rule with the aid of clients or tribal groups who have different ancestries. The relationship between kingship and group feeling is such that the ruler subsequently reneges against his own people. Once the dynasty is established, the people of his own group feeling are employed in the administrative services of the state. As the ruler centralizes his power, he attempts to distance himself from the people of his group feeling, disenfranchising them in the process. He instead brings clients and followers into the inner circle and assigns the important administrative positions to them[35] (*Muqaddimah*, I, 312–313 [I, 372–373]).

An example is the case of the Abbasids under al-Mu'tasim and his son al-Wathiq. When the Arab group feeling diminished, they ruled with the aid of Persians, Turks, Daylams, Seljuks and other clients. Client after client inexorably gained control over the provincial areas until the caliphs only controlled Baghdad and finally collapsed.[36]

The founding of a dynasty by a tribe sets into gear a process of social change which ensues in the weakening of 'asabiyyah. There are at least two ways in which this decline is brought about. One is where the second generation of tribesmen who founded the dynasty are born and brought up in sedentary society. The socialization in the new sedentary environment results in a change 'from the desert attitude to sedentary culture, from privation to luxury, from a state in which everybody shared in the glory to one in which one man claims all the glory for himself while the others are too lazy to strive for (glory), and from proud superiority to humble subservience. Thus, the vigour of group feeling is broken to some extent'. By the third generation 'asabiyyah dissolves completely.[37]

Secondly, 'asabiyyah also diminishes when the 'ruler gains complete control over his people, claims royal authority all for himself, excluding

---

[35] Ibn Khaldûn, *Ibn Khaldun: The Muqadimmah*, vol. 1, 372–3.
[36] Ibn Khaldûn, *Ibn Khaldun: The Muqadimmah*, vol. 1, 314–15.
[37] Ibn Khaldûn, *Ibn Khaldun: The Muqadimmah*, vol. 1, 344–5.

them; and prevents them from trying to have a share in it'.[38] The ruler attempts to proscribe his people from power. The cost is the difficulty of sustaining 'asabiyyah. The decline in 'asabiyyah ultimately undermines the capacity of the ruler to rule and cripples the state until it is finally occupied by another tribal group with superior 'asabiyyah. And so the cycle repeats itself.[39]

The Understanding of Reform

Ibn Khaldun's *Muqaddimah* is renowned as a work of what we may call political sociology, which deals with the rise and decline of the state. It is hardly considered that this theory is, at one and the same time, a theory of religious reform. The first to acknowledge this was probably the Spanish philosopher, Ortega y Gasset (1883–1955).[40] In a piece on Ibn Khaldun published almost a century ago, Ortega suggests that Ibn Khaldun's theory on the rise and decline of states can be employed to discuss the rise of the Wahhabi movement in Arabia. The founder of the Saudi Arabia, Abdul Aziz Ibn Saud (1876–1953), advocated an overarching religious ideology, Wahhabism, using this to unite nomadic tribesmen to form a militia known as the Ikhwan. With their aid Ibn Saud was able to unite various parts of Arabia under his control to form the state and kingdom of Saudi Arabia. Ortega was erroneous in likening the puritanism of the Wahhabis to Islam itself, although he was correct in pointing out the extremism of Wahhabism. He was also correct in acknowledging the pertinence of Ibn Khaldun's theory for the explanation of the role of the Wahhabi revival movement in the rise of the Saudi state.[41] Here it is important to refer to Ibn Khaldun on the role of religious leaders in the unification of the Bedouin.

---

[38] Ibn Khaldûn, *Ibn Khaldun: The Muqadimmah*, vol. 1, 353.

[39] Ibn Khaldûn, *Ibn Khaldun: The Muqadimmah*, vol. 1, 298–9.

[40] See also Syed Farid Alatas, *Applying Ibn Khaldun: The Recovery of a Lost Tradition in Sociology* (London: Routledge, 2014), chap. 5.

[41] Ortega y Gasset, José (1976–8) 'Abenjaldún nos revela el secreto', *Revista del Instituto Egipcio de Estudios Islámicos en Madrid* 19 (1976–8), 111–2.

When there is a prophet or saint among them, who calls upon them to fulfil the commands of God and rids them of blameworthy qualities and causes them to adopt praiseworthy ones, and who has them concentrate all their strength in order to make the truth prevail, they become fully united (as a social organization) and obtain superiority and royal authority[42] (Ibn Khaldūn, 1378/1981: 151 [1967: Vol. I, 305–306]).

As was mentioned earlier, the social cohesion or solidarity suggested by the concept of 'asabiyyah is not fully subject to kinship ties. Religion can also function to enhance such solidarity. The contest between the preurban Bedouin and the sedentarized tribes was not just over the economic wealth of the city. The Bedouin were also motivated by the view that the practice and belief of Muslims in the cities are morally depraved and are in need of reform. The preurban Bedouin, therefore, are highly determined to abolish what they considered to be morally unacceptable (taghyir al-munkar).[43] The abolishment of what is unacceptable, or unlawfully practiced religion or disregard for God has to do with the excesses of urban life.[44] But, the reform is transitory. The reform is seasonal. A tribe conquers a dynasty, founds a new one and rules until it is deposed by a leader inclined to reform who has the support of a new set of preurban tribes highly determined to reform and to profit from the city.

In such a cycle of rise and decline of dynasties, everyday people were entangled in a conundrum of dictatorial policies and conduct of royal authority on one hand and the possibility of conquest by bellicose Bedouin tribesmen led by a pious religious leader bent on 'abolishing what is objectionable', on the other. This Khaldunian cycle characterized many societies of Ibn Khaldun's world. The cycle ended only when the basis of state power was no longer tribal. However, the ending of the cycle was not something predicted by Ibn Khaldun, as he could not have likely anticipated modern developments that would lead to the

---

[42] Ibn Khaldûn, *Ibn Khaldun: The Muqadimmah*, vol. 1, 305–6.
[43] Ibn Khaldûn, *Ibn Khaldun: The Muqadimmah*, vol. 1, 323.
[44] Ibid., pp. 347–351.

elimination of conditions that caused the seemingly unending repetition of the cycle.

Gellner's attempt to combine Ibn Khaldun's theory with David Hume's oscillation theory of religion to yield a theory of reform is well known. Hume substituted his oscillation theory for the unilineal theory of the development of religion from polytheism to monotheism. According to the former, there was a flux and reflux of polytheism and monotheism.[45] The change from polytheism to monotheism was directed by a competitive sycophancy. The competition between worshippers to adulate the deities of a pantheon escalates till one of the deities assumes the status of the one and only God. The elevation of the God of Abraham, Isaac and Jacob to Jehovah and the creator of the world is an example that Hume gives. In time, however, this God is seen to be remote and unreachable, necessitating demi-gods and other lesser gods that can intercede between humans and the one true God. This is the swing to polytheism. Then, there is a swing back to monotheism as 'these idolatrous religions fall every day into grosser and more vulgar conceptions....'.[46]

Hume's theory tends to be psychologistic[47] and overlooks the role of social factors. This is where Ibn Khaldun's model becomes pertinent, providing the social basis for Hume's pendulum swing theory of religion. Ibn Khaldun's theory provides an explanation for how the urban setting provides for a scripturalist unitarian puritanism while the nomadic setting provides for a saint-mediated, hierarchical system.[48] Gellner presents Ibn Khaldun's theory of state formation as a theory of Muslim reform. Nevertheless, there are some issues with it. Gellner was correct to note that Hume's model was much too psychological. He attempted to correct this by way of providing a social basis for the theory through the merger of Hume and Ibn Khaldun. What Gellner failed to do, however, was to present Ibn Khaldun's concept of reform (*taghyir*

---

[45] David Hume, *The Natural History of Religion* (Oxford: Clarendon Press 1976), cited in Ernest Gellner, *Muslim Society*, Cambridge: Cambridge University Press, 1981), 9.

[46] Hume, *The Natural History of Religion*, cited in Gellner, *Muslim Society*, 10.

[47] Gellner, *Muslim Society*, 16.

[48] Gellner, *Muslim Society*, 41–2.

al-munkar) and examine how the religious change was linked with the larger societal change that took place in the context of war and conflict, a change in the state elite and regime and the ascent of a new ruling tribe. In other words, there was more to the social basis than what was examined by Gellner.

Ibn Khaldun's own examples are derived from the rise and decline of the many North African dynasties that he studied, including the Almoravids (A.D.1053–1147), Almohads (A.D.1147–1275) and Marinids (A.D.1213–1524). Founded with the support of Berber tribes, these dynasties declined according to the approach elaborated by Ibn Khaldun. The Almoravids established their state with the support of the Sanhajah tribes, but were eventually deposed by the Almohads, which started as a religious reform movement under Ibn Tumart with the support of the Masmudah tribes. The Almohads themselves were subjugated by the Marinids, whose basis of power was the Zanatah.[49]

There are general lessons from Ibn Khaldun's theory of Muslim reform that are still applicable today. Religious revival effectively takes place against the backdrop of regime change, the evolution of a new ruling class and the change of loyalties. Also, religious revival functions as an inclusive *'asabiyyah* that withstands tribalism, class and ethnicity and yet is inherent in them. For example, an Islamic *'asabiyyah* transcends all tribes, but is at the same time reliant on the *'asabiyyah* of the most influential tribe which appealed to religion. It is also interesting to note that the carrier of religious revival are those societal groups characterized by simpler modes of subsistence and less extravagant lifestyles. Referring to the Khaldunian model, Spickard noted that religious revival is the result of conflict between a lesser institutionalized religion-based solidarity (*'asabiyyah*) and an urban-based religiosity governed by institutions.[50] Spickard also makes the important point that the religious experience should be understood as not merely a psychological phenomenon. It must also be seen as a sociological phenomenon in that it is a

---

[49] Robert Montagne, *The Berbers: Their Social and Political Organisation*, (London: Frank Cass, 1931), 14–15.

[50] J. V. Spickard, 'Tribes and Cities: Towards and Islamic Sociology of Religion', *Social Compass* 48, 1 (2001), 109.

function of a particular type of *'asabiyyah*. The Khaldunian method is not grounded in individuals.[51]

The Marginalization and Recovery of Ibn Khaldun in Modern Sociology

Ibn Khaldun was first acknowledged in Europe in 1636, in a Latin translation of Ibn 'Arabshah's *Fi Akhbar Taymur 'Aja'ib al-Maqdur* (*Viate et rerum gestarum Timuri, qui vulgo Tamerlanes dicitur, Historia*). 'Arabshah mentions the momentous meeting between Ibn Khaldun and Tamerlane, the Mongol conqueror.[52] Following the Latin translation of 'Arabshah was the publication of Ibn Khaldun's biography in d'Herbelot's *Bibliotheque Orientale*.[53] However, it was only more than a hundred years later that a translation of Ibn Khaldun appeared in the form of a French and German translation of extracts.[54] The translation of the *Muqaddimah*, in French, appeared between 1862 and 1868.[55] Since the nineteenth century several scholars in the West acknowledged Ibn Khaldun as a founder of sociology.[56] He was

[51] J. V. Spickard, 'Tribes and Cities: Towards and Islamic Sociology of Religion', *Social Compass* 48, 1 (2001), 108.

[52] Simon, *Ibn Khaldun's Science of Human Culture*, 36–7.

[53] Barthélemy D'Herbelot de Molainville, 'Khaledoun', in *Bibliotheque Orientale* (Paris, 1697), II, 418.

[54] The French translation was undertaken by Silvestre de Sacy and appeared in 1810. See Baron Antoine Isaac Silvestre de Sacy, ed., trans., 'Extraits de Prolégomènes d'Ebn Khaldoun', *Relation de l'Egypt, par Abd-Allatif, médecin arabe de Bagdad* (Paris, 1810), 509–24 (translation), 558–64 (Arabic text). Around the same time, Joseph von Hammer-Purgstall published German translations of extracts of the *Muqaddimah*. See Joseph Freiherr von Hammer-Purgstall, 'Extraits d'Ibn Khaledoun', *Fundgruben des Orients* 6 (1818), 301–307; 362–364; Joseph Freiherr von Hammer-Purgstall, 'Notice sur l'Introduction a la connaissance de l'histoire, Celebre Ouvrage arabe d'Ibn Khaldoun,' *Journal asiatique* (Paris, 1 ser., 1 (1822), 267–78; Iv, 158–61.

[55] Ibn Khaldoun, *Histoire des Berbères et des dynasties musulmanes de l'Afrique septentrionale*, 3 Vols. Baron de Slane, trans. (Paris: Libraire Orientaliste Paul Geuthner, 1982).

[56] Alfred von Kremer, 'Ibn Chaldun und seine Kulturgeschichte der Islamischen Reiche', *Sitzunsberichte der Kaiserlichen Akademie der Wissenschaften* (*Philosoph.-histor. Klasse*) (Vienna) 93, 1979; Robert Flint, *History of the Philosophy of History in France, Belgium, and Switzerland* (Edinburgh, 1893), 158ff; Ludwig Gumplowicz, *Soziologische Essays: Soziologie und Politik* (Innsbruck: Universitats-Verlag Wagner, 1899/1928); Ludwig Gumplowicz, *The Outlines of*

continued to be seen as the originator of the discipline by Arab and other Muslim social scientists from the early years of the twentieth century.[57]

However, the level of recognition given to Ibn Khaldūn by Western sociologists of the nineteenth and early twentieth century was much higher than it is in the teaching of sociology and writing of the history of sociology today. Most students of Ibn Khaldun have not attempted to integrate his ideas into the theoretical frameworks of modern sociology, to develop a Khaldunian model and apply it to the study of historical and contemporary cases. The absence of Khaldunian sociology is all the more surprising when considering the fact that Ibn Khaldun developed theoretical tools and concepts that belong to the domain of positive sociology as opposed to the normative study of society. Nevertheless, there are not many works that have sought to go beyond merely comparing the ideas and concepts in Ibn Khaldun's work with those of modern Western scholars such as Marx, Weber and Durkheim

---

Sociology, Frederick W. Moore, trans. (Philadelphia: American Academy of Political and Social Science, 1899) [translation of Gumplowicz, 1899/1928], 90–114; René Maunier, 'Les idées économiques d'un philosophe arabe au XIVe siècle', *Revue d'histoire économique et sociale* 6 (1913); Franz Oppenheimer, *System der Soziologie*, Jena: Fischer, 1922–1935), vol. 2, 173ff; vol. 4, 251ff; Ortega y Gasset, 'Abenjaldún nos revela el secreto'. In 1938, Becker and Barnes in their *Social Thought from Lore to Science*, devote many pages to Ibn Khaldun and suggest that he was the first to apply modern-like ideas in historical sociology. See Howard Becker Harry Elmer Barnes, *Social Thought from Lore to Science*, 3 vols, 3rd ed. (New York: Dover Publications, 1961), vol I: 266–279.

[57] 'Abd al-'Aziz 'Izzat wrote his thesis in 1932 entitled *Ibn Khaldun et sa science sociale* under the guidance of Fauconnier and René Maunier in France. See Alain Roussillon, 'La représentation de l'identité par les discours fondateurs de la sociologie Turque et Egyptienne: Ziya Gökalp et 'Ali Abd Al-Wahid Wafi' in *Modernisation et mobilisation sociale II, Egypte-Turquie* (Cairo: Dossier du CEDEJ, 1992), 56, n. 48). He also published a comparative study between Ibn Khaldun and Emile Durkheim. See 'Abd al-'Aziz 'Izzat, *Etude comparée d'Ibn Khaldun et Durkheim* (Cairo: Al-Maktabat Al-Anglo Al-Misriyyah, 1952). 'Ali 'Abd al-Wahid Wafi embarked on a comparative study of Ibn Khaldun and Auguste Comte. See his *Al-falsafah al-ijtima'iyyah li Ibn Khaldun wa Aujust Kumt* (Cairo, 1951). He also wrote a renowned work on Ibn Khaldun as the founder of sociology which appeared as 'Ibn Khaldūn, awwal mu'assis li 'ilm al-ijtimā', in *A'mal Mahrajan Ibn Khaldun* (Proceedings of the Ibn Khaldun Symposium), Cairo: National Centre for Social and Criminological Research, 1962), 63–78. During the same period, Syed Hussein Alatas from Malaysia had referred to Ibn Khaldun as having founded the principles of modern sociology. See his 'Objectivity and the Writing of History', *Progressive Islam* 1, 2 (1954), 2.

towards theoretically integrating his theory into modern social science frameworks.[58]

It can be said, therefore, that Ibn Khaldun has been marginalized, particularly in the discipline of sociology. While there are many references to Ibn Khaldun spread across hundreds of works in various languages, these tend to be descriptive and historical rather than conceptual and theoretical. Where Ibn Khaldun is used in lectures and tutorial, he is generally only used in courses in Middle Eastern, Arab or Islamic studies. It is rare for Ibn Khaldun to be taught as a sociologist in sociology courses alongside Marx, Weber and Durkheim.

Part of the explanation for this indifference is that the Khaldunian sociological theory has not been developed over the centuries. There had not been efforts to make his work *qua* sociological theory not only more available but also applicable to the study of modern societies. Furthermore, it can be said that theoretical disregard is also caused by the prevalence of Eurocentric social science in global academia.[59] The fact that Ibn Khaldun is often limited to Middle East, North African or Islamic studies can attributed to the influence of Eurocentrism in sociology and other the social sciences. In many works on Ibn KhaldÉn, Ibn Khaldun appears as a provider of historical data rather than the origin of ideas that are relevant to contemporary studies. Ibn Khaldun appears as an object and much less as a knowing subject. In the works on the history of sociology, it is mostly Europeans thinkers who

---

[58] For some exceptions, see Abdesselam Cheddadi, 'Le Systeme du Pouvoir en Islam d`apres Ibn Khaldun,' *Annales, Eco., So., Civ.* 3–4 (1980), 534–550; Olivier Carré, 'A propos de vues Neo-Khalduniennes sur quelques systemes politiques Arabes actueles', *Arabica* 35, 3 (1988), 368–87; Yves Lacoste, *Ibn Khaldun: The Birth of History and the Past of the Third World.* London: Verso, 1984); Syed Farid Alatas, 'Ibn Khaldun and the Ottoman Modes of Production,' *Arab Historical Review for Ottoman Studies* 1–2 (1990), 45–63; Syed Farid Alatas, 'A Khaldunian Perspective on the Dynamics of Asiatic Societies', *Comparative Civilizations Review* 29 (1993), 29–51; Syed Farid Alatas, *Applying Ibn Khaldun: The Recovery of a Lost Tradition in Sociology* (London: Routledge, 2014).

[59] Some features of Eurocentrism, such as the subject/object dichotomy, the placing of Europeans in the foreground, the presentation of Europeans as originators and the dominance of European concepts and categories are discussed in Syed Farid Alatas, *Alternative Discourses in Asian Social Sciences: Responses to Eurocentrism* (New Delhi: Sage, 2006), 177–8. Eurocentrism functions to render non-Western thinkers like Ibn Khaldun irrelevant or peripheral.

are in the foreground and who are presented as the progenitors of sociology.

There is a need, therefore, to go beyond saying that Ibn Khaldun is a harbinger of the modern social sciences. It is possible to move beyond works that simply state that Ibn Khaldun was a founder of sociology or provide descriptive accounts of his works, and to move towards theoretical applications that include the integration of concepts and frameworks from Ibn Khaldun into contemporary social science theories. For example, Ibn Khaldun's theory of the dynamics of tribal state formation could be applied to a myriad of other historical cases outside of his geographical area and periods of interest. Examples would be Safavid Iran and the Ottoman empire.

Ibn Khaldun's theorization of the rise and decline of states is sociological as he speaks of the social characteristics of groups such as tribes, states and the ruling class. The concept of 'asabiyyah, around which Ibn Khaldun's theory centres, is also sociological as it refers to a type of social cohesion, in this case, one that is built on the knowledge of common kinship. But Ibn Khaldun's explanation of the circumstances and nature in which 'asabiyyah diminishes lacks any reference to the mode of organization of economic life. The notion and typology of the economic system is absent. It would be interesting to consider integrating a mode of production framework into Ibn Khaldun's theory of the rise and decline of tribal-based states.[60]

An interesting application of Ibn Khaldun would be to the modern state. One such application had been attempted by Michaud. He examines what he calls the Khaldūnian triad of 'asabiyyah, da'wah (call, invitation to Islam) and mulk (royal authority, absolute power) with reference to the modern Syrian state.[61] In Syria of the 1970s, power resides within the minority Alawite community, with President Hafez Al-Asad as head of state. One progresses down the hierarchy to find

---

[60] For an attempt to do this, see Alatas, 'Ibn Khaldun and the Ottoman Modes of Production'; Alatas, 'A Khaldunian Perspective on the Dynamics of Asiatic Societies'; and Alatas, *Applying Ibn Khaldun*, chaps. 6 and 7.

[61] Gerard Michaud, 'Caste, Confession et Societe en Syrie: Ibn Khaldoun au Chevet du 'Progressisme Arabe', *Peuples Mediterraneens* 16 (1981), 168.

family members of the President such as his brother, Rifaat, as well as others who have the highest positions in the intelligence services, army, air force and interior ministry. Power is not just attributed to membership in the Alawite community but also to clientele, alliances and, of course, blood ties (*nasab*), the key to '*asabiyyah*. Michaud notes that according to Ibn Khaldun, '*asabiyyah* not only does not preclude hierarchy but, as a result of the integration of several '*asabiyyah*, suggests it.[62] Blood ties are so important that they may result in a commandant having greater power than a general in the Syrian army.

Another Khaldunian application can be found in Carré's work, who discusses the typology of power in the Arab world. There are six possible means of the exercise of power in the resulting typology that Carré developed:

1. Rational power with external coercion, serving in the interests of the public. Repression is externally applied through enforcement of norms and codes, with the core of solidarity being tribal. Examples are the types of Baath regimes sponsored by Syria and Iraq under Saddam Hussein.[63]
2. Rational power with external repression, serving in the interests of the government. Examples are the Baathists regimes mentioned in (1) above, this time not as advocated by their leaders but as actually existing systems that act to maintain their power by leveraging on tribal agnatic ties.[64]
3. Rational power with external repression inspired by religion that functions in the interests of the ruled and is founded on the solidarity that is partly tribal, partly professional in the urban milieu. Examples are Nasserism and the Muslim Brotherhood.[65]

---

[62] Michaud, 'Caste, Confession et Societe en Syrie', 120.

[63] Olivier Carré, 'Ethique et politique chez Ibn Khaldûn, juriste musulman: Actualité de sa typologie des systèmes politique', *L'Année sociologique* 30 (1979–80), 122.

[64] Carré, 'Ethique et politique chez Ibn Khaldûn', 122.

[65] Carré, 'Ethique et politique chez Ibn Khaldûn', 123.

4. Rational power with external repression inspired religiously, but functioning to advance the interests of the ruling group and requiring military solidarity. An example is the Nasserist regime.[66]
5. The ideal power of the utopian city in which with internal control and repression is effected through faith in the virtue of egalitarianism as well as legal repression in the context of military solidarity and a prosperous urban sector. The example is South Yemen.[67]
6. The ideal power of the Medinan community during the time of the Prophet Muhammad founded on exclusively on internal control.[68]

Carré dwells on Khaldūnian concepts such as *'asabiyyah* as well as his distinctions between the ideal and rational, internal and external, and the interests of the ruled and those of the rulers, and innovatively applied them to the political times of contemporary Middle Eastern states.

Conclusion

While there is a systematic sociology that is to be found in the works of Ibn Khaldun, inadequate attention has been paid to Ibn Khaldun in introductory sociology texts and works on the history of sociology. Also, works of a theoretical and conceptual nature on Ibn Khaldun are few, especially where the discipline of sociology is concerned. I have proposed that the relative neglect of Ibn Khaldun, particularly in theoretical and conceptual terms, is attributed to the dominance of Eurocentrism in the social sciences. I discuss the possibility of developing Khaldunian sociology by merging his theoretical insights with those of modern sociology and systematically applying the resulting frameworks to both historical and contemporary empirical cases.

The purpose of this chapter is to showcase how the contributions of a social thinker may be thought of not just as an object of study in which

[66] Carré, 'Ethique et politique chez Ibn Khaldûn', 124.
[67] Carré, 'Ethique et politique chez Ibn Khaldûn', 124.
[68] Carré, 'Ethique et politique chez Ibn Khaldûn', 121.

his theories and concepts are described repetitively or in which his work is looked upon as a source of historical data, but as a source of theory that remains pertinent and that can be applied to both historical and contemporary settings. The examples of applications of Ibn Khaldun are few, especially when it is realized that Ibn Khaldun's works have been known for 600 years.

The task of developing Khaldunian sociology does require or call for the expunging of European categories and concepts from sociology and their replacement with Arab and Muslim ones. Rather, the objective is to enhance and universalize sociology by making accessible to the discipline a greater variety of ideas and perspectives.

Reference

Lacoste, Yves. *Ibn Khaldun: The Birth of History and the Past of the Third World.* London: Verso, 1984.

Karl Marx (1818–1883)

Syed Farid Alatas

Karl Marx was born on 5 May 1818 into a middle-class family in the German city of Trier near the border with France. His father was a Jew who converted to Christianity in order to maintain his career as a lawyer. Marx, in fact, was a descendant of a long line of Rabbis on both his mother's and father's side.[1]

Marx read a great deal about the French revolution and was also interested in the philosophy of Hegel. In addition to this, he had begun to read the works of the classical English political economists. In 1844, Marx drew up a proposal for a series of monographs that would deal with all these interests. The notes on these topics eventually came to be known as the 'Economic and Philosophic Manuscripts' or the 'Paris Manuscripts'.[2] It is these interests that eventually led Marx to become a foremost theorist of the capitalist system. Although many associate Marx as a theorist of communism and view Marx as a contemporary, he was

---

[1] Franz Mehring, *Karl Marx: The Story of His Life* (London: George Allen & Unwin, 1936), 1; David McLellan, *Karl Marx* (Harmondsworth: Penguin, 1978), 1.

[2] McLellan, *Karl Marx*, 5.

© The Author(s) 2017
S.F. Alatas, V. Sinha, *Sociological Theory Beyond the Canon*,
DOI 10.1057/978-1-137-41134-1_3

really a man of the nineteenth century, an analyst of the capitalism of his time and not a 'foresighted interpreter of historical trends'.[3]

Amidst the financial struggles, Marx had to slog at finishing his work on political economy. He penned a manuscript of more than 800 words, the *Grundrisse*, as it came to be known. The *Grundrisse der Kritik der Politischen Ökonomie* (*Outlines of the Critique of Political Economy*) consisted of copious notes and excursus, and made up of six parts. Marx only managed to continue work on the first part, expanding it into the three volumes of *Capital*, only volume 1 of which was published during Marx's lifetime, in 1867. The other two volumes were published posthumously.[4]

An Outline of Marx's Sociological Theory

Marx, like some of the social theorists featured in this book, was not a sociologist. There is, however, a social theory that can be identified and reconstructed from his works, which span many fields, particularly political economy and philosophy. Friedrich Engels was Marx's co-author and the co-founder of Marxist theory.[5] Engels' speech at the graveside of Marx at Highgate Cemetery in London on 17 March 1883 may serve as an introductory statement to Marx's sociology:

> Just as Darwin discovered the law of development or organic nature, so Marx discovered the law of development of human history: the simple fact, hitherto concealed by an overgrowth of ideology, that mankind must first of all eat, drink, have shelter and clothing, before it can pursue politics, science, art, religion, etc.; that therefore the production of the immediate material means, and consequently the degree of economic development attained by a given people or during a given epoch, form

---

[3] Jonathan Sperber, *Karl Marx: A Nineteenth Century Life* (New York: W. W. Norton, 2013), xiii.

[4] McLellan, *Karl Marx*, 13–14.

[5] So important was Engels as a founder of Marxist theory that Stedman Jones suggests that much of what we understand as Marxist theory was the construction of Engels. See Gareth Stedman Jones, *Karl Marx: Greatness and Illusion* (Cambridge, MA: Belknap Press, 2016).

the foundation upon which the state institutions, the legal conceptions, art, and even the ideas on religion, of the people concerned have been evolved, and in the light of which they must, therefore, be explained, instead of vice versa, as had hitherto been the case.

But that is not all. Marx also discovered the special law of motion governing the present-day capitalist mode of production, and the bourgeois society that this mode of production has created. The discovery of surplus value suddenly threw light on the problem, in trying to solve which all previous investigations, of both bourgeois economists and socialist critics, had been groping in the dark.[6]

Marx was first and foremost a theorist of capitalist society. Much of his work sought to understand the origins, essential features and function or impact of the capitalist mode of production and what its future was. Capitalism is a system in which wage labour is sold to the owner of capital. This engenders a relationship of exploitation between the capitalist and the working class. As the capitalist system expands and develops with technological advancements and the increase in plant size, labour becomes more specialized, routinized and interdependent. An important sociological phenomenon that Marx discussed regarding the work process is that of alienation. The state and exploitation and alienation of the working class eventually results in the members of this class becoming conscious of their state. They come to understand the working of capitalism, their role in the creation of value, the determination of wages and the definition of exploitation. In other words, they attain class consciousness. This consciousness, however, comes into conflict with the dominant ideas propagated by the ruling class, that is ideological in addition to politico-economic domination exerted by the ruling class.

At the same time, overproduction and underconsumption result in declines in profits, wages and employment, and the system experiences periodic crisis. This leads to final crisis in which labour leads the

[6] Frederick Engels, 'Speech at the Graveside of Karl Marx,' in *Marx and Engels through the Eyes of Their Contemporaries* (Moscow: Progress Publishers, 1972), 5.

revolution to take over the means of production and bring about the transition to socialism, a new and egalitarian mode of production.

Marx's approach can be gleaned from an oft-quoted statement:

> In the social production of their existence, men inevitably enter into definite relations, which are independent of their will, namely relations of production appropriate to a given stage in the development of their material forces of production. The totality of these relations of production constitutes the economic structure of society, the real foundation, on which arises a legal and political superstructure and to which correspond definite forms of social consciousness. The mode of production of material life conditions the general process of social, political and intellectual life.[7]

This statement can be said to summarize Marx's approach to the study of society, known as the materialist conception of history or historical materialism. The social relations that humans enter into must be understood in terms of the social or material production of their existence.

The first step to understanding the capitalist mode of production is to understand the nature of the society that it grew out of in Europe, that is feudal society.

Feudalism and the Rise of Capitalism

The Feudal System

In order to understand feudalism, capitalism or any other kind of system from the perspective of Marx, we need to begin with the concept of the mode of production.

Although Marx does not define the mode of production explicitly, this is an extremely important concept in his work. The mode of production does not merely denote an economic system. Humans cannot be reduced to *homo economicus*. The human being is social

---

[7] Marx, *A Contribution to the Critique of Political Economy*, 20–1.

animal who enters into social relations with other individuals in the production system. This is conveyed in a widely quoted statement of Marx. As humans engage in production, they 'inevitably enter into definite relations, which are independent of their will, namely relations of production appropriate to a given stage in the development of their material forces of production'.[8]

The mode of production, then, consists of the relations and forces of production. The relations of production refer to the mode of appropriation of the economic surplus and the economic ownership of the forces of production that correspond to that mode of appropriation of the economic surplus.[9] The forces of production are the means of production and the labour process. It refers to the labour process involved in the transformation of the raw material of nature into products by means of the tools, skills, organization and knowledge of the worker.[10] For example, in the capitalist mode of production the economic surplus is appropriated in the form of surplus value by a class of non-producers, the capitalists, which owns the means of production. Workers are forced to sell their labour power in return for wages as they do not own the means of production. Every mode of production has a determinate form of the relations of production and the forces of production.

What is important for sociology is that the mode of production does not just refer to physical process of production but the entire set of social phenomena and social relations that result from that process. These include alienation and class struggle to which we shall refer to later. In Marx's dialectical view of history, he understood the capitalist mode of production to have emerged out of a specific precapitalist modes of production, that is the feudal mode of production. It is not that the capitalist mode of production chronologically came after the feudal

---

[8] Karl Marx, *A Contribution to the Critique of Political Economy* (Moscow: Progress Publishers, 1970), 20.

[9] Tom Bottomore, *A Dictionary of Marxists Thought* (Cambridge, MA: Harvard University Press, 1983), 178; Hindess & Hirst, *Pre-Capitalist Modes of Production*, 9–10.

[10] Barry Hindess & Paul Q. Hirst, *Pre-Capitalist Modes of Production* (London: Routledge & Kegan Paul, 1975), 10–11; Eric Wolf, *Europe and the People Without History* (Berkeley: University of California Press, 1982), 75.

mode of production. Capitalism had its roots in feudalism in that the prerequisites of capitalism were found in the feudal system. But, the capitalist forces of production had to await the destruction of feudalism in order that they could be set free and the capitalist mode of production could be established. As Marx said:

> No social order is ever destroyed before all the productive forces for which it is sufficient have been developed, and new superior relations of production never replace older ones before the material conditions for their existence have natured within the framework of the old society.[11]

The feudal system is a system that emerged as a result of the weakening of the monarchical state in Europe. Feudalism is a mode of production in which land is the dominant means of production. There was private property in both land and urban manufactories. The fragmented nature of sovereignty was due to the independence of the landed nobility and the urban crafts from the state, which by the beginning of the tenth century had significantly weakened.[12] Central to the feudal mode of production as it was found in Europe was the institution of the fief. The fief was landed property granted by the owner to a vassal in return for military services.[13] The lord/vassal relationship is one aspect of the feudal relations of production. Another relation is that between the vassal and his dependents, the serfs, and is denoted by the term *seigneurie*.[14] The economic surplus is paid by the serfs to the knightly vassals in the form of a rent.

Medieval Europe between the ninth and fifteenth centuries was largely an agricultural society with a small proportion of people living in cities. The main features of feudalism were that the peasantries were

---

[11] Marx, *A Contribution to the Critique of Political Economy*, 21.

[12] Henri Pirenne, *A History of Europe*, 2 vols. (Garden City, NY: Double Day Anchor Books, 1956), vol. 1, 132.

[13] Henri Pirenne, *Economy and Social History of Medieval Europe* (New York: Harvest, 1937), 7; G. Poggi, *The Development of the Modern State* (Stanford, CA: Stanford University Press, 1978), 21–2.

[14] Poggi, *The Development of the Modern State*, 23. For more details on this, see Pirenne, *A History of Europe*, vol. 1, chap. 2.

tied to the land through obligations to the lords, the system was decentralized in that the king himself was an enfeoffed sovereign of his kingdom,[15] and that there was a separation between town and country. The seeds of destruction of feudal society were to be found within feudal society itself:

> The means of production and of exchange, on whose foundation the bourgeoisie built itself up, were generated in feudal society. At a certain stage in the development of these means of production and of exchange, the conditions under which feudal society produced and exchanged, the feudal organization of agriculture and manufacturing industry, in one word, the feudal relations of property became no longer compatible with the already developed productive forces . . . they were burst asunder.[16]

The towns or cities were very important for the rise of capitalism because it is here that merchants and artisans collected. Cities had not existed from the beginning of the feudal system. If by city is meant a locality in which the population lived primarily from commercial activity rather than the cultivation of the soil, cities began to emerge only after the tenth century.[17] Capital accumulated by the merchants was undoubtedly an important prerequisite for the rise of the capitalist mode of production. But, capitalism could not develop as long as merchant capital was separate from the production process and as long as the majority of labour was tied through feudal obligation to the land. According to Marx, monetary wealth turned into capital within the context of the dissolution of the feudal mode of production that creates free labourers.[18]

---

[15] Pirenne, *A History of Europe*, vol. 1, 132.

[16] Karl Marx and Frederick Engels, *Manifesto of the Communist Party* (Peking: Foreign Languages Press, 1973), 39.

[17] Henri Pirenne, *Medieval Cities, Their Origins and Revival of Trade* (Princeton: Princeton University Press, 1969), 57, 76.

[18] Karl Marx, *Precapitalist Economic Formations* (New York: International Publishers, 1965), 110–111.

The Rise of Capitalism

Generally speaking, for Marx there are four factors or preconditions for the development of the capitalist mode of production out of feudalism. They are the setting free of the peasantry,[19] the development of the urban crafts,[20] the accumulation of wealth derived from trade and usury[21] and the rise of manufactures.[22] All the four factors were crucial for the transition from feudalism to capitalism.

An important advancement in the division of labour is the separation of industrial and commercial from agricultural labour. For each stage in the development of the division of labour there corresponds a form of ownership.[23] In the case of the feudal form of ownership, which is based on an enserfed peasantry, its full development leads to antagonism with the towns.[24] The antagonism between the town and country expressed in terms of the union of workers in guilds is crucial for several reasons. Firstly, it left serfs who were unable to enter the guilds as unorganized, powerless day labourers.[25] Secondly, the existence of guilds made possible the existence of potential free labourers because of the development of the craft skill into not just a source of property, but property itself.[26] The rise of the craft-guild form of manufacture signifies a stage in the evolution of private property. In craft-guild labour, the 'fund of consumption' is co-possessed by the master and journeyman. The dissolution of this relationship in which the labourer is the 'proprietor of the instruments' leads to the relationship between labour and capital found in the capitalist mode of production.[27]

---

[19] Marx, *Precapitalist Economic Formations*, 104; Karl Marx, *The German Ideology* (New York: International Publishers, 1978), 69, 73.

[20] Marx, *Precapitalist Economic Formations*, 104–5.

[21] Marx, *Precapitalist Economic Formations*, 107–9.

[22] Marx, *Precapitalist Economic Formations*, 116–17; Marx, *The German Ideology*, 72–3.

[23] Marx, *The German Ideology*, 43.

[24] Marx, *The German Ideology*, 45–6, 69–70.

[25] Marx, *The German Ideology*, 70.

[26] Marx, *Precapitalist Economic Formations*, 104.

[27] Marx, *Precapitalist Economic Formations*, 97–8.

After the separation of town and country comes that of production and commerce and the rise of a distinct class of merchants. This leads to trade between towns and the further division of labour between individuals.[28] An immediate consequence of such a division of labour was the rise of manufacturing outside of the guild system. The manufacturers took in peasants who were both escaping the countryside and were leaving the guilds.[29] In conjunction with the rise of manufacturers and partly due to it was the dissolution of the manorial system, which provided free wage labour for the manufacturers.[30]

The main features of capitalism, that is the investment of merchant capital in the process of production and the separation of workers from the means of production, began to reveal themselves in the feudal period. The separation of peasants from the means of production was effected by the kicking out of feudal retainers/servants who lived on the manors in houses and castles, by lords driving peasants of the land because peasants were becoming more powerful in terms of the control over the land and the commodification of land whereby estates were bought and sold. This meant the separation of peasants from the land, that is from their rights to the land and their flight into the towns.[31] This was to create for the towns a mass of labourers, the proletariat. The capitalist themselves originated from artisans, craftsmen and even wage labourers. This was facilitated by the discovery of gold and silver in America in the fifteenth century[32] and the accumulation of merchant capital in the colonies by Spain, Portugal, Holland, France and England.

The relevance of Marx's discussion on the transition from feudalism to the capitalist mode of production is that it suggests that the presence of an emerging capitalist class in feudal societies and a weak decentralized feudal state were the preconditions for the rise of the capitalist system. This suggests that the preconditions were non-existent in

---

[28] Marx, *The German Ideology*, 71–2.

[29] Marx, *Precapitalist Economic Formations*, 73.

[30] Marx, *Precapitalist Economic Formations*, 105, 116–117; Marx, *Precapitalist Economic Formations*, 73–4.

[31] Marx, *The German Ideology*, 70.

[32] Marx, *The German Ideology*, 74–5.

non-European societies. Is Marx's way of understanding the evolution of Europe from Antiquity to the modern world problematic?[33] To what extent is this a Eurocentric view?

The Asiatic Mode of Production

Marx and Engels believed in the idea of the uniqueness of European feudalism for the development of the capitalist mode of production. Non-Western societies constituted barriers to the development of capitalism for various reasons. They made brief excursions into the history of India and other 'Oriental' societies in order to discover what they regarded as the barriers to capitalist development in these societies. Marx conceptualized the economic systems of these societies in terms of the Asiatic mode of production.

In contrast to the feudal mode of production, which was a decentralized system, in the Asiatic mode of production power was centralized in the state. The entire economic surplus is appropriated by the state and the state is the legal owner of landed and manufacturing property.[34] Such a state was extremely strong when it controlled a strategic element in the production process such as irrigation works or an army of superior military ability.[35] In addition to the centralization of power in the state, the Asiatic mode of production is defined in terms of the absence of private property in land,[36] and the combination of agriculture and manufacturing within a self-sustaining small community.[37] The centralization of power by the state,

---

[33] Jairus Banaji, *Theory as History: Essays on Modes of Production and Exploitation* (Chicago: Haymarket Books, 2011).

[34] Karl Marx, *Capital*, Vol. 3 (London: Lawrence & Wishart, 1970), 791; Karl Marx, 'India,' in Karl Marx & Frederick Engels, *On Colonialism* (Moscow: Progress Publishers, 1974), 79; Asaf Savas Akat, 'Proposal for a Radical Reinterpretation of the Asiatic Versus the European Social Formation', in Anouar Abdel Malek, ed., The Civilizational Project: The Visions of the Orient (Mexico City: El Colegio de Mexico, 1981), 70.

[35] Eric Wolf, *Europe and the People Without* History (Berkeley: University of California Press, 1982), 80.

[36] Marx, *Precapitalist Economic Formations*, 82.

[37] Marx, *Precapitalist Economic Formations*, 70.

the absence of private property and the absence of class differentiation and class struggle lead to the 'combination of manufacture and agriculture within the small community which thus becomes entirely self-sustaining and contains within itself all conditions of production and surplus production'.[38]

The basic ingredient of historical progression, class struggle, was missing and Asiatic societies were, as a result, stagnant.[39] What this means is that the internal contradictions to be found within the feudal mode of production, which eventually led to its dissolution in Europe, were not to be found in the Asiatic system. According to Marx, this accounts for the stagnation of Asiatic societies such as India, which has 'no history at all, at least no known history. What we call its history, is but the successive intruders who founded their empires on the passive basin of that unresisting and unchanging society'.[40]

Abrahamian, in his discussion on the Asiatic mode of production in Qajar Iran, finds two separate explanations for the power of the Asiatic state in Marx and Engels: '(1) The public works were the business of the central government; (2) the whole empire, not counting the few larger towns, was divided into villages, which possessed a completely separate organization and formed a little world in themselves.'[41]

Another trait of the Asiatic mode of production concerns the extraction of surplus directly from the dominated classes. In the Asiatic mode of production the state is both landlord and sovereign. Taxes and rent coincide in the sense that there was no tax that differed from ground rent.[42] The tax/rent couple is a result of the 'coupling of political sovereignty and landownership in the state which appropriates the surplus product through taxation which is simultaneously a land rent'.[43]

---

[38] Marx, *Capital*, vol. 3, 70.

[39] Marx, 'India,' 81.

[40] Karl Marx & Friedrich Engels, *On Colonialism* (Moscow: Progress Publishers, 1972), 81.

[41] Ervand Abrahamian, 'Oriental Despotism: The Case of Qajar Iran', *International Journal of Middle East Studies* 5 (1974), 6. The relevant citation is Marx's letter to Engels in D. Torr, ed., *The Correspondence of Marx and Engels* (New York: International Publishers, 1942), 70.

[42] Marx, *Capital*, vol. 3 (London: Lawrence & Wishart, 1970), 791.

[43] Bryan S. Turner, *Marx and the End of Orientalism* (London: George Allen & Unwin, 1978), 45–6.

With regard to 'Muslim society' Marx used 'Asiatic mode of production' in a most general manner that left Islam as one large, undifferentiated, stagnant social formation. Apart from being factually wrong about Islam at times, Marx's use of the Asiatic mode of production was much too general to yield detailed knowledge of the workings of Muslim economies and societies:

> The direct producer, according to our assumption, is to be found here in possession of his own means of production, the necessary material labor conditions required for the realization of his labor and the production of his own means of subsistence ... Under such conditions the surplus-labor for the nominal owner, the land can only be extorted from them by other than economic pressure, whatever the form assumed may be.[44]

According to Turner, there is an important dimension of Orientalism in the works of Marx:

> There is, however, a more fundamental relationship between the Orientalist problematic and Marx, namely, a correspondence between the historicism of the Orientalist approach and the historicism of Hegelian Marxism. Both forms of historicism are based on a model of history as a series of stages. For Hegelian Marxism, it is the process of feudalism, capitalism and socialism, which in Orientalism takes the form of Genesis and Fall. There is also the ideal typical contrast, fundamental to both historicisms, between the dynamic, conscious West and the static, uncritical House of Islam.[45]

Marx's views on non-Europeans come across very clearly in his statement about Oriental despotism. With reference to the Asiatic mode of production as it was found in India, he had stated that:

> [W]e must not forget that these idyllic village communities, inoffensive though they may appear, had always been the solid foundation of Oriental

---

[44] Marx, *Capital*, vol. 3 (London: Lawrence & Wishart, 1970), 790–1.
[45] Bryan S. Turner, *Marx and the End of Orientalism* (London: George Allen & Unwin, 1978), 7–8.

despotism, that they restrained the human mind within the smallest possible compass, making it the unresisting tool of superstition, enslaving it beneath traditional rules, depriving it of all grandeur and historical energies. We must not forget the barbarian egotism which, concentrating on some miserable patch of land, had quickly witnessed the ruin of empires, the penetration of unspeakable cruelties, the massacre of the population of large towns ... We must not forget that this undignified, stagnatory, and vegetative life, that this passive sort of existence evoked on the other part, in contradistinction, wild, aimless, unbounded forces of destruction, and rendered murder itself a religious rite in Hindustan. We must not forget that these little communities were contaminated by distinctions of caste and by slavery, that they subjugated man to external circumstances instead of elevating man to be the sovereign of circumstances, that they transformed a self-developing social state into never changing natural destiny, a thus brought about a brutalizing worship of nature, exhibiting its degradation in the fact that man, the sovereign of nature, fell down on his knees in adoration of Hanuman, the monkey, and the Sabbala, the cow.[46]

Given the nature of the Asiatic mode of production, the British colonialism had a 'double mission' to accomplish in India, that is 'the annihilation of old Asiatic society and the laying of the material foundations of Western society in Asia'.[47] This was the mission of destruction and regeneration; regeneration in terms of developing capitalism in India. Marx says:

What we call its [India's] history, is but the history of the successive intruders who founded their empires on the passive basis of that unresisting and unchanging society. The question, therefore, is not whether the English had the right to conquer India, but whether we are to prefer India conquered by the Turk, by the Persian, by the Russian, to India conquered by the Briton.[48]

---

[46] Karl Marx, 'The British Rule in India', in Karl Marx & Frederick Engels, *On Colonialism* (Moscow: Progress Publishers, 1974), 40–41.

[47] Karl Marx, 'The Future Results of the British Rule in India', in Karl Marx & Frederick Engels, *On Colonialism* (Moscow: Progress Publishers, 1974), 82.

[48] Marx, *'The Future Results of the British Rule in India'*, 81.

The various negative features of the Asiatic mode of production were to be destroyed and the positive aspects of capitalism to be introduced as a result of British colonial rule. It was to introduce private property and allow for capitalism to develop in India in order that socialism would follow.

Marx possibly, later changed his views. While in 1853 he was optimistic about the 'double mission of colonialism' in India, in 1881 he wrote that 'the extinction of the communal ownership of land was only an act of English vandalism which pushed the indigenous people not forward but backward'.[49] He began to see the destructive effects of colonialism. Colonialism did not develop capitalism but rather made India backward by destroying indigenous industries and tying India to the world market as an agricultural rather than manufacturing nation. Marx concluded that the British, far from developing the productive forces of India, were bleeding India by making profits within India as well as by taking money out in terms of dividends, rents, pensions, which Marx said was more than the total annual income of 60 million workers in India.[50] Marx had also later referred to anti-colonialists in India as revolutionaries and condemned the native allies of the British.[51]

What is not clear is whether Marx revised his views about the positive role of colonialism in destroying the Asiatic mode of production and preparing Asiatic societies for the evolution to socialism or simply noted that colonialism was not successful in the case of India. Nevertheless, Marx's earlier views on Oriental despotism and the Asiatic mode of production were taken up by others and weaved into an apology for colonialism in the name of Marxism.[52] A prominent example is the thought of the Israeli sociologist, Shlomo Avineri, whose work, Ghosh

[49] Karl Marx, 'Entwürfe einer Antwort auf den Brief von V. I. Sassulitsch', in Karl Marx and Friedrich Engels, *Werke*, Band 19 (Berlin: Dietz Verlag, 1962), S. 402; cited in Suniti Kumar Ghosh, 'Marx on India', *Monthly Review* 35 (1984), 46.

[50] Karl Marx and Friedrich Engels, *The First Indian War of Independence, 1857–1859* (Moscow: Progress Publisher, 1975), 163, cited in Ghosh, 'Marx on India', 46.

[51] Marx and Engels, *The First Indian War of Independence*, 103, 151, 178, cited in Ghosh, 'Marx on India', 48.

[52] For a recent study on the Orientalism of Marx, see Lutfi Sunar, *Marx and Weber on Oriental Societies: In the Shadow of Western Modernity* (Surrey: Ashgate, 2014).

correctly noted, functions as a 'blatant apology for colonialism in the name of Marxism'.[53]

Avineri seems to hold to the earlier view of Marx expressed in 1853 and discussed above. He takes the following view:

> Just as the horrors of industrialization are dialectically necessary for the triumph of communism, so the horrors of colonialism are dialectically necessary for the world revolution of the proletariat since without them the countries of Asia (and presumably also Africa) will not be able to emancipate themselves from their stagnant backwardness.[54]

Alienation

The development of capitalism in Europe and its spread throughout the rest of the world, either through colonialism or through other forms of imperialism resulted in a new kind of society with social phenomena and problems that did not exist in precapitalist societies. Marx's focus on and critique of capitalism was not confined to the economic aspects of the system but rather what we would call its sociological aspects. The form of production in capitalism results in certain forms of the relations of production that have implications for social life. The aspects of social and political life that are conditioned by the mode of production of material life include alienation, class, ideology and the role of the state. In order to appreciate the place of these phenomena in Marx's social theory, we need to have a rudimentary understanding of the economic aspects of Marx's theory. We begin with the theory of surplus value.

For most of human history, before the rise of the capitalist mode of production, production was not limited to the production of use values but included the production of exchange values or commodities. The use value refers to the utility or usefulness of a thing independent of the

---

[53] Ghosh, '*Marx on India*', 47.

[54] Shlomo Avineri, 'Introduction', in Shlomo Avineri, ed., Karl Marx on Colonialism and Modernization (New York: Doubleday, 1968), 12.

amount of labour that went into its production. The exchange value of a thing, on the other hand, refers to the value that is derived from its exchange in the market. In the process of the production of goods, labour is divided into two parts: necessary labour and surplus labour. Necessary labour is that part of labour that is required for workers to sustain their livelihood. According to the labour theory of value, a thing has value 'only because human labour in the abstract has been embodied or materialised in it'.[55]

Workers, however, work a full working day over and above what is necessary to reproduce themselves. The additional work is referred to as surplus labour. Surplus labour is the extra labour that goes into the production of extra goods that are traded in the market. This extra product produced by surplus labour is called the surplus product. Commodity production requires the use of a universally accepted means of exchange to facilitate exchange, money. This is a means of exchange against which all commodities are exchanged independently of each other.

When money appeared on the scene there appeared another social type, that is another player in social interaction and, therefore, relevant to sociology. This is the owner of money, otherwise known as the merchant/money-lender/usurer. When the peasant sells his produce in the market place he obtains money, which he uses to buy another commodity he needs. He sells in order to buy. On the other hand, when the money-owner or merchant goes to the market he buys in order to sell. He goes to the market place without any commodity but he owns money. Buying in order to sell makes sense only if the sale brings a higher value than what he bought it for.[56] This additional value is called a surplus value. The surplus value is simply the monetary form of the surplus product, above. The surplus product is produced by workers but is realized only by the merchant or capitalist who sells the surplus product and converts it to its monetary form, surplus value. The theory

---

[55] Karl Marx, *Capital: A Critique of Political Economy. Vol. 1 – A Critical Analysis of Capitalist Production* (New York: International Publishers, 1967), 38.

[56] Karl Marx, *Grundrisse: Introduction to the Critique of Political Economy* (New York: Vintage Books, 1973), 201–2.

of surplus value explains the relationship between the accumulation of profit and the exploitation of labour. Capitalist accumulation of profit takes place through the appropriation of surplus value, defined as the exploitation of labour.[57]

The key to capitalist production, therefore, is the production of surplus values. Without surplus values no capitalist would hire any workers, since buying labour power would not result in any profits. The nature of capitalism is such that labour is exploited through the production of surplus values.

It is important to note that the surplus product and surplus value are social categories because they refer not only to economic factors but also to the relationship between producers and those who appropriate the surplus, namely the landowners and merchants in precapitalist times and capitalists in modern capitalist societies. It is the understanding of this relationship that is the key to the sociology of Marx, to which we now turn.

Marx criticized bourgeois economists for only looking at circulation. By focusing on the sphere of circulation, they only saw an apparent equality between sellers and buyers because everyone is reduced to the common denominator of money.[58] But, the circulation and exchange of exchange values is merely 'the surface process, beneath which, however, in the depths, entirely different processes go on, in which this apparent individual equality and liberty disappear'.[59] In order to penetrate beyond the appearance of a phenomenon, it is necessary to think dialectically.

The core of the dialectic is the conception of the process by which change takes place. All things, whether natural or social, change as a result of the struggle of opposites or contradictions. But these contradictions must be searched for beneath a surface of apparent unity and harmony. To think dialectically is to think of phenomena in terms of appearances and reality where the internal contradictions lie. This idea

[57] Marx, *Capital*, vol. 1, 599.
[58] Marx, *Grundrisse*, 245.
[59] Marx, *Grundrisse*, 247.

Marx borrowed from Hegel. Things are continually in motion, but they give an appearance of rest or harmony. To think dialectically is to reveal the motion or contradictions that underlie the surface calm. Marx applied this method of thinking to the question of circulation and production. The appearance/surface of capital is understood in terms of circulation. The circulation of commodities in the market reveals a harmony. You find liberty and equality in the market. The distinction between buyers and sellers is not there. As Marx says: '[I]t is in the character of the money relation...that all inherent contradictions of bourgeois society appear extinguished...'.[60] Capitalism cannot be understood by remaining at the surface of capitalism. Circulation – the surface – 'is the phenomenon of a process taking place behind it'.[61] This beneath the surface process is that of production, where the contradictions of capitalism are to be found, that is exploitation, alienation and class struggle. The reference to the contradictions that are found beneath the surface phenomenon of circulation is an example of thinking dialectically. It is also possible to think about capitalism as a whole in dialectical terms. If we take the capitalist mode of production as a whole, the internal contradictions are such that the very system which results in the expansion of the capabilities of the forces of production (labour) and increases the productivity of labour, by doing so prepares the way for its own destruction (proletarian revolution and the rise of socialism), because the rise and development of the working class comes into the conflict with the relations of production, or class relations between them and capitalists, of the very same system. Dialectical thinking pervades the works of Marx and Engels. Sometimes it is explicit sometimes implicit in their works. The results of the contradictions of capitalism as they are manifested at the social level include pauperization and alienation.

The drive to the appropriation of surplus value creates competition among capitalists that has the effect of pauperization and alienation. An inherent feature of capitalism is a pool of unemployed and

---

[60] Marx, *Grundrisse*, 240.
[61] Marx, *Grundrisse*, 255.

partially employed labour. This reserve army of labour, helps to keep wages down.

> But in fact, it is capitalistic accumulation itself that constantly produces, and produces in the direct ratio of its own energy and extent, a relatively redundant population of labourers, i.e., a population of greater extent than suffices for the average needs of the self-expansion of capital, and therefore a surplus-population.[62]

Pauperization and income inequality are not the only consequences of capitalist exploitation. Central to Marx's thought regarding the consequences of capitalist exploitation is the problem of alienation. This is discussed in the *Economic and Philosophic Manuscripts*. Using the conceptual tools of political economy or bourgeois political economy, Marx says that has shown that the worker 'sinks to the level of a commodity and becomes indeed the most wretched of commodities' and that 'the wretchedness of the worker is in inverse proportion to the power and magnitude of his production'.[63] This is because the more the worker produces, the more surplus value is given up to the capitalist. The cause of this is the institution of private property. Labour increases the private property of the capitalist by giving up the surplus value. Marx criticizes bourgeois political economy for using the category of private property without explaining how it comes into existence.

Marx wants to understand the connection between private property on the one hand, and labour and capital on the other hand. He starts his argumentation from the economic fact of the present. The worker becomes poorer, the more wealth he produces, 'the more his production increases in power and size'. There is a relative pauperization taking place in that 'with the increasing value of the world of things proceeds in direct proportion the devaluation of the world of men' due to the production of more and more surplus value.[64] The realization of labour

---

[62] Marx, *Capital*, vol. 1, 630.

[63] Karl Marx, *The Economic and Philosophic Manuscripts of 1844* (New York: International Publishers, 1964), 106.

[64] Marx, *The Economic and Philosophic Manuscripts*, 107.

results in the production of commodities that are alien to labour, they are not his, they are appropriated as surplus product and converted to surplus value. Therefore, labour's product 'confronts it [labour] as *something alien*, as a *power independent* of the producer'. This refers to the power of capital.[65] It follows that the realization or accomplishment of labour turns into its opposite, that is the alienation of labour.

This refers to the first two forms of alienation, of which there are four. When we say that the realization of labour turns into its opposite, we mean that it represents the loss of the object. If labour is alienated from its object, it follows that the productive activity itself is alienating.[66] The more the worker '*appropriates* the external world, hence sensuous nature, the more he deprives himself of *means of life* in a double manner: first in the sense that the sensuous external world more and more ceases to be an object belonging to his labour . . . and secondly, in that it more and more ceases to be means of life . . . '[67]

Human beings are what Marx called species-beings. It refers to man's essential nature as humans with psychic and mental characteristics and the need to objectify himself, to create a world of objects through his activity. But now, his labour is an alienating process (in the two ways above). Therefore, man becomes alienated from his species-being, that is the human peculiarities setting him apart from animals become alienated or separated from him. This is the third form of alienation.[68] A consequence of these three forms of alienation is the alienation of man from man, the fourth form of alienation. [69]

Having established the fact of alienated or estranged labour, Marx then asks, 'If the product of labour is alien to me, if it confronts me as an alien power, to whom then does it belong?' It belongs to man but to some other man than the worker. Private property is, therefore the necessary consequence of alienated labour.[70]

---

[65] Marx, *The Economic and Philosophic Manuscripts*, 108.

[66] Marx, *The Economic and Philosophic Manuscripts*, 111.

[67] Marx, *The Economic and Philosophic Manuscripts*, 109.

[68] Marx, *The Economic and Philosophic Manuscripts*, 112–14.

[69] Marx, *The Economic and Philosophic Manuscripts*, 114.

[70] Marx, *The Economic and Philosophic Manuscripts*, 115–17.

Though private property appears to be the source, the cause of alienated labour, it is rather its consequence, just as the gods are *originally* not the cause but the effect of man's intellectual confusion. Later this relationship becomes reciprocal.[71]

Due to this relationship between alienated labour and private property, it follows that the economic and social emancipation of workers and the solution to alienation is the political emancipation of society from private property.[72]

Related to the idea of alienation is that of the fetishism of commodities. Drawing an analogy from religion, Marx says, 'the productions of the human brain appear as independent beings endowed with life, and entering into relations both with one another and the human race. So it is in the world of commodities with the products of men's hands. This I call the Fetishism which attaches itself to the products of labour, so soon as they are produced as commodities, and which is therefore inseparable from the production of commodities'.[73] In other words, humans make the world, but the world is not of their own making. This is because the market exchange of commodities functions to obscure or veil the real character of relations of production, that is between the property owners and the propertyless workers. The market takes on a function in the eyes of the actors that in reality only actors perform. Therefore, the fetishism of commodities gives to commodities and economic institutions like the market, an independent objective reality that is external to and coercive of actors. The fetishism of commodities is a specific case of the more general phenomenon of reification, which in turn is an aspect of alienation.

Although Marx did not use the term 'reification',[74] he describes the phenomenon:

A commodity is therefore a mysterious thing, simply because in it the social character of men's labour appears to them as an objective character

[71] Marx, *The Economic and Philosophic Manuscripts*, 117.

[72] Marx, *The Economic and Philosophic Manuscripts*, 118.

[73] Marx, *Capital*, vol. 1, 72.

[74] The term was used by Georg Lukács. See his *History and Class Consciousness: Studies in Marxist Dialectics* (Cambridge: MIT Press, 1971), 83ff.

stamped upon the product of that labour; because the relation of the producers to the sum total of their own labour is presented to them as a social relation existing not between themselves, but between the products of their labour. This is the reason the products of labour become commodities, social things whose qualities are at the same time perceptible and imperceptible by the senses ... It is only a definite social relation between men that assumes, in their eyes, the fantastic form of a relation between things.[75]

People do not realize that their own labour appears to be something objective and independent of them and that the relations among them and the social structures that define these relations are actually resulting from their own actions. This is a reflection of alienation, the separation between the producer and the product. The social world, actually a product of human action, appears to humans as something external to and coercive of them.

Class and Class Consciousness in Capitalist Society

Capitalism is maintained by the rule of one class over another, in both material and ideal terms. Marx did not explicitly define class but he uses the concept throughout his works. The *Manifesto of the Communist Party* by Marx and Engels was commissioned by the Communist League, an international association of workers. Published in 1848, it represents the theoretical and practical programme of the league.

The *Manifesto* begins by saying that the written history of all societies is the history of class struggles.[76] In other words, the motive force of history is class struggle and is characterized by the opposition between classes such as lord and serf, bourgeois and proletarian. Society has always been arranged in a manifold gradation of social rank. In feudal

---

[75] Marx, *Capital*, vol. 1, 72.

[76] Marx and Engels, *Manifesto of the Communist Party*, 32.

society there are lords, vassals, guild-masters, journeymen, apprentices, serfs. Marx and Engels refer to these as classes. Bourgeois society that arose from the ruins of feudal society had not done away with class conflict. It established new classes with new conditions of oppression. The new class structure is also simplified with two great hostile camps: bourgeoisie and proletariat.[77] Marx and Engels believed that just as the means of production, that is money as capital, developed in feudalism but became incompatible with feudal relations of production, that is the institution of serfdom, so were the bourgeois means of production becoming incompatible with the relations of production:

> Modern bourgeois society with its relations of production, of exchange and of property, a society that has conjured up such gigantic means of production and of exchange, is like the sorcerer who is no longer able to control the powers of the nether world whom he has called up by his spells.[78]

The very means of production, capital, that the bourgeoisie used to bring down feudalism, create now its own destruction, because capital pauperizes, immiserates, alienates and gets workers organized to overthrow capitalism and usher in a new mode of production, that is socialism. In order for this to develop, the proletariat or working class must develop class consciousness. Relevant here are two dimensions of class; that is subjective and objective class. The objective situation of a class refers to the membership of people in a class, and the role and function of this class in society.

The subjective class, however, refers to awareness of its members of their situation. In other words they are aware of exploitation based on appropriation of surplus value, aware of being alienated.

> [T]he great mass of the French nation is formed by the simple addition of homologous magnitudes, much as potatoes in a sack form a sack of

---

[77] Marx and Engels, *Manifesto of the Communist Party*, 33.

[78] Marx and Engels, *Manifesto of the Communist Party*, 39.

potatoes. Insofar as millions of families live under conditions of existence that separate their mode of life, their interests, and their culture from those of the other classes, and put them in hostile opposition to the latter, they form a class. Insofar as there is merely a local interconnection among these small-holding peasants, and the identity of their interests begets *no community*, no national bond, and no political organization among them, they *do not* form a class.[79]

A class is only a class, in the subjective sense, that is a class for itself, when it attains consciousness of the objective conditions under which it was created and exists. When a class is conscious of itself as a class and its interests, its attempts to realize its interests is referred to as class struggle, which takes various forms such as strikes, demonstrations and slow-downs. Class struggle can also take place in the context of the revolution to overthrow the state and the political economic order that it represents.

Capitalism and the State

The dominant view of the state in the thought of Marx and Engels is that it functions to maintain the rule of the bourgeoisie over the rest of society. In another oft-quoted statement they say, 'The executive of the modern state is but a committee for managing the common affairs of the whole bourgeoisie.'[80] This comes about because the state is dependent on the commercial credit which the bourgeoisie extends to it via the stock exchange, taxation and other means.[81] This view of the state has come to be known as the instrumentalist conception where the state is seen to act for and on behalf of the bourgeoisie as a result of its dependence on the bourgeoisie. While Marx never presented a comprehensive and systematic theory of the state, several statements on the subject have been understood to constitute what might be called the classical Marxist theory of the state.

---

[79] Karl Marx, *The 18th Brumaire of Louis Bonaparte* (New York: International Publishers), 124.
[80] Marx and Engels, *Manifesto of the Communist Party*, 35.
[81] Marx, *The German Ideology*, 79–80.

According to Marx, the modern state exists in societies where the bourgeoisie had become a class and is organized on a national level. The state is the form in which the numbers of the ruling class, here the bourgeoisie, assert their common interests.[82] The bourgeoisie, as a ruling class, is an economically dominant class which dominates other aspects of social life including the state. The bourgeoisie has ownership of and control over the means of production and in order to perpetuate this state of affairs it has to exercise state power. By this reading the state is a committee that manages the common affairs of the bourgeoisie. Unlike the liberal theory of the state, the state in classical Marxism is seen as an organization that is controlled by class interests and functions to advance these interests. A state may be democratic, but as long as it allows for private ownership of the means of production and the majority of people are selling their labour power, then the state is a machine for the suppression of labour by capital. What is understood as exploitation in Marxist terms is upheld by the state.

In the capitalist mode of production the state maintains the rule of the capitalist class over the working class. The capitalist is termed as the ruling class which has a specific relationship with the state. The capitalist class is the ruling class because it is the class which controls the major economic institutions of the country, and as a result of which dominates the state or governmental processes of the country. Therefore, when Marx says that state 'manages the common affairs' of the capitalist class, he means that the capitalist class is able to influence the state in formulating laws, rules, regulations and policies that favour the capitalist class. According to William Domhoff, there are four processes through which active members of ruling class influence the state. These are the special-interest process, the policy-planning process, the candidate selection process and the ideology process.[83]

In the special-interest process, members of the ruling class, the corporations get tax breaks, subsidies and other benefits through the

---

[82] Marx, *The German Ideology*, 80.

[83] William Domhoff, 'State and Ruling Class in Corporate America', *Insurgent Sociologist* 4 (1974).

lobbying process. Lobbies attempt to influence state policies by financing the electoral campaigns of members of parliament, by promising good jobs to legislators after they leave government service, by providing legislators with studies that provide legislators with arguments in support of the lobby's views, and by socializing with state officials in order to influence their views. The special-interest process implies that members of the ruling class, as capitalists, have positions that they take with regard to policies that should be implemented by the government on their behalf.[84]

The policy-planning process brings together members of ruling class in the form of various organizations, such as business councils and economic development committees. The objective is to familiarize themselves with general issues, resolve conflicts, hear the findings of hired experts and influence climate of opinion in government and the country in general.[85]

The candidate-selection process is one way of ensuring that the policies capitalists would like to be implemented actually get implemented. Since the government is elected by the people, does this not mean that the peoples' interests in general will be reflected in policies, not just the interests of capitalists? According to Marxist theory, this will not happen if members of the ruling class are also part of the state. The same people who direct major corporations and take part in the policy-planning process, fund candidates for elections who would then work to advance the interests of capital. Furthermore, the candidates themselves are from the capitalist class.[86]

Given these various processes that help to maintain ruling class domination over the state, why does the public accept this state of affairs? This is due in a large part to the ideology process. The strength of the capitalist system does not lie in its coercive powers but in the acceptance of the ruled of a conception of the world that is in harmony with the interests of capital. Through the ideology process, ideas, attitudes and values that reinforce the support of capitalism such as

---

[84] Domhoff, 'State and Ruling Class in Corporate America', 7–8.
[85] Domhoff, 'State and Ruling Class in Corporate America', 8–10.
[86] Domhoff, 'State and Ruling Class in Corporate America', 10–13.

democracy are propagated. For example, the idea that government is impartial and functions to advance the interests of all groups in society is ideological in that it conceals the complicit role of the state in capitalist exploitation.[87] These are the various ways in which the capitalist state becomes an instrument of the ruling class.

The instrumentalist theory of the state is not the only conception of the state to be found in Marx's works. There is another view of the state which emerged from Marx's observation of Bonapartism. The *coup d'etat* of Bonaparte led to an independent state.[88] This does not mean that Bonaparte was not representing any class. According to Marx, Bonaparte saw himself as a representative of both the bourgeoisie and the peasantry.

> But above all, Bonaparte looks on himself as the chief of the society of December 10, as the representative of the *lumpenproletariat* to which he himself, his *entourage*, his government and his army belong...
> This contradictory task of the man explains the contradictions of his government, the confused grouping about which seeks now to win, now to humiliate first one class and then another and arrays all of them uniformly against him.[89]

Taking his point of departure from Marx's view of the Bonapartist state, Alavi states that

> In the post-colonial society, the problem of the relationship between the State and the underlying economic structure is more complex than the context in which it was posed even in the Bonapartist State or other examples which arose in the context of the development of European society. It is structured by yet another historical experience and it calls for fresh theoretical insights.[90]

---

[87] Domhoff, 'State and Ruling Class in Corporate America', 13–15.
[88] Karl Marx, *The Eighteenth Brumaire of Louis Bonaparte* (New York: International Publishers, 1963), 122.
[89] Marx, *The Eighteenth Brumaire of Louis Bonaparte*, 132.
[90] Hamza Alavi, 'The State in Post-Colonial Societies: Pakistan and Bangladesh', *New Left Review* 74 (1972), 61.

Here, the class basis is much more complex. After the colonial period, the postcolonial state was left with three propertied classes with competing interests. In view of this, the state cannot be considered the instrument of a single class.[91] Rather, it is 'relatively autonomous and it mediates between the competing interests of the three propertied classes, namely the metropolitan bourgeoisies, the indigenous bourgeoisie and the landed classes'.[92]

The Role of Ideology

We have already touched upon the ideology process in connection with the Marxist view of the role of the state in capitalist societies. Ideology is an extremely important concept in the thought of Marx. For Marx, the term ideology has a negative connotation. It refers to the ideas connected with the material conditions of society as well as the interests of the ruling class. He chastised German philosophers for failing to 'inquire into the connection of German philosophy with German reality, the relation of their criticism to their own material surroundings'.[93]

Ideology should not be confused with political beliefs or the political culture of a collectivity. Ideology refers to beliefs that are integrated into a system of thought with ideas that are systematically connected with each other. Take the following beliefs – the essence of capitalism is giving; people who fail to led productive and prosperous lives have their own shortcomings to blame; private property is an inalienable right. When these beliefs are connected with each other to say that the failure of certain people or groups to lead a prosperous life in capitalist societies is not due to the capitalist system itself but due to certain negative cultural factors affecting the performance of these people (a culturalist rather than structuralist explanation) and their failure, therefore, to take advantage of their rights (to private property, for example), this becomes

[91] Alavi, 'The State in Post-Colonial Societies, 62; Hamza Alavi, 'State and Class under Peripheral Capitalism', in Hamza Alavi and Teodor Shanin (eds.) *Introduction to the Sociology of 'Developing Societies'* (London: Macmillan Education Ltd., 1982), 298.
[92] Alavi, '*The State in Post-Colonial Societies*', 62.
[93] Marx, *The German Ideology*, 41.

an ideology. This is a general definition of ideology which even non-Marxists would agree to. But Marxism goes beyond this to say that ideology is not just a systematic interconnectedness of ideas but also functions to support the interests of the group that espouses that ideology. An example is the ideology of liberalism which say that freedom and equality are found in the free market economy. This conceals the reality of inequality, alienation and exploitation that are found beneath the appearance or surface of circulation.

Marx was particularly interested in the ideology of the ruling class. In connection with this Marx made yet another famous statement:

> The ideas of the ruling class are in every epoch the ruling ideas, i.e. the class which is the ruling *material* force of society, is at the same time its ruling *intellectual* force. The class which has the means of material production at its disposal, has control at the same time over the means of mental production, so that thereby, generally speaking, the ideas of those who lack the means of mental production are subject to it. The ruling ideas are nothing more than the ideal expression of the dominant material relationships, the dominant material relationships grasped as ideas; hence of the relationships which make the one class the ruling one, therefore, the ideas of its dominance. The individuals composing the ruling class possess among other things consciousness, and therefore think. Insofar, therefore, as they rule as a class and determine the extent and compass of an epoch, it is self-evident that they do this in its whole range, hence among other things rule also as thinkers, as producers of ideas, and regulate the production and distribution of the ideas of their age: thus their ideas are the ruling ideas of the epoch. For instance, in an age and in a country where royal power, aristocracy, and bourgeoisie are contending for mastery and where, therefore, mastery is shared, the doctrine of the separation of powers proves to be the dominant idea and is expressed as an 'eternal law.'[94]

The ideas of the ruling class are not only a reflection of the material conditions of that class but also the material interests of those who believe in and articulate those ideas.

---

[94] Marx, *The German Ideology*, 64–5.

This brings us to the distinction between idealism and materialism. Marxist criticized German ideology for being idealistic and, therefore, veiling the material conditions of society. Marx's claim was that:

> It is not the consciousness of men that determines their existence, but their social existence that determines their consciousness. At a certain stage of development, the material productive forces of society come into conflict with the existing relations of production or – this merely expresses the same thing in legal terms – with the property relations within the framework of which they have operated hitherto. From forms of development of the productive forces these relations turn into their fetters. Then begins an era of social revolution . . . In studying such transformations it is always necessary to distinguish between the material transformation of the economic conditions of production, which can be determined with the precision of natural science, and the legal, political, religious, artistic or philosophic – in short, ideological forms in which men become conscious of this conflict and fight it out.[95]

Historical idealism sees ideas as sole or dominant motor of historical change. German ideology was idealist because in its attempt to understand social reality it started out with men's ideas, conceptions and consciousness. Historical materialism or the materialist conception of history, on the other hand, sees material factors, that is the mode of production, as the motive force in history. It is this material activity that determines the ideas of men and, therefore, ideology, not the other way around.

For Marx, the most important aspect of social existence is what is involved in the relations of production, in the productive process. Furthermore, the ideas of a group also reflect their material interests. Marx censured historians for not knowing what the simple shopkeeper knew:

> 'Whilst in ordinary life every shopkeeper is very well able to distinguish between what somebody professes to be and what he really is, our historians

---

[95] Marx, *A Contribution to the Critique of Political Economy*, 21.

have not yet won even this trivial insight. They take every epoch at its word and believe that everything it says and imagines about itself is true'.[96]

Thus, ideology refers to the thought that is so interest-bound to a situation; the real conditions of society are concealed or obscured by the collective unconscious of a given group and the given order being stabilized.[97] Ideologies are orientations that distort reality and attempt to conceal new realities by thinking of these new realities in categories more appropriate to the past. Therefore, ideologies are more geared towards preserving the status quo than transforming it.

Ideologies have a foothold in reality or praxis. Nevertheless, although their starting point is reality, ideologies present a fragmentary and partial reality. For example, bourgeois economics remains at the level of circulation and fails to unveil the contradiction of the economy that can be seen at the level of production.

Ideologies refract rather than reflect reality. Because only a partial reality is presented, the resulting representation is a refracted or distorted view of reality. An example is the claim of equality and freedom in capitalism. Ideologies also present themselves as universal ideas relevant and applicable to all groups and classes in a society. In this sense they are general and abstract. At the same time, however, they represent fixed and limited special interests.[98]

Conclusion

As we have seen, Marx had noted that the very means of production and of exchange, that were the foundation upon which the bourgeoisie built itself up, originated in feudal society. These means of production and of exchange upon reaching a certain stage of development become incompatible with the feudal organization of agriculture and manufacturing,

---

[96] Marx, *The German Ideology*, 67.
[97] Karl Mannheim, *Ideology and Utopia: An Introduction to the Sociology of Knowledge* (London: Routledge and Kegan Paul, 1936), 36–37.
[98] Henri Lefebvre, *The Sociology of Marx* (New York: Columbia University Press, 1982), 69–72.

that is with the feudal relations of property. The bourgeois revolution was to eventually destroy the feudal system within which its own means of production were generated.[99]

Marx believed that a similar process would take place in bourgeois society. The capitalist means of production and the organization of labour would reach a stage of development that would make them no longer compatible with the capitalist relations of property. A socialist revolution would eventually destroy the very system that gave rise to its own means of production and exchange. Capital would become more and more concentrated as the smaller capitalists who were unable to profit from the advantages of mass production get devoured by the bigger capitalists. Therefore, the average size of firms grows and capital becomes concentrated in fewer hands. The increasing concentration of capital means that the number of small self-employed people decreases and they join the ranks of the proletariat. For Marx, the fundamental contradiction in the capitalist system is that between labour and capital. He believed that at some point capitalism would be replaced by a more efficient and humane system that is not based on the production of surplus values and the exploitation of labour. But, Marx devoted very little time to discussing socialism or communism. Although he believed that a socialist mode of production would emerge from capitalism, just as the capitalist mode of production emerged from feudalism, Marx preoccupation was with analysing capitalist society rather than speculating about the nature and future of socialism.

While the socialist revolution ushering in a new mode of production as envisaged by Marx did not take place and capitalism was not overthrown, Marx remains relevant to sociology and the other social sciences for the concepts and method that he presented for the study of feudal capitalist and the so-called Asiatic societies. Although there are problems with his understanding of the nature of Asiatic societies, informed by his Orientalist standpoint, our attitude is that rather than exclude Marx, he needs to be rescued from himself, from his Orientalist assumptions, in order that what remains useful in Marx and be salvaged.

---

[99] Karl Marx and Frederick Engels, *Manifesto of the Communist Party* (Peking: Foreign Languages Press, 1973), 39.

Harriet Martineau (1802–1876)

Vineeta Sinha

Introduction

Harriet Martineau was an Englishwoman born in 1802 in the town of Norwich. She came from a middle-class family of devout Christian Unitarians and was largely home schooled with the exception of the year she spent in a girl's boarding school.[1] She wore an ear trumpet through most of her adult life, having been diagnosed with deafness at the age of 12. Her father's early death and the family's economic woes pressed Martineau into seeking employment. Fine needlework and writing were the two options available to women at the time and she excelled in both. As a woman in Victorian England, she faced numerous constraints and overcame personal adversity to achieve notable milestones professionally.

Martineau found great success in professional writing and supported herself financially through this. The writings she produced can be placed in the genres of travel and journalistic writing. Martineau was passionate

---

[1] Harriet Martineau, In *'Women in Sociology: A Bio-Bibliographical Sourcebook'*, Ed. Mary Jo Deegan, (New York, 1991), 290.

© The Author(s) 2017
S.F. Alatas, V. Sinha, *Sociological Theory Beyond the Canon*,
DOI 10.1057/978-1-137-41134-1_4

about writing, deriving immense satisfaction from putting pen to paper. She wrote scores of letters to newspapers,[2] journal articles, book reviews and essays, but as was the practice for women writers, her works appeared under pseudonyms in the early years.[3] Apart from writing for newspapers, Martineau experimented with fiction and produced novels, poetry, novelettes and short stories. While these found wide readership and brought her fame and popularity,[4] they were translated into meagre financial returns.[5] Martineau was part of a vibrant and lively intellectual circle, counting amongst her acquaintances and intimate friends, the likes of Charles and Erasmus Dickens, George Eliot, Thomas Carlyle, Florence Nightingale, Elizabeth Barrett Browning, William Wordsworth, Charlotte Bronte and Thomas Malthus.[6] Although engaged briefly to a suitor (who died unexpectedly), she remained single, reportedly happily.[7] She was a fiercely independent woman who worked her entire life, even during periods of illness. Martineau was plagued by a number of health problems throughout her life and died in 1876 at the age of 74. Martineau's three-volume autobiography was published posthumously in 1877.

As a young woman, Martineau was deeply religious and committed to Unitarianism. However, she found herself attracted to the disciplines of philosophy and metaphysics. She ultimately declared herself to be an atheist and found great appeal in positivism and science. Martineau captured the imagination of politicians, policy-makers, Members of Parliament and intellectuals of her time. She was an activist and openly voiced her position on such issues as slavery, women's rights,

---

[2] According to Hill and Hoecker Drysdale, (2002, 8), 'Martineau wrote more than 1,500 newspaper columns, of which only a few have been reprinted'.

[3] Francis E. Mineka, *The Dissidence of Dissent: The Monthly Repository, 1806–1838.* (Chapel Hill, 1944).

[4] R. K. Webb, *Harriet Martineau: A Radical Victorian*, (London, 1960).

[5] Mineka, *The Dissidence of Dissent*, (1944).

[6] Martineau collaborated with Florence Nightingale (McDonald 1994) and corresponded with George Eliot and Elizabeth Barret Browning (David 1987). She is also known to have developed deep friendships with Erasmus Dickens and Thomas Malthus (Hoecker-Drysdale 1992).

[7] Maria Weston Chapman, 'An Autobiographical Memoir.' In *Memorials of Harriet Martineau*, (Boston, 1877).

international affairs (such as British colonial policy in India) and various items of legislation (relating to poverty, health etc.), these being a few areas where her views had a bearing on current public opinion. Harriet Martineau is today by no means an unknown figure. Through the efforts of a dedicated group of scholars who have been working for more than four decades, her primary works have now been recovered, republished and made accessible. Critical commentaries on Martineau's primary works have also been growing steadily since the late 1960s[8] and gaining momentum through the 1980s[9] and 1990s.[10] Yet she has continued to remain on the margins of mainstream sociological theorizing. This chapter makes yet another case for recognizing the sociological and theoretical value of Martineau's works.

A General Outline of Martineau's Sociological Theories

Martineau's two-volume English translation of Auguste Comte's six-volume French original, *The Positive Philosophy* (published in 1853) was her closest encounter with the world of nineteenth-century academia. The task of translating Comte's volumes and rendering his ideas accessible to English-reading audiences is by no measure a small contribution in the history of the discipline. Yet, Martineau has received little attention from sociologists even in this connection apart from being named as a translator. This may have surprised Comte himself, given his highly favourable account of Martineau's translation of his work:

---

[8] Seymour Martin Lipset, 'Harriet Martineau's America,' in *Society in America*, Ed. SM Lipset, (New York, 1962); Webb, *Harriet Martineau*, 1960; Vera Wheatley, The Life and Work of Harriet Martineau, (London, 1957).

[9] See Rossi (1973); Deegan (1988); Hill (1987); Pinchanick (1990); Reinharz (1989); Riedesal (1981); Sanders (1986); Spender (1982), Terry (1983); Gayle (1985).

[10] Pioneering works include McDonald (1993, 1994), Hoecker-Drysdale, (1992, 1996, 2000), Deegan (1991), Hassett (1996), Hill (1998), Hill and Hoecker-Drysdale (2002), Hunter (1995), Niebrugge-Brantley and Lengermann (1996, 1998, 2002), Orazem (1999), Reinharz (1992, 1993), Sanders (1990), Weiner (1991, 1994). For a very recent edited volume on Martineau, see Sanders and Weiner (2016).

And looking at it from the point of view of future generations, I feel sure that your name will be linked with mine, for you have executed the only one those works that will survive amongst all those which my fundamental treatise has called forth.[11]

Martineau's belief in the moral value of philosophy of positivism was part of her motivation for undertaking this translation:

My strongest inducement to this enterprise was my deep conviction of our need of this book in my own country, in a form which renders it accessible to the highest number of intelligent readers. We are living in a remarkable time, when the conflict of opinions renders a firm foundation of knowledge indispensable, not only to our intellectual moral, and social progress, but to our holding such ground as we have gained from former ages.[12]

As a positivist, Martineau believed in social laws and the progressive evolution of society. Martineau had rejected that the universe was a divine creation and argued instead that it was determined by universal laws which only scientific inquiry could reveal. This was already expressed in the *Letters on the Laws of Man's Nature and Development*, a publication she co-authored with Henry Atkinson in 1851. In 'freely' translating and condensing Comte's philosophy, Martineau recognized the liberating potential of positivist philosophy in understanding and remaking society and was further committed to disseminating these ideas widely in society:

The supreme dread of every one who cares for the good of the nation or race is that men should be adrift for want of an anchorage for their convictions. I believe that no one questions that a very large proportion of our people are now so adrift. With pain and fear we see that a multitude, who might and should be among the wisest and best of our citizens, are alienated for ever from the kind of faith which sufficed for all in an

---

[11] Fredrick Harrison, Introduction, In *The Positive Philosophy of Auguste Comte*, 1 (London: 1895), 17–18.
[12] Martineau, Preface to Comte's translation of *The Positive Philosophy*, vii.

organic period which has passed away, and they cannot obtain for themselves, any ground of conviction as firm and clear as that which sufficed for our fathers in their day. The moral dangers of such a state of fluctuation as has thus arisen are fearful in the extreme, whether the transition stage from one order of convictions to another be long or short. The work of M. Comte is unquestionably the greatest single effort that has been made to obviate this kind of danger; and my deep conviction is that it will be found to retrieve a vast amount of wandering, of unsound speculation, of listless or reckless doubt, and of moral uncertainty and depression.[13]

Seeking independence of thought, she moved away from the confines of religious dogma and authority. She valued instead the search for truth on the basis of scientific principles and turned to reason, logic and empiricism as objective modes and methods of discovery.

Martineau's early writings appeared in the Unitarian magazine, *The Monthly Repository*. She also contributed letters, reviews of books and articles on education, women's rights and the abolition of slavery to newspapers and periodicals, like the *Daily News, Spectator, Weekly Chronicle, Quarterly Review, Tatler, New York Tribune* and the radical leftist *Westminster Review*. Martineau's published works have stimulated a great deal of interest amongst students of American history, Victorian life in nineteenth-century Britain, journalism, women's studies, religious studies, feminism and English literature. Between 1832 and 1834, Martineau produced her best known and popular writing, *Illustrations of Political Economy* (3,479 pages in 25 volume instalments), where 'she used fiction to explicate the new science of political economy'.[14] These stories were used to disseminate the workings of the structural processes of production, distribution, exchange and consumption amongst a lay readership. Martineau's first instalment of the political economy tales recorded a sale of 1,500 copies and '... by 1834, an average of 10,000 copies a month'.[15] She enjoyed a vast readership and her political economy tales were well received, not just amongst laypersons. These

---

[13] Martineau, Preface to Comte's translation of *The Positive Philosophy*, vii.

[14] Deegan, *Women in Sociology*, 290.

[15] Hoecker-Drysdale, *Harriet Martineau*, 33.

were exceedingly popular with readers of varied backgrounds and each instalment was eagerly awaited.

Apart from her political economy tales, Martineau wrote widely on issues close to her heart, including the universal need for a rational, systematic and scientific approach to life in all societal domains. An early and important document that carries Martineau's attraction to reason and systematic thought is carried in six compositions, entitled '*Essays on the art of thinking*'. These were written in 1829 but published in an anthology only in 1836 and described by McDonald as '[e]ffectively empiricism-for-all: how to think logically and bring appropriate evidence to bear on the problems of the day[16].' Her mature methodological reflections which outlined her systematic approach to observing society appeared later. In an era when it was not common for women to travel,[17] in 1834 Martineau embarked on a two-year trip to the United States of America (USA).[18] This journey produced a classic three-volume text, *Society in America*, which is favourably regarded by students of nineteenth-century American society for her astute and insightful observations of American life. Martineau added to the corpus of travel writing in this period from her 1846 travels through Egypt, Palestine and Syria. Her observations of customs and religious ideas of these places were published in *Eastern Life, Present and Past*, where she concluded a general trend towards atheism and which she saw as progress of rationality and positivist thinking.

Martineau valued the role of education, saw herself as a public educator and[19] addressed her writing largely to lay audiences of working-class and middle-class backgrounds. In 1822, as an almost 20-year-old, Martineau produced a piece entitled '*On Female Education*' where she outlined her feminist views about the value of women's education

---

[16] Lynn McDonald, *The Women Founders*, 168.

[17] Harriet Martineau, *Retrospect of Western Travel*, (London, 1838).

[18] In 1846, she also spent eight months in the 'Middle East' (including present day Syria, Egypt and Palestine), which is the basis of her 1848 book, *Eastern Life, Past and Present*. She also travelled to Ireland and Scotland.

[19] *Harriet Martineau on Women*, edited by Gayle G Yates, New Jersey: Rutgers University Press, 1985.

not just to women but to society as a whole. Martineau's 1848 book on *Household Education* offered 'moral and practical instruction'[20] to women for improving their household management skills. Her writings and analysis of the everyday lives of middle- and upper-class Victorian women as well as her scrutiny of domestic service reveal her analysis of social institutions. These writings reveal a theory and philosophy about 'work' and 'labour'. Martineau approached 'work' as an object of study; as a lens through which to study industrial, capitalist society. In concrete terms, she undertook detailed empirical studies of industries and occupations (e.g. domestic service). Martineau staunchly defended an individual's (and a woman's) right to work and the right to choose desired work. She present work as meaningful and honourable, as a medium of self-actualization and indeed speaks of work as a vocation, even as she argued that leisure was necessary. There are important parallels with Marx's theory of work here. Martineau was critical of 'idleness', an affliction of the middle classes, particularly women. This position was apparent in her fiction and non-fiction works.

While Martineau remained on the margins of the intellectual circle of would-be academics, she publicly and boldly articulated her views on the possibility of 'sociology,' 'moral sciences' and the 'social sciences',[21] taking root as a disciplined mode of inquiry, alongside the natural sciences. In 1858, in letters to *The Spectator* and *Daily News*, in an era before the social sciences were codified and formalized, Martineau was already asking the question 'What is social science?' and more importantly, providing her own answers. Her criticism of the 'National Association for the Promotion of Social Sciences' (NAPSS) was that it did not operate with a rigorous definition and understanding of 'science' and was grounded in her belief that the 'moral sciences' and 'social sciences' must be based on the model offered by the natural sciences, and envisioned it having a practical agenda for reform, progress and improvement of society.

---

[20] Yates, 1985, 87.

[21] While not a member herself, Martineau followed closely the affairs and activities of the National Society for the Promotion of Social Sciences (NAPSS), established in 1857 'by members of the British Association for the Advancement of Science, who wished to study political economy, education, and social issues' (Hoecker-Drysdale 1992, 135).

Fiction as Social Commentary

Martineau utilized different methodological principles in her writings. Typically, her early essays on the art of thinking and her *How to Observe* are cited as her contributions to sociological methods of inquiry. In addition, Martineau's *Illustrations of Political Economy* can be read for strategies she used in the task of public education. Martineau's political economy tales aimed to articulate, in simple language, the principles of political economy to laypersons, otherwise unable to access abstract, philosophical and theoretical tracts. Martineau translated the concepts and theories of Thomas Malthus, John Stuart Mill and Adam Smith into accessible language, but as she admits retrospectively, rather unintentionally. She notes in her 1877 *Autobiography* that she first encountered political economy in reading Jane Marcet's book on the subject:

> I took up the book chiefly to see what Political Economy precisely was; and great was my surprise to find that I had been teaching it unawares, in my stories about Machinery and Wages. It struck me at once that the principles of the whole science might be advantageously conveyed in the same way.[22]

The value of fiction and literature for conveying sociological ideas, and thus as a pedagogical tool, has enormous value. Martineau's methodology in the *Illustrations* was to utilize fiction as social commentary, to illustrate, educate and persuade readers. In her fictional stories, Martineau used the strategy of *demonstration* effectively. The overt didactic stories were constructed to reveal how and with what effect production, distribution and consumption processes functioned in everyday life. Martineau turned the analytic lens on everyday life in order to encourage appropriate attitudes and behaviours towards new economic and social developments. She was a professional writer and her writing was also meant to educate the public. Her intention disseminated amongst the masses a particular (mainstream) harmonious view of

---

[22] Martineau, *Autobiography*, 1877, Volume III, 138.

economics, capital/labour relationships, need for work discipline, regulation of wages, need for taxes, capitalism and industry. To be fair to Martineau, the messages in her stories were directed both at all classes – bourgeoisie and proletariat – as she implored the virtues of working harmoniously for the good of all.

Martineau's stories in the *Illustrations* reveal her conception and theorizing of industrial capitalism. For instance, embedded in '*The Moral of Many Fables*' are Martineau's conceptions of means of production, capital and labour and the relations amongst these. She certainly displayed a particular understanding of what these were and how they functioned:

CAPITAL is something produced with a view to employment in further production. Labour is the origin, and Saving is the support of capital. Capital consists of:

1. Implements of labour,
2. Material, simple or compound, on which labour is employed, [and]
3. Subsistence of labourers.

Since Capital is derived from Labour, whatever economizes labour assists the growth of Capital. Machinery economizes Labour, and therefore assists the growth of Capital. The growth of capital increases demand for labour. Machinery, by assisting the growth of Capital, therefore increases the demand for Labour. In other words, productive industry is proportioned to capital, whether that capital be fixed or reproducible. *The interests of the two classes of producers, labourers and capitalists, are therefore, the same; the prosperity of both depending on the accumulation of CAPITAL.*[23] (emphasis mine)

In this rendition, Martineau's ideas about capitalism are aligned more with Durkheim than with Marx. The former was equally optimistic about the possibility of organic solidarity in modern society, while Marx would disagree that: '*The interests of the two classes of producers, labourers and capitalists, are therefore, the same; the prosperity of both depending on*

---

[23] Martineau, 'The Moral of Many Fables', *Illustrations, 1832–1834.*

the accumulation of CAPITAL.' In a cynical and critical reading, Martineau's popularizing of political economy here served mainstream, conventional and established views of capitalism. It is no secret that Martineau admired British industry and saw capitalism as progressive. Martineau was a strong advocate of the free market and laissez-faire economics and saw advancement in industrialization and modernization of society. This was most clearly expressed in her defence of Britain's colonization of India. Like Marx's theorizing on the subject, Martineau too argued that colonialism (and the modernity it heralded) was good for India.[24] Yet, Martineau was ambivalent about British colonial rule in India. Martineau's eurocentrism is evident in the view of Western capitalism as universal, distinct and progressive and in the case of colonialism was aligned with Britain's civilizing mission.

Back home, Martineau could imagine industrial capitalism in idyllic and utopian modes. This despite considerable empirical evidence of industrial conflict and unrest in Britain through the period of her writing from the 1830s to the 1850s. Although social unrest and conflict were the overt subjects of her earlier stories 'The Rioters' and 'The Turn Out' as well as stories from the *Illustrations* 'The Hill and the Valley' (about machine breaking) and 'A Manchester Strike' (*Illustrations*), they were designed precisely to discourage conflict and unproductive and inefficient behaviour on the part of labour and to argue for an alignment of capital/labour interests. She presented a conservative and highly favourable view of capitalism and the industrial revolution, and argued in her stories that disruptions (like strikes, breaking of machines and other means of production as well as idling and refusal to work) were ultimately dysfunctional and unproductive.

Martineau's 'Science of Morals and Manners'

Martineau's travels to the USA were critical for shaping this 1838 work, which the American sociologist S. M. Lipset has described it as 'the first book on the methodology of social research in the then still unborn

---

[24] D. Logan, Martineau on India.

disciplines of sociology and anthropology' and proposed 'a separate scientific discipline, and called it the science of morals and manners'.[25] Martineau's *How to Observe Morals and Manners*[26] is an early document of sociological inquiry. Unsurprisingly, it has been recently compared with Durkheim's *The Rules of Sociological Method.*[27] It has been noted, somewhat belatedly, that Martineau's methodological text was written some 60 years *before* Durkheim's,[28] and that the two are 'nearly analogous'.[29] While this comparison is illuminating and significant from the point of view of history of ideas, it is as crucial to approach Martineau's text autonomously.

Here, Martineau lays forth the processes for systematic and methodical observations of society. She displays a concern here with outlining an intellectual programme she defines as the 'science of morals and manners',[30] an approach that seeks to uncover both observable manners as well as the more abstract morals. By 'morals' she refers to embedded values, norms and principles in which the more surface, observable practices, the 'manners' are rooted. This text is grounded in the methodological principles of empiricism, naturalism and objectivity,[31] which Martineau deems to be indispensable for studying society scientifically. Her method proposes the use of observation techniques (including participant observation), to elicit knowledge about a carefully demarcated subject matter. The book is divided into two parts: the first part is entitled 'Requisites for observation', that is how to observe, and the second part deals with the object of inquiry of a new science, that is what should be observed.

The text carries detailed instructions about *what* to observe and *how* to observe society. While attracted to rationalism and objectivity,

[25] Lipset, *Harriet Martineau*, 7.
[26] *How to Observe Morals and Manners*, edited by Harriet Martineau, (News Brunswick, New Jersey: Transaction Books, 1989).
[27] Emile Durkheim, *The Rules...*, (1895).
[28] Emile Durkheim, *The Rules of Sociological Method* (1895).
[29] Reinharz, *Teaching the History of Women*, 92.
[30] Martineau, *Retrospect of Western Travel*, (1838).
[31] Hill 1989, Lipset 1962; McDonald 1994, Riedesal 1981.

Martineau prioritized the 'instrument' of observation, that is the observer and the need to adopt an objective and non-judgemental stance. She cautions the observer against prejudices, quick generalizations and ethnocentrism (not her term), arguing that a sensitive and sympathetic predisposition is crucial to the task at hand. This adds a human dimension to the work of observation. Martineau's method is marked by a self-conscious and systematic approach for acquiring knowledge about strange, new, unfamiliar places/societies, recognizing that the act of observation requires two parties: the observer and the observed. Martineau places great emphasis on the observer as the 'instrument' of observation:

> The mind of the observer, the instrument by which work is done is as essential as the material to be wrought. If the instrument be in bad order, it will furnish a bad product, be the material what it may.[32]

Martineau outlined several methodological principles required for sound observation. The first of these she denoted as 'objectivity', emphasizing the need for avoiding prejudices and preconceived notions and value judgement, arguing that:

> Every prejudice, every moral perversion, dims or distorts whatever the eye looks upon.[33]

In contemporary language this would translate to cautions against ethnocentrism and the need for value neutrality. Given her attraction to positivism, she lists naturalism and empiricism as two tenets for objective accounting. For Martineau, the social world was ordered, patterned and functioned according to universal laws as was the natural world. She assumed that the former too could be analysed through systematic, logical, methodical efforts. Martineau held that science could lead to the discovery of these laws and thus lead to social reform. Martineau's commitment to positivism also privileged empiricism as the

---

[32] Martineau, *How to Observe*, 11.

[33] Martineau, *How to Observe*, 40.

tool for the acquisition of knowledge, that is, that all useful (and truthful) knowledge of society must come through sensory observation and concrete investigations. Like Comte and Durkheim, Martineau argued that systematic observation of an empirical field was the primary mode of acquiring knowledge about society. Thus Martineau dismissed whimsical, impressionistic and random commentary on social issues and insisted on distinguishing 'opinions' and 'facts', which meant that one had:

> to begin with the study of *things*, using the discourse of persons as a commentary upon them.[34]

In addition to these rules for observation, Martineau also listed 'practical advice' for the investigator. She noted the value of such implements as a 'daily journal' and a 'query list.' She advised that the latter should be prepared ahead of time and a regular entry be made in the journal. She added that a sympathetic and empathetic stance should be adopted by the observer. With the benefit of hindsight, the practical suggestions for doing research Martineau noted were subsequently systematized and codified as methodological guidelines for doing fieldwork in several disciplines, notably Anthropology and Sociology.

Martineau consciously crafted what she labels the 'science of morals and manners' and intends to apply the method she has outlined to a specific object of study, that is 'manners and morals' of a nation. By 'manners' she means 'patterned social relationships' as well as 'behaviour and institutions', which she denotes as 'observables', that is the empirical, objectified traces of institutional activity and social behaviour. For Martineau, the latter constitutes the starting points of observation, given that they are empirically graspable. But she adds that embedded and abstract 'morals' can be read from these 'surface' comportments. The latter reflected for Martineau the 'morals' investigators should seek, that is the collectively held norms, values, principles and sentiments. For Martineau, manners were a register of morals endorsed and sanctioned in society and were thus the real object of inquiry.

---

[34] Martineau, *How to Observe*, 73.

Substantively, Martineau outlined a vast field of 'manners' for empirical observation. These include: Epitaphs on graves in cemeteries, types of punishment, popular songs, types of work and industry, health, marriage and family, women and slaves, domestic servants, newspapers, charities, schools and so on.[35] She argued that a focus on any of these would reveal the logic and pattern of social organization, which were ultimately useful for discovering the moral underpinnings of society. While she distinguished between morals and manners, she highlighted their complex relationship and the folly of viewing them as distinct:

> that manners are inseparable from morals, or, at least, cease to have meaning when separated. Except as manifestation of morals, they have no interest, and can have no permanent existence ... To him, and to him only, who has studied the principles of morals, and thus possessed himself of a key to the mysteries of all social weal and wo, will manners be an index answering as faithfully to the internal movements, harmonious or discordant, of society, as the human countenance to the workings of the human heart.[36]

Martineau was keenly aware of the need to scrutinize social institutions in order to uncover the underlying moral base rather than rely on individual opinions to form judgement. A theory of social institutions can be abstracted from Martineau's narrative from *How to Observe Morals and Manners*:

> The institutions of a nation – political, religious or social – put evidence into the observer's hands as to its capabilities and wants, which the study of individuals could not yield in the course of a life time. The records of any society, by they what they may, whether architectural remains, epitaphs, civic registers, national music, or any other of the thousand manifestations of the common mind which may be found among every people, afford more information on Morals in a day than converse with individuals in a year. . . . General indications must be looked for, instead of

---

[35] Martineau, *How to Observe*, (1838).
[36] Martineau, *How to Observe*, (1838), 222.

generalisations being framed from the manners of individuals. In cities, do social meetings abound? and what is their purpose and character? Are they more religious, political or festive? ... Are women there? In what proportions ... In country towns, how is the imitation of the metropolis carried on? ... So, also, must every circumstance concerned with the service of society ... testify to the desires and habits, and therefore to the manners of a community, better than the conversation of any individual in society can do.[37]

The new science of society Martineau imagined was far from neutral. Instead she proposed for the sociologist a sympathetic stance based on sound empirical observations charged with producing truthful, objective knowledge in the service of creating a progressive society.

Martineau's Compromised Feminism?

Gayle Yates notes that Martineau avoided committing her position on the question of male/female equality and the nature-nurture debate. Yet she argued 'that women's intellectual inferiority to men is based on women's lack of mental training, others' expectations of women, and women's circumstances *rather than women's ability (emphasis mine)*.[38] Martineau was dedicated to the cause of women's education. In her *Autobiography* she reflected that there were specific structural conditions and societal expectations which shaped opportunities for her own education:

In discussing the subject of Female Education, it is not so much my object to inquire whether the natural powers of women be equal to those of men, as to shew the expediency of giving proper scope and employment to the powers which they do possess. It may be as well, notwithstanding, to enquire whether the difference be as great as is generally supposed between the mental structure of men and of women.[39]

---

[37] Martineau, *How to Observe*, 74–75.

[38] Gayle, 1985, 87.

[39] Martineau, 'On Female Education' *Monthly Repository* 17, October 1822, pp 77–81.

Martineau theorizes the differential progress made in educational spheres between boys and girls, highlighting gender-based normative practices and attitudes as causative factors, rejecting firmly any differences in natural abilities. Her argument is worth quoting in full:

> the boy goes on continually increasing his stock of information . . . while the girl is probably confined to low pursuits, her aspirings after knowledge are subdued, she is taught to believe that solid information is unbecoming her sex, almost her whole time is expended on light accomplishments, and thus before she is sensible of her powers, they are checked in their growth; chained down to mean objects, to rise no more; and when the natural consequences of this mode of treatment arise, all mankind agree that the abilities of women are inferior to those of men . . . Has it not been evident that the female mind, though in many respects differently constituted from that of man, may well be brought into comparison with his? If she wants his enterprising spirit, the deficiency is made up by perseverance in what she does undertake; for his ambition she has a thirst for knowledge; and for his perception, she has unwearied application. It is sufficient proof to my mind that there is no natural deficiency of power, that, unless proper objects are supplied to women to employ their faculties, their energies are exerted improperly. Some aim they must have, and if no good is one is presented to them, they must seek for a bad one.

However, there are strong shades of Androcentrism in Martineau's arguments. She continued to assert separate and distinct societal spheres for men and women, never doubting if these male and female provinces were socially constructed. As such, her feminism did not go far enough and she settled for the less radical outcome of 'better' performance of 'duties' and the 'strengthening' of the mind as reasons for making available 'stores of information' to women:

> I wish to imply by what I have said, not that great stores of information are as necessary to women as to men, but that as much care should be taken of the formation of their minds. Their attachments cannot in general be so great, because they have their own appropriate duties and peculiar employments, the neglect of which nothing can excuse; but I contend that these duties will be better performed if the powers be rationally

employed. If the whole mind be exercised and strengthened, it will bring more vigour to the performance of its duties in any particular province.[40]

She did not invoke the language of equality of the sexes or challenge regnant gendered division of labour in society, accepting in effect the view that women are meant to be wives, companions and mothers – and *naturally* superior in these roles. The rationale that women must be allowed to acquire knowledge rationally was ultimately for self-improvement so they could perform their given duties and responsibilities better:

> It must be allowed by all, that one of women's first duties is to qualify herself for being a companion to her husband, or to those with whom her lot in life is case. She was formed to be a domestic companion, and as such as one as shall give to home its charms, as shall furnish such entertainment that her husband need not be driven abroad for amusement. This is one of the first duties required from a woman, and no time can be misemployed which is applied to the purpose of making her such a companion . . . If their thoughts are continually occupied by the vanities of the world, if that time which is not required for the fulfilment of household duties in spent in folly, or even in harmless trifles in which the husband has no interest, how are the powers of pleasing to be perpetuated, how is she to find interesting subjects for social converse? If we consider the woman as the guardian and instructress of infancy, her claims to cultivation of mind become doubly urgent. It is evident that if the soul of the teacher is narrow and contracted, that of the pupil cannot be enlarged.[41]

Thus for Martineau it was imperative for women to improve themselves in order to be better wives and mothers. She argued thus:

> Let woman then be taught that her powers of mind were given to be improved. Let her be taught that she is to be a rational companion to

---

[40] Martineau, 'On Female Education', 1822, 79.
[41] Martineau, 'On Female Education', 1822, 80.

those of the other sex among whom her lot in life is cast, that her proper sphere is *home* – that there she is to provide, not only for the bodily comfort of the man, but that she is to enter also into community of mind with him; ... As she finds nobler objects presented to her grasp[42];

She continued in a vein that also ironically revealed her Androcentrism in presuming essentialist differences between men and women and that women cannot be equal to men:

> I allow that the acquirements of women can seldom equal those of men, and it is not desirable that they should. I do not wish to excite a spirit of rivalry between the sexes; I do not desire that many females should seek for fame as authors. I only wish that their powers should be so employed that they should not be obliged to seek amusements beneath them, and injurious to them. I wish them to be companions to men, instead of playthings or servants, one of which an ignorant women must commonly be. If they are to be called wives, a sensible mind is an essential qualifica- tion for the domestic character; if they remain single, liberal pursuits are absolutely necessary to preserve them from the faults so generally attrib- uted to that state, and so justly and inevitably, while the mind is buried in darkness.[43]

In *Society in America*, Martineau addressed women's status and educa- tion and expresses frustrations at the unnecessary restrictions that are placed on their desire to learn. She implored women to transcend these limitations:

> The intellect of women is confined by an unjustifiable restriction of ... education ... As women have none of the objects in life for which an enlarged education is considered requisite, the education is not given ... The choice is to either be 'ill-educated, passive, and subservient, or well-educated, vigorous, and free only upon sufferance'.[44]

---

[42] Martineau, '*On Female Education*', 1822, 80.

[43] Martineau, '*On Female Education*', 1822, 80.

[44] Martineau, *Society in America*, 1834, 292.

Martineau stepped outside the gender roles defined for women, going well beyond the domestic sphere, visible and influential in the public domain, through her writing and engagement with important political, economic and moral issues of the day. However, as her narrative on female education reveals, she was certainly a product of her times and operated within given normative frames vis-à-vis gender roles and notions of masculinity and femininity. Her Androcentrism is evident in her view that marriage was ideal for women, that women were tied to their biological functions and prone to excessive emotionalism. She also held the view that women were naturally and universally suited to domesticity, nursing, healing and teaching; she described nursing in particular as 'the most womanly of women's work' given by nature. At the same time, she was progressive in fighting for women's rights: for access to education, to work, to choose their vocation and to develop/cultivate the mind. Perhaps her stance can best be described as a 'compromised feminism.'

Martineau's Encounter with America

Martineau's insights about nineteenth-century American Society are carried in her three-volume work, *Society in America*. Interestingly, Martineau's preferred original title for the work was *Theory and Practice of Society* – which has a rather contemporary, even postmodern ring to it. But this title was rejected by her publishers as inappropriate for generating commercial interest in the book. Martineau's writings on America were thus conceptualized primarily as travel writing, a popular genre at the time, given European fascination with nineteenth-century America. In this book, Martineau sought to compare the stated *principles upon which* American nation had been founded with what she encountered of American society in *practice*. She describes her intentions in the 'Introduction':

> In seeking for methods by which I might communicate what I have observed in my travels, without offering any pretension to teach the English, or judge the Americans, two expedients occurred to me; both

of which I have adopted. One is, to compare the existing state of society in America with the principles on which it is professedly founded; thus testing Institutions, Morals, and Manners by an indisputable, instead of an arbitrary standard, and securing myself the same point of view with my readers of both nations. . . . The other method by which I propose to lessen my responsibility, is to enable my readers to judge for themselves, better than I can for them, what my testimony is worth. For this purpose, I offer a brief account of my travel, with dates in full; and a report of the principal means I enjoyed of obtaining a knowledge of the country.[45]

This account of American society was based on Martineau's travel to the USA, where she spent two years travelling extensively to different states, by stagecoach, by boat, by rail and on horseback. Here she encountered diverse sectors of American society. She interacted with men, women and children; met Americans of different class background, the wealthy and the poor; the disabled and the disempowered – including women, children and those who were enslaved; she met with elites as well – including politicians, mayors, judges and slave owners. In this offering, however, Martineau does demonstrate 'discrepancies between an actual condition and a pure and noble theory of society'[46] even if she refuses to 'decline the office of censor altogether.'[47] Martineau compares professed moral principles with actual social practices and found inconsistencies. She clarifies her 'means of information,' in passages that read like elaborations of fieldwork in specific sites and interactions with a range of different social groups to communicate that her sample did not suffer from a bias or partiality:

> In the course of this tour, I visited almost every kind of institution. The prisons of Auburn, Philadelphia and Nashville: the insane and other hospitals of almost every considerable place: the literary and scientific institutions; the factories of the north; the plantations of the south; the farms of the west. I lived in houses which might be called palaces,

---

[45] Martineau, *Society in America*, 48–49.

[46] Martineau, *Society in America*, 49.

[47] Martineau, *Society in America*, 49.

in log-houses, and in a farm-house. I travelled much in wagons, as well as stages; also on horseback, and in some of the best and worst of steamboats. I saw weddings, and christenings; the gatherings of the richer at watering places, and of the humbler at country festivals. I was present at orations, at land sales, and in the slave market. I was in frequent attendance on the Supreme Court and the Senate; and witnessed some of the proceedings of state legislatures. Above all I was received into the bosom of many families, not as a stranger, but as a daughter or a sister...It would be nearly impossible to relate whom I know, during my travels. Nearly every eminent man in politics, science and literature, and almost every distinguished woman, would grace my list. I have respected and beloved friends of each political party; and of nearly every religious denomination; among slave holders, colonizationists, and abolitionists; among farmers, lawyers, merchants, professors, and clergy. I travelled among several tribes of Indians; and spent months in the southern States, with Negros ever at my heels.[48]

She listed her deafness as her only disadvantage during these travels denying that her gender adversely affected her study of American society. In fact, she argued that being a woman placed her in an advantageous position:

I am sure, I have seen much more of domestic life than could possibly have been exhibited to any gentleman travelling through the country. The nursery, the boudoir, the kitchen are all excellent schools in which to learn the morals and manners of a people: and, as for public and professional affairs,-those may always gain full information upon such matters, who really feel an interest in them, – be they men or women.

The text carries a comprehensive, multi-dimensional account of her experience of American society, elicited through personal interactions from different categories of individuals in American society. Students of nineteenth-century America have reflected that compared to Tocqueville's *Democracy in America* (1835–1840), Martineau's work

---

[48] Martineau, *Society in America*, 53.

'is a better study of American life.'[49] It is not surprising that were indeed similarities between Martineau's and Tocqueville's narratives of American society. But these two observers of American social life differed on several important counts, including the extent/intensity of political participation and the status of women in American society. Tocqueville suggested that enhanced political participation (for him a distinct feature of liberal democracy) was universal in American society. Martineau questions this given that women, slaves and the poor could not vote and remained outside the realm of formal politics. The Frenchman was rather impressed with the extent to which the individual American citizen participated in the political governance of the country. Martineau, meanwhile, noted political apathy and indifference towards issues of collective and public interest, not to mention the presence of legal and juridical constraints which prevented universal political participation.

While the *American Declaration of Independence* emphasized equality, freedom and consent of the governed as part of its political process, in actuality Martineau demonstrated that there existed different kinds of inequalities and hierarchies in American society. She speaks of the 'political non-existence' of women and slaves, noting similarities in their structural location. Of course, their situations were far from identical given the dynamics of race and class. For instance, she highlighted the status of women and slaves and noted their *lack of political participation* in being denied the right to vote. Given her interest in exploring the *relationship between morals and institutions,* in her scrutiny of American political life, she wondered what kind of a value system supports the political structure of liberal democracy, typified with nineteenth-century America.

Martineau and Tocqueville were both intrigued with American liberal democracy. Tocqueville was interested in the contrast between the American version of liberal democracy and the French variety of despotic democracy. Martineau noted *serious gaps* between theory and

[49] Nisbet, *Reconsidering Tocquvelli's Democracy,* (1988), 173–4 and Kandal, *The woman question,* (1988), 73–74.

practice of American social life, which she argued produced tensions in society. She asked what moral logic/underpinnings of liberal democracy would justify prejudices and institutionalized discrimination against women and slaves and deny them to political agents in this democratic setup. This also led to her notice of various forms of domination in American society which served to eliminate the possibilities for individual autonomy.[50] She found the institution of slavery abhorrent:

> The personal oppression of the negroes is the grossest vice which strikes a stranger in this country. It can never be otherwise when human beings are wholly subjected to the will of other human beings, who are under no other external control than the law which forbids killing and maiming; – a law which it is difficult to enforce in individual cases.[51]

Martineau's critique of slavery was part of her narrative against structures domination in society which directed her attention women, children, slaves, prisoners and those in need of charity – as disenfranchised groups in society. She notes:

> though there appears to be a mockery somewhere, when we contrast slavery with the principles and the rule which are the test of all American institutions:- the principles that all men and born free and equal; that rulers derive their just powers from the consent of the governed; and the rule of reciprocal justice. This discrepancy between principles and practice needs no more words. But the institution of slavery exists; and what we have to see is what the morals are of the society which is subject to it.[52]

Tocqueville saw women in America as being content[53] with their purely domestic role, while Martineau noted the frustrations and limitations women faced in marriage and their working life and the implications

---

[50] See Lenggermann and Niebrugge, *The Women Founders; Sociology*, 37.

[51] Martineau, *Society in America*, 223.

[52] Martineau, *Society in America*, 219–220.

[53] In view of Tocqueville's notice that America women were satisfied with their lot in society, ironically 15 years after Tocqueville visited the USA, the largest women's Suffrage movement in the world was launched at the Convention on Women's Rights in New York.

these had for women's health. Martineau observed 'parallels' between the status of women and slaves arguing that both received 'indulgence' rather than 'justice'.[54] She argued that for America to become truly democratic, both of these disenfranchised groups would have to be given the right to vote and be treated as equal in the eyes of the law. Martineau devotes a chapter to the 'political non-existence of women' in *Society in America*, offering a scathing critique of the denial of full legal rights to women and their right to represent their own interests:

> The true democratic principle is, that no person's interests can be, or can be ascertained to be, identical with those of any other person... The interests of women who have fathers and husbands can never be identical with theirs, while there is a necessity for laws to protect women against their husbands and fathers... That woman has powers to represent her own interests no one can deny till she has been tried... The principle of the equal rights of both halves of the human race is all we have to do with here. It is the true democratic principle which can never be seriously controverted, and only for a short time evaded. Government can derive their just powers only from the consent of the governed.[55]

Speaking to the view that societies should be judged by their attitude to marginalized and disenfranchised groups, Martineau argued thus:

> If a test of civilisation be sought, none can be so sure as the condition of that half of society over which the other half has power, – from the exercise of the right of the strongest. Tried by this test, the American civilisation appears to be of a lower order than might have been expected from some other symptoms of its social state. The Americans, have in their treatment of women, fallen below, not only their own democratic principles, but the practice of some parts of the Old World... The unconsciousness of both parties as to the injuries suffered by women at the hands of those who hold the power is a sufficient proof of the low degree of civilisation in this important particular at which they rest. While woman's

---

[54] Martineau, *Society in America*, Volume II, 73-75.
[55] Martineau, *Society in America*, 126–128.

intellect is confined, her morals crushed, her health ruined, her weaknesses encouraged, and her strength punished, she is told that her lot is cast in the paradise of women . . . In short, indulgence is given her as a substitute for justice. Her case differs from that of the slave, as to the principle, just so far as this; that the indulgence is large and universal, instead of petty and capricious. In both cases, justice is denied on no better plea than the right of the strongest. In both cases, the acquiescence of the many, and the burning discontent of the few, of the oppressed testify, the one to the actual degradation of the class, and the other to its fitness for the enjoyment of human rights.[56]

Beyond a specific analysis of American society, Martineau's text offers broader sociological insights, which may today appear unremarkable or unsurprising, but were revolutionary within the context of Martineau's intellectual milieu. Her analysis of American society suggests that moral values shape social structures/social institutions; that the attendant tensions between theory and practice generate the conditions for reforming social and political institutions and that a society should be judged by its treatment of weaker groups in society, the latter two rather progressive ideas.

Freedom and Happiness

Martineau was concerned about the question of human happiness posing these queries: How could individuals be happy? How could society be organized to achieve maximum happiness for individuals? And on the basis of which moral principles? In her response, Martineau posited a relationship between the amount and distribution of happiness and the level of progress in any society. She saw the aspiration for happiness as a universal human condition and also the 'will of God':

That man should be happy is so evidently the intention of his Creator, the contrivances to that end are so multitudinous and striking, that the perception of the aim may be called universal. Whatever tends to make

---

[56] Martineau, *Society in America*, 291.

men happy, becomes a fulfilment of the will of God. Whatever tends to make them miserable, becomes opposition to his will. There are, and must be, a host obstacles to the express recognition of, and practical obedience to, these great principles; but they may be discovered as the root of religion and morals in all countries. There are impediments from ignorance, and consequent error, selfishness, and passion...but yet all men entertain one common conviction, that what makes people happy is good and right and what makes them miserable is evil and wrong.[57]

She viewed happiness as the capacity to be self-directing moral agents while engaged in an enterprise that involved human faculties. She saw the pursuit of wealth as leading to domination and diminished freedom for exercising moral agency. Here Martineau's ideas are akin to Durkheim's proposition that poverty does not necessarily signal misery, wealth does not guarantee happiness and that poverty in fact offers 'protection' from anomie.

One of her first pieces of writing was 'The Art of Thinking' – which was a call for the right of individuals to use reason and rationality; to arrive at judgements through logical, methodical thought rather than be pressured into accepting (without question) prearticulated rationale and theories. Martineau's conception of freedom is multi-dimensional. It includes the freedom to think and act autonomously, the right to work, political emancipation and empowerment and the capacity to challenge received, customary wisdom. Martineau's conception of freedom included political freedom and access to legal rights, which she argued were universally desired. This conviction is evident in Martineau's commitment and work towards abolishing slavery. In her Retrospect of Western Travel (1838), Martineau described the efforts and aspirations of a woman slave, Mum Bett, to be free and to be treated as an equal invoking the 'Bill of Rights' claiming liberty and her rights as 'one of the nation'.[58] In her famous short story, 'Demerara' (about a slave owner and his son), Martineau offered an economic, instrumentally driven critique of the institution of slavery arguing that it was inefficient and

---

[57] Martineau, How to Observe, 37.

[58] Harriet Martineau, Retrospect of Western Travel, vol. 2 [1838].

unprofitable for the economy. She argued that in comparison to slaves, free labourers were more efficient and productive workers. However, after witnessing slavery during her travels to the USA, Martineau called for abolition of slavery on social, ethical and political grounds.

Martineau included a chapter on 'The idea of liberty' in *How to Observe*. In arriving at a conception of the 'Idea of Liberty entertained by any society', she offers a list of indicators for empirical observation: police, legislation, classes in society, servants, imitation of the metropolis, newspapers, schools and objects and forms of persecution. Martineau here uses what Harold Garfinkel (working on ideas of Karl Mannheim and Alfred Schutz) has popularized as the 'documentary method' in ethnomethodology. This is a method interpretation in which the actual appearance of an entity is viewed as the document of, or suggest a deeper, underlying pattern. Using this logic, each of the eight indicators listed by Martineau can be approached as a 'document of' for the absence or presence of liberty. For example, she argues that the presence of the police, censorship of news and the extent of centralization suggest underlying forms of domination and thus signalled the absence of liberty:

> The Police of a country are a sure sign of the idea of liberty existing within it. Where the soldiery are the guards of the social order, it makes all the difference whether they are royal troops – a destructive machinery organized against the people – or a National Guard, springing up when needed from among the people, for the people's sake.[59]
>
> The idea of liberty must be low and feeble among a people who permit the government to maintain a severe censorship; and it must be powerful and effectual in a society which can make all its complaints through a newspaper, – be the reports of the newspapers upon the state of social affairs as dismal as they may be.[60]
>
> In despotic countries, the principle of centralisation actuates everything. Orders are issued from the central authorities, and the minds of the provinces are saved all the trouble of thinking for themselves. Where self-government is permitted to each assemblage of citizens, they are

---

[59] Martineau, *How to Observe*, 189.
[60] Martineau, *How to Observe*, 200–201.

stimulated to improve their idea and practice of liberty, and are almost independent of metropolitan usages.[61]

Martineau suggested that 'increase of knowledge is necessary to secure enlargement of freedom'.[62] The theme of liberty/freedom and its relationship to human happiness pervades Martineau's writings.[63] Lenggermann and Niebrugge note that Martineau is one of the few social thinkers who explicitly addressed the complex relations between individual freedom, human happiness, the pursuit wealth and the idea of progress.[64] Martineau asked how individuals could lead productive, efficient lives and achieve human happiness which she presumed was the ultimate goal for all social groups universally. In this effort she valued the role of education and the ethical task before Sociology of demonstrating how societal conditions could be created for the achievement of liberty and happiness. Based on this logic, Martineau's comparative studies focused on how 'morals and manners' could be developed to achieve happiness for individuals. As an astute observer of society, Martineau was deeply concerned with inequalities (including on the basis of gender, race and class) and dominations and their manifestation in the form of prejudices, discriminatory practices and unjust legal mechanisms and institutions. However, revealing her Eurocentric thinking, Martineau does not extend this argument to her theorizing of British rule in India nor call for an end to inequalities as a result of colonial domination.

Conclusion

Martineau was an important pioneering figure whose social thought was instrumental in shaping a discourse about the potential for understanding society through science, in an era long before sociology was

[61] Martineau, *How to Observe*, 199.
[62] Martineau, *How to Observe*, 206.
[63] Lenggerman 1998; Dryjanska 2008 and 2008a.
[64] Lenggermann and Niebrugge, *The Women Founders; Sociology*, 40.

systematized and formalized. Martineau had a firm sense of the 'society' as an object of study and she consciously crafted a method appropriate for studying this. Her efforts were empirical and analytical rather than abstract or speculative. Engaging with her ideas reveals that she had a profound and deep interest in theorizing social, economic and political domains, which she saw as complex and often contradictory. While being on the margins of professional sociology, Martineau thought systematically and methodically about society and proposed social reforms, moving away from theological and religious explanations of sociological phenomena. Martineau was a pioneering social thinker, theorist and methodologist. She carefully demarcated the subject matter of sociology, proposed a method of inquiry for scrutinizing society and offered a critique of forms of domination and inequalities in aspiring towards a progressive society. Sociology for Martineau was neither philosophical speculation nor abstract theorizing but had to have a practical, empirical impact. That is to enhance knowledge and under-standing produce the necessary social reforms for the greater good.

A. Rossi[65] in 1973 and then S. Hoecker-Drysdale in 1992 referred to Martineau as 'the first woman sociologist' and her biographer R. K. Webb declared that for years Martineau was 'preaching sociology with-out the name'.[66] A. Rossi in *The Feminist Papers* reaches a similar finale: 'Crusty, garrulous, a prodigious writer, forerunner of the discipline of sociology, not yet born, Harriet Martineau stands as an early ardent defender of women's rights, the first woman sociologist. ...'[67] The fact that Martineau is now at least mentioned and present in some intro-ductory sociology texts, sociology theory texts and encyclopaedias[68]

---

[65] Apart from a handful of feminists in the 1970s and 1980s (Poovey 1988; Rossi 1973; Spender 1982), Martineau's work have not been engaged by many contemporary feminist scholars. Part of the reason for this as reasoned by McDonald (1994) is due to the critique of empiricist methodology in feminist scholarship today. Empiricist, positivist approaches are defined as being antithetical to feminist methodology and research and are thus rejected. Martineau, given her methodological principles and her self-definition as a woman of science, is caught in the web of such a rebuff.

[66] Webb, *Harriet Martineau*, 308.

[67] Rossi, *The First Woman Sociologist*, 124.

[68] See Lengermann and Niebrugge-Brantley (1998), Zeitlin 1997, Ritzer 2000.

shows that some pressure has been brought to bear upon authoritative voices in the discipline that record the discipline's historiography. Moving beyond registering her presence, it is more important to ask how Martineau is included in narratives on history of sociological ideas.

Anticipating the likelihood of women thinkers and methodologists like Martineau fading once again, McDonald asks, what can be done 'to prevent another slide into oblivion?'[69] Part of the responsibility, she argues, rests with 'institutions to promote women's studies' while Terry has highlighted the crucial role played in this rethinking project by 'teachers, researchers and writers'.[70] Bureaucratic and administrative regimes in academia as well as its politics shape pedagogical norms and practices. Teaching is an appropriate arena for introducing new ideas. Listing Martineau alongside Marx, Weber and Durkheim, assigning her primary works to be read and criticized in tutorial discussions and setting term projects and exam questions on her ideas are important steps in the right direction. However, a comparative lens is an important pedagogical tool in this regard. Introducing Martineau alongside recognized classical sociological thinkers would be productive in demonstrating sociological thought and theories in her work. This chapter ends with an invitation to critically engage Martineau's works despite their Eurocentrism and Androcentrism, suggesting that her writings embody critical theorizing about class, work, happiness, gender, capitalism, democracy, freedom and colonialism – and much more.

Bibliography

Barnes, Harry Elmer. *An Introduction to History of Sociology*. Chicago: University of Chicago Express, 1948.

Collins, Patricia Hill. *Black Feminist Thought: Knowledge, Consciousness and the Politics of Empowerment*. Boston: Unwin Hyman, 1990.

Comte, Auguste. *Cours de philosophie positive*. Vol. 6. Paris: Bachelier, 1830–1842.

---

[69] McDonald, *The Women Founders*, 242.
[70] Terry, *Bringing Women . . .*, 259.

Coser, Lewis. *Masters of Sociological Thought*. New York: Harcourt Brace, 1977.

Coser, Lewis A., Charles Kadushin, and Walter W. Powell. *The Culture and Commerce of Publishing*. New York: Basic Books, 1982.

David, Deidra. *Intellectual Women and Victorian Patriarchy: Harriet Martineau, Elizabeth Barrett Browning, George Eliot*. New York: Cornell University Press, 1987.

Deegan, Mary Jo. 'Women in Sociology, 1890–1930'. *Journal of the History of Sociology* 1 (Fall 1978): 11–34.

Deegan, Mary Jo. 'Transcending a Patriarchal Past: Teaching the History of Early Women Sociologists'. *Teaching Sociology* 16 (1988): 141–159.

Deegan, Mary Jo. *Women in Sociology: A Bio-Bibliographical Sourcebook*. New York: Greenwood, 1991.

Dryjanska, Anna. 'Harriet Martineau: The forerunner of cultural studies.' In Marcia TexlerSegal, Vasilike Demos (ed), *Advancing Gender Reserch from the Nineteenth to the Twenty-First Centuries* (Advances in Gender Researh, Volume 12). Bingley, UK: Emaradl Group Publishing Limited, pp 63–77, 2008.

Farmer, Mary E. 'The Positivist Movement and the Development of English Sociology'. *Sociological Review* (1967): 5–20.

Harrison, Fredrick. 'Introduction'. Vol. 1, in *The Positive Philosophy of Auguste Comte*, edited by Harriet Martineau, v–xix. London: G. Bell, 1895.

Hassett, Constance W. *Siblings and Anti-Slavery: The Literary and Political Relations of Harriet Martineau, James Martineau and Maria Weston Chapman*. Signs 21, Winter 1996.

Hill, Micheal R. 'Harriet Martineau's Novels and the Sociology of Class, Race, and Gender'. *The Association for Humanist Sociology*. Typescript, 1987.

Hill, Micheal R. '*Empiricism and Reason in Harriet Martineau's Sociology.*' Vols. xv–lx, in *How to Observe Morals and Manners*, edited by Harriet Martineau, News Brunswick, New Jersey: Transaction Books, 1989.

Hill, Micheal R. 'Harriet Martineau'. In *Women in Sociology: A Bio-Bibliographical Sourcebook*, edited by Mary Jo Deegan, 289–297. New York: Greenwood, 1991.

Hill, Micheal R. 'Martineau in Current Introductory Textbooks: An Empirical Survey'. *The Harriet Martineau Sociological Society Newsletter* (Spring 1998): 4–5.

Hill, Micheal R. 'Empiricism and Reason in Harriet Martineau's Sociology.' In *Martineau H: How to Observe Morals and Manners*, xv–lx. New Brunswick: Rutgers University Press, 2002.

Hoecker-Drysdale, Susan. *Harriet Martineau: First Woman Sociologist*. Oxford: Berg, 1992.

Hoecker-Drysdale, Susan. 'The Enigma of Harriet Martineau's Letters on Science'. *Women's Writing* 2 no. 2 (Spring 1996): 155–165.

Hoecker-Drysdale, Susan. 'Harriet Martineau'. In *The Blackwell Companion to Major Social Theories*, edited by George Ritzer, 53–80. Malden: Blackwell, 2000.

Hoecker-Drysdale, Susan, and Micheal R. Hill, ed. *Harriet Martineau: Theoretical Methodological Perspectives*. London: Routledge, 2002.

Hunter, Shelagh. *Harriet Martineau: The Poetics of Moralism*. Aldershot, England: Scolar Press, 1995.

Kandal, Terry R. *The Woman Question in Classical Sociological Theory*. Miami: Florida International University Press, 1988.

Kineka, Francis E. *The Dissidence of Dissent: The Monthly Repository, 1806–1838*. Chapel Hill: University of North Carolina Press, 1944.

Lengermann, Patricia and Jill Niebrugge-Brantley. *Women Founders: Sociology and Social Theory, 1830–1930*, New York: McGraw Hill, 1998.

Lipset, Seymour Martin. 'Harriet Martineau's America.' In *Society in America*, S M Lipset (ed), New York, 1962.

March, Artemis. 'Female Invisibility and in Androcentric Sociological Theory'. *Insurgent Sociologist* IX, no. 2 (1982): 99–107.

Martindale, D. *The Nature and Types of Sociological Theory*. Boston: Houghton-MiiSin, 1960.

Martineau, Harriet. *The Positive Philosophy of Auguste Comte*. New York: William Gowans, 1853.

Martineau, Harriet, ed. *The Positive Philosophy of Auguste Comte*. London: Kegan Paul, Trench, Troebner, 1868.

Martineau, Harriet, ed. *The Positive Philosophy of Auguste Comte*. New York: AMS Press, 1893.

Martineau, Harriet. 'Harriet Martineau's America'. In *Society in America*, by Seymour Martin Lipset, 4–42. New Brunswick, NJ: Transaction, 1981.

McDonald, Lynn. *The Early Origins of the Social Sciences*. Montreal: McGill-Queens University Press, 1993.

McDonald, Lynn. *The Women Founders of the Social Sciences*. Ottawa, Canada: Carleton University Press, 1994.

Michie, Jonathan. *The Reader's Guide to the Social Sciences*. Vol. 1. London: New York: Routledge, 2001.

Niebrugge-Brantley, Jill, and Patricia Lengermann. 'Early Women Sociologists'. In *Classical Sociology*, edited by George Ritzer, 294–328. New York: McGraw-Hill, 1996.

Niebrugge-Brantley, Jill, and Patricia Lengermann. *The Women Founders: Sociology and Social Theory 1830–1930*. New York: McGraw-Hill, 1998.

Niebrugge-Brantley, Jill, and Patricia Lengermann. 'Early Women Sociologists.' In *Classical Sociology*, edited by George Ritzer, New York: McGraw-Hill, 2000.

Niebrugge-Brantley, Jill, and Patricia Madoo Lengermann. 'Back to the Future: Settlement Sociology.' *The American Sociologist* 33, no. 3 (2002): 5–20.

Niebrugge-Brantley, J., and P. Madoo Lengermann. 'Early Women Sociologists and Classical Sociological Theories: 1830–1990'. In *Classical Sociological Theory*, edited by G. Ritz and D. Goodman, 271–300. London: McGraw-Hill, 2004.

Nisbet, Robert. 'Tocquville's Ideal Types'. In *Reconsidering Tocquvelli's Democracy in America*, edited by S. Abraham Eisentadt, New Brunswick, NJ: Rutgers University Press, 1988.

Nisbet, Robert, and Tom Bottomore, ed. *A History of Sociological Analysis*. London: Heinemann, 1978.

Orazem, Claudia. *Political Economy and Fiction in the Early Works of Harriet Martineau*. Frankfurt am Main: Peter Lang, 1999.

Pinchanick, Valerie K. *Harriet Martineau: The Woman and Her Work, 1802–1876*. Ann Arbor: University of Michigan Press, 1990.

Poovey, Mary. *Uneven Developments; The Idological Work of Gnder in Mid-Victorian England*. Chicago: The University of Chicago Press, 1988.

Reinharz, Shumalit. 'Teaching the History of Women in Sociology: Or Dorothy Swaine Thomas, Wasn't She the Woman Married to William I'. *The American Sociologist* 20 (Spring 1989): 87–94.

Reinharz, Shumalit. *Feminist Methods in Social Research*. New York: Oxford University Press, 1992.

Reinharz, Shumalit, 'A Contextualised Chronology of Women's Sociological Work.' In *Women's Studies Program*. Waltham, MA: Brandeis University, 1993.

Riedesal, Paul L. 'Who Was Harriet Martineau'. *Journal of the History of Sociology* 3 (Spring–Summer 1981): 63–80.

Ritzer, George. *Classical Sociological Theory*. New York: McGraw Hill, 1996.

Ritzer, George, and Douglas J. Goodman. *Sociological Theory*. 6th edn, Indianapolis: McGraw-Hill, 2003.

Ritzer, George. *Sociological Theory*, MCGraw Hill, 2000.

Rossi, Alice S. 'The First Woman Sociologist: Harriet Martineau (1802–1876)'. In *The Feminist Papers: From Adams to de Beauvoir*, edited by Alice S. Rossi, 118–124. New York: Bantam Books, 1973.

Sanders, Valerie and Gaby Weiner (eds). *Harriet Martineau and the Birth of the Disciplines*. London: Routledge. 2016.

Sanders, Valerie, ed. *Harriet Martineau: Selected Letters*. New York: OXford University Press, 1990.

Sanders, Valerie. *Reason Over Passion: Harriet Martineau and the Victorian Novel*. New York: St. Martin's Press, 1986.

Serge, Denisoff, R. et al. *Theories and Paradigms in Contemporary Sociology*. Itasca: F. E. Peacock, 1974.

Sinha, Vineeta. 'Reading Harriet Martineau in the Context of Social Thought and Social Theory'. *Akademia* 59 (2001): 1.

Sinha, Vineeta. 'Decentering Social Sciences in Practise through Individual Acts and Choices'. *Current Sociology* 51, no. 1 (2003): 7–26.

Sinha, Vineeta, and Syed Farid Alatas. 'Teaching Classical Sociological Theory in Singapore: The Context of Eurocentrism'. *Teaching Sociology* 29, no. 3 (2001): 316–331.

Smith, Dorothy E. *The Everyday World as Problematic: A Feminist Sociology*. Boston: Northeastern University Press, 1987.

Spender, Dale. 'Harriet Martineau'. In *Women of Ideas and What Men Have Done to Them*, 125–135. London: Routledge & Kegn Paul, 1982.

Szacki, J. *History of Sociological Thought*. Westport: Greenwood Press, 1979.

Terry, James L. 'Bringing Women … A Modest Proposal'. *Teaching Sociology* 10, no. 2 (1983): 251–261.

Timasheff, S.N. *Sociological Theory: Its Nature and Growth*. New York: Random House, 1967.

Truzzi, Marcello. 'Definition and Dimensions of the Occult: Towards a Sociological Perspective'. *Journal of Popular Culture* 5 (1971): 635/7–646/18.

Webb, R.K. *Harriet Martineau: A Radical Victorian*. London: Heinemann, 1960.

Weiner, Gaby. *Controversies and Contradictins: approcahes to the studies of Harriet Martineau* (1802–1876), unpublished doctoral thesis. Open University: UK, 1991.

Weiner, Gaby. *Feminisms in Education: An introduction*, London: Open Univesity Press. 1994.

Weiner, Gaby. 'Introduction'. Vol. 1, in *Harriet Martineau's Autobiography*, edited by H. Martineau, 1–20. London: Virago Press, 1983.

Yates, Gayle G., ed. *Harriet Martineau on Women*. New Brunswick, NJ: Rutgers University Press, 1985.

Zeitlin, I.M. *Ideology and the Development of Sociological Theory*. 6th edn. Upper Saddle River: Prentice Hall, 1997.

Max Weber (1864–1920)

Syed Farid Alatas

Karl Emil Maximilian Weber was born in 1864 in the town of Erfurt in Prussia, Germany. He was a sociologist but had significant contributions to the field of political economy. In addition to that, he pioneered many ideas that influenced scholars in various disciplines such as history and jurisprudence.[1]

Weber was not as famous those days as he became posthumously. He was almost unknown in English-speaking world, little known in Europe, and was not considered a dominant scholar in Germany. It is generally agreed that Weber was often not understood. In fact Andreski says that although Weber was a great scholar and thinker, he was a 'thoroughly bad writer' and among the great founders of the social sciences 'scores the lowest in the skill of presentation'.[2] His standing today, however, is that of one of the major founders of modern sociology.

---

[1] Dirk Käsler, *Max Weber: An Introduction to His Life and Work* (Cambridge: Polity Press, 1988), ix.

[2] Stanislav Andreski, *Max Weber's Insights and Errors* (London: Routledge, 2013), 6.

© The Author(s) 2017
113
S.F. Alatas, V. Sinha, *Sociological Theory Beyond the Canon*,
DOI 10.1057/978-1-137-41134-1_5

An Outline of Weber's Sociological Theory

Weber's sociology was decidedly historical. The historical dimension was particularly important for accounting for the rise of modern capitalism in the West and the failure of modern capitalism to emerge in non-Western societies. The subject matter of Weber's sociology was the origins of modern capitalism and the nature of modern capitalist society. Weber inquired into the various factors that accounted for the emergence of capitalism in the West and also theorized about the factors that impeded the development of capitalism in non-Western societies. Weber's much cited and discussed Protestant ethic thesis was his attempt to understand the rise of capitalism in terms of the impact of Protestantism on the development of a specific type of work ethic that facilitated capital accumulation.

At a deeper abstract level, Weber's concern was with the pervasiveness of a certain form of rationality throughout the institutions of modern society. Modern capitalist society is characterized by a certain type of human. The creation of capitalism as an economic system and the capitalist has something to do with how Protestantism created the rational capitalist and in general the rational human. This rationalization was manifested in the various institutions of modern society, such as the state and authority, law, bureaucracy and the modern city. Rationalization refers to our attempt to understand the world around us, to connect events into a meaningful picture of the world. It is our attempt to master reality, to understand how the world works and, consequently, know how we should act in it.

Weber's sociology is a theory of the rise of capitalism and the nature of capitalist society based on the development and spread of rationalization into ever-increasing areas of life. Weber discusses the types of rationality and the types of social action that are informed by these types of rationality. The origins and nature of modern capitalism are explained in terms of the development and spread of one type of rationality. Furthermore, this type of rationality is problematic for modern society. The process of rationalization in modern capitalist society resulted in what Weber called the de-magification of society. This was a society in which rational goals defined life. Life was to be explained in terms of scientifically observable and measurable forces of nature, rather than in terms of the supernatural. The world became disenchanted or desacralized.

Therefore, Weber's theory of modern capitalist society was a theory of the rationalization of the world. Weber also looked at various aspects of modern capitalist society such as the state and authority, law, bureaucracy, the modern city, as part of the process of the unfolding of this rationality.

Methodology

It is appropriate to begin the account of Weber's sociology with his ideas on methodology. This is because Weber was explicit in addressing certain methodological issues that remain relevant to contemporary sociology. It is also necessary to understand his views on methodology in order to appreciate his social theory. Weber did not believe in methodology as a tool that was consciously used by the scholar to practice good scholarship. Instead, methodology

> can only bring us reflective understanding of the means which have *demonstrated* their value in practice by raising them to the level of explicit consciousness; it is no more the precondition of fruitful intellectual work than the knowledge of anatomy is the precondition for 'correct' walking.[3]

Weber insists that discussions on methodology should be reflective and are not the basis upon which the sciences are established. Rather, it is only when the substantive problems of the sciences are dealt with that both the sciences and their methods develop. However, pure methodological and epistemological discussions have never played a significant role in such developments.[4]

---

[3] Max Weber, *The Methodology of the Social Sciences*, Shils, Edward A. Shils & Henry A. Finch (trans. and ed.) (New York: Free Press, 1949), 115.

[4] Weber, *The Methodology of the Social Sciences*, 116.

Weber defines sociology as 'a science concerning itself with the interpretive understanding of social action and thereby with a causal explanation of its course and consequences'.[5] By social action Weber means the action of an individual of which its subjective meaning is oriented to the behaviour of others.[6] For Weber, the task of sociology was to achieve an understanding (*Verstehen*) of social phenomena, which referred to the understanding of social action. The German term, *Verstehen*, often translated as empathic understanding, refers to the understanding of the actions of actors in terms of the subjective meaning attributed to them in a given type of action. Such an understanding is made possible by our capacity to empathize with the thinking and motives of other human beings.[7] Weber's thinking on *Verstehen* as applied to the study of social phenomena was an extension of the German interest in hermeneutics, the discipline concerned with the interpretation of the meaning of texts as intended by the author. What Weber did was to extend this idea of interpretation to the study of social action and human interaction. This method of interpretation placed the human sciences at an advantage over the natural sciences, for it enables us to 'accomplish something which is never attainable in the natural sciences, namely the subjective understanding of the action of the component individuals'.[8]

Weber was not only interested in the meaning of social action but also the causal explanation of its course and consequences. Far from having a one-way causal explanation, Weber was committed to the idea of multiple causality. For example, in his study of the role of Protestantism in the development of modern capitalism, Weber was careful to point out that it was necessary to clarify the extent to which religious as opposed to other factors accounted for the development of material culture.[9]

---

[5] Max Weber, *Economy and Society: An Outline of Interpretive Sociology*. 2 Vols. G. Roth, & C. Wittich (eds.), (Berkeley, Los Angeles & London: University of California Press, 1978), 4.

[6] Weber, *Economy and Society*, 44.

[7] Weber, *Economy and Society*, 4; Sam Whimster, ed., *The Essential Weber: A Reader* (London: Routledge, 2004), 412.

[8] Weber, *Economy and Society*, 15.

[9] Max Weber, *The Protestant Ethic and the Spirit of Capitalism*, trans. Talcott Parsons (New York: Charles Scribner's Sons, 1958), 91–2, cited in George Ritzer, *Sociological Theory*, (New York: Alfred A. Knopf, 1983), 127.

One of Weber's most important methodological tools is the ideal type. The ideal type is an abstract, hypothetical concept constructed by the scholar to use for the systematic study of empirical phenomena. Ideal types should not be misunderstood to refer to the ideal of perfect in the moral or ethical sense. Rather, they refer to the common elements of a social phenomenon. Ideal types are analytical constructs that function as heuristic devices that enable the scholar organize the facts of reality into 'mental construct' (*Gedankenbilder*).[10]

As Weber wrote: 'An ideal type is formed by the one-sided accentuation of one or more points of view and by the synthesis of a great many diffuse, discrete, more or less present and occasionally absent concrete individual phenomena, which are arranged according to those one-sidedly emphasized viewpoints into a unified analytical construct...'[11]

An ideal type is formed from the traits and characteristics of a given social phenomenon, but is not meant to correspond to all of the elements of that phenomenon. The ideal type is constructed from empirical reality in a way that accentuates or exaggerates certain traits of a social phenomenon. If a certain relationship between social phenomena is suspected or hypothesized to exist, the precise nature of this relationship can be stated in a clear and understandable manner through the construction of ideal types.[12] The ideal type is a construct that functions as a yardstick that the analyst may use to examine the extent to which empirical phenomenon conforms to or deviates from the ideal or pure type. What defines the ideal type of a social phenomenon as such is its pure form as it exists in the mind of the analyst. It is through the ideal type that scholars can deal with certain problems that they raise about social reality.[13]

For example, let us consider the relationship between religion and capitalism. We may suspect and hypothesize the role of Protestantism in the rise of modern capitalism. We construct an *ideal type* of

[10] Max Weber, *The Methodology of the Social Sciences*, Shils, Edward A. and Finch, Henry A. (trans. and ed.), (New York: Free Press, 1997), 90.

[11] Weber, *The Methodology of the Social Sciences*, 90.

[12] Weber, *The Methodology of the Social Sciences*, 90.

[13] Lewis A. Coser, *Masters of Sociological Thought: Ideas in Historical and Social Context* (New York: Harcourt Brace Jovanovich, 1971), 223.

Protestantism, based on the various Protestant sects that existed during the Reformation. The elements that make up the ideal type are those that are suspected to be pertinent to capital accumulation and the emergence of capitalism. We then assess the extent to which empirical cases of Protestant traders or entrepreneurs, for example, confirm to or deviate from the pure type. This would allow us to make causal inferences regarding the relationship between Protestantism and modern capitalism.[14]

There are at least five types of ideal types in Weber's work. The first is individual ideal types, that is ideal types of historical individuals such as the 'Protestant ethic' or 'modern capitalism'. These are phenomena that occur only in specific cultural and historical contexts. The scholar selects elements from the particular historical context to construct an abstract intelligible entity. The second type is general ideal types. These ideal types are ahistorical abstractions or concepts. These can be applied to many historical and cultural contexts. The ideal type is constructed from elements from a large number of cases. The third type refers to the essence of an idea system. The core ideas are extracted to form a mental construct of the system. An example is Weber's construction of Calvinism. The fourth is ideal types of processes. An example is Weber's discussion of the historical process of the routinization of charisma. The fifth type of ideal types is 'rationalizing reconstructions of a particular kind of behavior'. Examples are propositions in economic theory that are ideal typical constructions of how people would behave if they were pure economic subjects.[15]

It is also important to mention Weber's contribution to discussions on the role of values in the social sciences. Much of our thinking today on the topic is influenced by Weber. Weber was against the teacher in the classroom making value judgements, taking the view that the lecture should be different from the speech. The task of the lecturer is to stimulate and

---

[14] Coser, *Masters of Sociological Thought*, 223–4.

[15] Raymond Aron, *Main Currents in Sociological Thought*, 2 Vols. (New York: Anchor Books, 1970), vol. 2, 246–7; Thomas Burger, *Max Weber's Theory of Concept Formation: History, Laws and Ideal Types* (Durham: Duke University Press, 1976), 118, cited in Ritzer, *Sociological Theory*, 130. This list of five is the result of collapsing Aron's three and Burger's four kinds of ideal types.

cultivate the students' capacity for observation and reasoning without burdening them with the lecturer's 'uncontradictable evaluation'.[16]

The distinction must be made between fact and value judgements.[17] For Weber, this position of value neutrality did not mean there was no place for values in the social sciences. That value judgements were to be withdrawn from scientific activities was a proposition to be rejected.[18] For Weber, there was such a thing as value relevance which meant that values had a role in the selection of the subject matter.[19] Without the values of the investigator there would be no criteria of selection of the subject matter.[20] Values also have a role to play in the use of the results of scientific investigation. This is where science has to withdraw. In the area of social policy, for example, science cannot provide justification for the norms and ideals that underlie policy.[21]

Weber said that it was essential to make the distinction between existential knowledge of what is and normative knowledge of what should be. Empirical knowledge may help in the determination of the means to given ends but it cannot provide scientific justification for the norms and ideals that underlie practical activity.[22] Objectivity does not refer to moral indifference[23] but to the understanding of the specific place of values in the process of research.

The Origins of Modern Capitalism

For Weber, modern capitalism was a system characterized by the provision of everyday wants by capitalistic methods. Capitalism refers to a specific method of enterprise that is characterized by 'capital accounting,

---

[16] Weber, *The Methodology of the Social Sciences*, 4–5.

[17] Weber, *The Methodology of the Social Sciences*, 9–10.

[18] Weber, *The Methodology of the Social Sciences*, 52.

[19] Weber, *The Methodology of the Social Sciences*, 11, 22, 77, 82.

[20] Weber, *The Methodology of the Social Sciences*, 82.

[21] Weber, *The Methodology of the Social Sciences*, 60.

[22] Weber, *The Methodology of the Social Sciences*, 51–2.

[23] Weber, *The Methodology of the Social Sciences*, 60.

that is, an establishment which determines its income yielding power by calculation according to the methods of modern bookkeeping and the striking of a balance'.[24] An entire system can be said to be capitalistic only if everyday needs are supplied capitalistically. As Weber said:

> A whole epoch can be designated as typically capitalistic only as the provision for wants is capitalistically organized to such a predominant degree that if we imagine this form of organization taken away the whole economic system must collapse.[25]

For Weber, it was only in the Occident that modern capitalism developed. The 'provision of everyday wants by capitalistic methods is characteristic of the occident alone...' since the nineteenth century.[26] Modern capitalism had originated in the West due to the presence of several conditions or factors to be found in feudal Europe. First, there is the appropriation of all physical means of production, which includes land, machinery and tools. These must be available as disposable private property to autonomous, private individuals.[27] Secondly, there must be freedom of the market. This refers to the absence of irrational, arbitrary limitations on market trade.[28] Thirdly, technology should be organized along rational lines. This refers to the calculability, to the highest possible degree, of technical conditions of production and also implies mechanization.[29] The fourth characteristic is calculable law. Rational law based on calculable adjudication and administration is required as opposed to arbitrary law. The former creates a stable environment for the rise of an independent trading class. The patrimonial states of Asia, the Greek city-state or even Europe in earlier times were characterized by 'cheap justice' where 'remissions by royal grace introduced continual

---

[24] Max Weber, *General Economic History*, Frank Knight, trans (New Brunswick & London: Transaction Books, 1981), 275.

[25] Weber, *General Economic History*, 275–6.

[26] Weber, *General Economic History*, 276.

[27] Weber, *General Economic History*, 276.

[28] Weber, *General Economic History*, 276–7.

[29] Weber, *General Economic History*, 277.

disturbances into the calculations of everyday life'.[30] The fifth characteristic is free labour. Only in a situation where there is a class devoid of
property, legally free and, therefore, forced to sell its labour for its
survival can modern capitalism exist. In fact, rational capitalistic
calculation would be impossible in the absence of free labour. This
is because it is only through the existence of free labour that the costs
can be 'unambiguously determined by agreement in advance'.[31] The
sixth and final condition is the commercialization of economic life.
This refers to the use of commercial instruments to represent share
rights in enterprise, and also property ownership, making capital more
available.[32]

But Weber does not stop at these six preconditions. In Weber's
historical and comparative analysis, the form of authority or domination
is a crucial comparative dimension accounting for the development of
modern capitalism. The bureaucratic-legal state is important for the
existence of modern capitalism because '[i]t is primarily the capitalist
market economy which demands that the official business of public
administration be discharged precisely, unambiguously, continuously,
and with as much speed as possible'.[33] Furthermore, the bureaucratic-
legal state with its rational law and adjudication frees land and labour by
opposing feudalism and maintains a free market. In general, the bureaucratic-legal state allows for the existence and the development of the six
preconditions of modern capitalism outlined earlier. The bureaucratic-
legal state is one form, and the purest, of rational legal authority. Legal
authority is characterized by Weber in terms of the rule-bound conduct
of official business; a defined jurisdiction; the hierarchical organization
of offices in which every office is under the supervision of a higher one;
an adequate amount of technical training for every office; the separation
of officials from the ownership of the means of production or administration; the absence of the appropriation of official positions by

---

[30] Weber, *General Economic History*, 277.

[31] Weber, *General Economic History*, 277.

[32] Weber, *General Economic History*, 277–8.

[33] Weber, *Economy and Society*, 974.

incumbents; and the recording of rules, decisions, and acts pertaining to adjudication.[34]

The Protestant Ethic and the Spirit of Capitalism

Thus far, Weber sounds like a materialist, attributing the origins and rise of capitalism in the West to structural rather than subjective or cultural factors. Elsewhere, however, Weber says that capitalism requires an attitude that he called the spirit of capitalism and that this attitude obtained its content from Protestantism. Weber defines the spirit of capitalism as an historical individual, that is, a 'complex of elements associated in historical reality which we unite into a conceptual whole from the standpoint of their cultural significance'.[35] Therefore, it cannot be defined in terms of the usual formula *genus proximum, differentia specifica*.[36] For Marx, the development of capitalism is explained primarily in materialist terms, that is ownership and control over the means of production, and class conflict between the emerging bourgeoisie and the old feudal classes. While Weber would probably not have disagreed with such a role of materialist factors, in his study on Protestantism and the rise of capitalism, Weber gives an idealist explanation of the rise of capitalism in Europe.

Notwithstanding the importance of the structural factors or conditions of modern capitalism listed earlier, Weber would add that the 'question of the motive forces in the explanation of modern capitalism is not in the first instance a question of the origin of the capital sums which were available for capitalistic uses, but, above all, of the development of the spirit of capitalism'.[37] Weber's capitalism, therefore, was clearly not a materialist interpretation of the origins of capitalism. Weber says, '[w]here it [spirit of capitalism] appears and is able to work itself out, it produces its own capital and monetary supplies as the means to its

[34] Weber, *Economy and Society*, 218–19.
[35] Weber, *The Protestant Ethic and the Spirit of Capitalism*, 47.
[36] Weber, *The Protestant Ethic*, 47.
[37] Weber, *The Protestant Ethic*, 68.

own ends, but the reverse is not true.'[38] In other words, the spirit of capitalism creates the institutions but not the reverse. The spirit of capitalism was a unique phenomenon that existed in a certain historical period in Europe and is crucial to the understanding of the origins of capitalism. It has specific traits which Weber describes before attempting a formal definition. He describes some statements of the American founding father and polymath, Benjamin Franklin, which convey the idea that the earning of more and more money is combined with the avoidance of spontaneous enjoyment of life. These statements include 'time is money', 'credit is money', '[t]good paymaster is lord of another man's purse' and 'money is of the prolific, generating nature'.[39] Weber formally defines the spirit of capitalism as an attitude which seeks profits rationally and systematically, a calculating form of profit-seeking, combined with the avoidance of spontaneous enjoyment.[40]

Central to the spirit of capitalism was that the practice of the acquisition of capital arose from the avoidance of the spontaneous enjoyment of life. Such acquisition was not for the satisfaction of material needs. Rather, there was a higher purpose behind it, as suggested by this quote from the Bible that Weber cites: 'Seest thou a man diligent in business? He shall stand before kings.'[41] Weber contrasted the spirit of capitalism with that of traditionalism. In traditionalism people do not wish to augment their wealth but wish to live as they are accustomed to and to earn as much as is necessary for that purpose.[42] The attitude behind traditionalism was deficient from the capitalistic point of view. The worker and capitalist alike were imbued with the spirit of capitalism and both regard work as an end in itself, as if it were a religious calling.[43] For capitalism to develop, traditionalism had to be overcome. Here, the distinction between the Catholic and Protestant worlds is important. In the successful merchant capitalist centres of trade in Florence, Italy in

[38] Weber, *The Protestant Ethic*, 68–9.
[39] Weber, *The Protestant Ethic*, 48–9.
[40] Weber, *The Protestant Ethic*, 53, 55.
[41] Weber, *The Protestant Ethic*, 53.
[42] Weber, *The Protestant Ethic*, 60.
[43] Weber, *The Protestant Ethic*, 63.

the fourteenth and fifteenth centuries, the capitalist spirit was considered ethically unjustifiable. In eighteenth-century Pennsylvania, on the other hand, there were very small, poor enterprises; the same attitude was 'considered the essence of moral conduct'.[44] Modern capitalism was to develop in those areas with the spirit of capitalism. The chances of this happening were greatest in areas where there was a Protestant religious upbringing. Methodical life in the pursuit of wealth can only come from a this-worldly asceticism. Asceticism itself referred to a life of severe self-discipline without the ordinary pleasures of life.

It was the attitude towards the acquisition of capital as a religious calling that made it possible for capitalism to become a systematic way of life. Protestantism instilled an attitude that was in people that was opposed to the traditionalism of Catholicism. While both espoused an ascetic way of life, there was an important difference between the two. In the case of Catholicism, it was founded on the idea that 'activity directed to acquisition [of capital] for its own sake was at bottom a *pudendum* which was to be tolerated only because of the unalterable necessities of life in this world'.[45] The traditionalism of Catholicism was based on an other-worldly asceticism which stressed retreat from worldly affairs. Neither could wealth acquisition be sustained by greed alone. People have been greedy for centuries, but this did not result in capitalism in terms of systematic and rational capital accumulation, that is planning, investing, frugality, the putting off of consumption, ploughing back of investments into the business and so on. Capitalism required an outlook on life that made the acquisition of capital a religious calling. Only then can it become a systematic way of life. For Weber, modern capitalism was the result of the merging of a capitalist enterprise and an ascetic Protestantism, above all, the Calvinistic version of it.[46] Economic activity as the pursuit of profit was seen as a spiritual end. These doctrines were not against worldly activity and did not frown upon wealth acquisition per se. Rather, the moral objection to wealth had to do with the

---

[44] Weber, *The Protestant Ethic*, 75.

[45] Weber, *The Protestant Ethic*, 73.

[46] Weber, *The Protestant Ethic*, 128.

'relaxation in the security of possession, the enjoyment of wealth with the consequence of idleness and the temptations of the flesh, and above all distraction from the pursuit of a righteous life'.[47] The spirit of capitalism was influenced by Calvinism in the sense that its this-worldly asceticism was a means of salvation. The effect of this was psychological in that it freed the acquisition of wealth from the inhibitions of the traditionalistic attitude.[48] Its asceticism was this-worldly in that it drove its adherents to hard work, discipline and frugality. It had this effect because the attainment of wealth as a fruit of labour in a calling was a sign of God's blessing. The practical result of all this was the ascetic compulsion to work hard, to avoid spontaneous enjoyment and, therefore, to save. It is this attitude towards life that Weber called the spirit of capitalism.

Calvinist doctrine dealt with the anxiety of salvation in two mutually connected ways. On the one hand, the faithful had a duty to believe that he was saved and to combat any doubts as to his salvation as temptations of the devil. On the other hand, attaining self-confidence regarding one's salvation could be achieved through intense worldly activity as '[i]t and it alone disperses religious doubts and gives the certainty of grace'.[49] The practical but anticipated result of such an outlook was the rapid accumulation of capital.

There are two important theoretical points to make about the effect of the Protestant ethic on the development of the spirit of capitalism. The first is that there was what Weber referred to as an elective affinity, correlation or congeniality between Protestantism and the modern capitalist attitude or ethic.[50] There is a connection between the irrational value commitments of Calvinism with rational, calculative economic conduct. This one seems irrational from the other's point of view but they come together in capitalism.

---

[47] Weber, *The Protestant Ethic*, 157.

[48] Weber, *The Protestant Ethic*, 171.

[49] Weber, *The Protestant Ethic*, 111–2.

[50] Weber, *The Protestant Ethic*, 91–2. The German term *Wahlverwandtschaft* was not translated as elective affinity but as correlation in Parsons' translation of *The Protestant Ethic and the Spirit of Capitalism*. Others, however, have preferred to use elective affinity, the term which has been an object of much discussion. See Andrew M. McKinnon, 'Elective Affinities of the Protestant Ethic: Weber and the Chemistry of Capitalism', *Sociological Theory* 28, 1, 2010: 108–126.

Secondly, the fact of congeniality is related to the idea that Calvinists did not consciously seek to create a capitalist system. Capitalism was an unintended consequence of the Protestant ethic, 'unforeseen and even unwished for results of the labours of the reformers'.[51] This is an important idea – what people intend by their actions may lead to a set of consequences that are at variance with their intentions.

Weber saw his theory of the Protestant ethic as a critique of historical materialism. The ideas did not simply correspond to the material conditions. One would have expected the spirit of capitalism to arise in Italy if that were the case and not in England, Germany and America. To say in this case that the material conditions are reflected in the ideal superstructure would be 'patent nonsense'.[52]

Weberian Orientalism

Given Weber's claim that it is only in the Occident that modern capitalism developed, that only the West had the prerequisites for the rise of capitalism and that it was a Western religion, Protestantism, that played a unique role in this rise, the question can be raised as to whether Weber took an Orientalist position according to which the West represented progress and the Orient backwardness. Indeed, a case for Weberian Orientalism can be made in two senses. One refers to Orientalism in the works of Weber himself, and the other to how Orientalism has been attributed to Weber by those who read him.

Weber's Orientalism

Weber's writings about the origin of modern capitalism in the West in his *The Protestant Ethic and the Spirit of Capitalism* should be read in the light of his comparative sociology of religion. His work on the Protestant ethic is

---

[51] Weber, *The Protestant Ethic*, 90.
[52] Weber, *The Protestant Ethic*, 75.

part of a larger project on the sociological study of religion in which Weber discussed other world religions such as Hinduism, Buddhism, Taoism, Judaism and Islam. In these works, Weber was not only interested in the relationship between religious ideas and economic activities but also the unique characteristics that make up Western civilization.[53] Above all, his concern was with whether the various non-Western religious traditions had the cultural resources that could give rise to the spirit of capitalism in the way that Puritanism did. Weber's sociology of religion began with *The Protestant Ethic and the Spirit of Capitalism* and then moves on to the analysis of *The Religion of China: Confucianism and Taoism*, *The Religion of India: The Sociology of Hinduism and Buddhism* and *Ancient Judaism*. While Weber did make references to Islam in his work, he died before being able to complete his project on Islam.

According to Weber, it was the peculiar features of European feudalism (*Lehensfeudalismus*) that led to the development of bureaucratic-legal authority in the West.[54] The dominance of formal law at the expense of patrimonial law was a result of the requirements of the feudal administration. Because of the consistent need of the ruler to pay the cost of his administration and because of the absence of provisions for raising these revenues, the Occidental feudal ruler had to frequently make new agreements that eventually led to the formation of corporate assemblies, turning temporary associations into permanent political structures. This is rather different from the Middle East where the 'legal insecurity of the tax-paying population *vis a vis* the arbitrariness of the troops to whom their tax capacity was mortgaged could paralyze commerce and hence the money economy, indeed, since the period of the Seljuks [ca. 1050–1150]'.[55] Only when there were conquests were there booty, and thus, a way for the administration to be financed. However, during periods of defeat, the army constituted a threat to the patrimonial ruler since he could not pay them wage arrears.[56]

---

[53] Reinhard Bendix, *Max Weber: An Intellectual Portrait* (London: Heinemann, 1960), chap. 3.

[54] Weber, *Economy and Society*, 259.

[55] Weber, *Economy and Society*, 1016.

[56] Bryan S. Turner, *Weber and Islam: A Critical Study* (London & Boston: Routledge & Kegan Paul, 1974), 123–4.

Weber's studies on religion were by no means unproblematic and display strong elements of Orientalism. For example, in *The Religion of India*, Weber's reading of caste and Hinduism as defining and distinct features of Indian society is problematic on two counts. It betrays a textual reading of the phenomena, and essentializes Indian society. Objections to Weber's account have been raised by scholars of Indian religion. Singer, who did a study on Madras entrepreneurs, concluded that Hindu industrialists did not experience a clash between their identity as Hindus and as entrepreneurs because of their adaptive strategy of compartmentalizing or separating their roles into different life-worlds.[57] In other words, modernity and tradition were combined through compartmentalization. Harriss, also looking at Madras entrepreneurs, disagreed with Singer's idea of compartmentalization. Instead, he noted the merging of a capitalist ethic, Hinduism and 'Tamil cultural politics'.[58]

Weber's writings on Chinese religion were also problematic. His reading of Confucianism and Taoism in *The Religion of China* is an instance of the imposition of the Judeo-Christian notion of 'religion' as if it were a universal category. Furthermore, Weber's characterization of Confucianism as 'world affirming' and of 'Confucian rationalism' as a 'rational adjustment to the world' contributes to the image of Chinese society as static and unchanging. This again betrays an Orientalist understanding of the non-West as passive, lacking a history and essentially different from the West. Also, Weber was at times factually wrong. It was noted above that Weber was of the view that historically there were no large private capitalist factories in China. C. K. Yang, in his introduction to *The Religion of China*, notes that in certain industries such as silk textile and chinaware, there were indeed factories of considerable size and complexity of organization.[59] Sometimes, the problem of empirical correctness is related to that of chronological discrepancy.

---

[57] Milton Singer, *When a Great Tradition Modernizes. An Anthropological Approach to Indian Civilization* (Chicago and London: The University of Chicago Press, 1972), 320–25.

[58] John Harriss, 'The Great Tradition Globalizes: Reflections on Two Studies of "The Industrial Leaders" of Madras', *Modern Asian Studies* 37, 2 (2003).

[59] C. K. Yang, 'Introduction', in Weber, *The Religion of China*, xxvii.

As Sunar notes, Weber often disregards gaps in time which may amount to thousands of years. When providing evidence for a fact, Weber might cite examples from antiquity and modern times side by side. For example, in his discussion on patrimonialism in Islam, Weber cites evidence from Prophet Muhammad in the seventh century, land tenure in the twelfth century and Ottoman *evkaf* (charitable endowments) in the sixteenth century, giving the impression that there were centuries of uninterrupted patrimonialism. Sunar suggests that Weber did not find this to be a problem if he assumed that Oriental societies were static.[60]

The Attribution of Orientalism to Weber

According to Weber, modern capitalism could only originate in the West because it required an attitude of commercial gain and profit, the spirit of capitalism, which generally emerged in Protestant-dominated areas of Europe. Weber acknowledged that although Islamic and Confucianist world views do stress frugality and hard work, the spirit of capitalism did not emerge in the Arab world or in China because of the absence of an ascetic compulsion to work. Third World consumption of Weber has been such that the discourse assumes that for Weber capitalism was an advanced, progressive economic system, and thus something 'good and desirable' and following from this that Western society was superior in this respect. As a result, some non-Western students and scholars took a defensive position and attempted to show that their own religions (Islam, Buddhism, Confucianism) were conducive to the development of capitalism or they were not against wealth acquisition.[61] This can be understood as the 'Orientalization' of Weber's Protestant ethic thesis. This refers to the faulty attribution of certain Orientalist ideas to Weber's views.

---

[60] Lutfi Sunar, *Marx and Weber on Oriental Societies: In the Shadow of Western Modernity*, Surrey: Ashgate, 2014, 159.

[61] Andreas Buss, 'Max Weber's Heritage and Modern Southeast Asian Thinking on Development', *Southeast Asian Journal of Social Science* 12, 1 (1984), 2.

An example of the Orientalization of Weber has to do with assigning an overdetermined role for Islam. In responding to Weber's thesis about the role of Protestantism in the rise of capitalism, some scholars assumed that Weber stressed the incompatibility of the Islamic ethic with capitalist development. Here, there is an attribution of essentialism to Weber, that is, that he regarded Islam as essential to and necessary for the function of the political economy of Muslim societies. In fact, as we saw earlier, Weber stressed more on the structural aspects of Muslim societies such as patrimonialism as barriers to capitalist development rather than any Muslim ethic. Jomo furnishes examples of such attribution. He refers to writers on Malay development who uncritically adopt Weber's view of Islam as an obstacle to capitalism. Based on this assumption, they attribute Malay peasant fatalism and backwardness to the religion of Islam, often ignoring the role of other factors.[62] We have seen, however, that Weber himself had stressed structural rather than ideological or cultural factors when he discussed Islam and its relation to capitalism. Furthermore, as noted by Syed Hussein Alatas, there are cases where Islam is not the decisive factor in the process of development. He cites the case of South Indian Muslims who have a pronounced capitalist spirit as opposed to the Malays who do not. Both are Muslims belonging even to the same jurisprudential school of Islam, that is the Shafi'is.[63]

The attribution of Orientalist ideas to Weber is due to misunderstanding about Weber's position with regard to the possibility of capitalism existing outside of the West. Weber had not claimed that capitalism could not exist beyond the Occident. His claim, rather, was that the attitude of commercial gain and profit based on rational calculation, that is the spirit of capitalism, could originate only in the West and was to be explained in terms of characteristics peculiar to the worldly asceticism of certain Protestant doctrines of the sixteenth and

---

[62] K. S. Jomo, 'Islam and Weber: Rodinson on the Implications of Religion for Capitalist Development', *The Developing Economies* 15, 2 (1977), 248–9.

[63] Syed Hussein Alatas, 'The Weber Thesis and South-East Asian', in Alatas, *Modernization and Social Change: Studies in Modernization, Religion, Social Change and Development in South-East Asia* (Sydney: Angus & Robertson, 1972), 19.

seventeenth centuries, particularly those of Calvin. In other words, what Weber did say was that there was no equivalent to the Protestant ethic in non-Western societies. Therefore, the spirit of capitalism could not originate outside of the West. This was not the same as saying that non-Western religions contained teachings that were not conducive to capitalism, a claim that Weber did not make.

Neither did Weber claim that there was a lack of the acquisitive drive among non-Westerners. As noted by Buss, Weber noticed that Indian and Chinese merchants may have had more acquisitive drive than the Protestant in the West.[64] But the point was not that acquisitive drive or love of wealth was necessary for the development of the spirit of capitalism. Rather it was the suppression of acquisitiveness that was necessary. Also, Weber did not claim that sobriety, honesty and thrift were absent among non-Western peoples. For the Protestant, however, frugality, thrift, the suppression of acquisitiveness and honesty, all existed in the context of an ascetic compulsion to be successful as if the soul depended on it.

Weber did not say that capitalism could not be implanted in non-Western societies. On the Chinese, he said:

> The Chinese in all probability would be as capable, probably more capable than the Japanese, of assimilating capitalism which has technically and economically been fully developed in the modern culture area.[65]

But this would be capitalism without the spirit. Finally, Weber did not say that capitalism was a superior system, certainly not in cultural or moral terms. Far from believing in the superiority of the West because it created capitalism, he saw Western civilization as an iron cage. He makes a Marxist sounding statement:

> Whoever takes only one penny of interest which others – directly or indirectly – have to pay, whoever owns a commodity or eats any food

---

[64] Buss, 'Max Weber's Heritage', 4.
[65] Weber, *The Religion of China*, 248.

produced with another person's sweat, lives of the machinery of that loveless and pitiless economic struggle for existence which bourgeois phraseology tends to call 'peaceful civilization'.[66]

Weber has been often misunderstood. In many academic communities, discussions on Weber's views on the development of capitalism are premised on the assumption that Weber considered capitalism to be an advanced system and, therefore, good and desirable. Based on this assumption, it was Weber's Protestant ethic thesis and his sociology of religion in general that was seen as an argument in favour of the superiority of Western civilization. Often unnoticed was the fact that Weber was extremely critical of modern capitalism and the order that it created. He lamented that humans of the modern age were born into an order based on technical and economic conditions of machine production and factory life. The bureaucratic division of labour that achieves this also creates a tension that is the basis of a modern pathology. This is the tension between the need for technical efficiency in administration on the one hand, and human values of freedom and autonomy on the other. What results is an enslavement of sorts:

> The Puritan wanted to work in a calling; we are forced to do so. For when asceticism was carried out of monastic cells into everyday life, and began to dominate worldly morality, it did its part in building the tremendous cosmos of the modern economic order. This order is now bound to the technical and economic conditions of machine production which today determine the lives of all the individuals who are born into this mechanism, not only those directly concerned with economic acquisition, with irresistible force. Perhaps it will so determine them until the last ton of fossilised coal is burnt. In Baxter's view the care for external goods should only lie on the shoulders of the 'saint like a light cloak, which can be thrown aside at any moment'. But fate decreed that the cloak should become an iron cage.[67]

---

[66] Max Weber, 'Between Two Ethics', in Weber, *Gesammelte Politische Schriften* (J. C. B. Mohr: Tubingen, 1958), cited in Buss, 'Max Weber's Heritage', 9–10.

[67] Weber, *The Protestant Ethic*, 181.

Social Action, Rationalization and the Metaphor of the Iron Cage

The problem of enslavement by rationality, as implied by the metaphor of the iron cage, is the pathology of modern society that Weber foregrounds. We saw earlier that at the more substantive level Weber was concerned with the role of the Protestant ethic in the development of capitalism. At a more abstract level this concern translates into a discussion on how the ethical substantive rationality of Protestantism gave rise to a system that was informed by a formal rather than substantive rationality. This formal rationality eventually became generalized across society, invading more and more spheres of life, replacing the substantive rationality that gave rise to it in the first place. In order to understand this argument, it is necessary to define Weber's types of rationality. For this we need to begin with the types of social action that Weber regarded as the subject matter of sociology. Rationalization is the attempt of humans to understand the world around them, to connect events into a meaningful picture of the world. It is the types of rationality, that is the ways in which humans master their fragmented and disconnected realities, that introduce corresponding types of social action.[68]

Social action is any action oriented to the behaviour of others, of which there are four types: (1) Instrumentally rational or means-ends rational (*zweckrational*) action is action that results from the actor's rationally pursued and calculated ends in which the behaviour of objects and other human beings in the environment are used as conditions or means for such calculation.[69] (2) Value rational (*wertrational*) action is action that is determined by a conscious belief in the value for its own sake of some ethical, aesthetic or religious behaviour independently of the prospects of success of the behaviour itself.[70] (3) Affectual action is

---

[68] Stephen Kalberg, 'Max Weber's Types of Rationality: Cornerstones for the Analysis of Rationalization Processes in History', *American Journal of Sociology* 85, 5 (1980), 1148.

[69] Weber, *Economy and Society*, 24.

[70] Weber, *Economy and Society*, 24–5.

action determined by actor's affects and emotional state. (4) Traditional action is action determined by habit. Neither affectual nor traditional action involves rationalization or rational processes. They involve automatic or uncontrolled reaction to habitual or exceptional stimuli rather than resulting from conscious rationalization.[71] Only value rational and instrumentally rational actions are guided by rationalization. Value rational action results from the human capacity of value rationality, while instrumentally rational action results from the human capacity of either formal or practical rationality.[72] So, what are the types of rationality?

Weber was careful to point out that rationalization may mean different things. On the one hand, it may refer to a 'theoretical mastery of reality by means of increasingly precise and abstract concepts'. This is a theoretical rationality involving abstract thought processes that do not directly lead to action, although it may indirectly introduce action.[73] Unlike theoretical rationality, the other types of rationality, that is substantive, practical and formal rationality, all directly result in patterns of action.[74] Practical rationality refers to the mastering of reality by way of 'precise calculation of adequate means' in order to achieve given and practical ends.[75] The world is viewed in terms of the person's pragmatic and egoistic interests. The given reality is accepted and the means are calculated to deal with that reality. Practical rationality is a manifestation of human's capacity for means-end rational action.[76] Formal rationality, while also a manifestation of means-end rational action, on the other hand, looks for the most precise and efficient means to achieve certain ends with reference to universally applied rules, laws and regulations and without regard for persons, as opposed to pragmatic self-interests.

---

[71] Weber, *Economy and Society*, 25.

[72] Kalberg, 'Max Weber's Types of Rationality', 1161.

[73] Weber, 'The Social Psychology of the World Religions', in *From Max Weber: Essays on Sociology*, trans. and ed. H. H. Gerth and C. Wright Mills (New York: Oxford University Press, 1946), 293; Kalberg, 'Max Weber's Types of Rationality', 1152–1155.

[74] Weber, *Economy and Society*, 85–6.

[75] Weber, 'The Social Psychology of the World Religions', 293.

[76] Kalberg, 'Max Weber's Types of Rationality', 1151–1152.

It involves the systematic and methodical application of rules and procedures to achieve certain goals and rejects arbitrariness.[77]

Although all three types of rationality introduce conscious regularities of action, it is only substantive rationality that results in methodical ways of life.[78] In substantive rationality reality is understood and acted upon in terms of criteria of ultimate ends that lie outside of the immediate sphere of action. These ultimate ends, which may be political, ethical, religious, feudal, hedonistic or whatever, are used to measure the results of action. In other words, action is assessed against the scales of value rationality or substantive goal rationality.[79] This is because it is only a unified set of values that can introduce methodicalness and continuity in life.[80] On the other hand, practical rationality fails to introduce a methodical way of life as it is based on subjective interests and merely reacts to changing situations rather than order life. Formal rationality too is unable to order life beyond the sphere of activity that it applies to, that is the profession of the civil servant, lawyer, businessman, scientist and so on. But, formal rationality fails to order life in others spheres, in the sphere of personal relationships, in the home and so on.[81]

The substantive rationality of the Protestant ethic introduced a methodical way of life by subjugating interest and mere orientation to rules to a unified configuration of values that ordered life. The religious outlook of the Puritan was such that people understood their success in capital accumulation as a sign of God's grace. The unintended consequence of this, however, was the creation of a new economic system, modern capitalism. Although the Protestant ethic gave birth to the spirit of capitalism, as capitalism developed the spirit of capitalism with its Protestant outlook on life lost ground. As John Wesley, the eighteenth century Anglican minister and theologian, said: 'Although the form of

---

[77] Kalberg, 'Max Weber's Types of Rationality', 1158; Weber, *Economy and Society*, 225–6, 975.
[78] Kalberg, 'Max Weber's Types of Rationality', 1164.
[79] Weber, *Economy and Society*, 85–6; Kalberg, 'Max Weber's Types of Rationality', 1155.
[80] Kalberg, 'Max Weber's Types of Rationality', 1164.
[81] Kalberg, 'Max Weber's Types of Rationality', 1164–65.

religion remains, the spirit is swiftly vanishing away.'[82] This was already evident in Wesley's time. By Weber's, people were already born into an order based on technical and economic conditions of machine production and factory life. The rational or systematic methodical nature of capitalism requires rational, systematic, methodical system of administration to run a modern capitalist society. This implies that the further advance of bureaucratization is inevitable. A tension develops between the need for technical efficiency in administration and human values of freedom and autonomy.

Asceticism redefined the world and made possible the great increase in production of material goods and capital accumulation. But today, capitalism is no longer based on a religious, ascetic ethic. Modern capitalist society, stripped of its religious and ethical meaning, consists of formally rational people and the institutions they run. The modern order is no longer governed by a religious ethic but by the bureaucratic norms of efficiency and calculability. In modern capitalist society people are less governed by a religious ethic and more by bureaucratic norms of efficiency and calculability. Bureaucracies have developed to the extent that they encompass almost all areas of life. For Weber, modern capitalist society was characterized by the formal rationalization of life which he also referred to as the problem of disenchantment. In his famous essay, 'Science as a Vocation', he writes that the fate of modern times is characterized not only by rationalization and intellectualization, but above all, by the de-magification of the world.[83] This refers to a kind of society guided by a rationality in which 'no mysterious incalculable forces come into play' – neither gods, other supernatural forces, nor magic are resorted to in order to understand the world, to master reality.[84] The world had become desacralized.

---

[82] Weber, *The Protestant Ethic*, 175.

[83] Max Weber, *From Max Weber: Essays in Sociology*, trans. and ed. by H. H. Gerth and C. Wright Mills, New York: Oxford University Press, 1946, 155. The German term *Entzauberung* is frequently rendered 'disenchantment'. Kalberg regards this as a mistranslation and prefers 'de-magification'. See Kalberg, 'Max Weber's Types of Rationality', 1146, n. 2.

[84] Max Weber, 'Science as a Vocation,' in *From Max Weber: Essays on Sociology*, trans. and ed. H. H. Gerth and C. Wright Mills (New York: Oxford University Press, 1946), 154.

The Sociology of Authority, Bureaucracy and Excessive Bureaucratization

At one level, Weber's work can be seen as a sociology of rationalization. He looked at how modern capitalist society changed from being dominated by a substantive to a formal rationality. Formal rationality in modern society is a manifestation of man's capacity for means-end or instrumental rational action. Formal rationality had historically resulted in institutionalized regularities of action that took the form of the legal-rational form of domination or authority. To the extent that authority is one of the most important elements of social action,[85] it is necessary to consider the types of authority that are found in society and to look at the type of authority that is founded on formal rationality and which engenders means-end rational action.

Social action, which involves a social relationship, very much depends on the belief in the legitimacy of the order.[86] This is also true of authority. Authority, defined as the 'probability that specific commands (or all commands) will be obeyed by a given group of persons', cultivates belief in its legitimacy. Authority is not based merely on force or the expectation of material gains. It is also based on one or another notion of legitimacy. There are three pure types of authority according to the claims of legitimacy they make. The claims to legitimacy may be made on rational, traditional or charismatic grounds. Three types of authority according to the claims of legitimacy they make are legal, traditional and charismatic authority. Legal authority is based on a belief in the legality of rules and the right of those in authority to issue commands. The probability that these commands will be obeyed by a group of persons depends on the belief in this legality. Traditional authority, on the other hand, is based on a belief in the sanctity of traditions. Those who have positions of authority in accordance with such tradition will be obeyed, for example, the rightful heir. The probability that a command will be obeyed

---

[85] Weber, *Economy and Society*, 941.
[86] Weber, *Economy and Society*, 31.

by a group of persons depends on the strength of tradition. Charismatic authority is based on devotion to the sanctity, heroism or exemplary character of an individual. The probability that a command will be obeyed by a group of persons depends on the strength of the personal trust that people have in his exemplary qualities.[87]

In the modern world, the legitimacy of authority based on rational grounds is far more widespread than that founded on traditional or charismatic grounds. In legal authority obedience is owed neither to tradition nor to an individual but to the legally established impersonal order. Obedience is owed persons who exercise the authority of an office by virtue of the legality of their commands. This in turn is delimited by the scope of the authority of the office.[88] In an organization based on legal authority members are required to be obedient to the rules of an impersonal order and not to the individual. The superior is herself subject to these rules. Furthermore, there is a specified sphere of competence or jurisdiction, meaning that specific functions are being performed by specific parts of the organization. Also offices are organized according to the principle of hierarchy. Each lower office is under the control and supervision of a higher one.[89] Legal authority, therefore, is founded on a formal rationality in that it seeks the most precise and efficient means to achieve certain ends by recourse to universally applied rules. This it does without regard for persons and by rejecting arbitrariness. The bureaucracy is the concrete manifestation of legal authority. As Weber says, '[t]he purest type of exercise of legal authority is that which employs a bureaucratic administrative staff.'[90] The administrative staff of a bureaucracy are subject to authority only with regard to their impersonal official obligations; they are organized in a hierarchy of offices which are clearly defined in terms of their respective spheres of competence; candidates selected for the office are required to have certain technical qualifications; the staff work for fixed salaries and are

---

[87] Weber, *Economy and Society*, 215–6.

[88] Weber, *Economy and Society*, 216.

[89] For these and other characteristics of legal authority, see Weber, *Economy and Society*, 217–20.

[90] Weber, *Economy and Society*, 220.

separated from the ownership of the means of administration, and are subject to systematic discipline.[91]

The institutionalization of legal-rational authority in the form of bureaucracy may lead to an organization being inflicted by excessive bureaucratization to the extent that deficiencies or bureaupathologies develop, rendering the organization unproductive.[92] This is a crucial aspect of the iron cage of rationality. The term bureaupathology refers to the pathology or shortcomings of the bureaucratic form of organization. Bureaucracies have many virtues which may become vices. These include specialization, hierarchy, rules and regulations and impersonality. The advantages of specialization are obvious but it often results in job fragmentation that limits activities, uses little of the total abilities of the staff, and does not allow for much variation in performance. As a result, there is little scope for initiative and work is experienced as boring.[93] Due to this dehumanization, there is little enthusiasm for work, which may even result in sabotage in the work place. Hierarchy is advantageous because its concentrates authority and provides direction and coordination. But, excessive hierarchy may lead to irresponsibility. At each layer of the hierarchy there is a fixed jurisdiction. Officials should be concerned with their own area of jurisdiction and not invade another's territory. It is assumed that the people at the top of the hierarchy know what is going on, but they may not.[94] Rules and regulations are necessary as they make for non-arbitrary, uniform and consistent decisions. But, the excessive following of rules can defeat the purpose they were meant for. An example cited by Caiden is a bus company that, in its bid to stick to a rigid timetable, had buses that did not stop at some bus stops in order to meet the overall schedule.[95] Impersonality is a positive and desirable feature of organizations because

---

[91] Weber, *Economy and Society*, 220–1.

[92] Gerald E. Caiden, 'Excessive Bureaucratization: The J-Curve Theory of Bureaucracy and Max Weber Through the Looking Glass', in Ali Farazman, ed., *Handbook of Bureaucracy* (New York: Marcel Dekker, 1994), 29.

[93] Caiden, 'Excessive Bureaucratization', 31–2.

[94] Caiden, 'Excessive Bureaucratization', 33–4.

[95] Caiden, 'Excessive Bureaucratization', 33–5.

it brings about impartiality. But, if carried too far, particularly in human service organizations, it reduces humans to files and numbers. For example, welfare clients need assurance that they will be taken care of by the state and should not be in fear that this help can be withdrawn at any time. Anonymity and impartiality reinforces these fears.[96] In other words, the bureaucracy can be irrational and dehumanizing.

According to George Ritzer, the ultimate irrationality of formal rationality is better exemplified in the fast food restaurant than the bureaucracy. Developing this point in an article entitled 'The "McDonaldization" of Society', Ritzer notes that the McDonalds fast food restaurant displays the various dimensions of formal rationalization.[97] These are efficiency, predictability, calculability, the substitution of non-human for human technology, greater control over uncertainty and irrationality.

McDonalds has an efficient way of preparing and serving food, in an assembly line fashion. Obsession with efficiency, however, may leads to goal displacement. When officials and workers become obsessed with efficiency they may forget the means were designed to achieve.[98] Predictability refers to the institutionalization of the most efficient way to perform task. McDonalds is very predictable in terms of its limited menu, the layout, the overall atmosphere, the dress and style of talking and its overall atmosphere. When these become institutionalized the organization becomes predictable.[99] Calculability refers to the emphasis on quantity rather than quality. McDonalds emphasizes the Big Mac, not the Good Mac. McDonalds would not be able to function efficiently if it was worried by quality because it wants to optimize speed, lower prices and increase profits.[100] Where the substitution of non-human technology for humans is concerned, while robots are not yet widespread, technology is increasingly used as a substitute for human thinking. An example is the McDonalds' programmed cash registers that

---

[96] Caiden, 'Excessive Bureaucratization', 37–8.

[97] George Ritzer, 'The "McDonaldization" of Society', *Journal of American Culture* 6, 1 (1983), 100–106.

[98] Ritzer, 'The "McDonaldization" of Society', 101–2.

[99] Ritzer, 'The "McDonaldization" of Society', 102–3.

[100] Ritzer, 'The "McDonaldization" of Society', 103–5.

minimize the need for the cashier to think.[101] The above dimensions of rationalization function to reduce uncertainty and allow for the greater control of humans both in and out of the workplace. This is required such that they fit in well with the rationalization processes going on.[102] Ultimately, rationalization produces irrationality. Formal rationalization is unreasonable because it dehumanizing.[103] This is because the norms of efficiency, calculability, predictability, control and substitution of non-human technology all tend to become ends in themselves and the ultimate goal of serving humans in a way that is fulfilling and meaningful is displaced.

Conclusion

Weber saw rise of modern capitalist society in terms of a dominant substantive rationality that took the form of the Protestant ethic. This had to give way to an encroaching formal rationality that manifested itself in the form of bureaucratization.

Therefore, at the theoretical level Weber was concerned with the process of the formal rationalization of modern society.

Weber saw his work on the Protestant ethic as a critique of historical materialism. The ideas did not simply correspond to the material conditions. As noted earlier, Weber himself did use materialist arguments in talking about the rise of capitalism. So, was Weber an idealist or a materialist? The Protestant ethic thesis seems to explain the rise of capitalism in terms of subjective motivations. He had referred to historical materialism as 'patent nonsense'. On the other hand, he stressed that it is not his intention to substitute a one-sided idealism for a one-sided materialism.[104] This question can be possibly answered by making a distinction between Weber's conception of sociology and how he actually did sociology.

---

[101] Ritzer, 'The "McDonaldization" of Society', 105.
[102] Ritzer, 'The "McDonaldization" of Society', 106.
[103] Ritzer, 'The "McDonaldization" of Society', 106–7.
[104] Weber, *The Protestant Ethic*, 183.

His conception of sociology was that it was an interpretive science – it looked at social action in terms of its meaning for actors, that is how actors consciously legitimate their actions by way of the various types of rationality. According to this approach, the rise of capitalism is understood in terms of what the world means to the Puritan and, therefore, how the Puritan thinks he should act. This led many, including Talcott Parsons to suggest that Weber was an idealist because of his alleged stress on the religious causes of the rise of capitalism.

There are at least three possibilities as to where Weber stands on the idealism/materialism issue. One is that he is an idealist given what he says about the aims of sociology and how he understood the role of religion in his work on Protestantism and capitalism. The second possibility is that he is neither an idealist nor a materialist as ideal and material factors interact with each other. This reading of Weber is strengthened by his statement that he does not want to substitute idealism for materialism. The third possibility is that Weber was an historical materialist, but one who did not ignore the role of ideal factors. He was not a materialist in the sense that he saw material factors as the cause of ideal factors. The relationship between material and ideal factors was one of elective affinity. Weber was possibly a materialist in the following sense: while there was an elective affinity between ideal and materialist factors, Weber looked at the interaction between the two in the overall context of materialism. In the *General Economic History*, Weber refers to many materialist preconditions of the rise of capitalism, as we saw earlier. It could be argued that the Protestant ethic was one ideal factor among several material factors that explain the rise of capitalism. A serious consideration of Weber's writings would at least lead one to steer away from a one-sided materialist or idealist approach.

José Rizal (1861–1896)

Syed Farid Alatas

The Filipino thinker and activist, José Protasio Mercado Rizal y Alonso Realonda (1861–1896), could be said to have been the first systematic social thinker in Southeast Asia. Although he was not a social scientist, it is possible to formulate a sociological theory based on his thought, a theory of colonial society that centres on the nature and conditions of Filipino colonial society and the requirements for liberation from colonial rule. He is most famous for his two novels, *Noli Me Tángere* (*Touch me Not*) and *El Filibusterismo* (*The Subversive*), but also authored numerous essays and poems and essays.

Rizal was a thinker and nationalist during the final days of the Spanish colonial period in the Philippines. He was an important member of the Filipino Propaganda Movement that pushed for political reforms for the Filipinos. Although an ophthalmologist by profession, he was an extremely talented writer who used his skill to write critically against the nature and effects of colonial rule on the natives. He was adept at painting, sketching and woodcarving, and made sculptures. He was also a polyglot and could speak 22 languages. He lived a short life but was an exceptionally productive thinker, unmatched by anyone in Southeast Asia, perhaps even Asia. Rizal is revered in the Philippines

© The Author(s) 2017
S.F. Alatas, V. Sinha, *Sociological Theory Beyond the Canon*,
DOI 10.1057/978-1-137-41134-1_6

as one of her greatest heroes. He wrote three novels, numerous poems and essays, and conducted studies in early Philippine history, Tagalog grammar, and even entomology. Rizal's literary and political writings together form the core of his analysis of colonial society and is the basis upon which we may reconstruct his social thought.

Outline of Rizal's Social Theory

The construction of a social theory from Rizal's works can be founded on three aspects of his substantive concerns. First, we have his views on the nature and conditions of colonial society. Secondly, there is Rizal's critique of colonial knowledge of the Philippines. Thirdly, there is his discussion on the meaning and requirements for emancipation.

For Rizal, the corruption of the Spanish colonial government and the Catholic Church in the Philippines was responsible for the oppression and exploitation of Filipinos. Spanish discourse, on the other hand, blamed the backwardness of the Filipinos on their alleged indolence. Rizal's agenda was to turn the Spanish argument on its head by showing that the backwardness of the Filipinos was in fact a consequence of colonial rule. In order to make this argument, Rizal had to show that in precolonial times the Filipinos were relatively advanced in comparison with their state in the colonial period. In other words, Rizal's observations on the problems of colonial society led him to critique the Spanish colonial construction of Filipino history as well as their image of the Filipinos, that is the image of the indolence of the Filipino.

The construction and elaboration of Rizal's social theory is built around the three aspects of Rizal's substantive concerns mentioned above. First, Rizal's observations about colonial society are discussed. Attention is drawn to specific problems in colonial society that he identified. The discussion then turns to Rizal's critique of the Spanish colonial construction of Filipino history as well as their image of the Filipinos, that is the image of the indolence of the Filipino. This leads up to an account of Rizal's views on freedom and emancipation. Finally, some remarks on Rizal's methodology are made.

Rizal's Views on Colonial Society

In Rizal's writings on the Philippines, one can identify three broad dimensions. First there are his thoughts on the nature and conditions of colonial society. Second, there is his analysis and critique of colonial knowledge of the Philippines. This includes the colonial construction of the image of the Filipinos as indolent people. Finally, there are his discussions on the significance and requirements for emancipation.

According to Rizal, the corrupt Spanish colonial bureaucracy and the Catholic Church brutally exploited the Filipinos, but blamed the underdevelopment of the Filipinos on their supposed indolence or laziness. Rizal's aim was to show that this was unfounded. The historical fact that proved Filipinos were a relatively advanced society in precolonial times suggested that their backwardness was a result of colonialism. Rizal's position is summed up in the following:

> Well now; in this unfortunate struggle between the friars who want ignorance and darkness like the bandit who lies in ambush at the night and in mystery and the educated and noble classes of the country who want light, union, direct understanding with Spain, the impolitic conduct of the government, lending itself as an arm of the monastic corporations, hurts the sentiment of the country and the true interests of the mother country. The people is undeceived; they see that they are isolated; that the government does not protect them, that it is afraid of its enemy towards whom it is complaisant. The people doubt, hesitate, their love for Spain threatens to go out, their hope in justice weakens, they are tired of extending their supplicating hands... Be careful. The people fight the friars; if the government puts itself on their side unconditionally, it becomes the enemy of the people, it admits that it is an enemy of their progress, and then the government itself will have opened a new and unfortunate era![1]

Here Rizal is criticizing the government for acting as the executive that manages the affairs of a corrupt clerical establishment. The

---

[1] José Rizal, 'The Truth for All', *Political and Historical Writings* (Manila: National Historical Institute, 1963), 37.

backwardness of the clergy is a recurring theme in the *Noli*. At a dinner, Ibarra is asked about what he learnt from his travels in Europe from which he had just returned. Here, Rizal has the Franciscan priest, Father Dámaso, mocking the idea of freedom. In response to Ibarra's statement that the 'prosperity or unhappiness of nations is in direct proportion to their liberties and their problems, and, by that token, to the sacrifices or selfishness of their ancestors', Father Dámaso says, 'Is that all?'. He adds, 'It wasn't worth throwing your fortune away to learn that! Any school-boy knows as much.'[2] After Ibarra took his leave, the priest remarks that Filipinos should not be allowed to leave the country and should not even be taught to read.[3] On another occasion, Ibarra listens to an account related by a schoolmaster about Father Dámaso. The priest had told the schoolmaster in Tagalog: 'Don't go around in borrowed clothes. Use your own native tongue and be happy with it. Don't go spoiling Spanish; it's not for you.'[4]

In addition to the low esteem in which the natives were held, there was also the corruption they had to endure. The poor, in particular, who hardly made enough money to make ends meet, had to bribe petty bureaucrats, clerks and guards. The church is also implicated in corruption. The following must have been the plight of a typical poor women in the Philippines of Rizal's time:

A poor widow, watching over her sleeping children somewhere in the own that night, worried about the money for the indulgences which would shorten the sufferings of her parents and husband. Every peso, she considered, meant a week of comforts for her children, a week perhaps of laughter and of fun, a, a month's savings, a dress for her daughter who was fast becoming a woman. Bu it was necessary to make sacrifices: the Church would not save the souls of her dear ones for nothing; indulgences were not given away, they must be paid for. She must work nights, sleep

[2] José Rizal, *The Lost Eden* (*Noli me Tangere*), Leon Ma. Guerrro, trans. (New York: W. W. Norton & Co., 1961). 19.a.
[3] Rizal, *The Lost Eden*, 20.
[4] Rizal, *The Lost Eden*, 98.

less; her daughter must bare her legs a little longer; they must eat less, if necessary; the cost of salvation was high.[5]

This is a damaging testimony to the corruption of the Church as it capitalizes on the salvation anxiety of the believers. It seemed that the Church, originally founded for the suffering, had 'forgotten her mission to comfort the afflicted and down-trodden and to humble the powerful in their pride; and were her promises now only for the rich, who could afford to pay?'[6]

Rizal, however, did understand the positive function of oppression. He says that the attempt to brutalize the Filipinos materially and morally would result in more Filipinos becoming educated and uprising.

> To try to plunge the Filipinos into darkness and brutalise them is materially and morally impossible. Our enemies can preach from their pulpits, go to the extreme in all kinds of measures – imprisonment, banishment, censorship, prohibitions, investigations, searches, etc. – but they will not attain their objective. The educated Filipinos, the liberals, who increase every day thanks to persecutions, and we the Filipino youth in Europe who have dedicated our strength to the benefit of our country, we guarantee it. They could simulate another uprising, like that of Cavite, and cut off the throats of so many educated heads, but from the blood thus spilled will sprout more numerous and fresher shoots. Before the catastrophe of 1872 there were fewer thinkers, fewer anti-friars. They sacrificed innocent victims and now you have the youth, women, girls, embracing the same cause. Let the hecatomb be repeated and the executioners shall have sealed their own sentence.[7]

Despite the claims of the colonial government and the Catholic Church, colonial policy was repressive and unjust. Rizal noted that the 'servant, the sacristan, the complacent tale-bearer of the parish priest, thanks to the omnipotent influence of the master in governmental

---

[5] Rizal, *The Lost Eden*, 80.
[6] Rizal, *The Lost Eden*, 80.
[7] Rizal, 'The Truth for All', 37.

spheres, often occupies the first position in the town with the contempt of the intelligent class, a contempt that the new petty tyrant pays with administrative charges, reports, etc., etc., aided by his master whom he also serves by serving his own passions'.[8] As for the priests themselves, Rizal spoke of them as the 'boasted ministers of God [the friars] and *propagators of light*(!) [who] have not sowed nor do they sow Christian moral, they have not taught religion, but rituals and superstitions'.[9]

Rizal was also critical of the pretentiousness of the Church. He called those priests vain and foolish who imagined that their miserable alms to God would 'clothe the Creator of all things', instead of helping the poor and feeding the hungry.[10]

Rizal also critiqued the Church in his 'Message to the Young Women of Malolos'. In criticizing the tendency of the Church to downplay the role of reason when it claimed that those who relied on their own reason were arrogant, Rizal suggested that '*more arrogant is he who wishes to subject another's will and dominate all men.* More arrogant is he who poses as God, who pretends to understand every manifestation of God's will. And exceedingly arrogant or blasphemous is he who attributes to God everything he says and desires and makes his personal enemies the enemies of God'.[11] Further oppression would only result in Filipinos becoming more educated about their conditions and developing more anticolonial consciousness.

The Critique of Colonial History

Rizal had to explore precolonial history in order to critique the colonial construction of Filipino history. His task was to show that precolonial Filipinos were relatively advanced and that their current state of

---

[8] Rizal, 'The Truth for All', 33.
[9] Rizal, 'The Truth for All', 38.
[10] José Rizal, 'Message to the Young Women of Malolos', *Political and Historical Writings* (Manila: National Historical Institute, 1963), 14.
[11] Rizal, 'Message to the Young Women of Malolos', 13.

backwardness under colonial rule was therefore due to the nature of colonial rule.

Rizal had concrete views about the problems of what we would call today Orientalist portrayals of Filipino society held by Spanish colonial and Filipino scholars. This comes across very obviously in his annotation and republication of Antonio de Morga's *Sucesos de las Islas Filipinas* (*Historical Events of the Philippine Islands*), a work that first appeared more than 200 years earlier in 1609. de Morga, a Spaniard, served 8 years in the Philippines as Lieutenant Governor General and Captain General. He was also a justice of the Supreme Court of Manila (Audiencia Real de Manila).[12]

Rizal's objective in annotating and republishing this work was to rectify what he understood to be erroneous reports and derogatory statements that could be found in most Spanish works on the Philippines. He also wanted to recover the precolonial past that was erased from the memory of Filipinos as a result of colonization. In his note to his Filipino readers, Rizal says:

Born and reared in the ignorance of our Yesterday, like almost all of you, without voice or authority to speak about what we did not see or studied, I consider it necessary to invoke the testimony of an illustrious Spaniard who governed the destinies of the Philippines in the beginning of the new era and witnessed the last moments of our ancient nationality. It is then the shadow of our civilization of our ancestors which the author is now evoking before you. I transmit faithfully to you his words, without changing or mutilating them, adapting them only whenever possible to modern orthography for greater clarity, and altering the somewhat defective punctuation of the original in order to make its perusal greater. The post, the nationality, and merits of De Morga, together with the data and testimonies furnished by his contemporaries, almost all Spaniards, recommend the book to your thoughtful consideration.

If the book succeeds to awaken your consciousness of our past, already effaced from your memory, and to rectify what has been falsified and

---

[12] de Morga, *Historical Events of the Philippine Islands*, xxx.

slandered, then I have not worked in vain, and with this as a basis, however small it may be, we shall be able to study the future.[13]

The violence done to the memory of the past includes the destruction of pre-Spanish records such as artefacts that would have shed light on the nature of precolonial society.[14] de Morga's work was different from others as it was the only civil, as opposed to ecclesiastical, history of the Philippines written during the Spanish colonial period.[15] Ecclesiastical histories were questionable not only because they tended to be biased but also because they 'abound in stories of devils, miracles, apparitions, etc., these forming the bulk of the voluminous histories of the Philippines'.[16] Rizal's annotations stressed the following: Filipino advances in agriculture and industry in precolonial times; the point of view of the colonized of various issues; cruelties perpetrated by the colonizers; the hypocrisy of the colonizers, particularly the Catholic Church and the irrationality of the Church's discourse on colonial topics. Hypocrisy is an important theme in Rizal's writings. In his famous 'Message to the Young Women of Malolos', Rizal remarks that Filipino women no longer bow their heads to every unjust order, smile at insults hurled at them by the friars and seek solace in their tears. They know very well that 'God's command is different from that of the priest, that piety does not consist in prolonged kneeling, long prayers, large rosaries, soiled scapulars, but in good conduct, clean conscience, and upright thinking'.[17]

Let us look at an example of the point of view of the colonized. In a section where de Morga discusses Moro piracy, Rizal notes that:

This was the first piracy of the inhabitants of the South recorded in the history of the Philippines. We say 'inhabitants of the South': for before

---

[13] José Rizal, 'To the Filipinos', in de Morga, *Historical Events of the Philippine Islands*, vii.

[14] S. Zaide, 'Historiography in the Spanish Period', in *Philippine Encyclopedia of the Social Sciences* (Quezon City: Philippine Social Science Council, 1993), 5.

[15] Ambeth R Ocampo, 'Rizal's Morga and Views of Philippine History', *Philippine Studies* 46 (1998), 192.

[16] de Morga, *Historical Events of the Philippine Islands*, 291 n. 4.

[17] Rizal, 'Message to the Young Women of Malolos', 12.

them there had been others, the first ones being those committed by the Magellan expedition, capturing vessels of friendly islands and even of unknown ones, demanding from them large ransoms.

If we are to consider that these piracies lasted more than 250 years during which the unconquerable people of the South captured prisoners, assassinated and set fire on not only the adjacent islands but also going so far as Manila Bay, Malate, the gates of the city, and not only once a year but repeatedly, five or six times, with the government unable to suppress them and to defend the inhabitants that it disarmed and left unprotected; supposing that they only cost the islands 800 victims every year, the number of persons sold and assassinated will reach 200,000, all sacrificed jointly with very may others to the prestige of than name Spanish Rule.[18]

Rizal also notes that the destruction of Filipino industry, the depopulation of the islands, Spanish plundering of gold from the Philippines and the enslavement of people were never seen as abusive acts among the Spaniards.[19] He noted that the Filipinos possessed sophisticated technologies before the arrival of the Spaniards. For example, in commenting on de Morga's account of Captain General Santiago de Vera's order to Pandaypira, an elderly Filipino, to cast artillery pieces. That Pandaypira was old suggested that he had acquired the skill of producing canons before the arrival of the Spaniards in Manila.[20]

Rizal's de Morga's project was sufficiently impressive for Blumentritt to comment in his prologue to the work that 'you [Rizal] have erected a *monumentum aere perennius*[21] to the name Rizal'.[22]

Given that such is the precolonial history of the Filipinos, what is to be made of the widespread view that Filipinos were indolent? Rizal's venture into precolonial history was meant to address the colonial

---

[18] de Morga, *Historical Events of the Philippine Islands*, 134 n. 1.

[19] de Morga, *Historical Events of the Philippine Islands*, 134 n. 1.

[20] de Morga, *Historical Events of the Philippine Islands*, 23 n. 1.

[21] 'A monument more enduring than bronze'.

[22] Ferdinand Blumentritt, 'Prologue', in Antonio de Morga, *Historical Events of the Philippine Islands by Dr Antonio de Morga, Published in Mexico in 1609, recently brought to light and annotated by Jose Rizal, preceded by a prologue by Dr Ferdinand Blumentritt*, Writings of Jose Rizal Volume VI (Manila: National Historical Institute, 1890/1962), viii.

accusation regarding the purported indolence of the Filipinos. This question was dealt with by Rizal in his famous essay 'The Indolence of the Filipino'.[23]

The Myth of Indolence

Rizal was very conscious of the fact that in Spanish colonial discourse, the backwardness of the Filipinos was blamed on their indolence. In general, the Spaniards had an extremely derogatory view of the Filipinos. On this Rizal said:

> That the sins of a few are attributed to the entire race is not a new thing for us. In order to vilify a country, it is only necessary to generalise the bad in her, just as to exalt her, it is enough to remind her of the good examples. The system as it can be seen produces fruits. Neither are we surprised that the mass of the Filipino people who feed with their sweat thousands and thousands of their brothers in the Peninsula and shed their blood for Spain, whose language they do not speak, are slandered and insulted with impunity behind a pseudonym. In the Philippines every insult from top to bottom is permitted; reply is prohibited. It seems that Castilian chivalry and nobility were damaged in the long voyage. In the Peninsula, he who insults a paralytic and a dumb would be a coward; in the Philippines . . . in the Philippines it is another thing.[24]

One of the derogatory views of the Spaniards was that the Filipinos had little devotion to work. But, as Syed Hussein Alatas noted, the unwillingness of the Filipinos to cultivate under the *encomenderos* was interpreted out of context and understood to be the result of indolence, which was in turn associated with their nature.[25] Rizal observes that the

---

[23] José Rizal, 'The Indolence of the Filipino', *Political and Historical Writings* (Manila: National Historical Institute, 1963), 111–139.

[24] Rizal, 'The Truth for All', 31.

[25] Syed Hussein Alatas, *The Myth of the Lazy Native: A Study of the Image of the Malays, Filipinos and Javanese from the 16th to the 20th Century and its Function in the Ideology of Colonial Capitalism* (London: Frank Cass, 1977), 125.

word 'indolence' was very much misused. He drew a parallel between the European medieval attribution of evil to whatever superstitious people could not understand and the Spanish attribution of indolence to the behaviour of Filipinos that had other causes. While those who sought to explain phenomena without recourse to the devil were persecuted in Europe, in the Philippines those who suggested alternative explanations suffered a worse fate.[26]

Rizal made some very intriguing observations that Alatas considered to be the first sociological treatment of the theme.[27] Rizal's aim was to 'study thoroughly this question without contempt or sensitiveness, without bias, without pessimism'.[28] Indolence was a panacea, like the devil. However, just because the idea of indolent Filipinos was misused, it did not mean that it did not exist.[29] Indolence, however, had to be understood in its proper context. Firstly, Rizal observed that the 'miseries of a people without freedom should not be imputed to the people but to their rulers. In order that one may be responsible, it is necessary that he is master of his actions, and the Filipino people is neither master of their actions nor of their thoughts'.[30] His many writings furnish instances of oppression and exploitation such as the expropriation of lands, appropriation of labour of farmers, high taxes and forced labour without payment, that explain the unwillingness of the Filipinos to work.[31] The Filipino farmer had to deal not only with natural calamities such as plagues but also with petty tyrants and robbers against which defence was not permitted.[32] To the extent that there was indolence, it was to be seen as not the cause of the disorder and backwardness, but rather as the effect of the disorder and backwardness created by colonial rule.[33]

---

[26] Rizal, 'The Indolence of the Filipino', 111.

[27] Alatas, *The Myth of the Lazy Native*, 98.

[28] Rizal, 'The Indolence of the Filipino', 111.

[29] Rizal, 'The Indolence of the Filipino', 111–112.

[30] Rizal, 'The Truth for All', 31–32.

[31] José Rizal, 'Filipino Farmers', *Political and Historical Writings* (Manila: National Historical Institute, 1963).

[32] Rizal, 'Filipino Farmers', 19.

[33] Rizal, 'The Indolence of the Filipino', 112.

Secondly, Rizal asserted that the Filipinos were not an inherently indolent people. Furthermore, to the extent that there was indolence this was not to be seen as a reason for backwardness. Rather it was the backwardness and exploitative conditions of colonial society that caused indolence. In precolonial times, the Filipinos were conscientious and diligent, controlling trade routes, tilling the land, mining and manufacturing. Their indolence, in the sense of the lack of love for work, grew when their destiny was taken away from them. Things were not the same in the precolonial period. The Filipinos

> worked more and they had more industries when there were no *encomenderos*, that is, when they were heathens, as Morga himself asserts . . . the Indios, seeing that they were vexed and exploited by their *encomenderos* on account of the products of their industry, and not considering themselves beasts of burden or the like, they began to break their looms, abandon the mines, the fields, etc., believing that their rulers would leave them alone on seeing them poor, wretched and unexploitable. Thus they degenerated and the industries and agriculture so flourishing before the coming of the Spaniards were lost.[34]

What is crucial to note here is Rizal's approach to the problem. In his treatment of the myth of the indolence of the Filipinos in his famous essay, 'The Indolence of the Filipinos', he defines indolence as 'little love for work, lack of activity'.[35] He then proceeds to discuss indolence in two different senses. First, there is indolence in the sense of the lack of activity that is caused by the warm tropical climate of the Philippines that 'requires quit and rest for the individual, just as cold incites him to work and to action'.[36] For similar reasons, that is differences in climate, the Spaniards are more indolent than the French, and the French are more indolent than the Germans. Rizal remarks that the same Europeans who accuse the natives of being indolent themselves live in the tropics surrounded by servants who perform every duty for them.

---

[34] de Morga, *Historical Events of the Philippine Islands*, 317 n. 2.
[35] Rizal, 'The Indolence of the Filipino', 111.
[36] Rizal, 'The Indolence of the Filipino', 113.

This enables the Europeans to live and eat better, to enrich themselves, and to have hope for the future, while the natives are compelled to work and toil for others and have no hope for their future.[37] Rizal continues:

> The fact is that in the tropical countries severe work is not a good thing as in cold countries, for there it is annihilation, it is death, it is destruction. Nature, as a just mother knowing this, has therefore made the land more fertile, more productive, as a compensation. An hour's work under that burning sun and in the midst of pernicious influences coming out of an active nature is equivalent to a day's work in a temperate climate; it is proper then that the land yield a hundredfold! Moreover, don't we see the active European who has gained strength during winter, who feels the fresh blood of spring boil in his veins, don't we see him abandon his work during the few days of his changeable summer, close his office, where the work after all is not hard – for many, consisting of talking and gesticulating in the shade beside a desk – run to watering-places, sit down at the cafes, stroll about, *etc.*? What wonder then that the inhabitant of tropical countries, worn out and with his blood thinned by the prolonged and excessive heat, is reduced to inaction?[38]

Rizal, therefore, made a distinction between being 'indolent' as a reaction to climate, for example, and indolence in terms of the lack of love for work or the avoidance of work.[39] The pace of life in the tropics was slower. Here, even the Europeans were forced to slowdown. What Rizal is alluding to here is the physiological reaction to the heat of a tropical climate which strictly speaking, as Syed Hussein Alatas noted, is not consistent with Rizal's own definition of indolence, that is 'little love for work'. The change in working habits to the tropical climate should not be understood as a result of laziness or little love for work.[40]

The second type of indolence that Rizal noted was a result of the experience of the Filipinos under Spanish rule. The fact that Filipinos

[37] Rizal, 'The Indolence of the Filipino', 113.
[38] Rizal, 'The Indolence of the Filipino', 113.
[39] Rizal, 'The Indolence of the Filipino', 111.
[40] Alatas, *The Myth of the Lazy Native*, 100.

were productive in the past meant that indolence must have social causes which are to be found in colonial rule. On indolence in the sense of the lack of activity and little love for work, Rizal says:

> The evil is not that a more or less latent indolence exists, but that it is fostered and magnified. Among men, as well as among nations, there exist not only aptitudes but also tendencies toward good and evil. To foster the good ones and aid them, as well as correct the[41] bad ones and repress them would be the duty of society or of governments, if less noble thoughts did not absorb their attention. The evil is that indolence in the Philippines is a magnified indolence, a snow-ball indolence, if we may be permitted the expression, an evil which increases in direct proportion to the square of the periods of time, an effect of misgovernment and backwardness, as we said and not a cause of them.[42]

Given that indolence is not inherent trait of the Filipino, Rizal's objective was to provide a detailed account of the various causes of indolence that were in effect during colonial rule.

We have already referred to Rizal's attribution of indolence to the tropical climate of the Philippines.[43] Rizal refers to this as indolence although it is strictly speaking not indolence and does not even confirm to his own definition of indolence. At any rate, to Rizal the lack of activity as a response to climate is not the main problem. The more serious problem is the loss for the love of work and the resulting inactivity as an effect of misgovernment and the backwardness of colonial society.[44] The proof that it was the conditions of colonial society, including the nature of colonial rule, that caused the indolence of the Filipinos was that Filipinos were not always indolent. For example, they were active in trade before the coming of the Europeans.[45] Rizal's question then is: 'How then and in what way was the active and

[41] Rizal, 'The Indolence of the Filipino', 120–123.
[42] Rizal, 'The Indolence of the Filipino', 114.
[43] Rizal, 'The Indolence of the Filipino', 113.
[44] Rizal, 'The Indolence of the Filipino', 114.
[45] Rizal, 'The Indolence of the Filipino', 116, 118–119.

enterprising heathen *Indio* of ancient times converted into a lazy and indolent Christian, as our contemporary writers say of him?'[46] To put it in other terms, Rizal suggested that there is a latent tendency or predisposition everywhere to be indolent. What are the causes that resulted in the awakening from its 'lethargy to this terrible predisposition'.[47]

The seventeenth century provides the context in which the factors causing indolence come into operation. The combination of wars, the execution of natives and the decline of agriculture led to the reduction of the population of the Philippines by one-third. Once flourishing farms were neglected.[48] Rizal notes that de Morga had stated that after 32 years of Spanish rule the Filipinos had lost much knowledge about agriculture, animal husbandry and handicrafts as compared to when they were 'pagans'.[49] In addition to this, pious but powerless priests often advised their poor parishioners to abandon their work in industries in order that they may escape the tyranny of the *encomenderos*. They were advised that the heaven was their sole hope.[50] As for the factors that served to foster indolence by creating a lack of love for work, there are several.

In fact, labour was actually discouraged in the Philippines. One reason is that the colonial government was weary of the frequent contact between Filipinos and other communities in the region such as the Malays, the Cambodians, the Thais and the Japanese. The fear was that the Filipinos may be influenced by their independence as these peoples were not colonized. The Malays of Borneo were accused by the colonial government of planning an uprising and many of them were executed. The discouragement eventual resulted in the Malays and others no longer coming to the Philippines. As a result, demand for Filipino goods was drastically reduced since they were the principal consumers of Philippines products.[51] Therefore, fewer opportunities to

---

[46] Rizal, 'The Indolence of the Filipino', 119.

[47] Rizal, 'The Indolence of the Filipino', 119–120.

[48] Rizal, 'The Indolence of the Filipino', 123.

[49] Rizal, 'The Indolence of the Filipino', 124.

[50] Rizal, 'The Indolence of the Filipino', 123.

[51] Rizal, 'The Indolence of the Filipino', 124.

work obtained, due to the decline in trade that resulted from obstacles put in place by the colonial government.

Rizal also notes the role of what he called 'absurd agriculture'. In the early days of colonialism, Filipinos were not allowed to work in their farms without permission from the Governor or the provincial authorities:

> Those who know how the administrative slowness and confusion in a country where the authorities work scarcely two hours a day; those who know the cost of going to and coming from the provincial capital to ask for a permit; those who are aware of the petty retaliation of the little office tyrants will understand how with this barbaric arrangement it is possible to have only the most absurd agriculture.[52]

There was also the problem of lack of security for the farmers. The government, for fear of hostility from the farmers, would deprive them of the right to carry weapons. Left without the means to defend themselves, they were left to the mercy of bandits. Farmers often abandoned their farms when confronted with banditry. This led to inaction and the turn to gambling as a means of making a living.[53] In fact, it seemed pointless to many farmers to attempt to be rich through bad work. They ran the risk of having their workmen and their farm animals being seized by the military chief of the town, or being forced to lend money to him. The rich farmer also ran the risk of being deported if there was an uprising. This also encouraged inaction on the part of the farmers.[54]

Yet another cause of indolence was the maltreatment by the *encomenderos* who had reduced many farmers to slavery, forcing them to work for their (*encomenderos'*) benefit, or compelling them to sell their products at low prices, or cheated them with false measures.[55] Bureaucracy also played its role in discouraging industry and agriculture among the Filipinos. Not only did the government not provide various kinds of

---

[52] Rizal, 'The Indolence of the Filipino', 125.
[53] Rizal, 'The Indolence of the Filipino', 125–126.
[54] Rizal, 'The Indolence of the Filipino', 128.
[55] Rizal, 'The Indolence of the Filipino', 126.

inducements and aid to encourage commerce and agriculture,[56] it also set up obstacles in the form of red tape. Apart from the umpteen documents that had to be provided and much paperwork that needed to be done, there was the ubiquitous problem of having to bribe officials so that the application would be sent up from one level to the next.[57] It was also the case that the best agricultural lands were in the hands of the friars, further compounding the problem of lower agricultural returns.[58]

The introduction of various forms of gambling and their encouragement by the government also served to breed dislike for labour.[59] Religious rituals played their part in engendering indolence. The large number of fiestas, lengthy Masses, the novenae, processions and rosaries often occupied Filipinos whole mornings, afternoon and nights.[60]

The combination of lack of demand from agricultural produce that resulted from colonial policies, exploitation and extortion by the authorities, the lack of inducement to work due to the uncertainties of decent returns, all contributed to the engendering of indolence, that is the love for works.[61] Rizal also makes the interesting point that there is the tendency of the colonized to imitate the ways of the rulers. This reminds us of Ibn Khaldun's observation that the 'vanquished always want to imitate victor in his distinctive marks, his dress, his occupation and all his other conditions and customs'.[62] This is because they believe in the perfection of those who have conquered them. Similarly, Rizal remarked that there was a pernicious influence of the Spanish rulers of the Philippines. They surrounded themselves with servants and despised manual labour, considering it unworthy of noblemen and the aristocracy. Consequently, there was the desire of the Filipinos to imitate the

---

[56] Rizal, 'The Indolence of the Filipino', 130–131.

[57] Rizal, 'The Indolence of the Filipino', 127.

[58] Rizal, 'The Indolence of the Filipino', 131.

[59] Rizal, 'The Indolence of the Filipino', 124, 130.

[60] Rizal, 'The Indolence of the Filipino', 130.

[61] Rizal, 'The Indolence of the Filipino', 130, 132.

[62] Ibn Khaldûn, *Ibn Khaldun: The Muqadimmah – An Introduction of History*, 3 vols., translated from the Arabic by Franz Rosenthal (London: Routledge & Kegan Paul, 1967), vol. 1, 299.

ways of their Spanish rulers. This desire to be like the Spaniards 'naturally produced aversion to activity and hatred or fear of work'.[63] The tendency to imitate the rulers had far-reaching consequences:

> Convinced through insinuation of his inferiority, his mind be wildered by his education – if the brutalization we discussed above can be called education – with only his racial susceptibility and poetical imagination remaining in him, the Filipino in the exchange of usages and ideas among the different nations, allows himself to be guided by his fancy and self-love. It is sufficient that a foreigner praise to him the imported merchandise and find fault with the native product for him to shift hastily, without thinking that everything has its weak side and the most sensible custom appears ridiculous to the eyes of those who do not follow it. They dazzled him, with tinsel, with strings of multi-colored glass beads, with noisy rattles, shining mirrors, and other trinkets, and in exchange he gave his gold, his conscience, and even his liberty. He changed his religion for the rituals of another religion, the convictions and usages dictated by his climate and his necessities for other usages and other convictions which have grown under another sky and under a different inspiration. His spirit, disposed to everything which seemed to be good, then was transformed according to the taste of the nation that imposed upon him its God and its laws; and as the trader with whom he dealt did not bring along the useful iron implements, the hoes to till the fields, but stamped papers, crucifixes, bulls, and prayer-books; as he did not have for an ideal and prototype the tanned and muscular laborer but the aristocratic lord, carried in a soft litter, the result was that the imitative people became clerks, devout, prayer-loving, acquired ideas of luxurious and ostentatious living without improving correspondingly their means or subsistence.[64]

In other words, for Rizal, indolence was by no means a condition that afflicted the Filipinos when they were encountered by the Spaniards on the eve of colonization. Rather, indolence was directly an outcome of Spanish rule. Included as one of the causes was the tendency of the Filipinos to imitate the lifestyle of their Spanish conquerors.

---

[63] Rizal, 'The Indolence of the Filipino', 128.
[64] Rizal, 'The Indolence of the Filipino', 136–137.

The above causes of indolence discussed by Rizal refer to the role of the government. Rizal also notes that there are causes that emanate from the people themselves. These include limited home education, a passive form of religiosity and the appointment of incompetent Filipinos to administrative posts.[65]

The eminent Brazilian sociologist, Gilberto Freyre, made a similar observation in the context of Brazil.

And when all this practically useless population of *caboclos* and light-skinned mulattoes, worth more as clinical material than they are as an economic force, is discovered in the state of economic wretchedness and non-productive inertia in which Miguel Pereira and Belisário Penna found them living – in such a case those who lament our lack of racial purity and the fact that Brazil is not a temperate climate at once see in this wretchedness and inertia the result of intercourse, forever damned, between white men and black women, between Portuguese males and Indian women. In other words, the inertia and indolence are a matter of race . . .

All of which means little to this particular school of sociology, which is more alarmed by the stigmata of miscegenation than it is by those of syphilis, which is more concerned with the effects of climate than it is with social causes that are susceptible to control or rectification; nor does it take into account the influence exerted upon mestizo populations – above all, the free ones – by the scarcity of foodstuffs resulting from monoculture and a system of slave labor, it disregards likewise the chemical poverty of the traditional foods that these peoples, or rather all Brazilians, with a regional exception here and there, have for more than three centuries consumed; it overlooks the irregularity of food supply and the prevailing lack of hygiene in the conservation and distribution of such products.[66]

To be sure, there are weaknesses in Rizal's understanding of the problem. Alatas argues that it is unreasonable to call the absence of the desire to work conditioned by the exploitative conditions of colonial rule

---

[65] Rizal, 'The Indolence of the Filipino', 131, 135, 138.

[66] Gilberto Freyre, *The Masters and the Slaves (Casa-grande & Senzala): A Study in the Development of Brazilian Civilization* (Berkeley & Los Angeles: University of California Press, 1986), 48.

indolence.[67] Indeed, there is a need to improve Rizal's definition of indolence. It should stress that the little love for work or lack of activity should be under conditions that are held to be favourable in order to qualify as indolence. Alatas did note, however, that Rizal's explanation of the lack of interest to work amongst the Filipinos by recourse to historical and sociological factors is on the whole sound.[68]

What was a negative attitude towards work and the lack of activity induced by the tropical climate of the Philippines Rizal wrongly referred to as indolence. He failed to distinguish this from true indolence, that is the lack of motivation to work. Nevertheless, his raising of the problem of indolence should be recognized as an important sociological contribution to the field of sociology. He dealt with the topic in a sociological manner. Of particular interest is his turning around of the dominant colonial view that indolence was a cause of the backwardness of Filipino society. Rizal argued that it was the backwardness and disorder of Filipino colonial society that caused indolence. In other words, indolence was a result of the social and historical experience of the Filipinos under Spanish colonial rule. As we saw above, Rizal had set himself the task of examining historical accounts by Europeans which suggested that the Filipinos were an industrious people. This includes the writing of de Morga which Rizal had annotated and republished. If these historical accounts were true, the only explanation is that the current day indolence of the Filipinos, that is the loss of love for work and their lack of activity, must have social causes that are to be found in the nature of colonial rule.

The theme of indolence or the idea of the lazy native in colonial scholarship is a crucial one that formed an important component of the ideology of colonial capitalism. Rizal was perhaps the first to deal with it systematically and sociologically. Rizal was clear that the idea of the indolence of the Filipinos had an ideological function. He said that the friars found the idea necessary to make themselves irreplaceable.[69] The exposé of the myth was taken up in greater depth by Alatas in his *The*

---

[67] Alatas, *The Myth of the Lazy Native*, 106.

[68] Alatas, *The Myth of the Lazy Native*, 105–106.

[69] Rizal, 'The Indolence of the Filipino', 111.

Myth of the Lazy Native, which includes a chapter entitled 'The Indolence of the Filipinos', in honour of Rizal's work on the same topic, 'The Indolence of the Filipino'.

Freedom of Thought and Emancipation

During his time in Spain at the Universidad Central de Madrid, Rizal became aware of controversies between liberals and conservative Catholics.[70] This undeniably led to his developing a greater commitment to the idea of the freedom of thought and inquiry.[71] In 1885, Rizal states in a letter to his mother:

> As to what you say concerning my duties as a Christian, I have the pleasure of telling you that I have not ceased believing for a single moment in any of the fundamental beliefs of our religion. The beliefs of my childhood have given way to the convictions of youth, which I hope in time will take root in me. Any essential belief that does not stand review and the test of time must pass on to the realm of memory and leave the heart. I ought not to live on illusions and falsehoods. What I believe now, I believe through reason because my conscience can admit only that which is compatible with the principles of thought . . . I believe that God would not punish me if in approaching him I were to use his most precious gift of reason and intelligence.[72]

Arguing that the underdevelopment of Filipino society was not due to any inherent shortcomings of the natives but rather to the backwardness of colonial rule, Rizal's position was that emancipation would come about from enlightenment. Colonial rule was oppressive due to the backwardness of the Church. The Church opposed the enlightenment,

---

[70] Raul J. Bonoan, S.J., *The Rizal-Pastells Correspondence*, (Quezon City: Ateneo de Manila Press, 1994), 13.

[71] Bonoan, *The Rizal-Pastells Correspondence*, 17.

[72] José Rizal, *One Hundred Letters of José Rizal to his Parents, Brother, Sisters, Relatives* (Manila: Philippine National Historical Society, 1959), 224, cited in Bonoan, *The Rizal-Pastells Correspondence*, 19.

the supremacy of reason. The European Enlightenment was good for Filipinos, while the Church opposed it because it established reason as authority, and not God or the Church itself. While thinkers such as Marx, Weber and Durkheim had recognized that reason had become unreasonable in the sense that modernity was disruptive, anomic and ultimately irrational, Rizal had a contrasting attitude to the Enlightenment and to reason. It is, therefore, interesting to note that while Rizal was also writing in the nineteenth century, he had a different attitude to the Enlightenment and to reason, in comparison to European thinkers such as to Martineau, Marx, Weber and Durkheim. His writings do not show disappointment with reason and he was not dissatisfied with modernity in the way that European thinkers of the same period were. His writings do not show the same kind of disillusionment or hesitancy with reason that is found in much of Western thought of the period. Why was this the case? This is probably because for Rizal the Philippines was not adequately modern, being held back by an anti-rational Church. To use Weber's terminology, Rizal would have wanted more formal rationalization, more bureaucracy, more efficiency, more calculability and more predictability because there were not enough of these in the Philippines.

We have already referred above to Rizal's discussion on the role of the Church in the oppression of Filipinos. In his correspondence, with Fr. Pablo Pastells, Rizal was apparently taken aback by Pastells' advice that he [Rizal] 'stop viewing his situation and predicament 'through the prism of his own judgement' in as much as 'no one sits in judgement in his own case [*nemo judex in causa propria*]'.[73] Rizal's response was interesting. He said that if people were not to view their situations through the prism of their own private judgement, they would have to do so through the myriad of prism of other. This would be a very impractical task as there are as many prisms as individuals. This would result in people 'running one another's houses, each one directing the activities of the other: there would be utter confusion, unless the small-

[73] Raul J. Bonoan, S. J., 'Introduction', in Raul J. Bonoan, *The Rizal-Pastells Correspondence* (Quezon City: Ateneo de Manila Press, 1994), 49.

minded among us should give up their own judgement and self-love – an act which in my humble opinion constitutes an offence against God since it should be a rejection of his most precious gifts'.[74] In other words, Rizal is suggesting that people ought not to give up their own judgement and self-love to the 'boasted ministers of God [the friars] and *propagators of light*(!) [who] have not sowed nor do they sow Christian moral, they have not taught religion, but rituals and superstitions.'[75]

Because of his critique of the Church, Rizal was seen as being against the Spanish flag, as a subversive. As Blumentritt noted, '[t]he parasites, the friars, and the Spanish gods of the Filipino world call you filibuster; thus you have been slandered by those who, for their madness for greatness, for the sake of their pockets, and for the bandage of their passions, are the indefatigable grave-diggers of the mother country.'[76] His rejection of the Church was seen as a rejection of colonial rule, which failed to modernize the Philippines but which kept her people backward. Therefore, if for Marx, Weber and Durkheim freedom meant the freedom to realize human potential, the freedom from the iron cage of rationality and the freedom from irrational passion, for Rizal freedom meant freedom in a more mundane way, from colonial rule, and from physical and intellectual oppression. The problem of modernity had nothing to do with the very nature of modernity such as capitalism or problems with the transition from traditional to modern society. Rather it had to do with the imposition of colonial rule and the colonial-imposed capitalist economic system.

Rizal's exhortations to the Spanish colonial government had always been of the following nature: 'And as we believe that one cannot serve a country better than to tell her the truth, we say this to the Mother Country so that she can apply timely remedy.'[77] It is as though Rizal believed in serving Spain. This led some to consider that Rizal was for reform to be undertaken by Spain and not revolution against the

---

[74] José Rizal, 'The First Letter of Rizal', in Raul J. Bonoan, *The Rizal-Pastells Correspondence* (Quezon City: Ateneo de Manila Press, 1994), 122.

[75] Rizal, 'The Truth for All', 38.

[76] Blumentritt, 'Prologue', ix–x.

[77] Rizal, 'Filipino Farmers', 22.

Spanish government. Indeed, when Rizal published the first novel, *Noli me Tangere* in 1887, he was only for breaking of civil power of friars. The title, *Noli me Tangere* or *Touch me Not* was taken from the Gospels. When related to one of the characters of the novel, Maria Clara, it symbolizes something that cannot be touched. In the Epilogue of the *Noli*, Maria Clara was cloistered at a nunnery. A representative of the authorities pays a visit to the nunnery to inquire about the nuns. One of the nuns, understood to be Maria Clara, appears in a wet and tattered habit and begs for protection from the official against the 'assaults of hypocrisy'.[78] Accepting the abbess, explanation that the woman was mad, the official elects not to intervene and leaves. Maria Clara saw the gates of the nunnery close 'as the damned might see the gates of Heaven close against them, if ever Heaven were as cruel and unfeeling as the world of men'. When the Governor General came to hear of this, he was inclined to rescue the woman. Now, however, the abbess refused any inspection of the nunnery and that was the end of the story of Maria Clara.[79] Maria Clara was not to be touched. She had become the symbol of clerical property, her story symbolizing the clerical dominance of the colony.[80]

The *Noli* of 1887 does not go so far into the issue as the *Fili* does. It only suggests the need to eliminate the civil power of friars. The Franciscan *padres* were the villains. The civil and military power administered by the Spanish Captain General, a colonial officer, is perceived as rational and progressive. Elias, a noble, patriotic and generous Filipino dies in the novel, while the egoist Ibarra survives. In the *Fili*, there seems to be a change in Rizal's thinking. There is the emergence of the *filibustero*, the 'dangerous patriot who should be hanged soon', in other words, a revolutionary. The revolution against Spanish rule and the Church seems imminent and appears to be the only means of achieving freedom. Rizal's second novel, *El Filibusterismo* (*The*

---

[78] Rizal, *The Lost Eden*, 406–407.

[79] Rizal, *The Lost Eden*, 407.

[80] Cesar Adib Majul, 'Rizal's Noli and Fili: Their Relevance to the Coming Millennium', in Gemino Abad et. al, *Centennial Lecture Series: Memories, Visions and Scholarship and Other Essays* (Quezon City: UP Center for Integrative and Development Studies, 2001), 67–68.

Revolution) is a remedy for revolution. The villains now include both the clergy, this time the Dominican priests, as well as the mercenary Captain General. The revolution does not succeed, this being a reflection of Rizal's evaluation of the lack of preparedness of the Filipinos for revolution. He had fears that those who would lead a revolution would be motivated by little more than self-interests rather than social commitment.[81] Rizal himself was hesitant to join the revolution, not because he was in principle against revolution. He did not support a revolution that was destined to fail due to the lack of preparation, the personal interests of the so-called revolutionaries and the absence of a united front. It can be claimed, however, that Rizal was revolutionary in his actions and writings. He paid the ultimate price for this when he was executed for charges of treason against Spain.

Rizal's Method of Argumentation

The method of argumentation refers to the method that is utilized to make truth claims about a particular subject matter. In the classical Greek, Islamic and medieval Europeans traditions, it was recognized that the process of thinking may take place in the right or wrong way. Therefore, the canon of logic was developed in order to present the methods of argumentation in a systematic manner to aid the process of reasoning. There are basically four legitimate kinds of reasoning. Demonstration refers to deductive or inductive reasoning that produces certain knowledge. Deductive reasoning, in particular, is held to yield certain knowledge as it is based on true or self-evident premises, causing the conclusions to be certain. What we refer to as the scientific method is made up of deductive and inductive reasoning. Dialectical reasoning, on the other hand, refers to disputation or reasoning that aims to silence an opponent. It may include deductive, inductive or other forms of arguments. However, there is an element of probability rather than certainty as the outcome of dialectics because they are founded on premises that

---

[81] Majul, 'Rizal's Noli and Fili', 68.

are generally accepted as true but are not necessarily true or self-evident. Dialectical arguments aim to establish a contradiction in order to silence an opponent. Poetic arguments refer to reasoning that has recourse to the use of figurative language and tropes such as analogy, metaphor, parable and similes with the aim of evoking images of in the mind, thereby stirring the imagination.[82] Rhetoric refers to reasoning that is directed towards influence or persuasion rather than instruction.

Rizal's principle methods were inductive, deductive and poetic. His political and journalistic writings were founded on inductive and deductive reasoning. Rizal was inductive when he wrote, for example, about the oppression of Filipino farmers. Such an observation was derived from his knowledge of numerous cases of oppression. Induction refers to reasoning from particular cases to a general truth.

Deduction, on the other hand, is a form of reasoning that proceeds from a general truth or premise and draws conclusions about particular cases. Rizal's statement that the 'miseries of a people without freedom should not be imputed to the people but to their rulers'[83] is an example of a general truth from which he makes conclusions about Filipino reality. This premise would lead to the conclusion that the underdevelopment of Filipinos in colonial society should not be attributed to the Filipinos themselves but to their Spanish colonizers. The premise suggests a line of interrogation that leads to such a conclusion.

Rizal's preferred mode of argumentation was poetic. His most important works were the *Noli Me Tángere* and *El Filibusterismo*. In these novels he employs a variety of figurative language and tropes to describe the situation of Filipinos under colonial rule not by providing factual information or theoretically informed arguments but by stirring the imagination through the evocation of images in the mind. As noted by Majul, it is the descriptions in the novels which are important because they reveal the character traits that reflect both a social malaise and praiseworthy social values. Although it is possible to identify certain

---

[82] J. Landau, 'Nasir al-Din Tusi and Poetic Imagination in the Arabic and Persian Philosophic Tradition', in Ali Asghar Seyed-Gohrab, ed., *Metaphor and Imagery in Persian Poetry* (Leiden: Brill, 2012), 42–43.

[83] Rizal, 'The Truth for All', 31–32.

characters in the novels with some of Rizal's contemporaries, what is more important is to see the characters as representing cultural and social institutions.[84]

Conclusion

Rizal's essay on the indolence of the Filipino can be said to form the basis of his sociology of colonial society. His critique of the colonial construction of indolent Filipinos is related to two other themes of sociological importance which, as we have seen, he himself dealt with. The first is the need to critically assess the dominant discourse, that is colonialist views concerning the Filipinos. Rizal included this to mean the study and critique of colonialist history as well as its reinterpretation to reclaim an alternative view of Filipino that was not founded on distortions and stereotypes. Secondly, Rizal was interested in examining the real causes of Filipino backwardness which he located in the nature of colonial rule.

Although Rizal wrote during the colonial period, much of what he said about the nature of colonial society and its problems remain relevant to the Philippines as well as other societies of the global South. In fact, it has been said that the task is to make Rizal obsolete.[85]

Rizal was probably the first thinker in the Malay world of Southeast Asia to think about social and political issues in a systematic manner. It could even be said that Rizal's thought about the nature and conditions of Filipino colonial society lay the foundations for an alternative approach to the sociology of colonial society. The reason behind promoting scholars like José Rizal and a number of other well known as well as lesser known thinkers in Asia, Africa and Latin America is to contribute to the universalization of the social sciences and humanities. These disciplines may be studied worldwide but are not universal as long as the various civilizational voices of our humanity that have something to say about society are not rendered audible.

---

[84] Majul, 'Rizal's Noli and Fili', 57.

[85] Renato Constantino, 'Our Task: To Make Rizal Obsolete', *This Week* 14(24), 14 June 1959, 40.

The examples of the works of José Rizal have demonstrated a number of features of what we might call an alternative tradition in sociology and the other social sciences. These can be listed as follows:

1. Rizal's work provides an alternative source of ideas that may suggest new research agenda and topics that are generally absent or marginal in mainstream social science research. The example from Rizal's own work is the study of laziness and indolence, and the ideologies that support them.
2. The focus on Rizal also draws attention to the notion that thinkers that are outside or on the margins of the canon are potential sources of ideas and concept. In other words, the 'Asiatic' or 'Oriental' is not to be seen merely as a topic of study or a source of data but also a source of ideas. Knowing subjects in social thought and social theory may not be restricted to Western European and North American white males. This chapter has shown that Rizal is not to be regarded as a mere source of data or information, but can also be considered as a knowing subject that furnishes us with concepts and theories to be taught as well as applied in research.
3. If significant attention is paid by sociologists and other social scientists, particularly by theorists, the thought of Rizal may later become mainstream in the sense of redefining the canon. Our project is not to replace the old canon with a new one but rather to replace the domination of European-derived concepts and theories with a multi-cultural coexistence of the same.

Such a sociology, if it were to emerge, would become part of what we may term alternative discourses in the social sciences. Alternative discourses may be defined as those which are informed by the local or regional historical experiences and cultural practices. The social scientists involved are conscious of the need to turn to philosophies, epistemologies, histories and the arts other than those of the Western tradition. These are all to be considered as potential sources of social science theories and concepts.[86]

[86] Syed Farid Alatas, *Alternative Discourses in Asian Social Science: Responses to Eurocentrism* (New Delhi: Sage Publications, 2006), 82.

Emile Durkheim (1858–1917)

Vineeta Sinha

Introduction

David Emile Durkheim was born on 15 April 1858 in the French town of Epinal, into a Jewish family, where his father and grandfather were rabbis. Durkheim himself attended rabbinical school, but by his teenage years had rejected the vocation and became an agnostic. His life-long interest in religion remained academic rather than personal. Despite a religious bent in his early education, he was schooled in literary and aesthetic subjects. Being dissatisfied with this training, he 'longed for schooling in scientific methods and in the moral principles needed to guide social life'.[1] He was educated in the most prominent French educational institutions, including the College d'Epinal and the prestigious Ecole Normale Superieure. While he was trained in philosophy, he rejected a traditional academic career in this discipline. As was the custom of the times in France, after graduation Durkheim taught in provincial high schools before moving on to university-level teaching.

---

[1] George Ritzer, *The McDonaldisation of society: An investigation into the changing character of contemporary social life* (Thousand Oaks, 1993) 18.

© The Author(s) 2017   **171**
S.F. Alatas, V. Sinha, *Sociological Theory Beyond the Canon*,
DOI 10.1057/978-1-137-41134-1_7

In 1885, Durkheim spent a term in Germany visiting universities in Berlin, Marburg and Leipzig. Here he was exposed to, and impressed by, scientific psychology, particularly through the work of William Wundt, who was already renowned as a psychologist. In 1887, Durkheim secured a teaching position at the University of Bordeaux in the Department of Philosophy, where he offered the first course in social science in a French university. By 1896, Durkheim had become a full Professor at Bordeaux. In 1906, he was named a Professor of Science of Education at the famous French university at the Sorbonne. In 1913, this title was changed to the Professor of Science of Education and Sociology. Notably, it was almost at the end of his academic career that a Chair in Sociology was created for Durkheim. He was married to Louise Dreyfuss and had two children. He is known to have been a sensitive, intensive and self-disciplined individual. His personal life was defined by the tragic death of his young son, Andre in World War I. His friends and family have written that Durkheim did not recover from the trauma of his son's early and violent passing. Durkheim himself died on 15 November 1917, at a relatively young age of 59, after suffering a stroke in 1916, but more importantly from a 'broken heart'.[2]

Emile Durkheim (1858–1917) and his sociological thought are less known to the lay public in the English-speaking world today than the name of Karl Marx and Marxist theories. Yet, Durkheim was a very influential figure in his lifetime in European intellectual and academic circles. Emile Durkheim and his works are today undoubtedly recognizable to Sociology students. This familiarity is a double-edged sword however. It has served to enshrine Durkheim as a household name in Sociological circles and also generated some inaccuracies and misreadings of Durkheim's work. The latter has to do with the ways in which Durkheim's works have been translated, disseminated, subsequently read and interpreted. In the first instance, his books were translated into English through the efforts of American sociologists and thus introduced his ideas to English-reading audiences the world over. The intention here is neither to essentialize Durkheim's ideas nor to

---

[2] LaCapra, *Emile Durkheim*, 116.

distil the 'real' sociologist in him. The presentation of his work is necessarily selective and focused on the following: his crafting of a methodology for Sociology and his analysis of the emergence of modernity.

A General Outline of Durkheim's Sociological Theories

Durkheim established Sociology as a distinct, independent discipline and helped to institutionalize it. Auguste Comte coined the term 'Sociology' but its legitimization and formalization of it within French academia was Durkheim's life work. Alongside the formalization of Sociology, Durkheim founded an important journal, *l'annee Sociologique* in 1898. An intellectual circle was formed around this periodical and a total of 12 volumes were published under Durkheim's stewardship. The primary aim of the journal was to explore and investigate the relationship between society and morality. In his first published article in this journal, Durkheim stated: '[o]f all the various branches of Sociology, the science of ethics is the one which attracts us by preference and which will command our attention first.'[3] This statement was an early but defining feature of all of Durkheim's sociological inquiries. His aspiration was to use this journal to articulate and demonstrate what Sociology could and must become. From the outset, Sociology (coupled with the methodology of science and an awareness of moral questions) was for Durkheim a discipline with a critical and reforming mission. While his contributions to developing Sociology in France are well known, his role in helping to institutionalize the Sociological Society in London is less known.[4] Brandford notes that the society's 'promoters enlisted the sympathy and aid of Durkheim'. Moreover, during the first session of the Society, he sent over a paper (prepared in co-operation with E. Fauconnet, a former pupil, become colleague) to be read on the 'Relation of Sociology to

---

[3] Emile Durkheim, *L'Année Sociologique*, 1 (1987), 1–70.
[4] Victor Brandford, 'Durkheim: A Brief Memoir', *The Sociological Review*, 10(2) (1918), 77–82.

the Social Sciences, and to Philosophy'.[5] Additionally, Durkheim attracted a band of followers, students and disciples. His interlocutors included such figures as Marcel Mauss (Durkheim's nephew), Henri Hubert, Francois Simiand, Georg Simmel, Paul Fauconnet, George Davy and Charles Bougle,[6] all of whom were independent thinkers in their own right.

Durkheim was an engaged academic, scholar and intellectual. He may have lacked the passionate and direct activism of Karl Marx, but he none-theless diagnosed the problems of modernity and sought to prescribe social reforms. He was active in French public life and imagined a 'practical' Sociology that was directed towards social progress. Durkheim was pro-foundly moved and disturbed by the foundational socio-economic and political changes that were occurring in nineteenth-century France and in other parts of Western Europe. Durkheim's conviction that the emerging modern, industrial society was defined by economic, social, political and moral crises led him to reflect on the fate of the individual under conditions of modernity. At the same time, he saw the promise of modernity. But Durkheim's thoughts differed from those of Weber and Marx fundamen-tally in positing solutions for the problems engendered by capitalist society *within* modernist frames. Durkheim was much more of an optimist and his theorizing suggested that the problems of modernity were temporary and could be averted. Yet scholars[7] have noted that, in a very serious way, Durkheim did not adequately address the socio-political complexities of his own era. Despite obvious awareness and experience of the terror and tragedy of war, for example, Durkheim did not theorize conflict and violence more thoroughly in his writings. Indeed, conflict and power are only marginally present in his key works, while the conceptual vocabulary for theorizing these remain seriously underdeveloped.

Durkheim was a prolific writer and the corpus of his work is wide-ranging. His foundational contributions as a social theorist and

---

[5] Brandford, *Durkheim: A Brief Memoir*, 79.
[6] For a complete list of contributors to the 12 volumes of The *Anne Sociologique*, see Steven Lukes, *Emile Durkheim, His Life and Work; A Historical and Critical Study*, (Stanford, 1972), 615–16.
[7] Lukes, *Emile Durkheim, His Life and Work*, (1972).

methodologist are evident in four of his key works: *The Division of Labour in Society* (*TDLS*, 1895), *Elementary Forms of Religious Life* (*TEF*, 1912),[8] *The Rules of Sociological Method* (*The Rules*, 1898) and *Suicide* (*1899*).

TDLS, Durkheim's doctoral thesis, carried an early statement about the structural analysis of 'modern' industrial, capitalist society. Empirically, the text was grounded in the concrete economic and socio-political transformations in Western European societies. This text carried both Durkheim's theory of social change as well as his analysis of modernity. However, Durkheim was not merely interested in the *structural* (social, economic, political) shifts. He was more interested in the forms of morality and solidarity generated by the emergent social structures. He pondered what would hold society together in the face of inevitable specialization of all societal domains and the 'division of labour'. Durkheim argued that a new form of solidarity would emerge and would be grounded in mutual interdependence, producing a specific kind of moral individualism. Speaking of *DLS*, Durkheim says, 'This book is pre-eminently an effort to treat the facts of moral life according to the method of the positive sciences.'[9]

Over the decades, sociologists have interpreted the book as Durkheim's tentative, exploratory essay that articulated core problematics that engaged him for the rest of his intellectual career.[10] However, others[11] see this as a flawed text in being abstract, ahistorical and theoretically frail. Yet Merton renders the text as 'one of the peak contributions of modern sociology'[12] and Tiryakian sees in this 'sociology's first classic'.[13] Upon publication, the book was noticed and made a

---

[8] Durkheim, E. (1912/1954). *The Elementary Forms of Religious Life*. (J. Swain, Trans.) New York: The Free Press.

[9] Emile Durkheim, *Division of Labour in Society*, (New York, 1933), 32.

[10] Steven Lukes, *Emile Durkheim: His life*, (Stanford, 1973).

[11] Dietrich Rueschemeye, 'On Durkheim's Explanation of Division of Labor,' *American Journal of Sociology* 88(2) (1982).

[12] Robert K Merton, 'Durkheim's Division of Labour in Society,' *American Journal of Sociology*, 40 (1934), 328.

[13] Edward A Tiryakian, Revisiting Sociology's First Classic: The Division of Labour in Society and its Actuality, *Sociological Forum*, (1994), 4.

significant impact, although at a professional cost. Durkheim was unable to secure a teaching position in Paris for some time after the appearance of the book, which displeased classical economists as Durkheim had challenged fundamental premises of their theorizing about human nature and capitalist economy. Despite being controversial, the book saw five French editions but was first published in English only in 1933.

In *The Rules*, Durkheim outlined his vision of the 'new science of society', that is 'Sociology' and proposed a scientific methodology to go with it. The strong underlying practical agenda here was to persuade policy-makers, educationists, university administrators and bureaucrats that Sociology was a 'distinct' science and should be established as an autonomous discipline within academia. Durkheim did not invent the label 'Sociology' nor was he the first to conceptualize its parameters as a field of study. Auguste Comte is rightly credited both of these achievements, and had described Sociology as a unique scientific discipline – studying the 'dynamics' and 'statics' of society. *The Rules* when first published, generated in Durkheim's words, 'a lively controversy'. This is not surprising as Durkheim questioned existing conceptions of Sociology here and offered critical commentaries on disciplines of Social Psychology, Philosophy and Political Economy. He offered instead his vision of Sociology as a 'science', as an autonomous, new discipline. After Durkheim's death, the book was largely ignored for its many contradictions and inconsistencies. More recently, however, there has been a renewed interest in Durkheim's methodology, even as the book remains controversial. Scholars[14] have raised new and different questions about *The Rules*. One novel approach comes from efforts of scholars like Lynn McDonald, Michael R. Hill, Susan Hoecker-Drysdale, Patricia M. Lenggerman and Gillian Niebrugge. They have offered historical contextualization for Durkheim's effort, which they suggest was not isolated, but part of a broader methodological project involving others like Henri de Saint-Simon, Pierre Simon Laplace, Auguste Comte and Harriet Martineau. This latter group was committed to positivism and to the scientific method and proposing a methodology for analysing society.

---

[14] Mike Gane, *A Fresh look at Durkheim's Sociological Method*, (London, 1994).

Durkheim's *Suicide* strived to demonstrate '*how to do Sociology*' by continuing the project begun in his methodological text, and aimed to concretize the abstract scientific methods he had proposed. The jury is, however, still out on whether he accomplishes this successfully. Despite this, the book continues to be important for two reasons: one methodological and the other theoretical. First, the book offered *evidence* that Sociology (as he has envisioned it) could be translated into practice. The effort was to show that the procedures could be applied effectively for the analysis of 'social facts'. By treating the phenomenon of suicide as a 'social fact', Durkheim applied positivist methods of analysis upon it, abstracting not only a typology of suicides but also the various social causes associated with these. Therefore, he argued, suicide as a social fact must be explained sociologically, that is scientifically, rather than resorting to biological or psychological factors. Relatedly, through this analysis Durkheim sought recognition and legitimacy for the discipline of Sociology. Theoretically, the book carried critical statements about the nature of 'modern society' and 'transitional society'. Durkheim asked how the transition to modernity was to be understood in the face of suicide, which he also saw as pathological and as abnormal. What did suicide reveal about the nature and structure of capitalist, industrial society? Using suicide as a lens, Durkheim made a larger statement about the emergence of modernity and about modernity itself. As a symptom, a sign, an index of pathology in modern society, suicide when analysed revealed the causes of disorder and disorientation in society. Durkheim's analysis further suggested 'remedies' to restore social order and stability and eliminate the various pathologies.

Durkheim's analysis of suicide is inspiring for two other reasons. First, his study suggests strongly that not all aspects of the 'social' are necessarily 'good' for the individual. This is clear, for example, in his discussion of 'altruistic suicide'. The latter Durkheim argued was the result of 'excessive' integration, when there is a high degree of collective conscience and too strong presence of the social. Mestrovic suggests that Durkheim stopped short of saying that 'active social life' is a contributing cause of suicide.[15] This prompts a rethinking of a conventional

---

[15] Emile Durkheim, *Suicide: A Study in Sociology*, (London, 1988), 128.

reading of Durkheim as 'anti-individual' and inevitably 'pro-society'. Second, although Durkheim suggested that some degree of voluntary death was 'normal' in all societies, for him 'suicide was an index of a more widespread state of pathology in society as a whole'[16] as rightly noted by La Capra. Durkheim viewed suicide not only as an endemic to transitional society but also as an essential part of 'normal' modern society. His rendering of suicide as 'normal' was aligned with his broader view of deviance and its role in modern society, which again nudges towards revisiting how Durkheim conceptualized the binary of 'normal/abnormal' and how the 'pathological' functions in modernity.

Durkheim's 1912 work on religion – in *TEF* – has been claimed as a foundational text by sociologists and anthropologists alike. Durkheim expressed a historical interest in this book, where he attempts to uncover the origins and development of 'primitive religion'. He explained: 'If we have taken primitive religion as the subject of our research... it is because it has seemed to us better adapted than any other to lead to an understanding of the religious nature of man, that is to say, to show us an essential and permanent aspect of humanity.' However, this method, the search for the original, essential, primordial, basic form of religion known to humanity, for understanding religion in its 'modern' manifestation has triggered criticism of this work.[17] Durkheim's commitment to social evolutionism and his Eurocentrism are evident in *TEF*. Here Durkheim defines the category 'sacred' and distinguishes it from the realm of the 'profane'. For him the sacred was, '... simply collective ideals that have fixed themselves on material objects... they are only collective forces hypostasized, that is to say, moral forces; they are made up of the ideas and sentiments awakened in us by the spectacle of society, and not of sensations coming from the physical world'.[18] However, it is also worth noting that Durkheim's interpretation of the

---

[16] LeCarpa, *Emile Durkheim*, 144.

[17] An early critique of the EF was offered by A. A. Goldenweiser *The Journal of Philosophy, Psychology and Scientific Methods. Lukes 1972 and Pickering 1984; Bloor 1984 – in defence of Durkheim*. For a more recent review of *EF* see Ken Morrison's piece in *Social Forces* 82.1 (2003) 399–404, Vol. 14, No. 5 (1 March 1917), pp. 113–124.

[18] Durkheim, *TEF*, 1912, p. 322.

sacred extended beyond the world of gods, spirits and supernatural beings. He argued that anything, including dimensions of the material or social world, could be sacred, this being governed by a set of attitudes rather than inherent essential properties. His famous dictum of the 'sacred' as that which is unambiguously 'set apart' from the world of profane, everyday routine activities, inspiring awe and reverence – remain controversial as does his assertion about the necessarily social character of religion. By now, students of religion have accepted that the sacred and profane are mutually constituted with no sharp dividing lines between them.[19] Durkheim saw religion as a foundational social institution and playing a positive function in society, overlooking its role in instances of social conflict and in producing asymmetrical power relations. According to Durkheim, 'A religion is a unified system of beliefs and practices relative to sacred things, i.e., things set apart and forbidden–beliefs and practices which unite in one single moral community called a Church, all those who adhere to them.'[20] In arriving at this formulation of a 'preliminary definition' of religion, Durkheim was mindful of regnant limited definitions of the same and rejected the belief in gods, spirits and the idea of the holy or *mysterium tremendum* as its core defining features. Yet his own understanding of what he called 'primitive' religion is problematic. Scholars from W.E.H Stanner to Arnold van Gennep to Clifford Geertz have critiqued Durkheim's conception of the sacred, his definition of religion, his social evolutionism and his method of treating the ethnography of the Australian aboriginal groups. While this text is undoubtedly central in a Eurocentric critique of the sociological canon, the brief discussion here invites readers to engage more fully the ideas and theories Durkheim presents in this book.

Not surprisingly, after more than a century of being in existence, generations of sociologists have critically engaged with Durkheim's works and ideas. His standing as a 'founding father' of the discipline and the canonical status accorded to his writings have both assured

---

[19] Talal Asad, Formations of the Secular, 2002.

[20] Durkheim, *TEF*, 1912, p. 62.

longevity and endurance to his theories and texts. The analysis of capitalist, industrial society that Durkheim advanced is thought-provoking and
controversial. A fundamental interrogation for Durkheim is aligned with
Georg Simmel's question: how is society possible? Durkheim was concerned with how a sense of social order could be achieved in moments of
crisis and change; how social solidarity could be possible and what kinds
of morality would this produce. Durkheim assumed that stable social
formations with the right kind of solidarity and morality would indeed be
possible even as he acknowledged that societies pass through transitional
moments defined by abnormalities and conflict. The disproportionate
levels of crime, deviance and suicide, abnormal division of labour,
assertions of egoism – were for him all indicative of the pathology of
modernity. Yet Durkheim viewed these as temporary. Durkheim's theorizing was embedded in a conception of human nature that was socially
determined and less complementary than Marx's but the individual was
also the site for resistance and non-conformity. The relationship
between the individual and the social is complex in Durkheim's theory
of society and a scrutiny of his concept of 'anomie' enables this complexity to be deconstructed. While Durkheim's theorizing of the transitional
moment was powerful, his argument about the combined role of moral
regulation and social integration in modern societies continues to be as
relevant and insightful.

Durkheim's Methodological Stance

In *The Rules*, Durkheim outlined a methodology of sociological positivism, arguing that Comte's version of Sociology had a 'philosophical
character'[21] and did not meet the conditions of 'positive science'. He
differentiated Sociology from existing conceptions of Sociology particularly that of Herbert Spencer and Auguste Comte.[22] Durkheim

---

[21] Emile Durkheim, *Emile Durkheim: Selected Writings*, Ed. Anthony Giddens (Cambridge, 1972), 55.
[22] Durkheim, *The Rules*, 63–64 & 71.

differentiated this new discipline from metaphysical, philosophical, introspective and reflective foundations by offering a scientific strategy for studying society. Like Comte, Durkheim too argued that Sociology was further different from preexisting disciplines in that it had its own separate subject matter. Durkheim denoted the latter 'the realm of the social' – and this was to be the focus of sociological investigation. The question of what constitutes the 'social' runs through all his writing. He further posits that his version of Sociology is different from discipline like Psychology, Philosophy, Political Economy and History. To take Psychology as an example, he used at least two distinguishing factors to make his case – object of study and mode of explanation. Firstly, he defined Psychology as 'the science of the individual',[23] concerned with states of the individual conscience. Sociology, however, dealt with the collective conscience and collective representations and was above all a science. Durkheim said 'the sociologist is engaged in scientific work and is not a mystic'.[24] Secondly, he saw psychological explanations in terms of 'organico-psychic' factors (given at birth outside of social influence), individual (as opposed to collective/social) factors and mental states/dispositions. Sociological explanations for him were rooted in identifying social facts as causal factors. Durkheim was committed to establishing Sociology as a scientific discipline and professionalizing it. He argued that the scientific method was relevant for studying social life, and would lead to the discovery of social laws and prescribe reforms for the good of society.

Durkheim's definition of the 'social realm' was crucial to his methodological project. Durkheim's efforts to delimit this 'objectively' given domain and his methodologizing of 'Sociology as science' continue to provoke and divide sociologists. Sociologists are still debating what constitutes Durkheim's 'social'. Durkheim himself invested considerable rigour in specifying its boundaries. He understood that establishing Sociology as a 'science' was premised on marking it as an 'independent' and 'distinct' discipline. Sociology had to claim its own specific subject

---

[23] Durkheim, *The Rules*, 135.
[24] Durkheim, *The Rules*, 159.

matter not already appropriated by other cognate disciplines. How did Durkheim delimit the boundaries of the 'social' realm? What properties does it have? For Durkheim, the 'social' had a special status and it had to be carefully delineated. To start, the 'social' realm for him was set apart from other aspects of human existence (psychological, philosophical etc.) but also not reduced to a sum of individual parts. This was 'data' for Durkheim's new science of society. Durkheim treated the word 'social' as a noun, as a thing, despite his awareness that studying society meant dealing with abstractions. For Durkheim, the 'social' was a

> category of facts which present very special and distinct characteristics: they consist of manners of acting, thinking and feeling external to the individual which are invested with a coercive power by virtue of which they exercise control over him. Thus they constitute a new species and to them must be exclusively assigned the term social.[25]

Social facts were institutionalized social norms, social organizations or structures of social relations, components of culture (legal and moral rules) and social currents (opinions, attitudes). Thus, defined, all social facts did not originate in individuals. There was no question for Durkheim that facts relating to social life existed; the question for him was what was 'social' about them? The 'social' domain is distinguished from the individual both in its psychological and biological/organic manifestations. For Durkheim, the social always suggested the 'collective' but this was not approached numerically. The 'social' had an objective reality; it was prior to the individual; it had a form/materiality/thingness; it was external to individual consciousness; it had coercive tendencies, that is restraints and controls individual behaviour and it could be internalized through socialization processes. Durkheim further posited that the domain thus identified lent itself perfectly to scientific analysis. The social was objectively given, and its presence taken-for-granted and non-problematic. This social reality was essentially knowable and did not resist being 'known' (analysed).

---

[25] Durkheim, *The Rules*, 52.

Durkheim's 'faith' in science and its methods shaped how he defined the object of inquiry, that is the realm of the social. The 'social' as the subject matter of sociology made the discipline both specific and independent. This realm had a unity, coherence and form. Its presence (distinguished from physical/empirical presence) could be sensed especially when individuals acted to transgress society's norms. Durkheim had to overcome a methodological hurdle by objectifying the 'social' – making it first empirically graspable to allow the methods of the positivist sciences to be applied. He says:

> Yet social phenomena are things and should be treated as such . . . Suffice to say that they are the sole datum afforded the sociologist. A thing in effect is all that is given, all that is offered, or rather forces itself upon our observation. To treat phenomena as things is to treat them as data, and this constitutes the starting point for science. Social phenomena unquestionably display this characteristic.[26]
> Indeed, we do not say that social facts are material things, but that they are things just as are material things, although in a different way.[27]

Durkheim the starting point for science had to be things not ideas. This is in part the evidence for Durkheim's positivism, but he was not a crude empiricist. He began with 'things' but only to allow him to derive concepts from them. What did Durkheim mean by a 'thing?' In the Preface to the 2nd edition of *The Rules*, he elaborated:

> The thing stands in opposition to the idea, just as what is known from the outside stands in opposition to what is known from the inside. A thing is any object of knowledge which is not naturally penetrable by the understanding. It is all that we cannot conceptualize adequately as an idea by the simple process of intellectual analysis. It is all that which the mind cannot understand without going outside of itself, proceeding progressively by way of observation and experimentation from those features which are the

[26] Durkheim, *The Rules*, 69.
[27] Durkheim, *The Rules*, 35.

most external and the most immediately accessible to those which are the least visible and the most profound.[28]

Here Durkheim distinguishes between 'things' and 'ideas', suggesting that the former were knowable only through direct observation not through reflection or intellectual analysis. However, unless Durkheim could make the abstraction of social reality 'concrete', 'objective' and 'empirical', his science of Sociology (given his positivism) could not be realized. Its method could only work with objectified data. This objectification of data was then the necessary precondition for the *possibility* of Sociology as a scientific discipline. Durkheim admitted no obstacles in any of the observational rules, which he stated rather matter-of-factly. He did not wonder if 'it is possible for a sociologist to discard all preconceptions' or 'how does one separate subjective observable data from objective ones'. These would be valid critiques of his methodology.[29] However, given the methodological assumptions of positivism, Durkheim could not admit these as legitimate queries.

Durkheim's emphasis on the methodical nature of this science suggests that there are rules and procedures to be followed in its practice. For Durkheim Sociology as a science was laborious, demanding, non-partisan, overcomes common sense, had a special competence and must eventually quell passions and dispel prejudices. Guided by the logic of scientific rationalism and positivism, Durkheim's sociological method was constituted of five basic sets of rules: for the *Observation* of Social Facts; for the *Distinction* of the Normal from the Pathological; for the *Constitution* of Social Types; for the *Explanation* of Social Facts and for the *Demonstration* of Sociological Proofs. His very choice of words like 'observation', 'demonstration' and 'proof' indicated a deliberate adoption of the language used in the Natural Sciences, which are offered as a

---

[28] Durkheim, *The Rules*, 35–36.

[29] *The Rules* triggered criticisms and Durkheim responded to them 'The role of General Sociology' (1905). For recent critics see Ronald Fernandez, *Mappers of Society: The lives, times and legacies of Great Sociologists*, (Westport: 2003), 49–52; Stephen Turner, 'Durkheim's The Rules of Sociological Method: Is it a Classic? Sociological Perspectives* 38 (2), (1995); Kenneth Thompson, Emile Durkheim, (New York: Tavistock, 1982), 101.

template for the sociological enterprise. These rules of observation, explanation and demonstration of proofs are central to Durkheim's conceptualization of sociological explanation and what he wanted to do with the knowledge produced. The 'realm of the social' was constituted of social facts, which were linked to each other, but these were not random associations. Durkheim described their specific relationship as bonds or connections. For Durkheim, sociological explanation thus amounted to elaborating the nature of this link between facts. Durkheim invokes the principle of causality (cause and effect relations) in explaining the links between social facts. Social facts were linked to each other (i.e. they had relationships, links and associations) which were manifested in discoverable social laws. These laws could be discovered and determined using methods developed in the positive sciences. The social realm is thus constituted by social facts that Durkheim treats as 'data' upon which scientific methods can be applied.

Contextualizing Durkheim's methodological efforts historically leads amongst others to Auguste Comte and Harriet Martineau. Durkheim's and Martineau's methodologies were uncannily aligned. Both were influenced by enlightenment thought and the intellectual tradition of scientific inquiry; they each crafted their methodologies in light of deep familiarity with the French positivist tradition, especially the writings of Auguste Comte. Two issues which demonstrate this sharedness merit further notice: one, the value of *observation* as the key starting point of sociological inquiries and two, the need for *scientizing* their interrogations of society. Both argue that observing social facts as 'things' requires one to systematically discard all preconceptions, as the philosophical spirit and basis of the scientific method. Like Martineau, Durkheim called for the elimination of common sense and preconceptions about objects under study, insisting that although sense experiences were the starting point for observation, they were ultimately unreliable. Thus, Durkheim cautions, 'It is a rule in the natural sciences to discard observable data which may be too personal to the observer, retaining exclusively those data which present a sufficient degree of objectivity.'[30]

---

[30] Durkheim, *The Rules*, 81.

What do Durkheim and Martineau mean by science and how is Sociology to be scientific? In invoking science, Durkheim was operating within the French tradition of positivism and highlighted two related themes: first, a 'certain attitude of mind'[31] and second, the application of methods of the positive sciences to social phenomena. Science for Durkheim was about 'making discoveries': the sociological enterprise is about discovering laws of the social world, which reveal underlying patterns and relations of causality. What was needed was the adoption of a *critical attitude* which required the suspension of common sense and taken for granted perspectives on social reality. This is because common sense he said 'imposes judgments upon us':

> His mind should always be conscious that the modes of thought 'with which he is most' familiar are adverse, rather than favourable, to the scientific study of social phenomena, so that he must consequently be on this guard against first impression.[32]

Secondly, Durkheim asked that sociologists assume a stance of 'ignorance' towards objects of study, as this is required for approaching phenomena scientifically. He elaborates:

> They are of necessity unknowns for us, things of which we are ignorant for the representations that we have been able to make of them in the course of our lives, since they have been made without method and uncritically lack any scientific value and must be discarded.[33]

Herein lay Durkheim's relativism, also shared by Martineau. In his discussions of law, morality and religion, Durkheim cautioned against transposing definitions of crime or religion from one society onto another. It is widely accepted today that predefining social phenomena prior to their investigation is methodologically unsound, today but Durkheim and Martineau were amongst pioneering figures in this

---

[31] Durkheim, *The Rules*, 36.
[32] Durkheim, *The Rules*, 31.
[33] Durkheim, *The Rules*, 36.

regard. Durkheim argued that a scientific attitude required the sociologist to rise above both individual/personal preferences as well as political and ideological motivations to produce universal, objective knowledge. The attention to 'social facts' and 'observables' generated concepts, which represented the world as it was in its full complexity. Further, the sociologist's presence and the application of the positivist method left the social domain untouched and unchanged. Durkheim argued that Sociology as science had to transcend ideologies and blind spots. Sociological knowledge offered liberation from all biases and prejudices given its non-partisan objectivity. Durkheim saw scientific inquiries as producing superior universal knowledge. Durkheim was interested in generating knowledge for a practical purpose: for explanation, control and prediction to enable social reform and practical intervention.

Theorizing the Emergence of Modernity

Durkheim's substantive writings were concerned with theorizing the *emergence* of modernity. He identified two types of normal, stable social forms: traditional society and modern society. These are akin to Max Weber's 'ideal types', and connote conceptually pure types of social formations. Each type was characterized by specific laws, morality, solidarity and social relations. Durkheim acknowledged that in real societies, combinations of these ideal type traits would be expected; but at a conceptual level, he retained the two social entities as distinct. Durkheim approached his analysis of 'modernity' and industrial society through the lens of 'division of labour (DOL)'. He argued that the great transformation affecting European societies could be seen in the increasing and inevitable process of economic, administrative, legal and judicial specialization in society. In other words, modernity was signalled by increasing DOL, a concept that Durkheim did not define explicitly but notions of specialization, differentiation, heterogeneity and fragmentation, 'division of responsibility'[34] are suggested in its usage. All of

---

[34] Paul Hirsch et al, A Durkheimian Approach to Globalization. In P. Adler (Ed.), *The Oxford Handbook of Sociology and Organization Studies: Classical Foundations,* (New York, 2009).

these are presented as inevitable, normal, natural and desirable processes that occur spontaneously in the march of historical change.

In Durkheim's schema, change was registered in the movement from 'traditional' to 'modern' society. Strains of social evolutionism[35] (and the requisite unidirectional moves from simple to complex and homogeneous to heterogeneous social formations) were reflected in his model of social change. Durkheim was certainly interested to theorize the *transition* from medieval society and feudal society towards industrial capitalism and the corollary shift from mechanical to organic solidarity. However, even in this dichotomous paradigm of change, there is tremendous theoretical potential in the idea of 'transitional society',[36] an idea that has received limited scholarly attention. There were two stages in Durkheim's logic of change: first, the move from 'traditional society' (normal and stable) to 'transitional society' (abnormal and unstable social formation) followed by a second shift to 'modern society' (normal and stable social formation). Durkheim located the empirical, historical experience of industrial, capitalist European societies within a 'transitional moment' (see Figure 1). This is where he situated the conflict, instability and crises of capitalist societies *en route to modernity*. Durkheim is convinced that these abnormalities are temporary and that the transition to 'modern society' – free from pathologies – will eventually be made. What has been defined as the 'problem of modernity' for Durkheim needs to be *conceptually delinked* from his vision of 'modern society' (as normal, stable and ideal). It is far more precise to see the crises identified by Durkheim embedded in the 'transitional society', a societal species dramatically different from his vision of a perfect, modern society. Durkheim does provide clues to enable an interpretation of this 'in-between' social entity in productive modes.

---

[35] According to Anthony Giddens (1984):

Functionalist thought, from Comte onwards, has looked particularly towards biology as the science providing the closest and most compatible model for social science. Biology has been taken to provide a guide to conceptualizing the structure and the function of social systems and to analyse processes of evolution via mechanisms of adaptation . . . functionalism strongly emphasises the pre-eminence of the social world over its individual parts (i.e. its constituent actors, human subjects).

[36] Tiryakian, *Revisiting Sociology's First Classic.*

With some rare exceptions,[37] Durkheim has been stereotypically read as a theorist who did not deal with social change.[38] Consequently, Durkheim's theories have been presented as static and ahistorical. This is ironic given that the question of social change was at the centre of his first major work in *TDLS*. The issue was more *how* Durkheim theorizes the emergence of modern society in the broader sweep of historical change. Durkheim was writing in a context when social evolutionary theories were in vogue and largely accepted by social scientists of the time. The stage theory of change, which presented societies as moving through set stages characterized by degrees of 'savagery' to 'civilization', was the norm. He too was influenced by such thinking. As such there are obvious problems with his theory of change. Durkheim's insistence that societal change was *natural* and *spontaneous* is conceptually weak and contradicted by history. For example, this conception does not address the processes of Western colonialism and imperialism in engendering coerced societal transformations, the effects of which Durkheim witnessed in his lifetime. Colonizing powers, including France, which were economically, militarily and technically superior forced colonized societies into adopting a different social, economic and political order through conquest. This coercive process was far from desirable and inflicted violence, destruction and death on subjugated populations. Durkheim was obviously aware of the excesses of colonialism, yet he did not systematically deal with its consequences in conceptualizing his theory of social change. This theorizing is limited in being untouched by the historical reality of colonial encounters between Europe and non-Europe. Neither did Durkheim theorize how Europe's capitalism and modernity were profoundly shaped by this encounter. Even European societies that Durkheim was theorizing (including France, Britain and Germany) had transited into industrial capitalism through revolutionary routes marked by chaos, disorder and turmoil. In his major works, at least, Durkheim was as silent about colonialism as he was about the

---

[37] J. Harms, Reason and Social Change in Durkheim's Thought: The Changing Relationship between Individual and Society, *Pacific Sociological Review*, 24 (4) (1981).

[38] T Parsons, *The Structure of Social Action* (Vol. III). Glencoe, 1937).

revolutionary struggles to overthrow feudal aristocracy in Europe. A comparative discussion of Eurocentric strains within the classical canon is productive here. What is problematic in Marx is his theoretical treatment of European colonialism and its relationship to capitalism. What is limiting in Durkheim is precisely his neglect of the colonial question for theorizing the emergence of capitalism in Europe. In a normative vein, Durkheim saw the transition from traditional to modern society as good and desirable; neither was there any turning back or away from this eventuality for Durkheim. In this sense he saw modernity as progressive and admired both capitalism and democracy, even though he argued for a version of socialism, which was rather different from Marx's vision.

Anomie, Egoism and Abnormal Division of Labour

Three core concepts in Durkheim's theorizing of European industrial capitalism are anomie, egoistic individualism and abnormal division of labour. Not surprisingly, the empirical presentations of all three concepts are found in the 'transitional moment', where Durkheim allowed for a number of sociological possibilities, otherwise inconceivable in his theoretical framework. As a theorist, Durkheim is interesting in suggesting the concept of 'transitional society', suspended in a state of liminality and societal in-between-ness. Durkheim acknowledged that the path to modernity was marked by conflict, chaos, anomie, egoism, inequality and moral crisis. It was in the *space between* 'traditional' and 'modern' societies that Durkheim's theorizing is most illuminating. Here he allowed for the possibility of different kinds of 'deviance', of individuals escaping society, maybe even of individual freedom and expression – which collectively complicate how Durkheim's theory of individualism is to be interpreted.

Anomie is probably the single most important concept in all of Durkheim's substantive writings, which he develops in *TDLS* and *Suicide*. It has been noted that anomie is to Durkheim, what alienation is to Marx and disenchantment is to Weber.[39] Anomie has been read as typifying the problem of modernity for Durkheim. But this is also the most misunderstood of Durkheim's concepts. Following Parsons' and Merton's readings, sociologists have attributed an interpretation of 'anomie' as a state of *normlessness, meaninglessness and powerlessness* – which would not have been agreeable to Durkheim himself. Mestrovic[40] offered an early powerful critique of this error, suggesting that anomie as a 'total social fact',[41] rather than 'positivist normlessness', is a more productive approach to the problematic. Gerber and Macionis define anomie as a 'condition in which society provides little moral guidance to individuals'.[42] The idea of 'normlessness' does not make sense within Durkheimian logic given that a society or a state of society *without* norms would be inconceivable for him. Durkheim's conception of anomie was influenced by the ideas of the French philosopher, Jean-Marie Guyau. He first developed the notion of anomie in his analysis of industrial capitalism, offering an explanation in *TDLS*:

> But on the contrary, if some opaque environment is interposed . . . relations [are] rare, are not repeated enough . . . are too intermittent. Contact is no longer sufficient. The producer can no longer embrace the market at a glance, nor even in thought. He can no longer see its limits, since it is, so to speak limitless. Accordingly, production becomes unbridled and unregulated.[43]

Durkheim introduced the term 'anomie' for the first time in the *DLS*. Stephen Marks argues that apart from *TDLS* and *Suicide*, '*Moral Education* . . . contains Durkheim's most sophisticated writing about

[39] Steven Lukes, Alienation and Anomie. In P. Hamilton (Ed.), *Emile Durkheim: Critical Assessments*, Vol. II (London, 1990).

[40] Mestrovic's *Anomie and the Unleashing of the Will:, In Emile Durkheim and the Reformation of Sociology*, (New Jersey, 1988).

[41] Mestrovic 1987, 567–583.

[42] *Gerber, John J. Macionis, Linda M. (2010). Sociology (7th Canadian ed.). Toronto: Pearson Canada. p. 97.*

[43] Durkheim, *DLS*, 368–369.

anomie, is probably his least known work'.[44] An etymological unpacking of the Greek term suggests that it can be translated as 'without name or identity'[45] but a literal interpretation would be a mistake. Durkheim described anomie rather as 'derangement' and as 'an insatiable will'[46] and the basis of conflict in modern society:

> It is this anomic state that is the cause, as we shall show, of the incessantly recurrent conflicts, and the multifarious disorders of which the economic world exhibits so sad a spectacle.[47]

Rescuing Durkheim's understanding of anomie from Parsonian and Mertonian readings is essential. Mestrovic offers the most sophisticated and nuanced interpretation of Durkheim's conception of anomie, and in doing so offers a critique of Merton's understanding:

> We will show that Merton is incorrect to attribute his understanding of anomie as 'normlessness' to Durkheim, and that the consequences of Merton's understanding are vastly different from Durkheim's. 'Normlessness' apparently causes no suffering; Durkheim's anomie does. 'Normlessness' apparently does not cause a weakening of the will to live but only deviance whereas Durkheim's understanding of what now passes for 'deviance' is more complex. 'Normlessness' assumes a rational agent capable of accepting society's goals and means, whereas Durkheim's anomie assumes that man's will is by nature dangerous to himself and to society. 'Normlessness' is difficult, if not impossible to imagine, for there will always be norms in any situation. But Durkheim's understanding of anomie as immorality can be conceptualized.[48]

[44] Stephen R. Marks. 'Durkheim's Theory of Anomie.' *American Journal of Sociology*, 80(2): 329–363, 1974, 329. Durkheim, E. (1925/1961). *Moral Education: A Study in the Theory and Application of the Sociology of Education.* (E. Wilson, & H. Schnurer, Trans.) New York: The Free Press.

[45] Mestrovic's, *Anomie and the Unleashing of the Will*, (1988).

[46] Mestrovic, Stjepan. *Emile Durkheim and The Reformation of Sociology.*

[47] Durkheim, *DLS*, 5.

[48] Mestrovic, *Anomie, the Unleashing of the Will*, 61.

Durkheim's understanding of 'anomie' emanated from a particular conception of human nature, which assumed a rather negative and pessimistic view of human beings. Durkheim argued thus:

> There are in each of us . . . two consciences: one which is common to our group in its entirety . . . the other, on the contrary, represents that in us which is personal and distinct, that which makes us an individual.[49]

> It is not without reason, therefore, that man feels himself to be double: he actually is double. . . . In brief, this duality corresponds to the double existence that we lead concurrently; the one purely individual and rooted in our organisms, the other social and nothing but an extension of society. (Durkheim (1914/1973, 162).

Mestrovic elaborated Durkheim's notion of *homo duplex* as the basis for Durkheim's theory of individualism and the need for the social regulation:

> But for Durkheim, egoism is the 'lower' side of homo duplex and is dangerous . . . One does not 'socialize' and 'regulate' such rebellion, because it is impossible to do so. Rather, for Durkheim, one establishes a social arrangement such that the 'lower' side of homo duplex is continually rules by the 'higher,' which is society.[50]

Following Schopenhauer, Durkheim argued that by nature, individuals have unlimited/infinite needs, passions and desires, which thus had to be controlled through appropriate social and moral codes. He says:

> The more one has, the more one wants, since satisfactions received only stimulate instead of filling needs.[51]

Under normal and stable social conditions, society itself provided a sense of restraint (through norms and values) on individual desires, thus regulating behaviour. However, under conditions of rapid, uncontrolled

---

[49] Durkheim, *DLS*, 129.

[50] Mestrovic, *Anomie, the Unleashing of the Will*, 65.

[51] Durkheim, *Suicide*, 248.

change, new appropriate moral codes did not emerge quickly enough to perform this critical function. It is this condition of unchecked individual desires and ironically their very satisfaction (which create further desires) that Durkheim recognized as anomie:

> Unlimited desires are insatiable by definition and insatiability is rightly considered a sign of morbidity. Being unlimited, they constantly and infinitely surpass the means at their command; they cannot be quenched. Inextinguishable thirst is constantly renewed torture.[52]

Conceptually then anomie refers to those conditions under *which limiting and regulating norms are absent,* thus producing a lack of legitimate sense of limits on individual behaviour. Mestrovic's poetic and graphic description renders anomie as an 'unleashing of the will'.[53] It is in the transitional moment that individuals freely express their infinite desires and try to actualize them without restraint. Additionally, for Durkheim there was an immoral dimension to anomie, with the individual ego as disobedient, willful and selfish. Another critical corrective needed with respect to conceptions of anomie is that it is a *structural* (i.e. due to the structure of social organization and social relations) rather than a *subjective* or a *psychological* or concept. Undoubtedly, the effects of anomie are felt and manifested in/by individuals: it leads to social and moral displacement is unsettling and disorientating for the individual, with experiences of anxiety, frustration, meaninglessness and powerlessness. Thus, for Durkheim the problem of modernity represented above all is a moral crisis and its alleviation was critical to the achievement of 'modern society' as he defined it.

This moral crisis was exacerbated by the presence of excessive individualism. That is, a condition in which the 'individual ego asserts itself to excess in the face of the social ego and at its expense'[54] found not only mostly in transitional society but also marginally in modern society.

---

[52] Durkheim, *Suicide,* 247.

[53] Mestrovic, *Anomie, the Unleashing of the Will,* 54.

[54] Cited in Lehmann, *Deconstructing Durkheim: A Post-post Structuralist Critique,* (London: 1993).

Here Durkheim described the atomized, self-interested and utilitarian individual who was motivated by pure and rational self-interest. The individual was 'freed' or detached from society and from collective sentiments, reflecting unrestrained passions and unlimited wants and the desire to realize these. But also in this moment, the individual did (albeit momentarily) stand *against* (as anti-social) and *outside* (as *unsocialized*) the social fabric. These ideas are conceptually powerful in acknowledging possibilities for individuals escaping society. Ultimately, though, Durkheim saw these as dangerous and unproductive, both for individual and society.

For Durkheim, the relationship between the individual and social was complex. Egoistic individualism suggested a decline in collective conscience and a detachment from the collective moral order, leading possibly to the disintegration of society. However, locating it in the transitional phase rendered it an atypical, abnormal occurrence. An alternative to egoism is carried in Durkheim's notion of 'moral individualism', which was rooted instead in the collective belief in the dignity and worth of individual differences. The latter was not utilitarian self-interest but a socially responsible individualism that was collectively sanctioned. Here the individual stood neither outside nor against the social. In Durkheim's words, this is 'individualism thus understood is the glorification not of the self but of the individual in general'.[55] This is reminiscent of the contemporary discourse of the 'rights of the individual', which has legitimacy in modern society, where collective conscience may be weaker. Moral individualism for Durkheim reflects a 'sympathy for all that is human'[56] with a 'belief in the sanctity of that which is common to all individuals to their humanity'.[57] A stereotypical view interprets Durkheim as a 'social determinist' and 'anti-individual'. These charges cannot be sustained in view of Durkheim's faith in 'moral individualism'.[58]

However, through much of his writing, using the language of social control Durkheim invoked the imagery of society *coercing, constraining*

---

[55] Cited in Lehmann, *Deconstructing Durkheim*, 114.
[56] Cited in Lehmann, *Deconstructing Durkheim*, 114.
[57] Cited in Lehmann, *Deconstructing Durkheim*, 114.
[58] Lehmann, *Deconstructing Durkheim*, (1993).

and *restraining* the individual. He described socialization processes which *penetrate* and *invade* individual consciousness. For Durkheim, the social is not by definition an evil, diabolical force, to be feared, fought and resisted; instead, he argued, it provided the necessary limiting and regulating norms, which were good for the individual. However, in his discussion of suicide and DOL, he suggested that not everything social is good for the individual. There is evidence of a *tension* in Durkheim's thought between the 'need for the social' and his 'admiration for moral individualism'. This struggle remained largely unresolved in his theorizing. One means by which Durkheim attempted to reconcile these is through the concept 'cult of the individual', suggesting the way forward thus:

> This is how it is possible, without contradictions, to be an individualist while asserting that the individual is a product of society rather than its cause.[59]

Here he was able to retain both collective conscience and his brand of individualism. They are for Durkheim not necessarily antagonistic, incompatible or mutually exclusive, calling the 'cult of the individual' the new collectivizing religion of modern society. Even in this formulation, however, Durkheim insists on the primary of social over the individual.

Finally, a turn to Durkheim's concept of 'abnormal division of labour'. While DOL is both inevitable and indeed desirable in its normal manifestation, Durkheim recognized that under certain historical conditions, this would not produce the right (normal) kind of solidarity. This notice was embedded in Durkheim's awareness of the contradictions within the existing industrial, capitalist societies of his time. Durkheim identified three forms of abnormal DOL: anomic, forced and 'alienated' (LaCapra's term not Durkheim's). Strikingly, Durkheim discussed abnormal DOL as pathological manifestations only in the last segment of the DLS and apparently in passing. However, this is possibly the most engaging section of the text. *Anomic DOL* is manifested during

---

[59] Cited in Lehmann, *Deconstructing Durkheim*, 114.

industrial and commercial crises and conflicts between labour and capital. Its root cause is anomie, interpreted as the absence of procedural rules that regulate relationships between different parts of a social system. Given insufficient contact and communication between its different parts, consensually agreed upon limiting norms were absent leading to social fragmentation rather than solidarity. Here Durkheim came closest to talking about exploitation and contradictions within capitalism. *Forced DOL* was a result of 'over-regulation' of the sphere of production as well as social relations. Durkheim notes the presence of what he calls 'illegitimate constraints', which he did not favour although social limits and restrictions by themselves are not necessarily problematic for him. Under this abnormal manifestation, rules and regulations *compel* one to work under threat and fear of violence. Furthermore, natural talents/skills are not the basis on which work and functions are allocated. Rather unjust and undemocratic criteria are applied. This Durkheim argued would not lead to solidarity but to conflict, disorder, disintegration and produce inequalities. Durkheim's solution was to eliminate 'illegitimate constraints' as well as ascribed status and arbitrary power differences. These, he argued, would ensure that equality of opportunity, meritocracy and other democratic ideals of social justice are upheld. Interestingly, the third category of abnormal DOL is left unnamed by Durkheim. LaCapra helps out by christening it alienated DOL, arguing that the Marx's idea of alienation expresses this idea well.[60] This occurs when 'functions "were distributed" in such a way that they did not offer sufficient material for the activity of individuals'.[61] Here, instead of being a 'permanent occupation' as well as a 'need', work does not produce solidarity but 'it limits the activity of each one, but also because it increases that activity'.[62]

Yet for Durkheim all these pathological forms were *exceptional, irregular* and a *deviation from the norm* and occurred only in the 'transitional moment'. The latter itself was an anomaly, was atypical and a temporary

---

[60] LaCapra, *Emile Durkheim*, (1972).
[61] LaCapra, *Emile Durkheim*, (1972).
[62] Durkheim, *Division of Labour*, 328.

moment that would eventually pass and stability established in the
culmination of modern society. This is Durkheim at his most optimistic
in presenting a utopian vision. But he acknowledged that this will not be
easy: 'We feel only too well how laborious a task it is to erect such a
society, one in which each individual will have the place he merits and
will be rewarded according to his deserts, where everyone will consequently co-operate spontaneously both for the common good and for
that of the individual.'[63] For Durkheim, the pathology of modernity was
curable through seeking appropriate moral codes to underpin social
interaction: 'In short, our first duty at the present time is to fashion a
morality for ourselves.'[64] Despite his rather negative judgement of
human nature, Durkheim nonetheless rejected the regnant view popularized through economic logic that individuals in industrial society were
connected and solidary only through contractual, exchange relations. In
contrast, Durkheim held the view that non-contractual relations, which
were more enduring and deep-seated, developed alongside[65] and had
moral dimensions creating obligations and solidarity amongst individuals. Arguing against the dominant economic logic, Durkheim noted:

> Yet if the division of labour produces solidarity, it is not only because it
> makes each individual an agent of exchange, to use the language of the
> economists. It is because it creates between men a whole system of *rights
> and duties joining them in a lasting way* to one another.[66]

Durkheim acknowledged the reality of anomie, egoism, conflict and
abnormal division of labour in the transitional moment, but conceptually all of these notions continue to be relevant in the analysis of
contemporary context – attesting to the endurance of his theorizing.
Frank Pearce offers a reassessment of Durkheim's views on socialism and
demonstrates elements of socialist thought in his theorizing. Durkheim's
rejection of Marx's ideas and the socialist promise of an ideal society

---

[63] Durkheim, *Division of Labour*, 339.
[64] Durkheim, *Division of Labour*, 340.
[65] Durkheim, *Division of Labour*, 155.
[66] Durkheim, *Division of Labour*, 338.

based on a moralistic critique of capitalism are well known. Pearce's book outlines Durkheim's critique of utopian socialism and communism, on grounds that it proposed unrealistic and impractical political projects, proposing instead his own notion of a corporate solidarism[67] akin to the ideas of guild socialism.[68] His version of socialism was decidedly non-Marxist but he did not advocate a centralized strong state. Instead, he argued for the development of intermediate, collective profession-based associations that would stand between the individual and the state. The basis of a new kind of organic solidarity would emerge from these groupings. Durkheim revealed a faith in the promise of modernity despite his awareness of the crises it generated arguing that these were temporary and would eventually be overcome.

Conclusion

Durkheim is possibly one of the best known but the least understood of the major classical sociological thinkers. Durkheim was essentially introduced to Euro-American audiences in the 1940s and 1950s through specific interpretations of prominent American sociologists like Talcott Parsons and Robert Merton. The mainstream received wisdom labels Durkheim as a functionalist, positivist and as politically conservative. Functionalist and structural-functionalist theories were the rage through the 1940s and 1950s. In the 1960s, however, they were heavily criticized for their inability to theorize conflict, structural contradictions and social change as well as their silence on inequalities produced by race, gender and class. By the 1980s, conflict, constructivist and interpretive theories had far greater appeal for sociologists not just in Europe but also in the North American Sociology circles. To-date functionalist theories (also known as consensus theory) have not recovered the respectability and influence they exercised in a historical moment when the sociological canon was being constructed. According to Barry Barnes, functionalist

---

[67] See Black 1984 for a fuller discussion.
[68] See Kaufman-Osborn 1986 and Alpert 1959.

theory is now as 'dead as the dodo'.[69] Part of the current attitude to Durkheim's theorizing has to do precisely with this legacy.

Durkheim was writing after both Karl Marx and Max Weber. Absent from Durkheim's work is any explicit engagement with Marx's writings, which were quite well known by then. Indeed, many of Durkheim's colleagues and students were not only reading Marx but also engaging critically with his ideas. LaCapra has denoted Durkheim's attitude to Marx as 'ritual avoidance of Marx'.[70] Durkheim seems to have approached much of Marx's writing as ideological rather than scientific and thus ignored the theoretical contribution of his scholarship. It has also been suggested that given Durkheim's stance to Marx's writings, his own analysis of modern society suffers from an inadequate treatment of the role of the economy, class structure and class conflict. Given the tenor of Durkheim's theory of social change, perhaps it is unsurprising that Marx's advocacy of class conflict as the engine of social change and its characterization as revolutionary, did not appeal to him. Gouldner argues against the view of Durkheim as a conservative or that his writings do not engage with conflict and social change, arguing that he may have been a 'moral conservative' but not a 'political conservative'.[71] Yet another slant presents him as a somewhat 'radical thinker'[72] and theorist against the dominant view that he was a 'functionalist' (narrowly and simplistically defined), 'anti-individualist' and 'politically conservative' thinker.

Given this historical backdrop, which has produced a specific image of Durkheim, is an alternative reading of his work possible? Perhaps more important than the questions of *if* and *why* Durkheim should be read today is *how* he should be read? A standard response would be that Durkheim and his scholarship merit attention because he was a founding father of Sociology. Certainly, despite the limitations noted in his work and the strongly normative tenor of much of his writing, his

---

[69] Barnes, B. 1995 *The Elements of Social Theory*. London: UCL Press. Reprinted in 2014 by Princeton University Press. Quoted in Jay J. Coakley, Eric Dunning, *Handbook of Sports Studies*.

[70] LaCapra, *Emile Durkheim*, 22.

[71] Gouldner in the Introduction to the English version *of Socialism and Saint-Simon*, 1959.

[72] Pearce F., *The Radical Durkheim*, (Canada. 2001).

substantive and methodological ideas have continued to influence generations of sociology students. A more meaningful question might be: how should Durkheim be *re-read* by contemporary sociologists. Some scholars who have re-read Durkheim from a fresh perspective are Stejpan G. Mestrovic, Edward Tiryakian, Jennifer Lehmann, Mike Gane and Frank Pearce.[73] Mike Gane's interpretations of Durkheim's methodological contributions challenge longstanding mainstream (mis)-readings of Durkheim's approach to methodology and demonstrate the continuing relevance of his approach. Critics have noted in Durkheim limited theorizing of the role of the state, the crisis of capitalism and the effects of bureaucratization on everyday lives of individuals. Gauging Durkheim's ideas in dialogue with other social thinkers of his time such as Auguste Comte and Harriet Martineau, both of whom shared overlapping substantive, conceptual and methodological interests with Durkheim, is further productive. In problematizing received wisdom about Durkheim, the intention is to seriously re-read his writings and bracket sociological common sense about him to enable a fresh tryst with his works. Approaching Durkheim in unconventional modes can prompt alternative and novel readings of his theoretical and methodological contributions.

Bibliography

Brandford, V. 'Durkheim: A brief memoir'. *The Sociological Review*, 10, no. 2 (1918): 77–82.

Catton, W. 'Emile Who and the Division of What?' *Sociological Perspectives* 28, no. 3 (1985): 251–280.

Cunningham, C. 'Finding a Role for Durkheim in Contemporary Moral Theory'. In *Philosophy of Education Yearbook*, edited by Scott Fletcher, 328–330, 2002.

---

[73] Mestrovic's, *Anomie and the Unleashing*, (1988); Tiryakiani, *Revisiting Sociology's First Classic*, 1994; Lehmann, *Deconstructing Durkheim*, (1993); Gane, *A Fresh look*, (1994); and Pearce, *The Radical Durkheim*, (2001); Gianfranco, *Durkheim*, (2000); Godlove, *Teaching Durkheim*, (2005); Jones, *Durkheim Reconsidered*, (2001); Lemert, *Durkheim's Ghosts*, (2006); Martins, *Debating Durkheim*, (1984).

Dietrich, R. 'On Durkheim's Explanation of Division of Labor'. *American Journal of Sociology* 88, no. 3 (1982): 579–589.

Durkheim, E. *Germany Above All; German Mentality and War.* Paris: A. Colin, 1915.

Durkheim, E. (1912/1954). *The Elementary Forms of Religious Life.* (J. Swain, Trans.) New York: The Free Press.

Emirbayer, M. 'Useful Durkheim'. *Sociological Theory* 14, no. 2 (1996): 109–130.

Emirbayer, M., ed. *Emile Durkheim: Sociologist of Modernity.* New York: Wiley Blackwell, 2003.

Fish, S.J. *Defending the Durkheimian Tradition: Religion, Emotion and Morality.* Aldershot: Ashgate, 2005.

Gane, M. 'A Fresh look at Durkheim's Sociological Method'. In *Debating Durkheim,* edited by P.A. Martins, 66–85. New York and London: Routledge, 1994.

Gianfranco, P. *Durkheim.* Oxford: Oxford University Press, 2000.

Giddens, Anthnoy. *The Constitution of Society.* Berekely: The University of California Press. 1984.

Godlove, F.T., ed. *Teaching Durkheim.* Oxford: Oxford University Press, 2005.

Harms, J. 'Reason and Social Change in Durkheim's Thought: The Changing Relationship between Individual and Society'. *Pacific Sociological Review* 24, no. 4 (1981): 393–410.

Hirsch, Paul. P. C.-G. 'A Durkheimian Approach to Globalization'. In *The Oxford Handbook of Sociology and Organization Studies: Classical Foundations,* edited by P. Adler, New York: Oxford University Press, 2009.

Jones, S. S. *Durkheim Reconsidered.* Cambridge: Polity Press, 2001.

LaCapra, D. *Emile Durkheim: Sociologist and Philosopher.* Cornell: Cornell University Press, 1972.

Lemert, C. *Durkheim's Ghosts: Cultural Logics and Social Things.* Cambridge: Cambridge University Press, 2006.

Lukes, S. *Emile Durkheim, His Life and Work; A Historical and Critical Study.* Stanford: Stanford University press, 1973.

Lukes, S. 'Alienation and Anomie'. In *Emile Durkheim: Critical Assessments,* edited by P. Hamilton, Vol. II 77–97. London: Routledge, 1990.

Martins, W.P., ed. *Debating Durkheim.* London; New York: Routledge, 1984.

Merton, R. 'Durkheim's Division of Labour in Society'. *American Journal of Sociology* 40 (1934): (318–328).

Mestrovic, S.G. 'Anomie and the Unleashing of the Will'. In *Emile Durkheim and the Reformation of Sociology*, edited by S. Mestrovic, New Jersey: Rowman & Littlefield, 1988.

Parsons, T. *The Structure of Social Action Vol. III.* Glencoe: Free Press, 1937.

Pearce, F. *The Radical Durkheim.* Canada: Canadian Scholar's Press, 2001.

Pickering, M. 'A New Look at Auguste Comte'. In *Reclaiming the Sociological Classics*, edited by C. Camic, Malden: Blackwell Publishers, 1998.

Pickering, M. 'Auguste Comte'. In *The Wiley-Blackwell Companion to Major Social Theorists*, edited by G.R. Stepnisky, Malden: Wiley Blackwell, 2011.

Pickering, W., ed. *Durkheim Today.* New York: Berghahn Books, 2002.

Scharff, R.C. *Comte After Positivism.* Cambridge; New York: Cambridge University Press, 1995.

Simpsons, E.D. *Division of Labour.* New York: Macmillan, 1933.

Tiryakian, E. 'Montesquieu's Contribution to the Rise of Social Science (1892)'. In *Montesquieu and Rousseau: Forerunners of Sociology*, edited by E. Durkhiem, (R. Manheim, Trans., Vol. 9),. Ann Arbor: The University of Michigan Press, 1960.

Tiryakian, E. 'Revisiting Sociology's First Classic: The Division of Labour in Society and its Actuality'. *Sociological Forum* 9, no. 1 (1994): 3–16.

Wilson, T.A., ed. *Reappraising Durkheim for the Study and Teaching of Religion Today.* Boston: Brill, 2002.

Said Nursi (1877–1960)

Syed Farid Alatas

The Life and Times of Nursi

Said Nursi was a late Ottoman theologian and thinker who lived well into the Turkish republican era. Following his own description, it is customary to divide Nursi's life into three periods, those of the Old Said, the New Said and the Third Said. This coincides with important periods in modern Turkish history, that is, the last decades of the Ottoman Empire, the first 27 years of the Republic of Turkey beginning in 1923 and the Democratic Party era (1950–1960).

Nursi was to suffer a great deal of persecution and hardship that took the form of exile, imprisonment and legal action. The authorities were forever alarmed by the popularity of Nursi's writings, which were read not only by religious students but by intellectuals and the military officers. Even at an advanced age, Nursi was sent into exile for allegedly violating laws mandating secularism but was acquitted of all these charges in 1956. Indeed, the period between 1926 and 1950 were years of exile and imprisonment for Nursi.

© The Author(s) 2017
S.F. Alatas, V. Sinha, *Sociological Theory Beyond the Canon*,
DOI 10.1057/978-1-137-41134-1_8

Outline of Nursi's Social Theology

The study of Nursi's life would reveal that he was concerned with the understanding the modern human condition in the modern world, the relationship between religious faith and modern life and the role of religion in negotiating the tension between tradition and modernity. At the more practical level, one of Nursi's main objectives was to revive Muslim ethics in a world that had become highly secularized. He believed in the possibility of an Islamic life in the modern world without reliance on political authority.

In this sense, Nursi differed from other Islamic thinkers of the twentieth century such as Mawdudi, Hassan al-Banna and Sayyid Qutb who advocated the idea of 'Islam as politics' rather than 'Islam as faith.'[1] Nursi writings constitute theology with a strong sociological dimension. For this reason, it is appropriate to define the social thought of Nursi in terms of social theology. The subject-matter of Nursi's social theology is said to be modern civilization and its ills and, in particular, the relative backwardness of Muslim society as Nursi saw it. The objective of Nursi's social theology was the reform of Muslim society via the revival of faith in Islam. Nursi believed that modern society required the demonstration of the truths of religious beliefs such as God's existence, prophethood, resurrection, justice and so on. The strengthening of those beliefs was necessary in order to deliver humans from the modern pathologies of unhappiness, despair, individualism and isolationism.

Nursi's theology was in fact oriented towards social reform. He lived in a time, the period of the end of the Ottoman Empire, when there was much consciousness of the decline of Muslim civilization and the backwardness of the Muslims in certain areas vis-à-vis the West. At the same time, Nursi was very critical of what

---

[1] Ibrahim Abu-Rabi, 'Introduction,' in Sükran Vahide, *Islam in Modern Turkey: An Intellectual Biography of Bediuzzaman Said Nursi*, edited and with an introduction by Ibrahim M. Abu-Rabi (Albany: SUNY Press, 2005), xv.

he understood to be the ills of modern civilization. Even Nursi's didactic approach had a social dimension to it. The many theological lessons that fill the *Risale-i Nur* are conveyed to the reader via analogies that involve accounts of relations between individuals in a modern setting.

Social theology takes as its point of departure the reality of the social, that is, the reality of social organization. It stresses the social dimension in human life but also employs traditional theology, to engage with the challenges of modern life. It may do this by laying emphasis on the relevance of theology for social life, for example, the impact of the Divine Attributes on human thought and action. More relevant to sociology, however, is the discussion of theological issues in terms of social categories such as class, the elite, the state, intellectuals, or social issues such as corruption, economic exploitation, political oppression, alienation and so on.

As a scholar rooted in the classical Islamic tradition of learning, Nursi's work does contain metaphysical, theological and ethical theories. Our main concern here, however, is with Nursi's empirical theory. Empirical theories offer generalizations about observable reality. The theory of Nursi that we are interested in here is his theory of the nature and characteristics of modern civilization. Nursi related theology to social life. On the Divine Attributes, Nursi emphasized their consequences for human action in this world, particularly in relation to the contest between good and evil.

The All-Glorious Creator of the universe has two sorts of Names, those pertaining to His Glory and those pertaining to His Beauty. Since these Names require to demonstrate their decrees through different manifestations, the Glorious Creator blended together opposites in the universe. Bringing them face to face, he gave them aggressive and defensive positions, in the form of a sort of wise and beneficial contest. Through making the opposites transgress one another's bounds, He brought conflict and change into being, and made the universe subject to the law of change and transformation and the principles of progress and advancement. In human kind, the comprehensive fruit of the tree of creation, he made that law of contest in even stranger form, and opening the door to striving, which would be the means of all human progress, He gave Satan's party certain faculties with which to be able to challenge God's party.[2]

Like many social theorists, for Nursi the basic nature of social reality is conflict. Societal progress is an outcome of the successful struggle against the people of misguidance. Progress is essentially a struggle between two types of groups, the party of Satan and the party of God. Here Nursi relates theology to social relations, as he does in the following:

> For one of the greatest results of the universe's creation is man's worship and his responding to Divine dominicality with belief and submission. However, due to the denial of unbelief, the people of unbelief and misguidance reject that supreme result, which is the ultimate cause of beings and the reason for their continued existence, and therefore perpetrate a sort of transgression against the rights of all beings.[3]

Unlike traditional theology, Nursi describes the consequences of unbelief not in terms of the fate of the individual soul but in terms of the transgression against the rights of all beings. It is also important to stress here that Nursi is not referring to the struggle of Muslims against non-Muslims. Rather, he is referring to that between those who affirm the rights of beings and those who deny those rights. Nursi's objective is to chart a 'new way in the life of human society' and to 'act in conformity with the natural laws in force in the universe.'[4] In fact, his objectives are set in very social terms. He refers to his origins as coming from the common people and declares that his objective is to work against the oppression and despotism of the capital-owning class.[5] Oppression and despotism indicate the absence of virtue.[6] It is therefore

---

[2] Bediuzzaman Said Nursi, *The Flashes Collection*, From the *Risale-i Nur* Collection 3 (Istanbul: Sözler, 2004), 115.

[3] Nursi, *The Flashes*, p. 119.

[4] Nursi, *The Flashes*, p. 225.

[5] Nursi, *The Flashes*, 226.

[6] Nursi, *The Flashes*, 227.

the restoration of virtue via belief that will contribute to the opposition of oppression and despotism. This can be said to be a summary statement of Nursi's social theology.

The Critique of Modern Civilization

The subject-matter of Nursi's social theology is the pathology of modern civilization. Nursi used the term 'illness' or 'sickness' (*al-amradh*)[7] in *The Damascus Sermon* when speaking of the problems of Muslim society. The term 'pathology' has been used in Western discourses on modern civilization, the idea here being to draw upon the body metaphor to talk critically about the human condition. Durkheim, for example, regarded suicide as a social pathology to the extent that it offends the public conscience. He regarded the rate of suicide in Europe as the index of a pathological state.[8]

Nursi saw two sides to modern Europe. 'Europe is two' referring to the distinction between a Europe founded on true Christianity and a Europe founded on the philosophy of naturalism.[9] As Michel noted, Nursi critique of modern civilization was directed at the second Europe.[10] Nursi discussed what he understood to be a central problem of modern civilization.

Referring to the second Europe, Nursi referred to it as a 'noxious, dissolute civilization' informed by a 'meaningless, harmful philosophy.' He summarizes the problem of European civilization in terms of five negative principles:

1. Its point of support is force, the mark of which is aggression.
2. Its aim and goal is benefit, the mark of which is jostling and tussling.
3. Its principle in life is conflict, the mark of which is strife.

---

[7] Nursi used the metaphor of illness (*mardh*, pl. *amradh*) and refers to the pharmacy of the Qur'an when discussing the lessons of the six 'words.' See *The Damascus Sermon* (Istanbul: Sözler, 2001), 26–27.

[8] Emile Durkheim, *Suicide: A Study in Sociology*, George Simpson, ed., John A. Spaulding

[9] Nursi, *The Flashes*, 160.

[10] Thomas Michel S.J. 'Grappling with Modern Civilization: Said Nursi's Interpretive Key,' in Michel, *Said Nursi's Views on Muslim-Christian Understanding* (Istanbul: Sözler, 2005), 82.

4. The bond between the masses is racialism and negative nationalism, which is nourished through devouring others; its mark is collision.

5. Its enticing service is inciting lust and passion and gratifying the desires. But lust transforms man into a beast.[11]

It is possible to understand Nursi's statement of the central problem of modern civilization in terms of the concept of desacralization. This logically follows from his criticism of naturalism, that is, a philosophy which explains everything is in terms of natural causes. This results in a kind of disenchantment in which 'minds become strangers' to non-material explanations.[12] For Nursi, the loss of belief in a Creator results in a sense of purposefulness. He says '[i]f there is no imagined goal, or if it is forgotten or pretended to be forgotten, thoughts perpetually revolve around the "I".'[13] The loss of purposefulness also removes hope and introduces despair to humans.[14]

The opposite of the meaninglessness of life is the meaningfulness of creation. Nursi explains the latter in terms of the distinction between two types of meaning, that is, nominal (*mana-yı ismi*) and significative (*mana-yı harfi*) meanings.[15]

According to the apparent meaning of things, which looks to each thing itself, everything is transitory, lacking, accidental, non-existent. But according to the meaning that signifies something other than itself and in respect of each thing being a mirror to the All-Glorious Maker's Names and charged with various duties, each is a witness, it is witnessed, and it is existent. The purification and cleansing of a person at this stage is as follows:

---

[11] This is presented in the collection of aphorisms entitled 'Seeds of Reality.' See Bediuzzaman Said Nursi, 'Seeds of Reality' in Nursi, *Letters –1928–1932* (Istanbul: Sozler, 2001), 548.

[12] Nursi, *The Words*, 496.

[13] Nursi, 'Seeds of Reality,' 546.

[14] Nursi, 'Seeds of Reality,' 547.

[15] Bediuzzaman Said Nursi, *Al-Mathanawi al-'Arabi al-Nuri* (Istanbul: Sözler), 62. See also Ibrahim Özdemir, 'Said Nursi and J.P. Sartre: Existence and Man – A Study of the Views of Said Nursi and J.P. Sartre,' 22–3. http://iozdemirr.blogspot.com/2009/12/said-nursi-and-j-p-sartre.html.

[i]f he relies on his individual existence and is unmindful of the True Giver of Existence, he has an individual light of existence like that of a fire-fly and is submerged in an endless darkness of non-existence and separation. But if he gives up egotism and sees that he is a mirror of the manifestations of the True Giver of Existence, he gains all beings and an infinite existence[16]

Meaning in life is derived from the recognition of the significative meaning of our lives as a mirror to the Divine Attributes. The absence or relaxation of moral restrictions and the experience of life as purpose-less and meaningless is a consequence of the living by five principles, particularly the principles of self-interest, the gratification for desires and the use of force to realize these interests and desires.

Nursi's critique of modern civilization was not confined to Europe or the West. It included Muslim societies. However, he had different criticisms of Muslim societies. When Nursi was writing, The Ottoman Empire was already integrated into the world capitalist system. The Turks and other Muslim societies were struggling to be modern, but their own pathologies were blocking their paths to the modern world. In addition to the negative principles of modern civilization, he believed that there were other problems in Muslim societies that accounted for the material backwardness of Muslims. These he referred to collectively as the six dire sicknesses of Muslim nations[17]:

1. The rising to life of despair and hopelessness in social life.
2. The death of truthfulness in social and political life.
3. Love of enmity.
4. Not knowing the luminous bonds that bind the believers to one another.
5. Despotism, which spreads, becoming widespread as though it was various contagious diseases.

---

[16] Nursi, *The Words*, 493
[17] Nursi, *The Damascus Sermon*, 26–7.

The central problem identified by Nursi is that of despair (al-ya's).[18] This in turn is related to the problem of disenchantment. Referring to the influence of Europe on the disenchantment of Muslims, Nursi says:

> At this time, however, due to the dominance of European civilization and the supremacy of natural philosophy and the preponderance of the conditions of worldly life, minds and hearts have become scattered, and endeavour and favour divided. Minds have become strangers to non-material matters![19]

At the same time, Muslims live in despair and hopelessness and 'suppose that "the world is the world of progress for Europeans and everyone else," but "it is the world of decline only for the unfortunate people of Islam!"'[20] Despair for Nursi was related to the loss of faith in the sense of the disenchantment of life. This can be seen from the following quotation:

> Despair is a most grievous sickness of communities and nations, a cancer. It is an obstacle to achievement and is opposed to the truth of the Sacred Hadith, 'I am with my bondsman who thinks favourably of Me.' It is the quality and pretext of cowards, the base and the impotent. It does not tell of Islamic courage.[21]

At the same time, Nursi relates the experience of despair to the failure of Muslims to adjust to the modern world. With reference to education, he says that the curriculum of the *medrese* system had become narrow and

---

[18] Nursi's Damascus sermon was delivered in Arabic. The Arabic term for despair used by Nursi is *al-ya's*. See Bediuzzaman Said Nursi, *Al-Khutbah al-Shamiyyah* (*The Damascus Sermon*) (Istanbul: Sözler, 2007), 28. In the Sufi tradition of Islam, *al-ya's* refers to the sense of hopelessness resulting from having lost contact with the Beloved, the Divine. See Amatullah Armstrong, *Sufi Terminology (Al-Qamus Al-Sufi): The Mystical Language of Islam* (Kuala Lumpur: A.S. Noordeen, 1995), 267. Nursi's usage of the term, however, is more in the modern sense of loss of purpose and meaning in life.
[19] Bediuzzzaman Said Nursi, *The Words: On the Nature and Purpose of Man, Life, and All Things*, Istanbul: Sozler, 2004, 496.
[20] Nursi, *The Damascus Sermon*, 39.
[21] Nursi, *The Damascus Sermon*, 44.

sterile on account of neglecting the modern sciences. The result was the production of ulama or religious scholars who believed in the clash between reason and revelation. This clash had caused 'feelings of hopelessness and despair, and had shut the door of progress and civilization.'[22] Nursi told the congregation in Damascus that despair was a 'grievous sickness [that] has entered the heart of the world of Islam.' Despair destroyed the morale of Muslims to the extent that the Europeans had been able to dominate them. Nursi appealed to the Arabs to overcome their despair and stand with the Turks in 'true solidarity and concord' and 'unfurl the banner of the Qur'an in every part of the world.'[23]

Indeed, as noted by the biographer of Nursi, Şükran Vahide, despair was for Nursi the central problem of Muslim society.[24] But, it is crucial to remember that for Nursi despair was not merely a worldly problem. It was related to the idea of the afterlife as well.

> The appointed hour is not known: in order to deliver man from absolute despair and absolute heedlessness, and to hold him between hope and fear and so preserve both this world and the Hereafter, in His wisdom Almighty God has concealed the appointed hour. The appointed hour may come at any time; if it captures man in heedlessness, it may cause grievous harm to eternal life. But illness dispels the heedlessness; it makes a person think of the Hereafter; it recalls death, and thus he may prepare himself.[25]

In other words, the question of despair is also one of faith. Belief in the hereafter relieves the death anxiety and gives hope. Without faith, the human mind is 'bewildered at the upheavals of the passing of the world, and laments despairingly.'[26] But, that hope is shaken when Muslims find themselves a conquered people and unable to feel comfortable in the

[22] Vahide, *Islam in Modern Turkey*, 45.
[23] Nursi, *The Damascus Sermon*, 43–45, cited in Vahide, *Islam in Modern Turkey*, 98.
[24] Vahide, *Islam in Modern Turkey*, 94
[25] Nursi, *The Flashes*, 274–275.
[26] Nursi, *The Words*, 229.

modern world. In a sense, failure in this world suggests failure in the next. For Nursi, life is defined in opposition to despair. That is, 'hope and thinking favourably of things are life itself. While to think the worst is despair, the destroyer of happiness and slayer of life.'[27]

Despair is an important theme in social theory, particularly since the nineteenth century and continues to be an important phenomenon today. In European thought, it is often treated under the category of anomie. Anomie refers to a state in which society fails to exercise sufficient regulation or constraints over the desires of individuals such that they are tormented at not being able to satisfy these desires. The unlimited desires and their insatiability due to the nature of things constantly renews the torture of individuals finally resulting in despair. This is the condition of the anomie discussed by Durkheim.[28] It is interesting to inquire how despair (al-ya's) in Nursi differs from Durkheim's anomie. Although despair and anomie are important phenomena in the Muslim world, they are under-researched. Nursi's identification of the phenomenon should result in serious conceptual and empirical attention to the problem.

Nursi clearly related the problem of despair to that of justice. In a discussion on 'the poor and the weak,' he notes that their suffering cannot be relieved by a nationalist patriotism. European philosophies increase the despair and suffering of the poor because they are founded on naturalism and promise nothing beyond this life. Faith, on the other hand, does promise salvation to those who believe.

It is only through the life of the hereafter that the elderly, who form half of mankind, can endure the proximity of the grave, and be consoled at the thought that their lives, to which they are firmly attached, will soon be extinguished and their fine worlds come to an end. It is only at the hope of eternal life that they can respond to the grievous despair they feel in their emotional child-like spirits at the thought of death. Those worthy, anxious fathers and mothers, so deserving of compassion and in need of

---

[27] Nursi, *The Words*, 744.
[28] Emile Durkheim, *Suicide: A Study in Sociology*, London: Routledge, 1989, 241–8.

tranquillity and peace of mind, will otherwise feel a terrible spiritual turmoil and distress in their hearts, and this world will become a dark prison for them, and life even, grievous torment.[29]

However, Nursi's position was not that the poor should accept their lot in this world and consider the rewards of the afterlife as just compensation for suffering here. Rather, he regarded a faith-based society as one that emphasized social justice.

Class, Exploitation and Justice

Although a theologian, Nursi's objectives are set in very social terms:

> Yes, by birth and the way I have lived I am from the class of common people, and I am one of those who by temperament and intellectually have accepted the way of 'equality of rights.' And due to compassion and the justice proceeding from Islam, I am one of those who for a long time have opposed and worked against the despotism and oppression of the elite class called the bourgeoisie. I therefore support total justice with all my strength, oppose tyranny, oppression, arbitrary power, and despotism.[30]

But, Nursi was not a supporter of socialism of the Bolshevik variety. His reason was as follows. The law of absolute equality that underlies socialism is contrary to human nature. Humans have the God-given capacity to perform the tasks of thousands of species. His faculties and senses are not unlimited like those of other animals. God 'left him free and gave him a capacity whereby they could roam through endless degrees, while being one species, mankind became like thousands of species. And for this reason, man was God's vicegerent on earth, the result of the universe, and monarch of the animals'.[31]

---

[29] Nursi, *The Words*, 111.
[30] Nursi, *The Flashes*, 226.
[31] Nursi, *The Flashes*, 226.

Nursi considered competition as the most important mechanism for the development of variety in humans. Competition allows humans to express themselves and realize true virtue. On the other hand, restricting competition, as done in socialism, would result in the removal of virtue because it changes human nature, extinguishes reason and annihilates the spirit.[32]

Modern society, however, had allowed competition to lead to oppression. This is due to the multiplication of desire and its consequences. Although the aims of modern civilization were to create the opposite, that is, a happy worldly life, what had come to past was the destruction of tranquillity.

> Mankind's happiness in life lies in frugality and endeavour, and it is through them that the rich and poor will be reconciled, I shall here make one or two brief points to explain this:
>
> In the nomadic age, man needed only three or four things, and it was only two out of ten people who could not obtain them. But now, through wastefulness, abuse, stimulating the appetites, and such things as custom and addiction, present-day civilisation has made inessential needs seem essential, and in place of the four things of which he used to be in need, modern civilised man is in need of twenty. And it is only two out of twenty who can satisfy those needs in a totally licit way; eighteen remain in need in some way...
>
> It perpetually encourages the desolate lower class to challenge the upper classes ... It has destroyed the tranquillity of mankind.[33]

The rich and the capital owning classes who should be the carriers of modesty and humility were oppressive and arrogant. At the same time, the poverty and powerlessness of the poor, rather than being the cause of compassion and bounty, resulted in their captivity and condemnation.[34]

---

[32] Nursi, *The Flashes*, 226.

[33] Said Nursi, *Emirdağ Lahikası* (Istanbul: Sinan Matbaası, 1959), 97–99, cited in Vahide, *Islam in Modern Turkey*, 318.

[34] Nursi, *The Damascus Sermon*, 102.

The practice of oppression, immorality and mercilessness by the
upper classes and the response of the lower classes in terms of hatred
and envy resulted in the struggle between capital and labour in Europe.[35]
Nursi advocated redistribution of wealth via the Islamic tithe, zakat, as a
solution to the problem of class conflict.

> *Zakat* is a most essential support of happiness not merely for individuals
> and particular societies, but for all of humanity. There are two classes of
> men: the upper classes and the common people. It is only *zakat* that will
> induce compassion and generosity in the upper classes toward the com-
> mon people, and respect and obedience in the common people toward the
> upper classes. In the absence of *zakat*, the upper classes will descend on the
> common people with cruelty and oppression, and the common people will
> rise up against the upper classes in rancour and rebellion. There will be a
> constant struggle, a persistent opposition between the two classes of men.
> It will finally result in the confrontation of capital and labour, as happened
> in Russia.[36]

For Nursi, every solution to a material problem involved not just material
but ideal solutions as well. Thus, zakat not only resulted in the fairer
distribution of income but induced compassion and generosity among the
wealthy. Elsewhere, Nursi spoke of the need for a conception of justice
that was intimately linked with theodicy.

In *The Words* life is conceived of as a journey in which humans
partake of God's bounty, gain knowledge from Him, remember and
thank Him. True believers would believe in God's mercy and be certain
of the existence of another realm beyond this world. It is impossible that
God, who established justice and balance in the cosmic order, would not
favour those who believe in that justice and who worship him.[37] The
afterlife, the promise of a goodly ending (*husn al-khatimah*) has to be
earned while we are in this world. This means living a life that is in line

---

[35] Nursi, *The Words*, 421–422.

[36] Nursi, *Letters*, 324.

[37] Nursi, *The Words*, 77. See also the Arabic translation of *The Words* which more accurately
reflects the use of Islamic terminology in the Turkish original – *Al-Kalimat* (Istanbul: Sözler,
1419/1998), 68.

with the Divine Law. This means emulate the attributes of God, one of which is justice (*'adalah*). Nursi did not only refer to God's justice but also to social justice, that is, justice conceived of and established, with God's instruction, by humans on this world.

The compulsion to justice, therefore, needed faith. The deeper problem, therefore, was not the lack of justice but the loss of faith. By the nineteenth century, Muslim faced unprecedented attacks on religious beliefs from the proponents of atheism and materialism. Nursi's response to these attacks was the *Risale-i Nur*, which was to expound on the Qur'an and tenets of belief in a way that was accessible to modern humans.

Religious Conflict and Reconciliation

Intra-Muslim Conflict

Another modern pathology identified by Nursi was the lack of cohesion in Muslim societies. There was an ignorance of the special bonds that bind believers or the luminous bonds (*al-rawabi al-nuraniyyah*).[38] This is relevant to the contemporary problem of Sunni-Shi'ite conflict. The division between Sunnis and Shi'ites is the oldest and most important of schisms in the history of Islam. This schism is mostly derived from different historical experiences and divergent views about the temporal succession of Muhammad as the leader of the young Muslim community after his death in the seventh century. The history of Islam is littered with instances of violence and hostility between Sunnis and Shi'ites. But, the scale of such conflicts was historically small. It is only in the twenty-first century that saw protracted conflicts between the two groups in not only the Middle East but also South Asia and the Malay World. Although the scale of Sunni-Shi'ite conflict was incomparable in Nursi's time to what had taken place recently in the twenty-first century, Nursi

---

[38] Nursi, *Al-Khutbah al-Shamiyyah*, 28.

had addressed the problem in a way that is relevant to the quest for reconciliation today.

In both Shi'ite theology and popular culture, far more attention is paid to the household of the Prophet (*ahl al-bayt*) than among Sunnis. The principle cleavage between the two groups surrounds the question of the succession of the Prophet Muhammad. Shi'ites maintain that the succession was supposed to devolve to Ali, the Prophet's nephew and son-in-law, and then subsequently to Ali's descendants, beginning with Hasan, Husayn and so on.[39] While members of the prophetic household such as Ali, Hasan and Husayn are revered by Sunnis as well, this reverence had receded into the background in Sunni consciousness and popular culture over the centuries. Nursi's role, as a Sunni theologian and thinker, was to bridge the gap between the two groups through his interpretation of the prophetic household and their role in history.

There are many traditions of the Prophet, common to both Sunnis and Shi'ites that attest to the crucial role of the family of the Prophet in the establishment and perpetuation of the revelation. The family of Prophet Muḥammad or the *ahl al-bayt* are referred to in the hadith as the *ahl al-kisa'* or the People of the Cloak. The hadith provides an account of an incident in which the Prophet gathered four members of his family, that is, Ali, Fatimah, Hassan and Husayn under his cloak. According to the tradition, it was at this time that the *ayat al-tathir* (the Verse of Purification; Qur'an 33:33) was revealed. Although there are different versions of the hadith, in essence they convey the same message and are found in both Sunni and Shi'ite sources.[40]

The *Narration of the Cloak* is well known in Islamic tradition and its significance was dealt with by Nursi. He explains the function of the *Narration of the Cloak* in the following manner. It was to exonerate the Prophet's family members of any wrongdoing that they were to

---

[39] See S. H. M. Jafri, *The Origins and Early Development of Shi'a Islam* (Beirut: Libraire du Liban, 1990).

[40] For Sunni sources see *Sahih Muslim, Kitab al-Fada'il al-Sahabah* (The Book Pertaining to the Merits of the Companions (Allah Be Pleased With Them) of the Holy Prophet (ص), (Book 31), 'The Merits of the Family of the Prophet (ص),' no. 5955, http://www.usc.edu/org/cmje/religious-texts/hadith/muslim/031-smt.php; *Sahih al-Tirmidhi*, v5, pp. 351,663. For a Shi'ite source see Shaykh 'Abbas Qummi, *Mafatih al-Jinan* (*The Keys of Paradise*) (Qom: Ansariyan Publications, 2001).

be accused of and console them for any hardship and calamities they were to suffer. The Prophet had foreknowledge of the internal strife that would afflict the Muslim community after his passing and the accusations that would be levelled against Ali, Hasan and Husayn as well as the suffering that they would endure. This made it impossible for true believers to deny the righteousness of the four, in the face of accusations, plots and intrigues against them after the passing of the Prophet.[41] Nursi in fact did cite the relevant traditions, in which the Prophet has foreknowledge of some trials and sufferings that were to befall members of the *ahl al-bayt*.[42]

Islamic tradition not only defines the *ahl al-bayt* but also accords to them a most significant role in the development of the Muslim community. The single most important narration that establishes this is the *Hadith al-Thaqalayn* or the *Narration of the Two Weighty Things*. Again, there are different versions of this hadith, but they convey similar meanings. A version narrated in Sunan Tirmidhi reads:

> Verily I am leaving in you that to which if you firmly hold onto you will not go astray after me; The Book of Allah and my family the Ahl al-Bait. These two will not be separated until they meet me at the Fountain (of Kawthar), so look at how you deal with them after me.[43]

Nursi himself strongly believed in the significance of the *Hadith al-Thaqalayn*. After quoting this hadith in *The Flashes*, Nursi relates the function of family of the Prophet to prophethood. What was required of the *ahl al-bayt* was the perpetuation of the practices or *sunnah* of the Holy Prophet. For this reason, it was necessary for the community of Muslims to gather around the *ahl al-bayt*. Nursi says that the Prophet knew that with the passage of time his descendants would become numerous and that Islam would become weak. Therefore, there was a need for a strong and cohesive mutual support group that would function as the means to

---

[41] Nursi, *The Flashes*, 131–132.

[42] See Nursi, *Letters*, 129, and Nursi, *The Flashes*, 132 for the relevant traditions. Nursi also mentions the Prophet's foreknowledge of the killing of Husayn at Karbala in *The Rays Collection* (Istanbul: Sözler, 1998), 596–597.

[43] *Sunan Tirmidhi*, vol. 5, 626, hadith no. 3788.

and centre for the spiritual progress of the Muslim world. It was with Divine permission that the Prophet arrived at this finding and urged the community to gather around his family, the *ahl al-bayt*.[44] Nursi also suggested that the Prophet foresaw the weakening of the Muslim community and recognized the need for a strong and mutually supportive group, the core of which should be *the ahl al-bayt*. The *ahl al-bayt* were the spiritual poles for the Muslim community in general and for the Sufi orders as well.[45]

The historical and social significance of the *Hadith al-Thaqalayn* as far as the role of prophethood is concerned can be understood by applying to our understanding of this hadith the idea of the conditional syllogism. Nursi draws our attention to this in *The Flashes* where he says:

> The sublime verse,
> *Say: 'If you do love God, follow me: God will love you'*
> proclaims in definite fashion just how necessary and important it is to follow the Practices of the Prophet (PBUH). Yes, among the syllogisms of logic, this verse is the most powerful and certain of the sort called hypothetical or conditional syllogisms.[46]

The logic of this is as follows. If a person loves God, he or she would follow God's beloved. If he does not follow God's beloved, it points to the conclusion that he does not love God. If a person loves God, it means that she will adhere to the *sunnah* of God's beloved.[47] The conditional syllogism can also be extended to the *ahl al-bayt*. It can be said that if a person loves God, he/she would follow God's beloved and his practices. Following God's beloved means loving the *ahl al-bayt*. Elsewhere, Nursi says that loving the *ahl al-bayt* is to love the Prophet and, therefore, God. Loving Ali, Hassan, Husayn and the *ahl al-bayt* will augment the love of the Prophet and become a means to love God.[48]

---

[44] Nursi, *The Flashes*, 38.
[45] Nursi, *The Flashes*, 38.
[46] Nursi, *The Flashes*, 83–84.
[47] Nursi, *The Flashes*, 83–84.
[48] Nursi, *Letters*, 138.

It is very clear that from Nursi's point of view that the role of the *ahl al-bayt* was bound up with the function of prophethood. Specifically, their role was to preserve and disseminate the Qur'anic decrees and the truths of Islam.[49] It was the *ahl al-bayt* that were the repositories and examples of the Holy Prophet's *sunnah*.[50] In the *ḤadÇth al-Thaqalayn*, the second of the two weighty things that the Prophet said he left behind is the *ahl al-bayt*. In other *aḤadÇth*, as noted by Cânan, it was his *sunnah* or practices that were the second thing he left behind.[51] Therefore, what the Prophet meant by 'weightiness' of his family was their embodiment of his *sunnah*. For example, Nursi says that the love and compassion that the Prophet had for Hasan and Husayn was not only due to the familial bonds between them but also because 'they were each the tip of a luminous thread of the function of prophethood, and the source, sample, and index of a community of great consequence which would receive the legacy of prophethood.'[52]

For those who would adopt Ali and Husayn as their historical ideals of life, their conduct would be informed by a certain ideal of excellence. In both Ali and Husayn the most significant aspects of their excellence may be enumerated as follows: (i) the striving to apply pure justice as opposed to relative justice; (ii) placing religion above politics; (iii) placing religion above nationalism; and (iv) the preparedness to suffer and die for one's principles. This can be considered as the most important dimension of the ideal of excellence, the willingness to sacrifice. Nursi makes a significant point with regard to this last aspect. The spiritual value and progress gained from the tragedy of Karbala for Husayn, his relatives and companions were of such a high value that the suffering they endured was 'easy and cheap.' Nursi likened their trial to that of a soldier who died a martyr after an hour's torture. The soldier would

[49] Nursi, *Letters*, 130–131.

[50] Nursi, *The Flashes*, 38.

[51] İbrahim Cânan, 'The Companions of the Prophet (PBUH) in Bediuzzaman's Works,' in *Proceedings of the Third International Symposium on Bediuzzaman Said Nursi – The Reconstruction of Islamic Thought in the Twentieth Century and Bediuzzaman Said Nursi*, Istanbul, 24–26 September 1995 (Istanbul: Sözler, 1997), 58.

[52] Nursi, *The Flashes*, 36.

have attained such a rank that another could reach only after striving for 10 years. The soldier gained so much for very little.[53]

Ali's virtue was that, according to Nursi, he was 'worthier of important duties other than politics and rule.' Had he been a complete success in government and politics, he would not have attained a spiritual role that continued long after his caliphate and his leaving this world.[54] The ugliness experienced by Ali and his supporters revealed the underlying beauty of his role and mission. The same is true of Husayn. His experience of the trials and tribulations of politics caused him to loose attachment to the world. Instead of becoming a commonplace caliph, he became one of the 'spiritual poles among the saints ... '[55]

Nursi views on the role of Ali and Husayn in early Islamic history provide a means to reconcile differences between present day Sunnis and Shi'ites. His message to Sunnis would be that they should pay more attention to the legacy of Ali and Husayn, as they are meant to. This is because of their spiritual role in Islamic history and the fact that they have a lofty place in the Qur'an as well as in Prophetic tradition. Nursi's advice to the Shi'ites, on the other hand, takes into account a distinction between the 'Sainthood Shi'ites' and 'Caliphate Shi'ites.'

> *If it is said* that the Shi'a are two: one are the 'Sainthood Shi'a,' and the other are the 'Caliphate Shi'a.' Through mixing hatred and politics the second group may have been unjust, but the first group were not concerned with resentment and politics. However, the Sainthood Shi'a joined the Caliphate Shi'a. That is, some of the saints of the Sufi orders considered Ali to be superior and they endorsed the claims of the Caliphate Shi'a.[56]

Nursi is less sympathetic to the Caliphate Shi'ites, that is, those who consider that the leadership of the community should have fallen

---

[53] Nursi, *Letters*, p. 77.
[54] Nursi, *Letters*, p. 75.
[55] Nursi, *Letters*, p. 76.
[56] Nursi, *The Flashes*, 39.

into the hands of the descendants of Muhammad. This is because his position was that the members of the *ahl al-bayt* were more worthy of important duties other than rule, as we saw above. He was more sympathetic to the Sainthood Shi'ites who emphasize the high degree of spirituality of Ali and express excessive devotion to him. On this Nursi says:

> For by reason of their way, those who follow the path of sainthood look towards their spiritual guides with love. And the mark of love is excess, it wants to see the beloved as greater than his rank. And that is how it sees him. Ecstatics may be forgiven excesses of love. So on condition their deeming Ali more worthy, which arises from their love, does not turn into disparagement of and enmity towards the other Rightly-Guided Caliphs and does not go beyond the fundamental teachings of Islam, it may be excused.[57]

If the Sunni's were to take Nursi's advice, they would find themselves close to what Nursi called the 'Sainthood Shi'ites.' Nursi appeal to the Sunnis and Alawis, a Shi'ite group in Turkey, was for them to end the 'meaningless, disloyal, unjust, and harmful dispute between you.'[58] Not doing so would result in the one being pitted against the other. Nursi considered sectarian differences as relatively unimportant when seen against the 'hundred fundamental sacred bonds between you which command brotherhood and unity.'[59]

Inter-religious Dialogue: Christianity and Islam

Nursi's hope for change, reform and progress was not directed solely at Muslim societies. He also believed that Europe would change for the better and that this change would come about as a result of dialogue with the Muslim world. As he once said famously:

---

[57] Nursi, The *Flashes*, 40.
[58] Nursi, *The Flashes*, 43.
[59] Nursi, *The Flashes*, 43.

So, supported by the fact that the clever fields of Europe and America have produced crops of brilliant and exacting scholars like Carlyle and Bismarck, I say with all assurance:

Europe and America are pregnant with Islam; one day they will give birth to an Islamic state. Just as the Ottomans were pregnant with Europe and gave birth to a European state.[60]

He further speculated that true Christianity, as a result of the dialogue, would unite with Islam.[61] Nursi did not elaborate on the meaning of the statement 'Europe and America are pregnant with Islam.' One possible interpretation takes Christian-Muslim dialogue a step further to the idea of a Judeo-Christo-Islamic civilization. In the current and prevalent notion of Judeo-Christian civilization, the Islamic dimension is missing. Nursi's statement suggests that an alternative, post-Orientalist conceptualization of Western civilization as Judeo-Christo-Islamic is necessary in order to transcend the Occidentalist-Orientalist divide. The evidence for the construction of a Judeo-Christo-Islamic civilization comes from the history of the interaction between Muslim societies and EuroAmerica in various fields and arenas of life.

It is not only resonant with Said Nursi's views on the relationship between Islam and the West but is also founded on a more inclusive definition of the self. This conception of Western civilization also has implications for dialogue between Islam and the West. The role of dialogue in the establishment and sustainability of tolerance and peace will be limited if dialogue merely emphasizes similarities and parallels between Islam and the West. It is well known that ethnic and religious groups that share many similarities with each other still go to war against each other and enter into extremely hostile relations. The role of dialogue, therefore, must go beyond the statement and assertion of similarities and parallels.

The term 'Judeo-Christian' appeared in the later eighteenth and early nineteenth century but in those days referred to the integration of Jewish

---

[60] Nursi, *The Damascus Sermon*, 35.
[61] Nursi, *The Damascus Sermon*, 36.

and Christian beliefs as well as Jewish converts to Christianity. The way in which it is generally understood today, that is, a reference to a more inclusive conception of American culture that combines its Christian and Jewish elements, was a later development. It was much promoted during the ascendency of Nazism by groups in America opposed to anti-Semitism,[62] such as the National Conference of Christians and Jews. The New English Weekly in 1939 made a reference to the 'Judaeo-Christian scheme of morals.'[63] As a candidate in 1952m Eisenhower said: 'Our Government has no sense unless it is founded in a deeply felt religious faith, and I don't care what it is. With us of course it is the Judeo-Christian concept, but it must be a religion that all men are created equal.'[64] The term is not always used in its inclusivist sense. Some contexts call for a more exclusivist understanding of 'Judeo-Christian.' For example, American political conservatives and others emphasized America's Judeo-Christian heritage in opposition to communism, socialism, Third World opposition to global capitalism.[65]

In an effort to correct this exclusivist perception, Richard Bulliet makes a case for Islamo-Christian civilization which he defines as a single historical civilization that is comprised of Christian society of Western Europe and Muslim society of the Middle East and North Africa.[66] The term 'Islamo-Christian civilization' first appeared in Bulliet's 2004 book, *The Case for Islamo-Christian Civilization*. He coined the term for two reasons. First of all, following the September 11 terrorist attacks, Bulliet proposed the notion of Islamo-Christian civilization as a way of focusing on the shared history and characteristics of the Christian and Muslim religious communities, in order to correct the one-sided emphasis on the historic enmity between them. It built on

---

[62] Richard W. Bulliet, *The Case for Islamo-Christian Civilization* (New York: Columbia University, 2004), 5–6.

[63] *New English Weekly* 237(2), 1939.

[64] Cited in Thomas A. Bruscino, *A Nation Forged in War: How World War II Taught Americans to Get Along* (Knoxville: University of Tennessee Press, 2010), 202.

[65] Lisa McGirr, *Suburban Warriors: The Origins of the New American Right* (Princeton: Princeton University Press, 2002), 172–173.

[66] Bulliet, *The Case for Islamo-Christian Civilization*, p. 10.

the idea of 'Judeo-Christian civilization' that emerged in the aftermath of Nazism to forge inter-faith relations between Christians and Jews. Secondly, Bulliet proposed the idea as a means of encouraging conceptual and historical research into the relations, similarities and parallel growth between the Christianity and Islam that was manifested in a variety of way over several centuries. Bulliet states the following as an axiom: 'The greater the recognition of a sibling relationship between Islam and Christianity, the better the prospects for peaceful coexistence in future years.'[67]

Bulliet proposed the idea of Islamo-Christian civilization to oppose Samuel Huntington's clash of civilizations thesis and the 'Islamophobia' that it encouraged. The idea of clash of civilizations veiled the common heritage that Christians and Muslims shared. Bulliet claims that the use of 'Islamo-Christian civilization' would render Huntington's 'clash of civilizations' definitionally meaningless, suggesting that reconciliation between hostile parties within Islamo-Christian civilization would be facilitated by the presumption of common heritage.[68] The argument is weak for a number of reasons. The mere existence of similarities and parallels between different societies does not warrant their being categorized under the same civilization. Also, the notion as put forward by Bulliet does not include Muslim societies outside of the Middle East and North Africa.

An alternative approach would be for the West to see itself as Judeo-Christo-Islamic, that is, to think of Islam as part of its civilization and not merely to note similarities and parallels with Islam. More important than establishing Muslims and the West as one civilization on the basis of a shared tradition, similarities or interactions is the question of whether the West sees Islam as a part of its heritage. To put it in Nursi's terms, to what extent does the West see itself as pregnant with Islam?

The case for the West as a Judeo-Christo-Islamic civilization can be made by recourse to historical evidence for the role of Islam in the

---

[67] Richard Bulliet, Islamo-Christian Civilization, Institute for Social Policy and Understanding, Policy Brief, December 2012. http://www.ispu.org/pdfs/ISPU_Brief_IslamoChristianCiv_1212.pdf
[68] Bulliet, *The Case for Islamo-Christian Civilization*, 11.

making of Western civilization. Many examples of this can be provided from the field of education, culture and religious life.

The story of the origins of the medieval university and its Islamic roots is a case in point. To the extent that Muslim educational institutions such as the *madrasah* and *jÅmi`ah* influenced the rise of medieval universities and colleges in Europe, the modern university must be seen as a multicultural product. The university was also the site of inter-civilizational encounters. For example, Frederick II (1194–1250 A.D.), Holy Roman Emperor of the Hohenstaufen dynasty, came into contact with Muslims in Sicily and during the Sixth Crusade (1228 A.D.). He was so impressed with the culture that he adopted Arab dress, customs and manners. More importantly, he admired their philosophic works. He was apparently able to read these works in the original Arabic.[69] In 1224 A.D. Frederick founded the University of Naples. This was to specialize in translating the scientific works of Muslims from Arabic into Latin and Hebrew.[70] It was through the encouragement of Frederick that Michel Scot spent time in Toledo in 1217 and translated some works of Ibn Rushd (Averroes) on Aristotle.[71] The great Christian theologian, St. Thomas Aquinas, himself had studied at the University of Naples, was exposed to the works of the Muslim philosophers and their commentaries on Aristotle there, and frequently entered into theological debates with them.[72] By the middle of the thirteenth century almost all the philosophical writings of Ibn Rushd had been translated into Latin. A peculiarly Christian appropriation of Ibn Rushd began to develop in Europe and came to be known as Latin Averroism, establishing itself in various European universities such as Bologna, Padua and Paris.[73]

The Islamic educational institutions were degree (*ijazah*) granting. This predates degree granting in European medieval universities. It is

---

[69] De Lacy O'Leary, *Arabic Thought and Its Place in History*, rev. ed. (London: Kegan Paul, 1939), 280.

[70] O'Leary, *Arabic Thought and Its Place in History*, 281.

[71] O'Leary, *Arabic Thought and Its Place in History*, 281.

[72] O'Leary, *Arabic Thought and Its Place in History*, 285–286.

[73] O'Leary, *Arabic Thought and Its Place in History*, 290–291, 294.

possible that the idea of the degree came from Islam. In 931 A.D. the Abbasid caliph, al-Muqtadir, had all practicing physicians examined and those who passed were granted certificates (Ar. sing. *ijazah*). In this way, Baghdad was able to get rid of its quacks.[74] The *ijazah* was the principle means by which scholars and Sufis passed on their teachings to students, granting them permission to carry on their teachings. In the 1930s, the renowned Orientalist, Alfred Guillaume, noted strong resemblances between Muslim and Western Christian institutions of higher learning. An example he cited is the *ijazah*, which he recognized as being akin to the medieval *licentia docendi*, the precursor of the modern university degree.[75] Guillaume suggested that the Latin *baccalaureus* may have originated from the Arabic *bi haqq al-riwayah* (the right to teach on the authority of another) but was unable to go beyond this speculation.[76] Later, Ebied and Young, aware of Guillaume's suggestion, discussed the appearance of the exact phrase *bi haqq al-riwayah* as a technical term in documents called *ijazah* that conferred on the recipient the right to teach.[77] The theory is that the phrase *bi haqq al-riwayah* was assimilated to *baccalaureus*.[78]

Numerous examples of the influence of Muslim learning and educational institutions on Europe can be given. The influence of Islam on the arts of Europe is also evident and well known. There is evidence of the use of Turkish carpets in medieval Europe from Renaissance paintings.[79] These carpets were used in secular as well as religious settings. Examples of the latter include *The Marriage of the Virgin* (unknown, early fifteenth

---

[74] Philip K. Hitti, *History of the Arabs* (Houndmills: Macmillan, 1970), 364.

[75] Alfred Guillaume, 'Philosophy and Theology,' in Sir Thomas Arnold & Alfred Guillaume, eds., *The Legacy of Islam* (London: Oxford University Press, 1931), 244.

[76] Guillaume, 'Philosophy and Theology,' 245n.

[77] R.Y. Ebied & M. J. L. Young, 'New Light on the Origin of the Term "Baccalaureate",' *Islamic Quarterly* 18, 1–2 (1974), 3–4.

[78] See also Mesut Idriz, 'From a Local Tradition to a Universal practice: *Ijazah* as a Muslim Educational Tradition,' *Asian Journal of Social Science* 35, 1 (2007), 84–110.

[79] Donald King and David Sylvester, eds. *The Eastern Carpet in the Western World, From the 15th to the 17th century* (London: Arts Council of Great Britain, 1983), 9–28, 49–50, & 59. Cited in 'Islamic Art,' http://en.wikipedia.org/wiki/Islamic_art#Rugs_and_carpets. Accessed 19 January 2014.

century), *The Virgin and Child Enthroned* (Gentile Bellini, 1470), *The Mass of St. Giles* (Master of St. Giles, c.1500) and *Annunciation with St. Emidus* (Carlo Crivelli, 1486).[80] It is interesting that it was apparently not considered anomalous to employ these Islamic artistic creations in Europe's churches and to feature them in paintings portraying Christian subjects.[81] The use of geometric structures such as spirals and arabesques expressed not only an Islamic aesthetic but also its theological and philosophical conception of creation.[82]

It is also interesting here to mention something of the influence of Islam in America. Foley has provided an interesting account of how Euro-Atlantic discourse between the fifteenth and eighteenth centuries on religious, literary and political issues was shaped by the context of Muslim military power. Intellectuals like Martin Luther, John Locke and Thomas Jefferson educated themselves about Islam and utilized Islam to justify reforms in their societies.[83] Jefferson purchased an English translation of the Qur'an. The translator, George Sales, states in his introduction that knowledge of the Qur'an was an important element of contemporary knowledge.[84] Foley demonstrates how, for Locke and Jefferson, the very prominence of Muslim civilization in their time and their familiarity with Islamic law contributed to their arguing for a more universal vision of human rights and political freedom that did not privilege people on the basis of religious affiliation. Jefferson did not believe that Americans were free because they were Protestants. In his vision of human rights, he had to show that the values he espoused applied equally to Muslims and others if this vision was to be credible.[85] Referring to Virginia's Bill for Establishing Religious Freedom that Jefferson proposed in 1779, he said it protected the rights

---

[80] John Mills, *Carpets in Paintings* (London: National Gallery, 1983), 11, 16, 20, 20, 22, 24.

[81] Mills, *Carpets in Paintings*, 18.

[82] Alexandre Papadopoulo, *Islam and Muslim Art* (New York: Harry N. Abrams, 1979), 247–248.

[83] Sean Foley, 'Muslims and Social Change in the Atlantic Basin,' *Journal of World History* 20, 3 (2009), 379.

[84] *The Koran*, George Sales, trans., 5th ed. (Philadelphia: J.W. Moore, 1856). Cited in Foley, 'Muslims and Social Change in the Atlantic Basin,' 394.

[85] Foley, 'Muslims and Social Change in the Atlantic Basin,' 392, 395.

of 'the Jew, the gentile, the Christian and Mahometan, the Hindoo, and infidel of every denomination.'[86]

Even in the area of everyday life, there were significant contributions of Muslims. During the Crusades, for example, the Europeans were introduced to sugar, silk, spices, incense and dyes, gold coinage and methods of banking. The English word 'sugar' comes from the Arabic word *sukr*. 'Sherbet' comes from the Arabic *sharbat*, referring to water sweetened with sugar and flavoured with fruits. 'Syrup' comes from the Arabic *sharab* that is a medicated sugar solution.[87]

Nursi did not expand on the meaning of his idea that Europe would give birth to an Islamic state. One possible meaning is that Europe will recognize its Muslim roots and that such recognition would contribute to the Christian-Muslim dialogue.

The Methodology of the *Risale-i Nur*

Nursi employed the traditional methods of the theologians that had developed in the classical period of Muslim scholarship. These include the various types of analogical reasons such as allegorical comparisons (*kiyas-ı temsili*).

Nursi's is, in fact, what we may call a traditional approach that is to be seen among the early Sufis of Islam such as al-Ghazali, Mevlana Celaleddin-i Rumi and Farid al-Din 'Attar. Still, as noted by Şükran Vahide, Nursi was not content to confine himself to the method of the great Sufis but wanted to combine both heart and mind in his approach.[88] Furthermore, Nursi's thought would be a more recent example of such an approach that is especially important for us because he lived in the modern period and was familiar with the kinds of social and moral problems that confront us today. The result of Nursi search

---

[86] Denise A. Spellberg, 'Could a Muslim be President? An Eighteenth Century Constitutional Debate,' *Eighteenth Century Studies* 39, 4 (2006), 490–491.

[87] Hitti, *History of the Arabs*, 335.

[88] Şükran Vahide, *Islam in Modern Turkey: An Intellectual Biography of Bediuzzaman Said Nursi*, Albany: State University of New York Press, 2005, 166.

for an appropriate approach is a perspective that combines the intense concern for morality among the Sufis with the injunction to establish justice by the jurisconsults. As Nursi once said in the presence of a student, Mustafa Sungur:

> Sixty years ago, I was searching for a way to reach reality that was appropriate for the present age...First I had recourse to the way of the philosophers; I wanted to reach the truth with just the reason. But I reached it only twice with extreme difficulty...Then I had recourse to the way of Sufism and studies it. I saw that it was truly luminous and effulgent, but that it needed the greatest caution. Only the highest of the elite could take that way. So, saying that this cannot be the way for everyone at this time, either, I sought help from the Qur'an. And thanks be to God, the *Risale-i Nur* was bestowed on me, which is a safe, short way inspired by the Qur'an for the believers of the present time.[89]

The *Risale-i Nur* is full of the use of analogies. Consider the following. Two soldiers had received an order to go to a distant city. They travelled together until they reached a fork. There a man explained to them about the two possible roads they could take. The road to the left has no one in authority and no rules. The soldier may travel without baggage and arms to make the journey easier. Whereas the road to the right, being under military order, required the soldier is required to carry to take are compelled and sufficient fire power to deal with any problems on the way.

After listening to the man, the two soldiers went on their way. The one who took the right road had a heavy load to carry but travelled with a light heart free of worry. The soldier who took the left road did so because he did not want to conform to order. There being no rules, he travelled light but was weighed down by fear and indebtedness as he had to beg for help along the way. Upon reaching his destination he was punished as a deserter. The other soldier, on the other hand, loved the order of the army, remained obliged to no one, feared no one and reached

---

[89] Cited in Vahide, *Islam in Modern Turkey*, 167.

his destination with independence. There he was rewarded as an honourable soldier. He represents 'those who submit to the Divine Law, while the other represents the rebellious and those who follow their own desires.'[90]

The analogy is only persuasive to those who are already believers. This was Nursi's assumption. His task was not to convert people to belief but to reinvigorate the belief of Muslims whose faith he feared was under threat by the Westernizing and secularizing reforms of the Turkish Republic.[91] In a sense, his task was to prove the truths of Islam to those who believed in Islam to begin with.

The method of allegorical comparison is not only an effective didactic tool but is also in harmony with the Qur'anic approach which is founded upon the analogy of travel and forms the basis of all Sufi literature. The basis of this approach lies in the distinction between *mana-yı ismi* and *mana-yı harfi*, the aspect of things that look to themselves, and the aspect that looks to God. As Nursi notes, this is explained in all books on Arabic grammar and is something basic. Nursi's explanation of the distinction, by way of analogy, is very instructive.

When you look in the mirror, if you look at it for the glass, you will intentionally see the glass; in it, Re'fet will strike the eye secondly, indirectly. Whereas if your purpose is to look at the mirror in order to see your blessed face, you will intentionally see lovable Re'fet. You will exclaim: '*So blessed be God, the Best of Creators!*' The glass of the mirror will strike your eye secondly and indirectly.

Thus, in the first instance, the glass of the mirror is 'the meaning which looks to the thing itself', while Re'fet is its 'significative meaning'. In the second instance, the glass of the mirror is 'the significative meaning', that is, it is not looked at for itself, but for another meaning; that is, the reflection. The reflection is 'the meaning which looks to the thing itself.'

[90] Nursi, *The Words*, 29–30.

[91] Şükran Vahide, 'Proof of the Resurrection of the Dead: Said Nursi's Approach,' in Ibrahim M. Abu-Rabi,' ed., *Theodicy and Justice in Modern Islamic Thought: The Case of Said Nursi* (Surrey: Ashgate, 2010), 41.

That is, it is included in one respect in the definition 'it points to a meaning in itself.' While the mirror verifies the definition of its 'significative meaning', which is 'it points to the meaning of another.'[92]

Nursi goes on to explain that according to the Qur'anic view, all things in the universe are letters that have *mana-yi harfi* or significant meaning. They point to the names and attributes of the Maker. This is to be contrasted with materialist or what Nursi calls soulless philosophy that points to a meaning in itself. The consequence of Nursi's method of allegorical comparison is the contribution to the development of a culture of multidimensional interpretation.

Conclusion

Nursi inspired a religious revival movement in Turkey that has several million followers in Turkey and among the Turks and others who live in the around the world.[93]

The social theology of Bediuzzaman Said Nursi is at the same time a theology of reform. The two main aspects of this theology concern the negative principles of Western civilization which he saw to have also affected Muslim societies, and the six pathologies of the Muslim world. Nursi's theology provides a diagnosis of modern civilization and suggests areas for reform. Nursi dealt with wide range of issues, some of which are more relevant to us today than during Nursi's own time. In this chapter, relatively more attention was paid to Nursi's views on sectarianism. This was not a major preoccupation with Nursi as sectarianism was not as serious a problem in his time as it is today.

The reconstruction of Nursi's social theology requires going beyond what is already stated in the *Risale-i Nur*. There are concepts in the *Risale-i Nur* that need to be further defined and elaborated. This can

---

[92] Nursi, *The Flashes*, 155–6.

[93] Şerif Mardin, *Religion and Social Change in Modern Turkey: The Case of Bediuzzaman Said Nursi*, Albany: SUNY Press, 1989), 23.

only be done with reference to the contributions of both Muslim and non-Muslim scholarship. For example, Nursi's discussion on despair (*al-ya's*) can greatly benefit from comparisons with the concepts of alienation and anomie. The elaboration and further refinement of Nursi's critique of European civilization requires mastery of many non-Muslim classics that deal with similar issues. Examples are the works of Marx, Durheim, Rizal and Dostoevsky. Others can be included such as Max Weber, Franz Kafka, Ivan Turgenev, Alexander Herzen, Nikolai Gogol and Ortega y Gasset.

There are also themes in Nursi's work that have generally not been dealt with in Western thought. An example is that of laziness or indolence. Although this had been discussed by Rizal and later by Syed Hussein Alatas,[94] it remains marginal to the interests of Western social science.

The project of developing the social theology of Nursi requires work in at least three areas. First, more themes or topics concerning the social in Nursi's writings need to be identified. Examples would be class, ethnicity and tribe, or the social consequences of religious factors. Secondly, comparisons and contrasts should be made between Nursi and other Muslim thinkers. Examples I have in mind are Jamaluddin Afghani, Syed Shahkh al-Hady and Ali Shari'ati. Thirdly, there is much benefit to be derived by comparing Nursi's thought to the Catholic tradition of liberation theology.

Nursi said that 'ninety-nine percent of the *shari'ah* is concerned with morality, worship, the hereafter, and virtue.'[95] Clearly, Nursi did not reduce the *shari'ah* to rules and regulations. He was not legalistic in his approach. He considered virtue, love, mutual attraction, co-operation, unity and solidarity to be among the principles underlying the *shari'ah*.[96] More can be said elsewhere on the relationship between the *shari'ah* and morality, and religion and modern science. Furthermore,

---

[94] See the chapter on Rizal.

[95] Şükran Vahide, *Islam in Modern Turkey: An Intellectual Biography of Bediuzzaman Said Nursi*, Albany, 2005, 67.

[96] 'Gleams,' in Nursi, *The Words*, 745–746.

there are other themes in Nursi's work such as freedom that are also related to the theme of justice. Nursi regarded Islam as a vital force that should underlie the planning of a society's development. Only Islam could hold greed, extravagance and corruption in check. Nursi saw the problems of Turkey as resulting from a moral crisis that could only be resolved via the implementation of the *shari'ah*, understood in the broader sense as a code of ethical conduct. This should not be confused with the clamouring for a vaguely conceived 'Islamic' state that is often found among many modernist agitators. These are some of the ingredients that would go into the definition and conceptualization of Nursi's understanding of the reform of Muslim societies.

Pandita Ramabai Saraswati (1858–1922)

Vineeta Sinha

Introduction

Pandita Ramabai Saraswati was born on 23 April 1858 in the forest of Gungamal in the Indian state of Maharashtra. Her father, Anant Shastri Dongre, was a Brahmin scholar who was committed to the cause of female education. He taught his own young wife, Lakshmibai, and his young daughter, Ramabai – Sanskrit and the Hindu scriptures. Ramabai had no formal education but was taught by her parents and could recite the *Puranas* proficiently from a very young age. The wisdom imparted to her was largely religious rather than secular and from texts. After her parents passed away between 1874 and 1877, she traveled across India with her brother, giving lectures in Sanskrit

Ramabai's name appears in various forms in the literature: Pandita Ramabai Saraswati; Pandita Ramabai Mary Saraswati (in her Christian persona); Ramabai Dongre Medhavi (connecting to her parentage and marital identity).

© The Author(s) 2017
S.F. Alatas, V. Sinha, *Sociological Theory Beyond the Canon*,
DOI 10.1057/978-1-137-41134-1_9

and engaging religious experts on a variety of social and spiritual matters.[1] At the end of her travels, she arrived in Calcutta and spent a significant part of her adult, creative life in this city. It was here that she was honoured by Brahmins of Calcutta with the title 'Pandita' – which translates to 'eminent scholar and teacher' – on the basis of her knowledge of sacred Hindu texts. She was also seen as a modern-day incarnation of Saraswati – the Hindu goddess of learning. The conferring of these two titles, produced the name by which she was to be subsequently remembered. In addition to Sanskrit, she could read and write Marathi, Kanarese, Hindi and Bengali. She was also interested in studying medicine and turned to the Anglo-Indian community in India for support in actualizing this ambition. In 1880, her brother died leaving her without any family. At age 22, Ramabai chose to marry a friend of her brother's, a lawyer by profession, and a man outside her caste community of *Chitpavan* Brahmins – thus breaking with convention. She had a daughter, Manorama in 1881, but lost her husband to cholera the following year when their child was just six months old.

In 1883, Ramabai left for England with her two-year-old daughter, Manorama. She enrolled at the Cheltenham Women's College to study the natural sciences, mathematics and English but her ambition was to qualify as a medical doctor. Unfortunately her dream remained unrealized as she developed deafness due to a health condition while in London.[2] To support herself in a foreign land, she taught Sanskrit and Marathi at the Cheltenham Female College to women missionaries who were planning to work in Maharashtra, India. Within a few months of arriving in England, Ramabai had converted to Christianity. While in Poona she had already been exposed to English missionaries and had expressed misgivings and disillusionment about orthodox Hinduism. Unsurprisingly, her conversion created much controversy back in India. She was resoundly criticized for rejecting her Hindu identity

---

[1] Meera Kosambi, *Pandita Ramabai through her own words: Selected works* (New Delhi: Oxford University Press, 2000), 117.

[2] Public interest in India in Ramabai's overseas activities remained intense and were reported in the Indian media routinely. For example, even the news of her ill health and deafness was reported in *The Times of India*.

even by some of her staunch admirers and supporters.[3] After almost four years of studies in England, in 1886 she sailed to the USA. to attend the graduation of her distant relative, Dr. Anandibai Joshi (considered the first Indian woman medical doctor),[4] at the University of Pennsylvania. In 1887, the 'American Ramabai Association'[5] was formed in Boston and raised substantial funds to establish a school for widows in India. Ramabai spent about three years traveling and observing life in America. She was lauded here as the heroine for the oppressed and exploited Hindu woman and was enthusiastically received in progressive reform circles. In 1889, Ramabai returned to India to continue her work towards the upliftment of Indian women. Ramabai led a packed and committed life, intellectually and spiritually, and died on 5 April 1922 just before her 64th birthday.[6]

General Outline of Ramabai's Work

The body of Ramabai's work is diverse and multidimensional. She has left a legacy of works, ideas and contributions that requires careful intellectual unpacking. Ramabai was a prolific writer producing documents in the form of numerous books, pamphlets, lectures, brochures, newspaper articles, her testimony as a witness before the Hunter

---

[3] Letters and editorials in *The Times of India* archives reveal tremendous public interest in Ramabai's activities abroad and, especially, the news of her conversion to Christianity. Her reform work upon her return to India in 1889 was plagued first in being funded by American donations and by accusations that the 'secular' and religiously neutral institution like Sharada Sadan that she had established for the education of widows were in fact engaged in missionizing activities. These led her supporters – Ranade, Tilak, Bhandarkar, Deshmukh, Pandit and Telang to dissociate themselves from the institution.

[4] Joshi had begun her medical studies in the USA when she was 17 and returned to India years later as an M.D. She tragically died of tuberculosis six months after she arrived in India. She had requested that her remains be sent to the USA for burial and her family acceded to this. Ramabai attended Joshi's graduation ceremony and delivered a lecture on the status of women.

[5] In addition, a total of 63 'Ramabai Circles' were also formed across the country by 1888 and offered spiritual and material support to Ramabai's work in India, raising substantial funds. By 1890 more than 75 such circles had been established, 'demonstrating the pervasive appeal of Ramabai's cause to a wide spectrum of age groups and regions.' (Kosambi 2003, 23).

[6] When she died she was remembered variously, not least as one of the 'makers of modern India' (*The Times of India*).

Commission, religious writings in Hindi and Marathi and her translation of the Bible to Marathi. She offered an unyielding critique of Hindu orthodoxy, caste and patriarchy and argued that educating Indian women would culminate in raising the status of Hindu women. Her work also includes her efforts in building institutions for social reform and education of Indian women. Upon her return to India in February 1889 (via China and Japan), Ramabai initiated educational reform for women and established institutions for abandoned woman and widowed women/girls. Institutions she founded include the following: 'Sharada Sadan,' (Home of Learning, a school for widows; Established in Bombay 1889 but moved to Poona in 1890); the 'Arya Mahila Samaj' (School for Women, in Pune, 1 June 1882); 'Kripa Sadan' (Home of Mercy, for prostitutes and victims of sexual abuse, which served lower caste women and engaged in humanitarian work; in Kedgaon in 1903) and 'Mukti Mission' (Home of Salvation; in Bombay, in 1905 Bombay). As she traveled through different parts of India, she lectured on women's causes and also appeared as a witness before the Hunter Commission on Education.[7] In 1904, she started translating the Bible from the original Greek and Hebrew to Marathi. She also produced religious writings in Hindi and Marathi, as well as poetry and was seen as a pioneering figure in Marathi literary circles of the late nineteenth century. She was well read and exposed to scholarly literature within her field of interest. One good example of this is the scholarship on religion. For example, already in an essay she wrote in 1886 on the subject of 'Indian Religion,' Ramabai was familiar with the writings of Max Muller, Monier Williams, Wheeler Talboy, and so on.

Ramabai's overseas travels produced reflections about the places she visited and the cultures she encountered. These writings document her observations about the societies she encountered and embody her critique of slavery, racism, patriarchy and institutionalized religion (including religious structures in Christianity) and her comparative observations about the status of women in India and the USA. Some

---

[7] This was the first Indian Education Commission, set up on 3 February 1882 under the Chairmanship of Sir William Hunter, a member of the Executive Council of Viceroy. Ramabai gave her testimony before the committee in Poona on 5 September 1882 (Kosambi 2003, 242).

prominent examples of her writings are The Cry of Indian Women (The Cry, 1883), *Stri Dharma Neeti (SDN, 1882), An Autobiographical Account (September 1883), The High Caste Hindu Woman (HCHW, 1886), Indian Religion (1886), The Peoples of the United States (TPUS, 1889)* – which included *Religious Denominations and Charities in the USA* and *The Condition of Women in the USA.* Ramabai's later writings include 'Famine Experiences' (1897), 'To the friends of Mukti School and Mission' (1990), 'A short history of Kripa Sadan or Home of Mercy' (1903), *A Testimony of our Inexhaustible Treasure (1907)* and 'The Word Seed' (1908).[8]

According to Frank Conlon, Ramabai 'was a pioneer champion of women's causes in India'[9] while Nicol MacNicol's 1926 biography of Ramabai appears under the auspices of the series 'Builders of Modern India.' According to the prominent historian A. B. Shah, Ramabai was 'the greatest woman produced by modern India and one of the greatest Indians in all history . . . the one to lay the foundations for a movement for women's liberation in India.'[10] Despite this high acclaim, others have noted that Ramabai has 'a surprisingly hazy presence in contemporary consciousness – if she is indeed a presence at all.'[11] But in the year 2016, Ramabai is captured in scholarly and lay discourses relating to travel,[12] Indian social reform and education,[13] nationalism and anti-colonial movements,[14] women's emancipation and feminism,[15] Christian

---

[8] All of these primary writings are available in English translation through the efforts of Kosambi in a resource text, Pandita Ramabai through her own words,2000, New Delhi: OUP.

[9] Conlon, Book review of Padmini Sengupta's, *Pandita Ramabai Saraswati, Pacific Affairs* 44 (4): (1970), 632.

[10] A.B. Shah (ed.), *The letters and correspondence of Pandita Ramabai* (Bombay: Maharashtra State Board for Literature and Culture, 1977).

[11] Susie Tharu and K. Lalita. (eds.), *Women writing in India, 600 B.C to the Present.* 2 vols (Oxford University Press: New Delhi, 1995), 243.

[12] Grewal, *Home and Harem,* 1996.

[13] Clementia Butler, *Pandita Ramabai Sarasvati: Pioneer in the movement for the education of the child-widow of India* (Fleming H. Revell Company: New York, 1922), Geraldine Forbes, *Women in Modern India* (Cambridge: Cambridge University Press, 1996).

[14] Bannerji 2000, Butler 1922, Chakravarti 1996, Chakravarti 1998, Chakravarti 2001, Dyer 1900, Grewal 1996, Hedlund et al. 2011, Kosambi 1992, Kosambi 1988, Macnicol and Mangalwadi 1996.

[15] Fuller 1939, Kosambi 2000b, Robinson 1999, Sengupta 1970.

conversion, missionizing, literary studies[16] and evangelical work in India.[17] In recent years substantial writings on Ramabai's life and ideas have been published.[18] Ramabai is further conspicuous on various popular, lay, journalistic, Christian and missionary Internet sites and archives. Additionally, primary translations of Ramabai's non-English writings and reprints of her English material, which have been made available through committed scholarship, have been critical in enabling practitioners (educationists and researchers) to narrate Ramabai's story beyond the remit of received wisdom about her. Ramabai has a visibility and an international name-recognition today even though she is less familiar and her ideas less well known than those of other Indian social reformers of her time.

Ramabai's life and writings reveal an explicit and engaged social reformist tone. Her primary concern was the status of women, in particular, the status of high caste Hindu women, whose lives, she argued, were constrained by a highly rigid and patriarchal social arrangement. She was not thus speaking of the condition of all Hindu women in Indian society. She was distinct amongst her contemporaries for her direct critique of patriarchy, its ideologies and institutions. She challenged long-held discriminatory social and cultural practices and their debilitating effect on girls, i.e the institution of child marriage for girls, enforced widowhood and restrictions on education of girls. Her rallying call encouraged women to be self-reliant, urging them to lead autonomous, self-reliant and independent lives. Ramabai was instrumental in establishing schools for girls – an act that was interestingly opposed by some male and female reformers of her time. She also founded institutions that provided food and shelter to homeless widows and other needy women to reduce their dependence on often hostile and non-supportive families. Being an exemplar, she encouraged

---

[16] Dharwadker 2002.

[17] Blumhofer 2008, Case 2012, Ganachar 2005. Hedlund et al Kosambi 1992, McGee 1999, Symonds 1993, Symonds '2004, Viswanathan 1998.

[18] Midgley 1998, 101. Ramabai's contributions to women's upliftment are recorded in volumes on Indian women: Desai and Thakkar (2001) mention Ramabai in passing once, while Forbes' 1996 text carries a substantial discussion of Ramabai's biography, efforts at building educational institutions for women, her conversion to Christianity as well as some of her publications.

women to participate in public life and take an interest in political issues, taking the lead herself in running large organizations and addressing public gatherings on issues of social and political relevance. She was a staunch nationalist and her opposition to British colonial rule was publicly articulated.

Ramabai's Method/Approach to Social Reform

Ramabai was a social thinker and reformer who valued and advocated freedom of thought and action and worked tirelessly so that equality and progress could be achieved for Hindu women. Ramabai's work is approached here first and foremost as *social commentary*. She offered a scathing critique of her present, of the blindspots existing religious dogma and social norms, identified the causes of these phenomenon and imagined altered social structures and a better future. These she argued would materialize only through concerted efforts, collective and institutional. The – commentary and critique of society – carried in the substantive body of Ramabai's work, is radical and marked by self-reflexivity. This reading of her works suggests strongly that her diagnosis of the problem of the high caste Hindu women was rooted in a recognition of structural factors and assumed that the problematic of women's oppression could be *allievated*. She highlighted education (and lack of it), morality and religious orthodoxy and dogma in diagnosing societal problems, like the status of women. The remedies she proposed were educational reforms and cultivating and disciplining the individual mind. Broadly she argued that it was concerted human actions and the individual capacity to exercise freedom that would engender change through individual, collective and institutional interventions. Her 'work' can be productively interpreted through feminist frames. Kosambi narrates her own discovery of Ramabai in engaging the sociocultural space of late nineteenth-century Maharashtra and her 'puzzlement' as she

stumbled upon the militant feminist rhetoric of Pandita Ramabai. She seemed to have inhabited the same age but not shared the same social space; her thoughts resonated well with late twentieth (sic) century thinkers – at least feminist ones – but have been almost erased from mainstream records of history. This enigma paved the way for my gradual retrieval of her obscure – and obscured – writings, in the hope of several simultaneous agendas:...correct the imbalance in historical discourse, and to reclaim a significant part of our feminist heritage.[19]

Ramabai did not invoke what would be recognizable as feminist terminology, but in *intent*, she sought to bring about concrete changes in the status of women, recognizing their oppression and subordination. The autobiographical method (and the use of life history as methodology) is a well-established mode of inquiry in qualitative research. This logic here is grounded in approaching a range of empirical material – interview data, letters, diaries, memoirs, autobiographical narratives, visual images – as documents from which to read the intimate connections between the 'individual' and 'social.' Amongst anthropologists 'Autoethnography' as a methodology makes similar arguments about the emplacement of the personal in the social and vice versa. Strong proponents of this method of mapping personal experiences onto a broader sociopolitical canvass, Elllis, Adams and Bochner explain it thus:

Autoethnography is an approach to research and writing that seeks to describe and systematically analyze (*graphy*) personal experience (*auto*) in order to understand cultural experience (*ethno*) (ELLIS, 2004; HOLMAN JONES, 2005). This approach challenges canonical ways of doing research and representing others (SPRY, 2001) and treats research as a political, socially-just and socially-conscious act (ADAMS & HOLMAN JONES, 2008). A researcher uses tenets of *autobiography* and *ethnography* to *do* and *write* autoethnography.[20]

[19] Kosambi 2000, 2.
[20] Ellis, carolyn, Tony E Adams and Arthus P Bochner, 'Autoethnography: An Overview' Volume, 12, No 1, January 2011 (http://www.qualitative-research.net/index.php/fqs/article/view/1589/3095, accessed 10 May 2015).

She would likely find support from radical feminists of later years in her privileging of individual experiences, which she uses this rather effectively in her approach to social reform. Without using this contemporary language, Ramabai invokes her own life narrative (and experiences and stories of those around her) to represent persuasively the situation of Hindu women in India and enlist support for her specific social reform projects. A scrutiny of her autobiographical narratives reveals her to be intensely self-reflexive. In her memoirs she dissected assiduously her personal experiences and the life events that produced the person she became but also in the process, isolating the role of various structural factors (social norms about gender, religious orthodoxy and dogma, denial of educational opportunities to women). Ramabai's views on education, child marriage and treatment of widows were mediated by her biographical experiences – her own as well as that of her mother, Lakshmibai's – having seen intimately the value of education for the cultivation of the mind and for the capacity for independent thought. Several of her writings – *An Autobiographical Account (September 1883), A Testimony of our Inexhaustible Treasure (1907) and Famine Experiences (1897)* – *communicate* details of her personal and familial life as well as detailed narratives of her religious conversion. It was precisely in the *examplification of her life* that broader insights about society emerge:

But for Ramabai, *social analysis was a precondition to – and a means of – reform*. It was therefore a way station on the path to her fulfillment as an activist whose life proceeded directly from her religious devotion . . . But at the same time, a social science utterly particular is equally problematic, denying as it does the validity of others' experience. The roots of humane social science thus lie in translation, in making the systematic leap from one social standpoint to another. Of this leap Pandita Ramabai Sarasvati provides a profound example, both in her writing and in her life.[21] (emphasis mine)

---

[21] Celarent 2011.

B. Celarent's 2011 review essay specifies the difference between Ramabai's social reformist project and the late-nineteenth-century social science agendas of theoretical knowledge production. She writes:

> Pandita Ramabai produced her view of America not because she was *theoretically interested in improving a body of common knowledge called social science, but because she had an ambition to change the place of women in India.* She thus takes a place beside the many reformers of the late 19th century whose work laid the foundations of sociology in the United States (foundations quite different from the historical and positivistic foundations in Germany and France, respectively). Most of that reform work disappeared from the sociological canon, partly for want of method, but mostly for want of 'theoretical concerns,' the trope by which an emerging academic discipline came to define itself (emphasis mine).[22]

To some extent, the marginalization of social reform agendas from the core discourse on sociological theory *has* produced the false and untenable dichotomy of 'pure' and 'applied' research. Celarent argues that 'analysis' and 'reform' were not alienated for Ramabai but integrally related. In this her position was aligned with those of the classical sociological theorists as well as that of Nightingale, Martineau and Sarkar – presented in this volume. In fact, echoes of Durkheim's and Martineau's theorizing reverberate strongly in Ramabai's stance. Celarent's idea of the production of 'haphazard' social science grounds the reading of Ramabai offered here. Celarent writes, 'So we often find *social science texts issuing haphazardly from lives* whose logic quickly drove their protagonists elsewhere. *This haphazard social science is all the more important for its commitment.* A social science from nowhere lacks humanity: no human lives in nowhere.'[23] Ramabai's works and writings can no doubt be criticized on various grounds, but they cannot be accused of lacking humanity and commitment.

---

[22] Celarent 2011, 360.
[23] Celarent 2011, 360.

Ramabai: The Cry of Indian Women[24]

A scrutiny of Ramabai's work reveals her engagement with two related substantive domains: first, with the 'world and experiences of high caste Hindu women' (girls, child brides and widows) and the second, with the world of religious orthodoxy, dogmas and authority. The first translated concretely into Ramabai's social reformist efforts: as Grewal notes 'Ramabai's discourse of reform takes as its subject the high-caste Hindu woman.'[25] The second emanated from her own remarkable religious trajectory, in the move from a Hindu identity to her baptism as a Christian. Her critique of religious structures of authority was not confined to Hindu orthodoxy. Despite her embrace of Christianity and her subsequent interpretation of her own life through predominantly Christian frames, Ramabai was as critical of the racism, patriarchy, authoritarianism and conservatism of the Anglican Church. Her later work is focussed on questions of religious identity, spirituality, with explicit comparisons between her religion of birth and her chosen religion. These comparative statements on Hinduism and Christianity make interesting reading, but Ramabai's judgement (especially about Hinduism) is mediated by her conversion experience. Ramabai's correspondence with Sister Geraldine (her spiritual mentor in London) reveals that she felt restricted, controlled and micro-managed during her time in England. A strong message she received was that being properly Christian meant 'submission to authority,' something that was jarring to her given her rather unorthodox personal and familial background, not to mention that in India she had pushed boundaries and broken with custom and convention. With due respect to her English friends, benefactors and guardians, Ramabai expressed her desire for freedom and independence, citing divine inspiration for her questioning spirit and its legitimacy.[26]

Here only the first of Ramabai's thematic interests can be elaborated in its complexity. Kosambi speaks of the 'evolution' of Ramabai's

---

[24] Ramabai, 'The Cry of Indian Women,' June 1883.

[25] Grewal, *Home and Harem, 1996*, 185.

[26] Bapat, *Pandita Ramabai*, 1995.

'feminist consciousness' over time.[27] Shades of her feminism are evident in the three of her earliest writings, *The Cry, SDN* and *HCHW* where different nuances of her feminist thinking are revealed. Kosambi articulates the continuing value and relevance of 'Ramabai's troping of oppressed Indian womanhood' which she says

> started with 'The Cry of Indian Woman' and continued through *The High Caste Hindu Woman* and beyond has still not lost its power because of her revolutionary, objective critique of Hindu doctrines and customs (to the extent that they can be homogenized) with a concrete programme to redress women's oppression resonate well with most Indian feminists today. If, lacking today's language of feminism, she couched her analysis in different terms, she still succeeded in 'naming' the problem.

Ramabai's emergent feminist consciousness lies in this very 'naming' of the 'problem' and is important to highlight. Her *conceptualization* of Indian women's oppression and the need for redress constitute her critique of patriarchal norms given in caste, religion and convention-based gender discrimination. Ramabai's articulation of the problem is expressed in one of her earliest writings, 'The Cry of Indian Women' (1883). This is the title of a long letter that Ramabai wrote as a member of the committee of the Arya Mahila Samaj while she was in London. It was addressed to Sir Bartle Frere, the former Governor of Bombay Presidency, to bring to his attention the plight of women in India and to enlist his help in raising funds in Britain for building homes for destitutes in India. In Ramabai's words, 'the object of the letter is . . . to present you the picture of the female community of India, as to their condition' and 'to give you an idea of the life of a Hindoo woman.'[28] The picture she paints is indeed dismal, stating that 'the condition of women in India is not better than that of animals in hell.'[29] She paints a graphic picture of the abhorrence of the girl child, the practice of child marriage, the denial to girls of equal opportunities for education and the

---

[27] Kosambi 2000, 16.
[28] Ramabai, 'The Cry,' Kosambi (ed), 2000, 106.
[29] Ramabai, 'The Cry,' Kosambi (ed), 2000, 106.

ill-treatment of young widows. Hindoo[30] women are presented as crushed under the weight of centuries of conservative and backward religious, social and cultural thought. Ramabai constructs these women as 'helpless creatures' in 'distress' in imploring British intervention on moral, religious and political grounds – but eventually enlisting financial support from 'English brethren' for building institutions for widows and destitutes. In constructing women as victims and subjects with no agency, she will no doubt be criticized from postcolonial perspectives. Yet while there is clearly a deliberate polemical and strategic tone to this document, it did convey the lived realities of women's experiences. In this Ramabai also puts her finger on the pulse of Indian society – in identifying a core problematic – one that persists in contemporary Indian sociological and feminist debates.

It is striking (and disturbing) that many of her sharp observations about attitudes to the 'female community' in India penned in 1883 in this document reverberate in contemporary India. The status of Indian women remains a powerful issue in India's public domain today – and the problems of female infanticide, valuing of sons over daughters, denying educational opportunities to the girl child, challenges of a patriarchal joint family living arrangement for women – continue to be relevant. This attests to Ramabai's ability to identify a core problematic in the Indian context – the status of women – and a deep-seated one at that and reaffirms that her ideas have an endurance and applicability beyond the context in which she was writing.

Ramabai wrote *SDN* in Marathi in June 1882. The book's dedication reads, 'This small book, written by the grieving widow of Babu Bipin Behari (Das Medhavi), MA, BL, in memory of her very dear late husband, is dedicated to her countrywomen with love.' Kosambi suggests that in *SDN*, there is evidence of anti-feminist and seemingly even anti-women ideological stance' – a discovery by which she herself was 'shocked.'[31] Kosambi's reading complicates Ramabai's explicit critique

---

[30] In this letter, Ramabai switches between speaking of 'Hindoo women' and 'Indian females' – using them interchangeably.

[31] Ramabai, *SDN*, Kosambi (ed), 2000, 7.

of Hindu patriarchal norms, demonstrating that Ramabai operated with essentialist notions of gender (male and female) and class. In addition, Ramabai internalized and perpetuated the image of the oppressed Indian women in need of being rescued. In sum, *SDN* reflects Ramabai's complex and contradictory views about Hindu women. Its polemical tone is designed to achieve a kind of 'consciousness-raising'[32] amongst men and women alike. It is possible to read it as revealing early feminist sensibilities calling upon Hindu women to strive for autonomy and self-reliance. In the *Preface* to the first edition, Ramabai stated her project in the book thus:

> The present condition of women in our unfortunate country is too sad for words and will undoubtedly make every thoughtful; person's heart melt with grief. The women of this country, being totally helpless and lacking education, do not understand how to achieve their own welfare; it is therefore necessary for learned people to explain it to them and make them conduct themselves accordingly.[33]

After stating the problem thus, Ramabai proceeds to diagnose this by identifying its chief causes:

> Knowledge of morality and conduct confronting thereto are the doors to human progress, and both are lacking in womankind at present, the chief reason being their ignorance of the *shastras*.[34]

In *SDN*, Ramabai expresses her admiration for the Hindu *shastras* and indeed suggests that in order for women to lift themselves out of an ignorant and oppressed existence, they must turn to a proper under-standing of women's roles in society as elaborated in these texts. The book is divided into eight sections: The foundation, education, modesty, true religion, conduct for brides, domestic duties and the nurture and care of children. In the segment on education Ramabai lists the

---

[32] Ramabai, *SDN*, Kosambi (ed), 2000, 7.

[33] Ramabai, *SDN*, Kosambi (ed), 2000, 36.

[34] Ramabai, *SDN*, Kosambi (ed), 2000, 36.

following branches of knowledge as essential: grammar of a language, history, dharma shastras, physics, geography, political economy and moral science, medicine, culinary art and arithmetic. Her emphasis on political economy reminiscent of Martineau's maxim that all lay people should understand the processes of production, distribution and consumption in society. The sections on conduct of brides, care of children and domestic duties read like manuals of sorts about how women in their various roles as wives, mothers and homemakers should systematically and methodically care for themselves, those in their charge and the home. These are similar to the Victorian etiquette and advice manuals and household management manuals directed at middle class and upper class women. But interestingly, there are also ethnographic insights here about patterns of socialization and kinship relations in Indian households of the day. The book is directed at women themselves and implores them to achieve independence and self-reliance and reject received wisdom about the nature of womanhood:

> Some people claim that women are ignorant and weak to begin with, besides being in a state of subjection, and that they do not know what path to follow in order to achieve advancement and knowledge; what can they do in this condition. But proper consideration shows that there is no room for such doubts.[35]

Ramabai makes a case for the universal 'capacity to exercise freedom in achieving their welfare,' extending this to 'mute and ignorant creatures, such as animals and birds.'[36] Unfortunately Ramabai could not shake off the storm caused by her religious conversion. She had to deal with the controversy her Christian identity created during her lifetime. But even more important, her commitment to improving the lives of Indian women was mediated by her Christian identity. Given her connection with missionaries and her own religious conversion, her social reform narratives and discourses (which she continued to express while she was

---

[35] Ramabai, *SDN*, Kosambi (ed), 2000, 39.
[36] Ramabai, *SDN*, Kosambi (ed), 2000, 39.

abroad) were received with suspicion. Clare Midgley notes that 'many scholars consider her coming to consciousness within a religious framework.'[37] She has been labeled a 'rebel in religion'[38] and a 'religious revolutionary.'[39] But this radicalism and break with tradition carries complex resonances. Notably, Ramabai fought religious orthodoxy of all kinds – Hindu and Christian. Her conversion to Christianity was more complex and by no means a passive, unreflexive acceptance of Christian doctrine or norms and practices of the Church. For example, in response to the Bishops' view that, while in England, Ramabai should not be teaching boys, her retort was,

> I have just with great effort freed myself from the yoke of Indian priestly tribe, so I am not at present willing to place myself under another similar yoke by accepting everything which comes from the priest as authorized command of the most high.[40]

Interestingly and perhaps ironically, despite having rejected a Hindu identity in converting to Christianity – Ramabai returns to her Indian and Hindu roots to offer counter-arguments:

> It was the example set by the good Brahmos which kindled my spirit and made me able to plead the cause of women before my countrymen . . . I am not anxious to give lessons to young men, but I am anxious to do away with all kinds of prejudices which deprive a woman in India of her proper place in society.[41]

She articulated a most modern idea that 'self-improvement depends only on oneself. Every human being is free to achieve his welfare by concentrating his mind and intellect on a suitable goal. This proves that

[37] Clare Midgely, *Gender and Imperialism*, 1988, *101*.

[38] A.B. Shah, 'Pandita Ramabai: A rebel in religion,' In A.B. Shah (ed) Religion and Society in India, Bombay: Somaiya, 1981.

[39] See Bapat 1995.

[40] Ramabai in a letter to Sister Geraldine, 12 May 1885, in A.B. Shah Letters and Correspondences of Pandita Ramabai, 59.

[41] Ramabai to Sister Geraldine, A.B Shah, *The letters and correspondence*, 59.

all human beings possess the capacity to independently achieve advancement through self-reliance.'[42] She also counselled women to not 'sit idle,' 'avoid sloth,'[43] 'learn self-restraint' and 'be humble.' It is the latter that Ramabai prescribes as a 'remedy . . . for achieving the progress of our women.'[44] She implored women to apply themselves to attain virtues such as 'knowledge' and 'industry,' by delivering a clarion call:

> So, my dear sisters, let us now together exorcise the ghost of animal-like ignorance which has entered our bodies, with the help of the powerful incantation of diligence. And let us exert ourselves to attain the divine virtues which can be acquired through education. Then, we will shortly get out of our sorry state and achieve a happy state. Do you not feel shame to remain in this inferior condition?[45]
>
> How can you not make an effort to uplift yourselves when you have fallen into this dark well of ignorance? Every woman must exert herself courageously for her own advancement, relying as much as possible on herself.[46]

Ramabai's insistence that it is women themselves who must act to change their dismal circumstances is telling. This is to be achieved, for Ramabai through education, which she described as 'indestructible wealth.'[47] These narratives reveal an embedded conception of 'freedom' as the desire and capacity to achieve self-reliance, self-determination, independence and autonomy through knowledge, industry and dedication and, above all, exercising reason – reminiscent of enlightenment discourse. In offering an ultimate solution, Ramabai's narrative does posit a glorious past for Indian women in the 'good old days' when men were enlightened and did not deny women knowledge and

---

[42] Ramabai, *SDN*, Kosambi (ed), *Pandita Ramabai through Her Own Words*, 39.

[43] Ramabai's condemnation of women who are slothful, idle and avoid industry is akin to Martineau's critique of middle-class Victorian women.

[44] Ramabai, *SDN*, Kosambi (ed), 2000, 40.

[45] Ramabai, *SDN*, Kosambi (ed), 2000, 45.

[46] Ramabai, *SDN*, Kosambi (ed), 2000, 46.

[47] Ramabai, *SDN*, Kosambi (ed), 2000, 47.

acquisition of desirable qualities and virtues. Ramabai explained why women's 'ancestors . . . were so brilliant':

> The reason was that in their time nobody thought of women as servants. They imparted knowledge to women, and inculcated in them qualities such as brilliance, (etc). They did not behave licentiously and in a self-willed manner contrary to the interests of women. *They protected the rights of the women.* Therefore women acquired virtues, lived in contentment, and were happy like queens, even (while) in poverty . . . Now, if the people of our country want to restore this old state of affairs, they should give up their misguided selfishness, and improve the fundamentals. They should try to inculcate virtues in women and should not deprive them of *their just rights.*[48] (emphasis mine)

Ramabai's invocation of women's 'just rights' (albeit, in translation) and the need to protect them are quite striking. It is possible to abstract from *SDN*, a theory for gender rights and gender justice, which are premised on the recognition of women's subjection and oppression. Ramabai's *HCHW* in many ways moves these ideas towards fruition. Ramabai's *HCHW* is probably the most well known and popular of her writings in India and internationally. The book saw two editions in Ramabai's lifetime. She herself noted in the *Preface* to the second edition the success of the book in its public reception and discussion in the media. Ramabai writes, 'This indicated that in spite of its many faults, the book also contains useful portions. I think this has made my efforts worthwhile. In view of these useful portions, the Hon'ble Director [of Education] bought 500 copies of the first edition and the rest were bought by the general public. Therefore this second edition has been published, in which many of the faults of the wording and structure have been removed.'[49] The book was written while she was in England. It helped to pay part of her passage to the USA, where her reputation was built on the widespread publicity of the book and the message it carried. It seems to have captured the imagination of the American public, especially in

---

[48] Ramabai, *SDN*, Kosambi (ed), 2000, 92.
[49] Kosambi 2003, 37–8.

Christian and missionary circles and had the effect of making visible the plight of the high caste Hindu woman, as articulated in Ramabai's narrative. The latter culminated not only in intense expressions of admiration for the courageous heroine – the now Christian Ramabai – but also generated sympathy for her cause which translated into various kinds of support (including financial) for alleviating women's condition back in India. It sold 10,000 copies and did much to promote and raise public consciousness about her mission and agenda, particularly outside India.

Sociologically too, this book is salient. Scholars have argued that on the basis of this text, Ramabai should be considered the first sociologist of kinship and family in India.[50] The book takes the reader through the various crucial moments in the life of a high caste Hindu woman – from childhood to married life to widowhood, with a view to outlining their place and status in society. Here, Manu's Code of Laws – the text and its author – are both filtered through Ramabai's feminist lens and found to be limited. She is unforgiving in her critique of Manu's outlined social codes for women and his pejorative and disrespectful characterization of women and their 'flaws.' Using straightforward, direct (almost simplistic) language Ramabai communicated graphically the everyday life of a Hindu girl/woman in India. She reflected on the consequences, the social roles, duties and sanctions against women for men, families and society in general. The book is descriptive and empirical but also analytical in documenting the various discriminations and oppressions faced by high caste Hindu women in their daily lives as well as highlighting their primary cause in being sanctioned by Hindu texts. Kosambi and Shah make a strong case for reading her as a pioneering figure who directed scrutiny and analysis to the domain of kinship and family in Hindu society. For instance, in *HCHW*, she questioned the ascription of women's roles exclusively through marriage and the institution of the family and their confinement to the domestic domain.

---

[50] Meera Kosambi, 'Women, Emancipation and Equality: Pandita Ramabai's Contribution to Women's Cause.' *Economic and Political Weekly* 23 (44), (1988), Shah, *The letters and correspondence*, 1977.

She encouraged women's move into the public domain, applauded their greater political participation and worked to raise women's self-awareness about these issues.

Scholars have identified a strongly feminist stance in such thinking, which challenged patriarchy and discrimination of women, calling for their emancipation and equal treatment. The feminist tone of her writings in the critique of Hindu orthodoxy and patriarchal structures therein together with that of British colonialists is impossible to miss. Yet, Indian feminists have not received her enthusiastically, as a pioneering radical thinker who challenged stereotypes of Indian women, discrimination and oppression. While Bapat notes her radicalism and revolutionary tenor in religious matters, he declares that she is 'certainly not a feminist.'[51] Celarent suggests one possible explanation for this:

> But all the same, it is an audience of women and, more particularly, reform-minded women that Ramabai takes for granted. Women's experience is the touchstone of her writing, and she is, for Indian women at least, the figure who first systematized the feminist case against 'traditional' Hindu institutions. What made her difficult for later feminists to swallow was her explicit Christian commitment, which increased with time and which, despite her own efforts to contain it, would at times become overbearingly evangelical.[52]

Grewal observes that in addressing the various forms of oppression faced by Hindu women, Ramabai had no choice but to participate in the larger colonial discourse on women in India and thus inevitably reproduced the Hindu woman as the site of colonial, missionary civilizing projects as well as the nationalist reformist agenda. Grewal adds rightly that Ramabai as 'almost the greatest champion of women's struggles in nineteenth century India, which may be seen as the early beginnings of feminism, reveals that there were indeed no neutral spaces.'[53]

[51] Bapat, *Pandita Ramabai: Faith and Reason*, 1995.
[52] Celarent, *The High Caste Hindu Woman*, 357.
[53] Grewal, *Home and Harem, 1996*, 179-180.

The final chapter of *HCHW* is entitled 'How the condition of women tells upon society' – a theme that carries huge sociological significance and connects Ramabai to other social thinkers who have made a similar observation. A good, close at hand example is Harriet Martineau whose arguments are based on her observations about the status of women in America. What is particularly striking here is, Ramabai's insight that women's status (and their treatment by society) is an index of the broader structural ethos. She argued that a society cannot progress until it acknowledged the unjust and inhumane treatment doled out to the most vulnerable and oppressed members of society, including women. She also made a powerful statement in the text about how the 'degradation of women' affected not just women but also men, since their existence is mutually interdependent and shaped the future of that society. According to Kosambi there is, in her work, a 'causal connection between the condition of women and the state of the nation.'[54] Ramabai herself declared:

> Those who have done their best to keep women in a state of complete dependence and ignorance, vehemently deny that this has anything to do with the present degradation of the nation.[55]
>
> The seclusion, complete dependence and the absolute ignorance forced upon the mothers of our nation have been gradually and fatally telling upon the mental and physical health of the men, and in these last times they have borne the poisonous fruit that will compel the Hindu nation to die a miserable and prolonged death if a timely remedy is not taken to them.[56]

Ramabai returned to this theme in her observation of American society in theorizing relations between men and women. Notwithstanding the assumptions she made about women being weaker by nature, she suggested an almost natural propensity for the physically powerful to

[54] Kosambi, *Women, Emancipation and Equality* . . . , 43.

[55] Ramabai, *HCHW*, 1887,

[56] Ramabai, *HCHW*, 1887, 98.

also exercise political domination. She made a powerful argument that according respect to less robust and vulnerable groups in society is a sign of moral victory:

> How true is the claim of many Western scholars that a civilization should be judged by the conditions of its women! Women are inherently physically weaker than men, and possess innate powers of endurance; men therefore find it very easy to wrest their natural rights and reduce them to a state that suits the men. But, from a moral point of view, physical might is not real strength, nor is it a sign of nobility of character to deprive the weak of their rights . . . [A]s men gain wisdom and progress further, they begin to disregard women's lack of strength to honor their good qualities, and elevate them to a high state. Their low opinion of women and of other such matters undergoes a change and gives way to respect. *Thus, one can accurately assess a country's progress from the condition of its women*[57] (emphasis mine).

The final appeal that Ramabai made to her audience by narrating the 'sad story of my countrywomen,'[58] comes to rest on her judgement that, 'We, the women of India, are hungering and thirsting for knowledge; only education under God's grace, can give us the needful strength to rise up from our degraded condition.' It is timely now to turn to Ramabai's account of America, where she saw women as emancipated and equal members of society, in large measure through educational reform.

Ramabai's Comparative Sociological Insights

Kosambi describes Ramabai's *The People's of the United States* (TPUS), as a 'critical ethnography of American society.'[59] The text was conceived while Ramabai was still in the USA, observing at close range different

---

[57] Ramabai, *TPUS*, 1889, 169.

[58] Ramabai, *HCHW*, 1889, 98–107.

[59] Kosambi 2003.

facets of life therein. But the book was published after she returned to India, only to be translated into English more than a century after its first publication. Crafted for an Indian audience, the text carried chapters on the system of government, social and domestic conditions, spheres of education, commerce and industry, politics and religion as well as the status of women in American society. Kosambi's *Introduction* to the English translation of the Marathi original is accurately entitled 'Returning the American Gaze: Situating Pandita Ramabai's American Encounter.' It is an atypical narrative that simultaneously achieves several reversals: a post-Orientalist perspective through an Indian scrutinizing American culture; the emergence of a female and feminist gaze upon the Occident (*ibid.*). It stands out as a rare commentary (by a colonized subject, a woman with feminist leanings) on a 'Western' society in the nineteenth century.[60] Interest in America during these years was of course intense in Europe as well as non-Europe. The French aristocrat and scholar, Alexis de Tocqueville and the British social thinker, Harriet Martineau were prominent observers of American life in the early decades of the nineteenth century. Ramabai's narrative conveyed details of American sociopolitical, cultural and religious landscape more than six decades later.

Ramabai noted the problems of constructing an accurate account of society based on travel narratives alone. She highlighted the problems of perspective and the impossibility of producing objective accounts. A productive comparison here is with the methodological principles articulated in Martineau's manual on the need to avoid prejudicial readings in observing strange, unfamiliar cultures. The following statements from *TPUS* confirm these parallels:

> It is impossible for a person to see all the sides of an object while sketching it; the same applies to the description of the social conditions in a country. A single person is not able to see all aspects of a society; therefore one person's opinion of it cannot be assumed to be infallible.[61]

---

[60] Kosambi, *Pandita Ramabai Through Her Own Words*, 2002a.

[61] Ramabai, *TPUS*, 1889, 95.

Some English and American people have traveled in India and written descriptions of our customs and manners and social conditions. A perusal of these clearly shows that a foreigner sees the people of the country he visits in a very different light from how the inhabitants see themselves. Therefore, I have refrained from presenting any firm and final conclusion that such-and-such is the nature of American society and that it has only these many types. Instead, I intend to describe how they appeared to me. This is the objective of this chapter and of the book as a whole.[62]

Substantively, its overtly comparative perspective maps societal forms in England, India and the USA, mediated by Ramabai's first-hand, direct experience of these societies. It is also a layered text which carries both Ramabai's admiration as well as her critique of American social and political life. It was impossible for her to deny slavery as well as discriminatory treatment of African Americans. She had to admit that

racial discrimination and prejudice, which are most inimical to all progress and civility, are not altogether absent in this country.[63]

But assuming a progressive stance, she proceeded almost immediately to note in a laudatory and optimistic tone that:

Not a single right which is available to the White citizen of the United States is now denied to the Black; and there are favorable signs that the obstacles to social intercourse between the Black and White people which exists today will soon disappear.[64]

But her positive assessment of American society is somewhat idealistic and polemical; she only reluctantly mentioned its inherent problems, such as slavery, racism and the non-political participation of women[65]:

[62] Ramabai, *TPUS*, 1889, 95.
[63] Ramabai, *TPUS*, 1889, 114.
[64] Ramabai, *TPUS*, 1889, 115.
[65] Kosambi, *Returning the American Gaze*, 2003.

The throne of the Goddess of Liberty, and the home of knowledge and progress . . . is the United States. It is no wonder that the sight of this land also fills the heart of a proud but enslaved person with joy, allows him to forget his sorry state for a brief while and be immersed in the heavenly happiness of freedom; and makes him earnestly wish that all the people in all the countries of the world would acquire such a system of government, such liberty, equality and fraternity.[66]

But above all Ramabai focused on the 'public spiritedness' of political institutions and equality she observed in the USA. She stated in glowing terms:

This vast country has overcome all kinds of obstacles and calamities in such a short time, and become more advanced and prosperous than all other countries on earth, on the strength of a system of government whose greatness is indescribable! The creator of this system of government, the source of all happiness and the real force of humankind, is Liberty, whose statue stands in the New York Harbour – the Delhi Gate of the United States and in such a short time. – and captures the minds of the whole world by her serene, pure brilliance.[67]

Her approach is to utilize these observations to reflect on forms of inequality in Indian society under British colonial rule and contemplate possibilities for eliminating them. Ramabai openly admired the anti-colonial ideology, liberal democratic principles and the equality of gender relations she found in the USA. This is in stark contrast to her anti-British sentiments, negative appraisal of the style of governance, the rigid hierarchical ordering of society and the ideology of colonialism in England.[68] Celarent argues that Ramabai accepted Western arguments for progress and change but was ambivalence about colonialism:

---

[66] Ramabai, *TPUS*, 1889, 93.
[67] Ramabai, *TPUS*, 1889, 93.
[68] Kosambi, *Returning the American Gaze*, 2003.

Thus Ramabai had a theory of decline. Yet at the same time, she accepted the 19th-century West's profound belief in progress, an acceptance which is evident not only in her accounts of American trade, industry, and agriculture, but also in her belief that most social problems can be overcome by sufficient education and by an end to ignorance and mutual distrust.[69]

This book would currently hold a different resonance in the context of post-colonial, post-orientalist and post-modernist debates and discourses that clearly could not have dictated Ramabai's depiction of American society. Within the context of this volume, reading Ramabai and Martineau comparatively reveals convergences in their life experiences and connections in their ideas. Further it is intriguing that Ramabai had read Martineau's text based on her American travels and even cites her in *TPUS*:

> Some months ago I chanced to see the book *Society in America*, written by the famous and scholarly Englishwoman Harriet Martineau. After visiting America in 1840[70] and observing the society here, she wrote the book upon her return home.

The accounts of these two women observers of American life were separated by more than half a century. In chapter 'Pandita Ramabai Saraswati' of *TPUS*, Ramabai offered, in summary, Martineau's views on the 'condition of native women,' which differed dramatically from her own assessment:

> They (the women in this country) receive no higher education at all, moreover, all avenues for acquiring it are blocked for them. The highest reach of their education consists of singing, playing musical instruments, a little reading and writing, and needlework. They enjoy no social or political freedom. Should they suffer the misfortune of widowhood or poverty, they have no recourse but to undertake work like sewing,

---

[69] Celarent, HCHW, 2011.

[70] Ramabai is mistaken about the date of Martineau's visit to the USA.

cooking, domestic service, or similar lowly work; or to marry or remarry against their will. The laws of the country take no cognizance of women's existence at all. Women are mere prisoners of men, like slaves. There is no exception to this is political matters in the eyes of the law, only in social life might there be an exception, though a very rare one.[71]

Ramabai acknowledged that this described the 'pitiable and dreadful plight of native women about fifty years ago'[72] but that 'courage, powers of endurance and unceasing effort which enabled these women to lift themselves out of this condition.'[73] Essentially, Ramabai presented Martineau's verdict on the status of American women as being of historical interest. She lists the milestones in the status of American women at the end of the nineteenth century: they had been emancipated in being granted access to higher education, the right to work to and organize themselves politically. Ramabai's account was more aligned with Tocqueville positive pronouncements (also made for America in the 1830s) about the status of women in America.

Concluding Remarks

In 1919, the British Government, on behalf of Queen Victoria, honoured Pandita Ramabai Saraswati with the *Kaiser-i-Hind*[74] medal for community service. In 1922, the Episcopal Church (USA) declared 5 April as a 'feast day in its religious calendar, a day which honours Pandita Mary Ramabai, described as a 'Prophetic witness and Evangelist in India.'[75] In 1932, the Wilson College of Mumbai

---

[71] Ramabai, *TPUS*, 1889, *167*.

[72] Ramabai, *TPUS*, 1889, 168.

[73] Ramabai, *TPUS*, 189, 168.

[74] 'The Kaiser-i-Hind Medal for Public service in India' was a 'decoration' awarded by the British Monarch between 1900 and 1947 (it ceased to exist in 1947) to 'any person without distinction of race, occupation, position, or sex... who shall have distinguished himself (or herself) by important and useful service in the advancement of the public interest in India.' (*The London Gazette*, 11 May 1990, 2996).

[75] http://satucket.com/lectionary/Alpha_list.htm (accessed 12 August 2015).

established a girls' hostel and named it 'Pandita Ramabai Hostel.'[76]
While complimentary narratives that mark Pandita Ramabai Saraswati
as the 'first Indian woman' to address the historic 1899 session of the
Indian National Congress[77] can be found, accounts that counter them
also abound.[78] In the post-1947 period, there are limited instances of
state-led efforts to canonize Ramabai in India. But some examples do
exist. On the centenary of her birth in 1858, the 'Pandita Ramabai
Centenary Celebrations Committee, Bombay planned to raise a fund of
one lakh rupees for the publication of a memorial volume in aid of
destitutes and scholarships.'[79] In 1964, her 'admirers' presented a portrait of her to the University of Poona, imploring those 'who cherish the
Pandita's memory to contribute to the Portrait Fund.'[80] On 26 October
1989, the Department of Post India issued a commemorative stamp in
her honour (see Fig. 2). Soon after, the Government of India named her
the 'Woman of the Millennium' in recognition of her contributions to
the advancement of Indian women.

Ramabai was a prominent public and international figure in her
lifetime. She has been described as a woman ahead of her times, living
in an age that was not ready to accept her radicalism and critique of
society – both Indian and British – in her overt confrontation of Hindu
orthodoxy, patriarchy and British imperialism. The profile presented
here reveals Ramabai as a complex and multidimensional figure. She has
most often been described in the literature as a social reformer, educa-
tionist, feminist and an activist. Despite the large body of secondary
writings about Ramabai, she is typically seen as having worked for

---

[76] The hostel was dedicated to the memory of Ramabai and made possible by a financial 'gift' from
the American Ramabai Association to Wilson College. The association had 'held certain invested
funds in Bombay, the interest of which was used for the maintenance of work more or less on the
lines that the Pandita undertook.' (*The Times of India*, 5 February 1932, 15).

[77] Tarabai Sathe, *The Times of India* (2 September 1964), 8.

[78] K.S.Abhayankar offers the corrective that although Ramabai was one of nine to ten lady
delegates attending the 1899 Indian National Congress session, she in fact addressed a session
of the 'National Social Conference' (condemning the disfigurement of child widows), which was
held alongside the INC session (*The Times of India*, September 1964, 6).

[79] *The Times of India* (17 April 1958), 3.

[80] Tarabai Sathe, *The Times of India* (2 September 1964), 8.

women's education and widow remarriage. There is now an increasingly visibility of her ideas in other spheres. Some even consider her a pioneering feminist thinker.

Returning to the classroom where our interest in Martineau and Ramabai was first triggered, there is tremendous potential in bringing together comparatively say the three narratives of Tocqueville, Martineau and Ramabai – about social and political life in nineteenth-century America. Furthermore, it would be provocative and productive to bring together Ramabai and Martineau in conversation – two women social thinkers separated temporally and culturally, but with many converging ideas. In many ways, there are parallels between Ramabai and Florence Nightingale. Given their reputation and recognizability, neither could be justifiably defined as a 'missing person' in Lynn McDonald's terms. The continued presentation of Nightingale as 'the lady with the lamp' and Ramabai as a Christian convert is problematic in selectively emphasizing specific aspects of their work at the expense of obscuring their other contributions. In making a case for viewing her as an independent social thinker, it has been crucial to abstract her intellectual thought from her writings and her reformist work. Her efforts were focused and committed to particular social and political agendas relating to improving lives of Indian women. Her activism was daring and effective and grounded in a body of social and political thought. Neither was she just an arm chair critic. She tried to translate into concrete terms her condemnation of outdated and non-progressive practices of the treatment of Indian women, by initiating relevant structural changes.

References

Bannerji, Himani. "'Projects of Hegemony: Towards a Critique of Subaltern Studies" "Resolution of the Women's Question."'. *Economic and Political Weekly* 35 (11) (2000): 902–920.

Bapat, Ram. 'Pandita Ramabai: Faith and Reason in the Shadow of the East and West.'. In *Representing Hinduism: The Construction of Religious Traditions and National Identity*, edited by Vasudha Dalmia and Heinrich von Stietencron, 224–252. New Delhi; Thousand Oaks, CA: Sage Publications, 1995.

Blumhofer, Edith. 'Consuming Fire: Pandita Ramabai and the Global Pentecostal Impulse.' Chapter 9. In *Interpreting Contemporary Christianity: Global Processes and Local Identities*, edited by Ogbu U. Kalu and Alaine Low, Grand Rapids, Mich.: William B. Eerdmans Pub. Co, 2008.

Butler, Clementina. *Pandita Ramabai Sarasvati: Pioneer in the Movement for the Education of the Child-Widow of India*. New York: Fleming H. Revell Company, 1922.

Case, Jay Riley. *An Unpredictable Gospel*. New York: Oxford University Press, 2012.

Celarent, Barbara. 'Book review of Pandita Ramabai Sarasvati's The High Caste Hindu Woman by; Pandita Ramabai's America: Conditions of Life in the United States (United Stateschi Lokasthiti ani Pravasvritta)', edited by Pandita Ramabai Sarasvati, Kshitija Gomez, Philip C. Engblom, and Robert E. Frykenberg, *American Journal of Sociology* 117 (1) (2011): 353–360.

Chakravarti, Uma. Review Literary Trust. "'The Myth of 'Patriots' and 'Traitors': Pandita Ramabai, Brahmanical Patriarchy and Militant Hindu Nationalism". In *Embodied Violence: Communalising Women's Sexuality in South Asia*, edited by Kumari Jayawardena and Malathi De Alwis, 190–239. London: Zed Books, 1996.

Chakravarti, Uma. *Rewriting History: The Life and Times of Pandita Ramabai*. New Delhi: Kali for Women in association with the Book Review Literary Trust, 1998.

Chakravarti, Uma. "Wifehood, Widowhood, and Adultery: Female Sexuality, Surveillance, and the State in Eighteenth-Century Maharashtra". In *Of Property and Propriety: The Role of Gender and Class in Imperialism and Nationalism*, edited by Himani Bannerji, Shahrzad Mojab, and Judith Whitehead, Toronto: University of Toronto Press, 2001.

Desai, Neera and Usha Thakkar. *Women in Indian Soicety*. India: National Book Trust, 2001.

Dharwadker, Vinay. 'English in India and Indian Literature in English: The Early History, 1579–1834'. *Comparative Literature Studies* 39 (2) (2002): 93–119.

Dyer, Helen S. *Pandita Ramabai. The Story of Her Life*. London: Morgan & Scott, 1900.

Forbes, Geraldine. *Women in Modern India*. Cambridge: Cambridge University Press, 1996.

Fuller, Mary Lucia Bierce. *The Triumph of an Indian Widow: The Life of Pandita Ramabai*, 3rd edn. Havertown, Penn: American Council of the Ramabai Mukti Mission, 1939.

Ganachari, Aravind. 'Dilemma of a Christian Convert: Pandita Ramabai's Confrontation with Apologists – Hindu and Christian' Chapter 10. In *Nationalism and Social Reform in a Colonial Situation*. Delhi: Kalpaz Publications, 2005.

Grewal, Inderpal. *Home and Harem: Nation, Gender, Empire, and the Cultures of Travel*. London: Leicester University Press, 1996.

Hedlund, Roger E., Sebastian Kim, and Rajkumar Boaz Johnson. eds. *Indian & Christian: The Life and Legacy of Pandita Ramabai*. Delhi: ISPCK, 2011.

Kosambi, Meera. 'Women, Emancipation and Equality: Pandita Ramabai's Contribution toWomen's Cause.' *Economic and Political Weekly* 23 (44) (1988): 38–49.

Kosambi, Meera. 'Indian Response to Christianity, Church and Colonialism: Case of Pandita Ramabai'. *Economic and Political Weekly* 27 (43/44) (1992): 61–71. WS61-WS63+WS65-WS71.

Kosambi, Meera. *Pandita Ramabai Through Her Own Words: Selected Works*. New Delhi: Oxford University Press, 2000a.

Kosambi, Meera. 'Motherhood in the East-West Encounter: Pandita Ramabai's Negotiation of 'Daughterhood' and Motherhood.' *Feminist Review* 65 (2000b): 49–67.

Kosambi, Meera. 'Returning the American Gaze: Pandita Ramabai's "The Peoples of the United States, 1889"'. *Meridians* 2 (2) (2002): 188–212.

Kosambi, Meera. *Returning the American Gaze; Pandita Ramabai's The People of the United States*. New Delhi: Permanent Black, 2003.

MacNicol, Nicol. *Pandita Ramabai: The Story of her Life*. Calcutta: Association Press, 1926.

Macnicol, Nicol, and Vishal Mangalwadi. *What Liberates A Woman? The Story of Pandita Ramabai: A Builder of Modern India*. 1926; reprint. New Delhi: Nivedit Good Books, 1996.

McGee, Gary B. '"Latter Rain" Falling in the East: Early-Twentieth-Century Pentecostalism in India and the Debate over Speaking in Tongues.'. *Church History* 68 (3) (1999): 648–665.

Midgley, Clare. ed. *Gender and Imperialism*. New York: St. Martin's. 1998.

Robinson, Catherine A. *Tradition and Liberation: The Hindu Tradition in the Indian Women's Movement*. New York: St. Martin's Press, 1999.

Sengupta, Padmini S. *Pandita Ramabai Saraswati: Her Life and Work*. Bombay: Asia Publishing House, 1970.

Shah, A.B. ed. *The Letters and Correspondence of Pandita Ramabai*. Bombay: Maharashtra State Board for Literature and Culture, 1977.

Shah, A.B. 'Pandita Ramabai: A Rebel in Religion.' In *Religion and Society in India*, edited by A.B. Shah. Bombay: Somaiya, 1981.

Symonds, Richard. *Far Above Rubies; The Women Uncommemorated by the Church of England*. Herefordshire: Fowler Wright Books, Chapter on Ramabai and Florence Nightingale. 1993.

Symonds, Richard. "Ramabai, Pandita Mary Saraswati (1858–1922)". In *Oxford Dictionary of National Biography*. Oxford: Oxford University Press, 2004.

Tharu, Susie, and K. Lalita. eds. *Women Writing in India, 600 B.C to the Present 2 vols*. New Delhi: Oxford University Press, 1995.

Viswanathan, Gauri. 'Silencing Heresy'. Chapter 4 In *Outside the Fold: Conversion, Modernity, and Belief*. Princeton: Princeton University Press, Ramabai is discussed here with regards to Christianity 1998.

Florence Nightingale (1820–1910)

Vineeta Sinha

Introduction

Florence Nightingale was born on 12 May 1820 to Fanny and William Nightingale. They christened their younger daughter after the Italian city she was born in.[1] Nightingale was raised in the lap of luxury, in a privileged family background of social prestige and considerable financial standing. She received a classical education from her father who enthusiastically taught both his daughters history, philosophy, mathematics as well as Greek, Latin, Italian, French and German. Nightingale's interest in learning mathematics was not supported in this by her mother who felt that knowing mathematics would be useless to a married woman. Neither did she find an ally in her otherwise liberal and progressive father. It was only at the intercession of an aunt who favoured her that she was finally allowed to have tuition in mathematics. She learned arithmetic, geometry and algebra enthusiastically long before she came to nursing.

---

[1] Woodham-Smith 1950, 6.

© The Author(s) 2017
S.F. Alatas, V. Sinha, *Sociological Theory Beyond the Canon*,
DOI 10.1057/978-1-137-41134-1_10

Nursing was seen as a demeaning occupation and associated with working class women in Victorian England. Despite her family's strong objections to this career choice, Nightingale remained steadfast and embarked on a nursing career eventually. At the age of 31, in 1852, she travelled to Germany to study nursing at the Institute for Protestant Deaconesses at Kaiserswerth. Nightingale volunteered her services as a nurse during the Crimean War. In November 1854, with 38 nurses Nightingale reached the Selimiye Barracks at Scutari where she established an efficient nursing department. It is her work here that led to Nightingale being christened 'the lady with the lamp' given her habit of walking the wards at night with a lamp and attending to the wounded soldiers. Those who hail Nightingale as the heroine of the Crimean War highlight that through her concerted reforms in nursing practices she reduced the mortality efforts in Scutari considerably.[2] Nightingale, guided by miasma theory but rejecting the germ theory of disease, focused on sanitary reform by highlighting the lack of ventilation, defective sewerage system and overcrowding as causative factors.[3] Nightingale's formal association with social science and academia were limited but significant: She regularly submitted papers to the British Association for the Promotion of Social Science and she was the first woman member of the London Statistical Society.[4] Her work was directed primarily at medical reform, intended to register improvements in hospitals, nursing and sanitary conditions. Nightingale successfully established modern nursing as a secular profession: through training and education of nurses and, opening it to women of working class and middle class backgrounds and rescuing it from the stigma of a demeaning, discredited occupation and bestowed respectability.

---

[2] Stephen Paget. 'Nightingale, Florence' In Sidney Lee (ed) Dictionary *of National Biography*, *Supplement 3. London: Smith, Elder & Co, 1912.*

[3] Hugh Small, *Times Literary Supplement* (2000).

[4] Other encounters include the following: Reading a paper 'Life or death in India' at the meeting of the *National Association for the Promotion of Social Science*, in Norwich in 1873; Being appointed an honorary member of the Bengal Social Science Association (formed in 1867 and dissolved in 1878) in 1869, L. McDonald and G. Vallee, Florence Nightingale on Health in India (vol 9), 2006, 32–35.

Nightingale was not bound by existing wisdom about vocations open to Victorian women. She determined her career choices autonomously although she struggled in this journey. Her call to service was triggered in her early twenties when she became 'conscious of the world of misery and despair.'[5] Despite her privileged background, Nightingale was moved to serve humanity and turned to nursing as a calling from God.[6] She remained deeply religious and her desire to serve others defined her entire life's work. She had a productive public career and was reported to be a workaholic. Nightingale suffered from various health problems throughout her life. She died in London on 13 August 1910 at the age of 90. Her family declined an offer of a burial at Westminster Abbey and she was buried in the graveyard at St. Margaret Church in Hampshire.

General Outline of Nightingale's Work

Florence Nightingale's legendary and iconic stature pervades the dominant discourse in nursing, public health and sanitary reform, given the enormity of her contributions to these fields. Lynn McDonald notes that androcentrism in the historiography of the social sciences is expressed in varied modes. This ranges from denying the very presence of women as social thinkers, theorists and methodologists to problematic acknowledgements of women's contributions to misrepresentations of their identities. The latter, in particular, deny the presence of women as producers of knowledge about society and as analysts and thinkers.[7] Nightingale has been precisely the victim of this method of misrecognition. Her inclusion in a text on sociological theory will most certainly trigger surprise. The corpus of Nightingale's work translated into concrete projects on mortality and public health, nursing reform, management of the domestic space,

---

[5] Woodham-Smith 1951, 48.
[6] Woodham-Smith 1951, 48.
[7] See (McDonald 1993, 1994, 1998), Strachey 1928a, Women Founders of the Social Sciences, Carleton University Press.

homes (for effective nursing), health promotion and preventive medicine, contagious diseases, famines, poverty alleviation and British rule in India and views on women. This chapter presents Nightingale as an astute observer of society, who was concerned with a number of social issues, including health and sanitation, status of women, poverty, unemployment and prostitution, and worked towards solving social problems of the day. It is productive to approach Nightingale as a methodologist and social reformer. Her works and endeavours were embedded in a set of ideas about society, its structure and functioning. This is evident in her causal analysis of famine and poverty, for example. Furthermore, as a methodologist she used statistics and scientific knowledge to diagnose problems in society and proposed appropriate reforms.

Nightingale has left a legacy of more than 200 books, pamphlets, reports and letters[8] even though she clearly prioritized action and results over mere words: 'You ask me why I do not write something . . . I think one's feelings waste themselves in words; they ought all to be distilled into actions and into actions which bring results.'[9] Only a small portion of her writings were published in her lifetime, and that too privately with few copies in circulation. In a short crisp early piece, William J. Bishop notes, 'at least 15,000 original letters of Florence Nightingale are known to exist and the total may be more than 20,000; but the Nightingale correspondence is likely to prove to be the most extensive collection of letters ever written by any one person. Fortunately, her handwriting is beautifully clear and bold, every letter being so well formed that there is never any doubt as to its interpretation.'[10] Bishop noted the 'overwhelming size and range'[11] of her correspondence and that 'Some of her letters extend to 40 or more pages,'[12] with Nightingale herself reporting that 'she was writing eight letters a day.'[13] Nightingale wrote

---

[8] See the following primary source 'A Selection of Letters Written by Florence Nightingale.' University of Kansas Medical Center. January 2001. http://clendening.kumc.edu/dc/fn

[9] (See NIghtingale 1911), Nightingale in a letter to a friend cited in E.T. Cook, 1913, 94.

[10] Bishop 1957, 607.

[11] Bishop 1957, 607.

[12] Bishop 1957, 607.

[13] Bishop 1957, 607.

to and received letters from a range of personalities and public figures of her time.[14]

Her ideas and thoughts are embodied in letters,[15] private papers as well as autobiographical notes, not all of which have been comprehensively analysed. Some examples include Mary Andrews' *A Lost Commander: Florence Nightingale* (1929) which reveals her private thoughts and feelings during the Crimean War and portrays Nightingale's life through her letters. E.T. Cook's detailed and oft-cited 1950 text reconstructs a narrative of her life using correspondence between Nightingale and her family and friends. Lois Monteiro's *Letters of Florence Nightingale* (1974) is an excellent primary resource for researchers providing samples of her letters as well as complete copies of three letters written by Nightingale. Lynn McDonald's efforts have offered access to Nightingale's biblical annotations, sermons, journal notes, essays and letters – a gold mine for researchers – in her ongoing project to surface the collected works of Nightingale.[16]

Nightingale also penned innumerable reports on health and sanitation in Britain and her colonies. Amongst her first writings was a pamphlet of 1851, *The institution of the Kaiserswerth on the Rhine: for the practical training of deaconess under the direction of the Rev. Pastor Fliedner, embracing the support and care of a hospital, infant and industrial schools and a female penitentiary*. In 1858 she wrote and privately published *Notes on matters affecting the health, efficiency and hospital administration of the British Army* and *Subsidiary notes as to the introduction of female nursing into military hospitals in peace and in war* (based on her experience of the Crimean War) and presented them to the Secretary of State for War. Upon her return to England, she collaborated with leading Victorian public figures and experts in this field, namely, William Farr and Edwin Chadwick. The very influential *Notes on Hospitals* appeared

---

[14] This included for example, 'Queen Victoria, the Crown Prince of Prussia. Secretaries of state and viceroys of India; the heads of the Army and the Navy; intellectuals like the great Benjamin Jowett of Balliol College, Oxford, and John Stuart Mill; and of course Sidney Herbert' (Bishop 1957, 608). See Kelly 1998.

[15] Her *Letters from Egypt: A Journey on the Nile 1849–1850* was privately published in 1854.

[16] McDonald, Lynn. *Collected Works of Florence Nightingale* Vols 1–16, Ontario, Canada: Wilfrid Laurier University Press.

in 1859 followed by *Notes on Nursing in 1860*. In 1863 she prepared the two volume *Report of the Royal Commission on the Sanitary State of the Army of India* as well as the *Sanitary Statistics of Native Colonial School and Hospitals*. Back home she directed her efforts at the poorest sector of British society by writing *Suggestions on the Subject of Providing, Training, and Organizing Nurses for the Sick Poor in Workhouse Infirmaries in 1867*. In 1871 she wrote *Introductory notes on lying-in institutions together with a proposal for organizing an institution for training midwives and midwifery nurses*.[17] These reports were long and detailed documents based on data she had painstakingly collected, analysed and generated statistics therefrom. Her reports often used numbers, percentages, charts and graphs, designed to persuade those in positions of power to enact informed laws and policies to improve the lives of individuals. Above all, Nightingale was engaged in a call to service and moved from one concrete project to another. She held that a given social order was governed by general laws and divinely given but which could nonetheless be changed through human intervention.

Nightingale's Methodology: Reform Through Statistics

Probably one of the earliest scholars to note Nightingale's attraction to statistics was E.T Cook who describes her as a 'passionate statistician.' Numerous others since Cook have argued that Nightingale was an 'accomplished statistician'[18]and a 'reverent statistician.'[19] Calabria and Macrae note that 'Florence Nightingale is best known as a woman of action: as the founder of modern nursing, a reformer in the field of public health, and a pioneer in the use of statistics.'[20] However, Cohen

[17] See Dossey (2000, 2005), Other writings of sociological value include her *Notes on Nursing for the Labouring Classes* (1861) and an essay on '*The Family*,' published in *Fraser's Magazine* (1870).
[18] Schuyler 1992, 4.
[19] Calabria and Macrae 1994 xii.
[20] Calabria and Macrae 1994, i.

notes that this competence of Nightingale is 'Less well known, because it has been neglected by her biographers' in comparison to her accomplishments in the field of medical reform and public health. He highlights 'her equally pioneering use of the new advanced techniques of statistical analysis in those battles.'[21] Calibria and Macrae opine that, although Nightingale was an empiricist unlike Comte, she did not see the need to abandon her belief either in God or in religion and sought to unify science and religion.[22]

Given her comprehensive classical education and her own sharp intellect, Nightingale critically received the writings of such luminaries as Dante, Bacon, Hegel, Kant, Comte, Mill, Newton Plato and St. John. They offered provocation and inspiration for formulating her own independent and critical thinking. The combination of religious dedication with scientific knowledge infused the spirit of reform in the nineteenth century. Schuyler observes that:

> Historians of the 19th Century wrote that it was the combined force of scientific knowledge and Idealism that enabled reformers of the time to succeed as never before. It was this combination that made Nightingale so successful. She used empirical evidence to illustrate the need for reforms and her belief in philosophical and religious ideals spurred her on to push the needed reforms into reality.[23]

The enlightenment legacy had bequeathed primacy to human reason and intellect which were deemed capable of making discoveries and using scientific principles to improve human existence. However, Nightingale distanced herself from the notion of free will and the view that no divine guidance was needed in this effort arguing that, 'She agreed with the Idealists and Positivists that God had a plan for people to use their reason to understand the social and moral laws that would lead them to perfection.'[24] In this stance she differed radically from

---

[21] Cohen 1984, 128.
[22] Calabria and Macrae 1994, ix.
[23] Schuyler 1992, 13.
[24] Schuyler 1992, 13.

Comte, Durkheim and Martineau. She saw no contradiction and incompatibility in her mutual commitment to scientific knowledge and belief in God. Indeed she was passionate about the science of statistics and expressed a passion this:

> Because of Nightingale's natural predilection for collecting and analyzing data, her interest in mathematics turned into a passion for statistics. She enjoyed reading statistical tables, particularly those dealing with nursing and public health, as most people enjoy reading novels.[25]

Scholars have noted that Nightingale was influenced by the work of Lambert-Adolph-Jacques Quetelet (1796–1874), the Belgian astronomer and natural scientist and the founder of modern social statistics.[26] Nightingale met Quetelet in 1860 during his visit to England. She was also a member of the International Statistical Congress which he founded in 1853. She had read Quetelet's text, *Physique Sociale*, admired him and considered him the founder of 'the most important science in the whole world'[27] and held that 'upon it depends the practical application of every other [science].'[28] Cohen further argues, 'To her, laws governing social phenomena, "the laws of our moral progress," were God's, laws, to be revealed by statistics.'[29] Predictably, God is not factored out of this logic but is seen to have organized the universe through a particular set of organizing principles, which she held could be discovered through scientific inquiries. 'To understand God's thoughts we must study statistics, for these are the measure of His purpose'[30] and that, 'Statistics is thus a sacred science that allows one to transcend one's narrow, individual experience and read the thoughts of God.'[31] The

---

[25] Calibria and Macrae 1994, xi.
[26] Calibria and Macrae 1994, xii; Schuyler 1992; Cohen 1984, 133.
[27] Cohen 1984, 137.
[28] Cohen 1984, 137.
[29] Cohen 1984, 137.
[30] Brian Everitt, *Chance Rules: An Informal Guide to Probability, Risk, and Statistics*, 1999, 137. See Vicinus 1996.
[31] Calibria and Macrae, 1994, xii

following narrative by Brian Everrit offers a cogent summary of Nightingale's spiritual commitment to statistics:

> Her statistics were more than a study, they were indeed her religion . . . Florence Nightingale believed – and in all the actions of her life acted upon that belief – that the administrator could only be successful if he were guided by statistical knowledge. The legislator – to say nothing of the politician – too often failed for want of this knowledge. Nay, she went further; she held that the universe – including human communities – was evolving in accordance with a divine plan; that it was man's business to endeavor to understand this plan and guide his actions in sympathy with it. But to understand God's thoughts, she held we must study statistics, for these are the measure of His purpose. Thus the study of statistics was for her a religious duty.[32]

While much has been written about the far-reaching and enduring effect of her wide-ranging medical reforms, it is less widely known that she relied predominantly on the empirical method and the science of statistics to influence legislators and policy makers to accept the recommendations she proposed in the reports she diligently and meticulously prepared. An early illustration is found in the 1000-page report she wrote to convince the Secretary of War, Lord Panmure, the need to establish a Royal Commission to investigate and reform the health administration of the British army.[33] As Calibria and Macrae note, 'In a lengthy report entitled *Notes on Matters Affecting Health, Efficiency and Hospital Administration of the British Army* (1858), she pioneered the graphical representation of statistics, illustrating with charts and diagrams how improved sanitation decreased the rate of mortality.'[34] Schuyler corroborates this view in observing that 'She used statistical data to compile reports explaining the need for each reform that she pursued. She demonstrated how mortality rates increased in institutions

---

[32] Francis Galton in *The Life, Letters and Labours of Francis Galton* (1924) by Karl Pearson, Vol. II
[33] Schuyler 1992, 5.
[34] Calibria and Macrae 1994, xi.

with unsanitary conditions. During the process of collecting data on certain hospitals, she recognized a need for uniform statistics on hospitals.'[35]

Nightingale's contributions as a methodologist can be abstracted from selections from *Notes on Nursing* (1860) and *Suggestions for Thought* (3 volumes), which she wrote in her thirties (as a young woman, considering that she lived to be 90). Like Quetelet, Nightingale assumed that human behaviour was patterned and shaped by social circumstances rather than random and haphazard, was subject to the laws of probability and could be predicted with some degree of accuracy. She expressed the confident view that, 'If we could entirely know the character and circumstances of a man...we might predict his future conduct with mathematical precision.'[36] Adhering to the principles of naturalism, she held that the social universe was governed by a set of laws which governed human will. She further believed that changing social conditions through human efforts (legislation and policies) could produce 'perfection' in individuals and improve society. Nightingale offers her interpretation of laws thus:

> Law is the continuous manifestation of God's presence – not reason for believing him absent. Great confusion arises from our using the same word law in two totally distinct senses...as the cause and the effect. It is said that to '*explain away*' everything by law is to enable us to do without God. But law is no explanation of anything; law is simply a generalization, a category of facts. Law is neither a cause, nor a reason, nor a power, nor a coercive force. It is nothing but a general formula, a statistical table. Law brings us continually back to God instead of carrying us away from him.[37]
>
> Newton's law is nothing but the statistics of gravitation, it has no power whatever.

---

[35] Schuyler 1992, 9.

[36] Calibria and MacRae 1994, xii.

[37] *Suggestions for Thought: Selections and Commentaries* (1994), edited by Michael D. Calabria and Janet A. MacRae, 41.

Let us get rid of the idea of power from law altogether. Call law tabulation of facts, expression of facts, or what you will; anything rather than suppose that it either explains or compels.[38]

In expressing these views, Nightingale stood apart from many of her contemporaries who saw no room for religion in discussions of naturalism, empiricism, positivism and the scientific method. Nightingale pioneered the development of a pie chart[39] or polar area diagram and the rose diagram, to depict visually, graphically and pictorially mortality rates, analysis of deaths in the Crimean War and in Indian famines. McDonald goes so far as to say that a 'Nightingale methodology' can be identified in her work:

Read the best information available in print, especially government reports and statistics; interview experts; if the available information is inadequate sendout your own questionnaire; test it first at one institution; consult practitioners who use the material; send out draft reports to experts for vetting before publication.[40]

The embedded methodological logic revealed the rather radical idea for the times that human behaviour and social phenomenon could be quantified, measured and anlaysed mathematically and also *predicted* and *regulated*. In this she would have found an ally in Durkheim and Martineau who shared a similar set of beliefs and methodological principles: the objectification of social phenomena, their close, systematic observation and the need for informed scientific research in order for effective human intervention. However, Nightingale demonstrated far greater faith and confidence in the power of statistical analysis to reveal the workings of different societal domains than many of her peers and possibly far more who are sceptical today. But it is critical to remember

---

[38] *Suggestions for Thought: Selections and Commentaries* (1994), edited by Michael D. Calabria and Janet A. MacRae, 41.

[39] Hamilton notes that Nightingale called this 'coxcomb,' 2015, 63.

[40] McDonald, Lynn 'Florence Nightingale as a Social Reformer.' *History Today*, 56(1): 9–15, 2006.

that, for Nightingale, statistical methods and logic were crucial in advancing a higher goal, i.e. her agenda for social reform and perfection. She was an early proponent of the view that statistics could be utilized effectively to analyse social and economic problems in and construct effective and meaningful policies and laws.

The Problematic of Gender, Family and Marriage

According to Holton, although gender was a 'central problematic'[41] for Nightingale, her views on women were complex and ambiguous, producing tensions and contradictions in her narratives. This has made it challenging to contemporary feminists to either easily claim or reject her as a 'feminist':

> Florence Nightingale has been rendered at one and the same time a symbol of women's emancipation from conventional femininity and an ideal example of true womanhood – a duality which appears paradoxical by today's standards of women's liberation.[42]

Ray Strachey is of the view that Nightingale 'had only an incomplete and easily exhausted sympathy with the organized Women's Movement.'[43] He is, but, one example from a long list who deny that Nightingale can be read as a feminist or even a precursor. Elaine Showalter notes that 'Nightingale vehemently refused to join the J S Mill's women's suffrage committee; she was notoriously critical of female ignorance, laziness, incompetence and lack of moral purpose.'[44] Cecil Woodham-Smith notes her disagreement with Martineau on the issue of women's rights thus:

---

[41] Holton 1984, 59.
[42] Holton 1984, 59.
[43] Strachey 1978, 24.
[44] Showalter 1981, 395.

She (Harriet Martineau) was a passionate supporter of the movement for 'Women's Rights', unlike Miss Nightingale who, though she did more to open new worlds to women than perhaps any other woman, was not a feminist. Miss Nightingale dedicated herself to the cause of the unfortunate, the weak, the suffering and the defenceless, and it was a matter of indifference to her whether they happened to be men or women.[45]

She counted Harriet Martineau[46] and John Stuart Mill as her acquaintances who supported her liberal reform agenda through using their own strategies and connections, even as she disagreed with them in specific areas. Her religious views differed from Martineau's and Mill's. Nightingale's politics has been demonstrated to be of a liberal variety,[47] yet she apparently did not support the call for legal, political and educational equality of men and women. Stark suggests that this 'anti-feminist' stance had more to do with her view that women's 'economic struggle was more important than suffrage'[48] and 'it will be years before you obtain the suffrage for women.'[49] In the meantime, Nightingale was dedicated to solving what she saw as more pressing problems facing women. Already in 1860, Nightingale had articulated her view on women's rights thus:

I would earnestly ask my sisters to keep clear of both the jargons now current everywhere (for they are equally jargons); of the jargon, namely, about the 'rights' of women, which urges women to do all that men do, including the medical and other professions, merely because men do it, and without regard to whether this is the best that women can do; and of

---

[45] Woodham-Smith 1951, 315–16.

[46] McDonald notes that the two women 'worked together constructively for many years' (2005, 79) but also that differences in their religious and philosophical views stalled their partnership beyond a point. Although sharing a Unitarian Christian family background, Martineau differed from Nightingale in moving from 'Unitarianism to agnosticism' (p 79) while the latter remained a committed believer even as she embraced empiricism and Science unreservedly. Also see McDonald 1996, 1998a for an elaborate discussion of the collaboration and political dynamics between Nightingale and Martineau.

[47] See Bostridge 2008; McDonald 2006.

[48] Stark 1979, 18.

[49] Stark 1979, 18.

the jargon which urges women to do nothing that men do, merely because they are women, and should be 'recalled to a sense of their duty as women,' and because 'this is women's work,' and 'that is men's,' and 'these are things which women should not do,' which is all assertion and nothing more. Surely woman should bring the best she has, whatever that is, to the work of God's world, without attending to either of these cries.[50]

Despite Mill's request she refused to join the 'National Society for Women's Suffrage' although she finally agreed to lend her name to the cause upon his continued insistence. However, looking beyond the rhetorics of her rejection of women's rights, Nightingale's understanding of liberation must be understood within the historical context of her experience and measured against the weight of the actual work she did to create alternative spheres of women's action. Questions about how one understands women's worlds and women's rights in the nineteenth century are neither new nor recent. Women of those times, like Nightingale, Jex-Blake and Martineau were in their own ways creating new societal sites for women's occupation and consequently proposing new roles for them. This requires appreciating what denial of freedom meant for women in Victorian England and how they overcame obstacles. Holton suggests that Nightingale strived to 'widen women's spheres while at the same time accepting certain constraints placed upon such a goal by given gender definitions.'[51] Looking beyond organized women's movements surfaces multiple agents and participants in the field and complicate conceptions of feminist ideology and praxis. Women thinkers featured in this volume – Harriet Martineau, Pandita Ramabai and Florence Nightingale – each in their own way chipped away at the sedimented weight of gender stereotypes and prejudices applied to women in their specific societal contexts. They conceptualized alternative ways of being women, often offering their own lives as exemplification of the need for self-determination and autonomy.

---

[50] From *Notes on Nursing* cited in McDonald, *Collected Works of Florence Nightingale*, Vol 12, 684–85.
[51] Holton 1984, 59.

The three-volume *Suggestions for Thought to the Searchers After Truth Amongst Artizans of England* was a 829-page original work. As only a few copies were privately published in 1860, it has been inaccessible to reading audiences.[52] Well into adulthood, Nightingale laboured under the weight of familial expectations and social custom, dictated ironically by her privileged background. Rather than grant her freedom of inquiry, thought and expression, her cultured middle-class background obliged her (as she and many of her female contemporaries saw it) to a life of idleness and inactivity. Her protests against domesticity and lack of ambition imposed on women are carried in an essay she wrote, entitled *Cassandra*[53] (parts of which are uncannily autobiographical), the only piece of 'fiction' Nightingale produced in the mountain of writing she left behind. *Cassandra* was written in 1852 and was reprinted in 1979 by The Feminist Press, with an introduction by Myra Stark. Interestingly, this latter reprint presents Nightingale's essay as 'Florence Nightingale's angry outcry against the forced idleness of Victorian women.' Stark describes this semi-autobiographical essay as a political document, starting with despair and frustration and ending in rebellion. Its radicalism is evident as Nightingale sounds the clarion call to women, 'Awake, ye women, all ye that sleep, awake!'[54] and rousing them to act, 'The time has come when women must do something more than the "domestic hearth," which means nursing the infants, keeping a pretty house, having a good dinner and an entertaining party.'[55] The latter is achieved by referring to her 'fictional' essay, *Cassandra*, embedded in *Suggestions*, which embodies her spiritual philosophy. In *Cassandra*, Nightingale expresses her critical views on men, women, marriage, children and the institution of the family. She articulates her frustrations with the Victorian ideal of women's role in society. She criticizes the idleness and

---

[52] Calabria and Macrae, 1994, x.

[53] Nightingale sent the draft of *Suggestions for Thought* to JS Mill which included the essay *Cassandra*. The draft made clear Nightingale's attack on the 'jargon of women's rights' and Mill in fact requested her to revise this which she did not do in the version that she sent to him a second time. See Evelyn Pugh 1982 for a fuller discussion of the exchanges between Nightingale and Mill on this issue. See Mak and Waaldijk 2009, Pugh 2002, Smith 1981, Strachey 1928b.

[54] *Cassandra*, 1979, 52.

[55] Cassandra, 1979, 52.

inactivity that were institutionalized as appropriate and legitimate for middle and upper class Victorian women, their lack of ambition and freedom of thought. Apart from being read as an early articulation of women's emancipation from social restrictions, the text carries socio-logical insights about family, marriage and gender relations. Assuming a self-reflexive, stance and drawing on her own familial experiences, she implored women to exercise their divinely given capacity for thought and action. She uses a combination of sarcasm and humour to drive home her pointed message:

> Suppose we were to see a number of men in the morning sitting around a table in the drawing room, looking at prints, doing worsted work, and reading little books, how we should laugh! Now, why is it more ridiculous for a man than for a woman to do worsted work and drive out in the carriage every day? Is man's time more valuable than a woman's Or is the difference between man and woman this: that woman has confessedly nothing to do?[56]

Nightingale wrote the first edition of *Notes on Nursing: What It Is, What It Is Not* in 1859 to explain nursing. The 136-page book eventually served as the first textbook for nurses (which was translated into many languages) although it was written specifically to instruct the self to care for others at home.[57] In *Notes on Nursing*, Nightingale implored women not to reject 'activity' and tasks which societal norms deemed 'unsuitable' for women, holding instead that 'you want to do the thing that is good, whether it is "suitable for a woman" or not. It does not make a thing good, that it is remarkable that a woman should have been able to do it. Neither does it make a thing bad, which would have been good had a man done it, that it has been done by a woman. Oh, leave these jargons, and go your way straight to God's work, in simplicity and singleness of heart.'[58] Phyllis Malpas makes

---

[56] Cassandra, 1979, 32.

[57] The book was very popular and 15,000 copies of the first edition were sold (E Pugh 1982, 121)

[58] Cited in McDonald, *Collected Works of Florence Nightingale*, Volume 12, 2009, 685.

the observation that Nightingale was founding an independent field of study, a new discipline:

> ... Florence determined that 'nursing,' a practice every woman engaged in, was not simply a matter of kindness and care, but rather a body of knowledge, an art and a science. She never lost sight of her goal that nursing should become a profession in its own right, and not a branch of medicine.[59]

However, it is also not a secret that Nightingale reinforced the image of nursing as a female/feminine space. She expressed frustration and disappointment that not more women were enthusiastic about entering a site that she had created and where they could excel, given their natural role as care givers.[60] She also objected the women's rights call for women to be allowed to do 'men's work' including entry into the medical profession. But this non-feminist stance is complicated by the rather progressive advice she offers to young women, by referring to herself in a self-deprecating mode:

> I have no peculiar gifts. And I can honestly assure any young lady, if she will but try to walk, she will soon be able to run the 'appointed course'. But then she must first learn to walk, and so when she runs she must run with patience. (Most people don't even try to walk.) But I would also say to all young ladies who are called to any particular vocation, qualify yourself for it as a man does for his work. Don't think you can undertake it otherwise.[61]

Nightingale's fictional essay *Cassandra* offers a critique of social restraints on women in Victorian England as well as the institutions of marriage and family. In this work, Nightingale – like Harriet Martineau and Jose Rizal – uses fiction as social commentary. She ponders, 'Why have women passion, intellect, moral activity – these three – and a place in

---

[59] Phyllis Malpas, 'Florence Nightingale: Appreciating Our Legacy, Envisioning Our Future.' Gastroenterology Nursing, 2006, 29(6):447–452. See Whittaker and Olesen 1967.

[60] Stark 1979, 18.

[61] Florence Nightingale, letter published in the *Englishwoman's Review* (January, 1869)

society where no one of the three can be exercised?'[62] and that 'these three have never been satisfied in a woman. In this cold and oppressive conventional atmosphere, they cannot be satisfied. To say more on this subject would be to enter into the whole history of society, of the present state of civilisation.'[63] In this analysis, she turned the analytic lens on regnant gender ideologies and institutions which have denied women opportunities for work, education and intellectual engagement. She concludes that it is 'the stimulus, the training and the time, are all three wanting to us; or, in other words, the means and inducements are not there.'[64] She rejected the view that women were limited either by nature or inherent moral failing, highlighting instead modes of thought and social structures which have produced the feebleness and dependence of women. She offered nothing short of a scathing critique of women's lack of activity, thought and ambition in this sociopolitical and intellectual milieu, except to perform dutifully the domestic roles that has been crafted for them:

> Women are never supposed to have any occupation of sufficient importance not to be interrupted, except 'suckling their fools'; and women themselves have accepted this, have written books to support it, and have trained themselves so as to consider whatever they do as not of such value to the world or to others, but that they can throw it up at the first 'claim of social life.' They have accustomed themselves to consider intellectual occupation as a merely selfish amusement, which it is their 'duty' to give up for every trifler more selfish than themselves.[65]

She paints a graphic, dismal picture of the everyday lives women lead. In enacting their given roles she says 'they sink to living from breakfast till dinner, from dinner till tea, with a little worsted work, and to looking forward to nothing but bed.'[66] She suggests that even thinking women

---

[62] Cassandra 1979, 25.

[63] Cassandra 1979, 29.

[64] Cassandra 1979, 30.

[65] Cassandra 1979, 31.

[66] Cassandra 1979, 35–36.

who would want to live their lives differently find themselves constrained by convention and custom. Speaking metaphorically and almost poetically, she argued that sustenance for the spirit and intellect is even more important than that for the material body:

> To have no food for our heads no food for our hearts, no food for our activity, is that nothing? If we have no food for the body, how do we cry out, how all the world hears of it, how all the newspapers talk of it, with a paragraph headed in great capital letters, DEATH FROM STARVATION! But suppose one were to put a paragraph in '*Times*,' Death of Thought from Starvation, or Death of Moral Activity from Starvation, how people would stare, how they would laugh and wonder! One would think we had no heads nor hearts, by the total indifference of the public towards them. Our bodies are the only things of any consequence.[67]

Nightingale documented the limited status and role of women in Victorian society and suggested a different future for them. Indeed a theory of change which identified the attendant tensions as the engine for transforming society is discernible in her writings. She declares further that it is the women themselves who have to act:

> The progressive world is necessarily divided into two classes – those who take the best of what there is and enjoy it – those who wish for something better and try to create it. Without these two classes the world would be badly off. They are the very conditions of progress, both the one and the other. Were there none who were discontented with what they have, the world would never reach anything better.[68]

In an alternative social order, she imagined women being able to exercise freedom of thought, and be self-determined and autonomous actors, expanding their horizons beyond the narrow confines of domesticity and the socially acceptable roles of wives, daughters and mothers. She displayed a keen awareness of how social institutions prescribed specific

---

[67] Cassandra 1979, 41.
[68] Cassandra 1979, 29.

social roles for men and women which had been internalized by both groups but had a more debilitating effect on women's lives, declaring the fate of women as 'Suffering, sad "female humanity!"':

> What women suffer – even physically – from the want of such work no one can tell. The accumulation of nervous energy which has had nothing to do during the day makes them feel every night, when they go to bed, as if they were going mad.[69]

Nightingale found it disturbing that women themselves internalized and normalized apathy, indifference and passivity in the acceptance of their given roles and duties. As a woman of action and intellect herself she pleads, 'Give us back our suffering, we cry to Heaven in our hearts – suffering rather than indifferentism; for out of nothing comes nothing. But out of suffering may come the cure. Better have pain than paralysis!'[70] Avoiding naturalistic and biological arguments current at the time, Nightingale assumed instead that in a primordial state, women were divinely granted capacities which have been denied by particular social structures. But in her logic, human, societal intervention could restore women to this originary state:

> Jesus Christ raised women above the condition of mere slaves, mere ministers to the passions of the man, raised them by His sympathy, to be Ministers of God. He gave them moral activity. But the Age, the World, Humanity, must give them the means to exercise this moral activity, must give them intellectual cultivation, spheres of action.[71]

It is less important to settle the debate about whether Nightingale can or should be labelled a feminist or not. If so, what kind of feminist politics did she engage in? If not, what politics prevented her from supporting J. S. Mill's project of enfranchising women and participating in organized women's movements of the time or even lending her name to this

---

[69] Cassandra 1979.
[70] Cassandra 1979, 29.
[71] Cassandra 1979, 50.

cause. Her views and actions clearly suggests that she supported social reform movements and critiqued the enforced idleness of middle-class Victorian women, a project in which she did not stand alone.[72] Nightingale was critical of the institutions of patriarchy (although she did not use the term), family and marriage. She lamented that women rejected the idea of 'equality of duties and rights' with men. They instead subordinated themselves to men's needs and work and, 'behind his destiny woman must annihilate herself, must be only his complement. A woman dedicates herself to the vocation of her husband; she fills up and performs the subordinate parts in it. But if she has any destiny, any vocation of her own, she must renounce it, in nine cases out of ten.'[73] Her own experience of intensely difficult familial relations – with her mother and sister – are clearly expressed in her interpretation of how families functioned not in the interest of the individual but in supporting a set of mores and norms. She does not use the language of affection, solidarity and mutual interdependence in her evocations of the family, pronouncing instead that:

> The family? It is too narrow a field for the development of an immortal spirit, be that spirit male or female. The family uses people, not for what they are, not for what they are intended to be, but for what it wants for – its own uses. It thinks of them not as what God has made them, but as the something which it has arranged that they shall be. This system dooms some minds to incurable infancy, others to silent misery.[74]

Her interpretation of the family is more aligned with conflict theorists than with functionalist theorists if one were to use contemporary theoretical frames for locating her ideas. The family as she saw it thwarted ambitions of individual members (men and women) subjecting and disciplining them into normativity. The institution of marriage, deemed to the most desirable aspiration for Victorian women, is not spared by Nightingale either. She deconstructed and demythologized the ideal of

---

[72] Stark 1979, 14–15.
[73] Cassandra 1979.
[74] Cassandra 1979, 37.

romance, sanctity and nobility of a marital union between a man and woman and invited the reader to 'Look round at the marriages which you know. The true marriage – that noble union, by which a man and woman become together the one perfect being – probably does not exist at present upon earth.'[75] She continues 'It is not surprising that husbands and wives seem so little part of one another. It is surprising that there is so much love as there is. For there is no food for it. What does it live upon – what nourishes it?'[76] She argues that for there to be 'real communion between husband and wife'[77] there must be friendship, intellectual camaraderie, mutual respect and discourse beyond domestic issues and children. As with her motivation for nursing reform, this too was part of an 'emancipatory project,' offering women a way out of the narrowly defined sphere of domesticity, to which they had confined themselves. Ultimately, for Nightingale the tragedy would be if women 'no longer had the strength to dream'[78] or 'are left without the food of reality or of hope'[79] but concluded that ambition alone was unproductive and inconsequential – 'out of activity may come thought, out of mere aspiration can come nothing.'[80]

On India: Colonialism, Industry and Progress

Nightingale's writings on India are varied and extensive. This interest in India engaged her energies for a good part of her active working life and she worked closely with numerous Indian collaborators. Ramanna rightly observes that Nightingale was alarmed by the health of the British army – the 'backbone 'of colonial rule – and its capacity to 'hold' India.[81] She further argues that Nightingale's equation of British notions of sanitation with civilization suggests that her campaigns for health and

---

[75] Cassandra 1979, 44.
[76] Cassandra 1979, 44.
[77] Cassandra 1979, 45.
[78] Cassandra 1979, 49.
[79] Cassandra 1979, 49.
[80] Cassandra 1979, 51.
[81] Ramanna 2002, 46.

sanitary reform in India cannot be read uncritically.[82] On the one hand Nightingale expressed humanitarian concerns about the plight of the Indians but on the other hand she also approached 'hygiene as a handmaiden of civilisation,'[83] working with the assumption that best practices from the British experience of sanitation and hygiene would also be applicable to the Indian context. A turn to Nightingale's views on colonialism is helpful in articulating her Eurocentrism and the assumed benefits of imparting lessons from a 'higher civilisation'[84] to colonized populations. Her narrative on India also offers support for reading her as a social thinker.

Nightingale's sympathetic stance towards India, her support of Indian nationalists and a free India are also evident in the efforts to introduce reforms through legislation – for the benefit of Indian populations. She had an early interest in India's health scene but focused as well on other issues like famine, poverty and death in India. The latter led her to write papers on the state of irrigation, water supply and salt taxation in India. However, Nightingale's views on India moved from a non-problematized Imperialist position where she displayed 'optimism'[85] about colonial rule to eventually one where she saw the limitations, gaps and flaws of colonial policies and their devastating effects on health and mortality of Indians. In particular the British governments mishandling and mismanagement of famines and droughts in India led her to call for 'power sharing with Indians'[86] and ultimately independence from British rule. Nightingale argued that the 'laws of political economy'

> if really discovered, are of course as immutable as the laws of nature, but at present there is scarcely any extravagance which political economy is not made to father, for example the workhouse test, which probably has made

[82] Mridula Ramanna, 'Florence Nightingale and Bombay Presidency.' Social Scientist, 30(9/10): 31–46, 2002.

[83] Raymond G. Herbert, *Florence Nightingale, Saint, Reformer or Rebel*, Florida, 1981, 170. Cited in Ramanna 2002, 45. See Ichikawa 2011.

[84] McDonald 2010, 159.

[85] McDonald 2010, 159.

[86] Jharna Gourlay, *Florence Nightingale and the Health of the Raj.* 2003.

more paupers than anything else – the theory that supply and demand will always under all circumstances, in all countries, answer to each other – which made the Orissa famine possible under our "enlightened rule".[87]

In suggesting that that these laws do not operate always in the same ways, not least under colonial rule, Nightingale articulates the vested interests of a colonial government and the disregard for the welfare of colonized populations. Nightingale's cynicism is in her 1878 piece, here evident as she makes an ethical argument for the responsibilities of a colonial government towards improving the everyday lives of the rural poor in Indian villages:

> We do not care for the people of India. This is a heavy indictment: but how else to account for the facts about to be given? Do we even care enough about their daily lives of lingering deaths from causes we could remove? We have taken their lands and their rule and their rulers into our charge for state reasons of our own.[88]

Nightingale does not hold back from a scathing critique of the colonial government, noting its hypocrisy and double standards:

> Is it not strange, that under a country boasting herself the justest in the world and the abolisher of the slave trade, a poverty, an impecuniosity, an 'impropertyness' leading to virtual slavery, should be growing up – actually the *consequence* of its own laws – which outstrips in miserable results, because it enslaves and renders destitute a land-possessing peasantry (in southern and western India) anything except the worst slave *trades*? (emphasis in the original)

As McDonald elaborates, Nightingale's views on the role and work of the government were complex.[89] she notes that in imploring action, Nightingale called for governments to offer solutions to the social

[87] Martineau, cited in McDonald *Florence Nightingale at First Hand*, 2010, 36.
[88] Florence Nightingale, 'The People of India' in Nineteenth Century, Aug., 1878, p.193–221.
[89] McDonald, *Florence Nightingale at First Hand*, 2010.

problems of the day, but after due assessment of the effectiveness of laws and policies:

> Above all it is governments which dispose of life. Is it not then the first, the most essential step to have a political science, to raise it, if it a science as all, into an *exact* science? . . . A government, in modifying laws, should collect with care documents to prove, at a future state, whether the results obtained have answered their expectation. Laws are made and with such precipitation that it is most frequently impossible to study their influence.[90]

In an effort to advocate grounded reforms, she highlighted the role of irrigation, adequate water supply and transportation in fighting famine and poverty in India. In seeking to account for India's poverty, Nightingale poses the problematic as a puzzle:

> . . . how is it that whole peoples, amongst the most industrious in the world, on perhaps the most fertile soils in the world, are the poorest in the world; how is it that whole peoples always in a state of semi-starvation are from time to time on the brink famine? and if not actually swept away by famine, it is by their rulers giving food, not water wholesale. Is their any fatal necessity for this? Is it not due to two or three causes, not only preventible, but which we, their rulers, having ourselves induced, either by doing or not doing, can ourselves gradually remove?[91]

The 'two or three causes' she then lists include: moneylending, water (irrigation, cheap canal communications, improved methods of agriculture, forest plantations) and land tenure. Ending poverty Nightingale argued is crucial to not just to 'material' but also 'moral' progress:

> This great essential work of the regulation of water of India is perhaps at this moment the most important question in the world, or rather not question – action. Nothing can compare with it for the material progress

---

[90] Martineau cited in McDonald, *Florence Nightingale at First Hand*, 2010, 36.

[91] Martineau, 'The People of India' (1878), L. McDonald and G. Vallee, Florence Nightingale on Health in India (vol 9), 2006, 786. See McDonald 2004.

of the people, and their moral progress is greatly dependent upon it; for, till the people are in a measure relieved from their bondage to poverty and want, they cannot attend to other things.[92]

Nightingale was sympathetic towards *ryots*, the Indian peasants, and had an interest in India's rural landscape for a variety of reasons. On the specific causes of famine and emiseration of the rural poor, Nightingale isolated the role of political and economic factors rather than natural or environmental ones, and certainly did not propose shortage of food as a casual factor. McDonald notes that Nightingale offered 'social causes'[93] of famine and called for 'interventionist strategies' including changes to irrigation policies, rather than adopt a hands-off approach, given in the regnant *laissez faire* liberalism:

> But it is that in India the loss of life by famine is the test, the type of the condition of people, a test so striking, a type so awful that, if it does not move the Government of India and the people of England to action, the case is indeed hopeless – a test and a culmination which, thank god, can exist in no other country, not even in Ireland in days gone by under our rule. It is a test, because it is not precluded that there was not food to be had in this Indian famine, if there had been money to pay for it. And the large quantities of grain poured in from the irrigated districts of Godavary, Kistna and Kaveri (Tanjore) are matters of official report.[94]
>
> Water, if we had given them water, we should not have had to be giving them bread and not only this but to have seen millions perishing for want of it. It is said that thrift must save the Indian *ryot*. This is what the Secretary of State for India says. We have heard of the horse being made to

---

[92] Martineau, 'Appendix to Life and Death in India; How to make irrigation healthy.' Included in Lynn McDonald (ed) *Florence Nightingale on Health in India (Vol 9) The Collected works of Florence Nightingale*. Waterloo, Ontario, Canada: Wilfrid Laurier University Press, 2006, 745.

[93] McDonald 2010, 167.

[94] Martineau's letters to Sir Louis Mallet, Balliol College, 12 March 1879. Included in Lynn McDonald (ed) *Florence Nightingale on Health in India (Vol 9) The Collected works of Florence Nightingale*. Waterloo, Ontario, Canada: Wilfrid Laurier University Press, 2006, 837.

live on straw a day; but I do not think that we ever heard before that the horse ought to exercise thrift and save his one straw a day.[95]

The cause of irrigation has received a frightful significance from this Bengal famine, irrigation being literally a matter of life and death. Not whether we will have irrigation or not, but how to make it healthy, and how to pay for it are our questions. Wherever water for irrigation exists, famine is effectually met.[96]

She notes 'bribery, oppression, corruption, bullying' in the supervision of public works, like water supply and irrigation. Yet even in her sharp political and sociological analysis of India's famines, Nightingale makes an argument for the benefit that irrigation would have for boosting the manufacture sector, and its added value for promoting industrial capitalism in the provision of 'cheap labour, cheap power, cheap carriage and cheap food':

Another very important point, and ultimately connected with irrigation in all ways, has to be taken up, and that is the subject of manufacturing in India. There are at this moment at least 100,000 horse water power available and made no use of in the great irrigation canals. The canals will convey the goods to and from manufactories, and the irrigation will set free millions from agricultural labour for such work. With cheap labour, cheap power, cheap carriage and cheap food, India will have the highest advantages for manufacture, for civilization and also for life and all that makes life worth having to those whom God has created higher than the brutes and only a little 'lower than the angels.'[97]

Nightingale noted that specific laws and practices which prevented capital in India from encouraging industrial and commercial growth of the economy, as it should and had elsewhere:

---

[95] Monica Bayly [ed.] As Nightingale Said, London, 1991, 43–44.

[96] Martineau, 'Appendix to Life and Death in India; How to make irrigation healthy.' Included in in Lynn McDonald (ed) *Florence Nightingale on Health in India (Vol 9) The Collected works of Florence Nightingale.* Waterloo, Ontario, Canada: Wilfrid Laurier University Press, 2006, 723.

[97] Martineau, 'Appendix to Life and Death in India; How to make irrigation healthy.' Included in in Lynn McDonald (ed) *Florence Nightingale on Health in India (Vol 9) The Collected works of Florence Nightingale.* Waterloo, Ontario, Canada: Wilfrid Laurier University Press, 2006, 745.

The tacit encouragement given to usury by our existing laws tends to transfer land to the moneylender, a transfer by which, as can be shown, the land does not gain. The landlord is still, of course, the usurer, making the hardest terms possible with his tenant, who is also his debtor, and often little better than his slave. But not only this; this same encouragement ties up the capital in usury instead of letting it flow into commerce, India's great want; In India *capital creates pauperism*, not prosperity through manufacture, trade and commerce or new industries. No one flourishes but the capitalist and *his* flourishing means power of absorbing other people's property. It means reducing to utter misery and slavery a well-to-do and hardworking peasantry. It means that the enormous interest guaranteed, one may say, by or own courts to the usurer – with no risk but that of being murdered and this but very seldom, only when the debtor gets desperate – prevents the moneylender or capitalist from doing anything useful with his money, from putting money into honest enterprise, manufacturing, commercial or even agricultural. It means that the use of riches is to make the *people poor*, to make them beggars and even to sell them for slaves (emphasis in the original).[98]

For figures like Harriet Martineau and Florence Nightingale, much like Karl Marx and Emile Durkheim, the imperialist project was a given, a 'fact.'[99] There were no 'ifs and buts' about the logic of colonialism or its value. Adopting the critical lens of Eurocentrism reveals that Nightingale's position on India, Indians and British colonial rule was complex and marked by contradictions. Like Martineau and Marx, albeit for different reasons, for the most part. Nightingale too assumed initially that colonial rule would benefit the natives. However, she was recognized the failures of colonial policies that over a period of advocated independence and self-rule, supporting the freedom efforts of the Indian National Congress.

---

[98] Martineau, 'The People of India' (1878), L. McDonald and G. Vallee, Florence Nightingale on Health in India (vol 9), 2006, 795.
[99] McDonald 2010, 159. See McDonald 2005, Williams 2008.

Concluding Remarks

Florence Nightingale is a familiar name even to contemporary audiences, possibly one of the most famous women of nineteenth-century Britain. She is hailed as the heroine of the Crimean War, idolized as the champion of the poor and the impoverished and above all a compassionate nurse. Her canonization in this image began during her lifetime and continues into the present, notwithstanding that the 'true' nature of her legacy has been mired in controversies. Even though she did not have much training in nursing she is legendary in nursing circles today. She did not have qualifications and credentials and did not hold any official position in government, but was yet able to influence those in power – administrators, bureaucrats, policy makers, legislators and governments – to effect reforms. Even Queen Victoria was reportedly impressed with her intellect and had exclaimed, 'Such a head . . . I wish we had her at the War Office.'[100]

Florence Nightingale has been claimed as a pioneering figure by generations of mathematicians, statisticians, epidemiologists, nursing professionals, public health practitioners, hospital administrators and even management gurus. With some rare exceptions, she has mostly remained invisible in social science discourses. Neither her ideas nor her work is even known amongst sociologists or demographers, let alone engaged with or used either in teaching or research efforts. Few sociologists have acknowledged her as a social thinker while her identity as a methodologist and statistician or an applied social scientist remains unknown to most practitioners. Interestingly, quantitative sociologists have not turned to Nightingale either, possibly due to the rather primitive science of statistics practiced by Nightingale, now deemed old fashioned or out of date. Feminists and women's studies scholars also receive her with scepticism both because she did not articulate the 'right' feminist politics (in her refusal to publicly support the struggle for women's rights) and due to her attraction to the scientific method.

Nightingale, whom history has immemorialized as the 'lady with the lamp,' remains 'imprisoned' in this persistently powerful image, famous

---

[100] Stark 1979, 7.

in this guise both in official historical records and in lay public imagination to the extent that even school children the world over recognize Nightingale primarily if not exclusively as a nurse. This remains true both in efforts which sanctify her as a compassionate healer and in projects that present her as a committed social reformer. This, Lynn McDonald observes, is the outcome of a particular mode of remembering women's contributions which has selectively emphasized (even *overemphasized*) specific features of Nightingale's identity and which *veil* her other achievements. Nightingale's multifarious expertise and capabilities as a hospital and public health administrator, statistician and methodologist, consultant to the War Office in London and an engaged intellectual who brought into the public arena issues relating to prostitution, poverty, nursing, army hospitals, sanitary reform, public health, Indian famines, British rule in India, workhouses, infirmaries, etc. have typically not been highlighted in mainstream discourses about her. Her persona as a nurse denies Nightingale's contributions a rightful place in the history of ideas, production of knowledge and social reformist efforts. This characterization is limited not because it is inaccurate but because it is highly selective and disregards or misrepresents her 'other' accomplishments in the face of overwhelming evidence offered in the pages of this chapter.

References

Andrews, Mary. *A Lost Commander: Florence Nightingale.* (1929).

Bishop, William J. 'Florence Nightingale's Letters'. *The American Journal of Nursing* 57 (5) (1957): 607–609.

Bornstein, David. 'The Fixed Determination of an Indomitable Will: Florence Nightingale, England: Nursing.' Chapter 4. In *How to Change the World*, ed. Bornstein, David,. New York: OUP, 2007.

Bostridge, Mark. *Florence Nightingale: The Woman and Her Legend.* London: Viking, 2008.

Boyd, Nancy. *Three Victorian Women Who Changed their World: Josephine Butler, Octavia Hill, Florence Nightingale.* Oxford: Oxford University Press, OUP, 1982.

Calabria, Michael. 'Florence Nightingale and the Libraries of the British Army'. *Libraries and Culture* 29 (4) (1994): 367–388.

Calibria, Michael and Janet Macrae. eds. *Suggestions for Thoght by Florence Nightingale.* Phil: University of Pennsylvania Press. 1994.

Cohen, Bernard. 'Florence Nightingale.' *Scientific American* 250 (3) (March 1984): 128–137.

Dossey, Barbara Montgomery. *Florence Nightingale: Mystic, Visionary, Healer.* Springhouse, PA: Springhouse Corp, 2000.

Dossey, Barbara Montgomery. *Florence Nightingale Today: Healing, Leadership, Global Action.* Silver Spring, MD: American Nurses Association, 2005.

Gourlay, Jharna. *Florence Nightingale and the Health of the Raj.* Aldershot, Hants, England; Burlington, VT: Ashgate, 2003.

Grint, Keith. 'Nursing the Media: Social Leadership in the Crimean and English Hospitals' Chapter 4. In *The Arts of Leadership*, ed. Grint. Keith,. New York: OUP, 2000.

Holton, Sandra. 'Feminine Authority and Social Order: Florence Nightingale's Conception of Nursing and Health Care'. *Social Analysis: The International Journal of Social and Cultural Practice* 15 (1984): 59–72.

Ichikawa, Chieko. 'Writing as Female National and Imperial Responsibility: Florence Nightingale's Scheme for Social and Cultural Reforms in England and India'. *Victorian Literature and Culture* 39 (1) (2011): 87–105.

Kelly, Heather. 1998. *Florence Nightingale's Autobiographical Notes: A Critical Edition of BL Add. 45844 (England).* Wilfrid Laurier University.

Mak, Geertje, and Berteke Waaldijk. 'Gender, History, and the Politics of Florence Nightingale.' In *Doing Gender in Media, Art and Culture*, eds. Rosemarie Buikema and Iris Van Der Tuin. New York: Routledge, 2009.

McDonald, Lynn. *The Early Origins of the Social Sciences.* Montreal; Buffalo: McGill-Queen's University Press, 1993.

McDonald, Lynn. *The Women Founders of the Social Sciences.* Montreal: McGill-Queen's University Press, 1996.

McDonald, Lynn. 'Classical Social Theory with the Women Founders Included'. In *Reclaiming the Sociological Classics*, ed. Charles Camic, Malden, MA: Blackwell Publishers, 1998.

McDonald, Lynn. *Women Theorists on Society and Politics.* Waterloo, On: Wilfrid Laurier University Press, 1998a.

McDonald, Lynn. ed. (to present). *Collected Works of Florence Nightingale.* Waterloo: Wilfrid Laurier University Press, 16-volume project 2001.

McDonald, Lynn. ed. *Florence Nightingale on Public Health Care.* Waterloo, On.: Wilfrid Laurier University Press, 2004.

McDonald, Lynn. 'The Nightingale-Martineau Collaboration: Differeences of Philosophy and Religion.' *Sociological Origins* 3 (2) (2005): 79–80, 120.

McDonald, Lynn. 'Florence Nightingale as a Social Reformer'. *History Today* 56 (1). http://www.historytoday.com/lynn-mcdonald/florence-nightingale-social-reformer. Retrieved 25 Sep 2013 (2006).

McDonald, Lynn. ed. *Florence Nightingale: The Crimean War*. Waterloo, ON: Wilfrid Laurier University Press, 2010.

Monteiro, Lois. *Letters of Florence Nightingale*. 1974.

Nightingale, Florence. *Notes on Matters Affecting Health, Efficiency and Hospital Administration of the British Army*. 1858.

Nightingale, Florence. *Notes on Nursing*. 1860.

Nightingale, Florence. 'Florence Nightingale's Letter of Advice to Bellevue'. *The American Journal of Nursing* 11 (5) (1911): 361–363.

Nightingale, Florence. *Cassandra: An Essay*. New York: Feminist Press, 1979.

Penner, Louise. *Victorian Medicine and Social Reform: Florence Nightingale Among the Novelists (Nineteenth Century Major Lives and Letters)*. London: Palgrave Macmillan, 2010.

Pugh, Evelyn L. 'Florence Nightingale and J.S. Mill Debate Women's Rights'. *Journal of British Studies* 21 (2) (1982): 118–138.

Pugh, Martin. *The March of the Women: A Revisionist Analysis of the Campaign for Women's Suffrage, 1866–1914*. Oxford: OUP, 2002.

Ramanna, Mridula. 'Florence Nightingale and Bombay Presidency'. *Social Scientist* 30 (9/10) (2002): 31–46.

Schuyler, Constance. In F. *Nightingale, Notes on Nursing, what it is and what it is not*, 3–17. Philadelphia: J. B. Lippincott, 1992.

Showalter, Elaine. 'Florence Nightingale's Feminist Complaint: Women, Religion, and "Suggestions for Thought"'. *Signs* 6 (3) (1981): 395–412.

Smith, Fances T. 'Florence Nightingale: Early Feminist'. *The American Journal of Nursing* 81 (5) (1981): 1020–1024.

Stark, M. *Florence Nightingale's Cassandra*. New York: Feminist Press, 1979.

Strachey, Lytton. *Eminent Victorians: Cardinal Manning, Florence Nightingale, Dr. Arnold, General Gordon*. London: Chatto & Windus, 1928a.

Strachey, Ray. *'The Cause': A Short History of the Women's Movement in Great Britain*. London: G. Bell & Sons Ltd, 1928b.

Strachey, Ray. *The Cause: A Short History of the Women's Movement in Great Britain*. London: Virago, 1978.

Vallee, Gerard. ed. *Florence Nightingale on Social Change in India*. Waterloo: Wifrid Laurier University Press, 2007.

Vicinus, Martha. '"Tactful Organising and Executive Power": Biographies of Florence Nightingale for girls.' Chapter 7. In *Telling Lives in Science: Essays on Scientific Biography*, edited by Michael Shortland and Richard Yeo. New York: CUP, 1996.

Whittaker, Elvi Waik, and Virginia L. Olesen. 'Why Florence Nightingale?' *The American Journal of Nursing* 67 (11) (1967): 2338–2341.

Williams, Keith. 'Reappraising Florence Nightingale'. *BMJ: British Medical Journal* 337 (7684) (2008): 1461–1463.

Woodham-Smith, Cecil. *Florence Nightingale, 1820–1910*. London: Constable. 1950.

Woodham Smith, Cecil *Florence Nightingale*. London: Constable, 1951.

Zaleznik, Abraham. ed. 'A Change Agent: Florence Nightingale and Medical Reform'. In *Hedgehogs and Foxes: Character, Leadership and Command in Organizations*. New York: Palgrave Macmillan, 2008.

Benoy Kumar Sarkar (1887–1949)

Vineeta Sinha

Introduction

Benoy Kumar Sarkar was born on 26 December 1887 in the district of
Malda in the-then Indian part of Bengal. At the young age of 13 he
distinguished himself by topping the entrance exam of the Calcutta
University. He was educated at the Presidency College in Calcutta,
where in 1905 he topped the undergraduate cohort with a double
honours degree in History and English, completing a Master's degree
in 1906. He had a long and illustrious career as an academic: he was
appointed lecturer at the Department of Economics of University of
Calcutta and rose the ranks to become Professor and Head of
Department. Sarkar was a prolific writer, with tremendous intellectual
output, straddling a range of social science perspectives from Economics
to Political Philosophy, History, Sociology, Literature, Demography,
Political Science and Anthropology.[1]

Apart from his solid academic credentials, he was a prominent public
figure and well-regarded in Bengali academic and intellectual circles.

---

[1] Mukherjee 1953.

© The Author(s) 2017
S.F. Alatas, V. Sinha, *Sociological Theory Beyond the Canon*,
DOI 10.1057/978-1-137-41134-1_11

Committed to nationalist, socialist and social service agendas, Sarkar was embedded in the patriotic stance of securing for India political freedom from British colonial rule. To this end, he was active in both the *Swadeshi* (self-rule) and the National Education movements in Bengal. Sarkar was instrumental in professionalizing the discipline of Political Science in India and an institution builder, establishing several cultural, political and academic institutions in Calcutta. The years 1914–1925 saw Sarkar spend considerable time outside India. He visited Egypt (1914), England, Scotland, Ireland (1914), the USA (1914–1915; 1916–1920), Hawaii (1915), Japan (1916), Korea and Manchuria (1915), China (1915–1916), Japan (1916), France (1920–1921), Germany (1921–1923; 1924–1925), Austria (1922–1923), Switzerland (1923–1924) and Italy (1924 and 1925).[2] During his long travels, he visited premier American and European tertiary institutions and engaged with scholars and intellectuals there. In Germany and Italy he acquired linguistic competence in French, German and Italian. This in addition to already having mastered English, Bengali and Hindi, a truly impressive linguistic feat. In these travels, he delivered lectures in German, French and Italian, and also published scholarly works in the same.

He doubled up as an ambassador for India (and Asia, more broadly speaking) and tried to facilitate greater understanding on both sides of the East-West divide. After his long stay abroad, Sarkar returned to India in 1925, was appointed lecturer at the Department of Economics, Calcutta University, and promoted to Professor and Head of Department in 1947. After retirement in 1948, he travelled to the USA in 1949 – a trip arranged by the Institute of International Education, New York, and the Watamull Foundation, Los Angeles. During this trip, he lectured in various American universities (including Harvard University) and research institutes and addressed business

---

[2] Benoy Kumar Sarkar, *The Positive Background of Hindu Sociology* (Allahabad, 1914 & 1921). The publisher's note in this book records that Sarkar wrote a book in Bengali on every country that he visited, for the benefit of Bengali audiences. Comprising a total of 4,500 pages or so: These reports were published in monthly and weekly journals of Calcutta during 1914–1925. They became the basis of his twelve books under the common title, *Varttaman Jagat* (*The Modern World*).

organizations and political centres on the subject of East-West relations, amongst other issues. This hectic tour took a toll on his health. In October 1949 he suffered chest pains, and passed away a month later at the Freedman's Hospital in Washington, DC.[3]

General Outline of Sarkar's Works

Sarkar's intellectual works have been carefully documented by his peers and students.[4] Satardu Sen's *Benoy Kumar Sarkar: Restoring the Nation to the World*[5] is the most recent narrative on Sarkar's ideas and theorizing. Sen says of Sarkar that he was a 'notoriously contrarian thinker' and also '"out of step" with the nationalist mainstream of contemporary India', but nonetheless Sarkar 'gives us glimpses into alternative possibilities of thinking and being.'[6] Descriptors like anti-imperialist, nationalist, internationalist, pragmatist have been applied to Sarkar. Sen argues that Sarkar's anti-imperialism and internationalism were compromised given that his 'model of nationhood and power is indebted to right-wing European ideologies and political developments.'[7] Manu Goswami's efforts have produced to-date the most nuanced proclamation on Sarkar's contribution to sociological thought.[8] Unearthing and making visible Sarkar and his scholarship are pivotal to Goswami's project of thinking about the relationship between postcolonial theory and Sociology. She marks Sarkar as 'a premature postcolonial sociologist' as well as 'the most prominent social scientist in interwar colonial India and a fierce critic of dominant nationalism.'[9]

Attempting a comprehensive account of Sarkar's scholarship is a tall order. Sarkar published predominantly in English and Bengali, but his

[3] Mukhopadhyay 1979.
[4] Bandhopadhyaya 1984, Behn 2004, Dass 1939, Dutt 1932, Ghoshal 1939, Mukherjee 1953, 1995, Mukhopadhyaya 1979.
[5] Sen 2015.
[6] Sen 2015, 1
[7] Sen 2013.
[8] Goswami 2013.
[9] Goswami 2013, 147.

works also appeared in several European languages, including German, French and Italian. He wrote 53 books in English (many of which were published in Europe, the USA, China and Japan by presses based there) and countless articles in leading Indian, American and European journals and periodicals. Some examples of the latter include: *The Calcutta Review, Modern Review* (Calcutta), *Political Science Quarterly* (New York), *American Sociological Review, American Political Science Review, International Journal of Ethics, Indian Historical Quality* and *Insurance and Finance Review*. He published in what are today considered top peer-reviewed journals in the disciplines of Economics, Political Science and Sociology in the USA. But at the time these were pioneering journals in these fields of study. Sarkar's works were not only published but also reviewed, debated and often criticized in the pages of these publications. Sarkar also reviewed works of European and Indian scholars and which appeared in academic journals[10] and periodicals, both in India and beyond.

Sarkar was writing in an intellectual context (in the closing decades of the nineteenth and opening decades of the twentieth century) alongside figures who would later be rendered the founding fathers of Sociology and whose writings (by the 1950s and 1960s) would be canonized as classical texts for the discipline. As a theorist of modernity, he advanced his characterizations of capitalism as well his response to it. He theorized the industrial revolution, both for 'Euro-America'[11] and the 'East,' but for the latter within the context of colonialist and imperialist experiences. Stolte and Fischer-Tine[12] refer to Sarkar as the 'Calcuttan *homo universalis*' and as one of '"Young Asia's" ... most important prophets in India,'[13] noting further:

This economist and sociologist from Calcutta, all but forgotten today, wielded considerable influence during his lifetime and had a significant

---

[10] Verney Lovett, *A History of the Indian Nationalist Movement* (Cornell: Cornell University, 1920), reviewed by Benoy Kumar Sarkar, In *the Political Science Quarterly*, 3 (1) (Mar 1921), 136–138.

[11] Sarkar used "Eur-America' as a synonym for 'West'.

[12] Stolte and Fischer-Tine, 2012.

[13] Stolte and Fischer-Tine, *Imagining Asia in India*, 88.

impact on intellectual life in his Bengali homeland as much as he formed the image of India in Europe and the United States.[14]

In a review of Swapan Kumar Bhattacharya's 1990 text, *Indian Sociology: The Role of Benoy Kumar Sarkar*, Andre Beteille described Sarkar as 'one of the founders of sociology in modern India' notes:

> Reading about him, one might suspect that there cannot be anything new about sociology, for most of the ideas discussed by sociologists in India today were expounded, advocated, criticized or demolished by him in the first half of the present century. Yet he is all but forgotten today. Professor Bhattacharya has renewed a service to his discipline by bringing Sarkar's work to attention again.[15]

However, in his lifetime, Sarkar and his works received tremendous public visibility (including outside India) and were popular. The weight of his contributions to social science scholarship was probably unrecognized even by his peers. While evidence of sociological and political thought can be abstracted from the huge corpus of Sarkar's writings, this task has yet to be undertaken systematically and comprehensively. The term, 'Sarkarism' was coined by his peers to refer to his unique intellectual and theoretical stance. Ghoshal holds that 'Sarkarism is out and out a doctrine of energism and progress.'[16] He highlights three constitutive elements of Sarkar's doctrine: *shaktiyoga* (energism), *charaiveti* (march on) and *digvijaya* (world-conquest) – which he sees as lending a coherence to the body of his work. The term 'Sarkarism' has also been typically invoked as a metaphor, a perspective or an orientation rather than a grand theorizing or a totalizing logic. But as has been rightly noted, unpacking 'Sarkarism' reveals the inconsistencies and contradictions of his theorizing.[17]

---

[14] Stolte and Fischer-Tine, *Imagining Asia in India*, 88.
[15] Andre Beteille, *Sociological Bulletin*, Vol 40, No ½, (1991). 205–207.
[16] Ghoshal, *Sarkarism: The Ideas*, 5.
[17] Bandyopadhyay 1979, 120–123.

A small selection of Sarkar's works is presented here to demonstrate his standing as a theorist of modernity.[18] These include sections from *The Positive Background of Hindu Sociology (PHS)*,[19] *Chinese Religion Through Hindu Eyes (CR)*,[20] The *Futurism of Young Asia (Futurism)*,[21] *Villages and Towns as Social Patterns (VT)*[22] and *Political Philosophies since 1905 (PP)*.[23] Apart from producing these key texts, Sarkar also contributed regularly to journals, magazines and newspapers, including periodicals like *Young India*[24] and *The Hindusthanee Student*. His articles and commentaries in English and Bengali appeared regularly in the pages of these publications alongside those of Annie Besant, Lajpat Rai, Charles T. Hallinan, Sarojini Naidu, amongst others. Sarkar had sustained editorial associations with the monthly journal of nationalism and world culture, the *Grihastha* (Bengali, The Householder) and the *Collegian*, the fortnightly educational journals of Calcutta.

Sarkar wrote on a variety of subjects: ideas, political institutions, economic development, education, sociology of population, social structure of town and villages and social transformations. He also translated several social science books by European authors into English and Bengali, and translated Sanskrit texts into Bengali. Given his cosmopolitan interests, Sarkar did not confine himself to 'Indian' problematics. His substantive focus was often on issues concerning 'Asia' but he also offered analyses of social, economic, cultural and political issues in European settings. In no sense did he see himself narrowly as an 'Indian social scientist,' qualified to speak exclusively to 'local' concerns. He did not shy away from engaging ideas of prominent American and

---

[18] See Bandyopadhyay, 1984, for a comprehensive list of Sarkar's corpus of writings.
[19] Sarkar 1914 & 1921.
[20] Sarkar 1916.
[21] Sarkar 1922.
[22] Sarkar, 1941.
[23] Sarkar 1941a
[24] Sarkar's essay, 'International India' was published in *Young India*, February 1918, a lecture originally delivered at Columbia University in March 1917; 'Buddhism in Hindu Culture' appeared in *Young India*, February 1919, II (2); 'Specimens of Hindu Literature' was published in *Young India*, I (10) (October 1918).

European social scientists of his time, critiquing and challenging their theories. In Ghoshal's estimation, 'Even his smallest essay embodies a constructive challenge to accepted notion.'[25]

Sarkar was not an armchair intellectual. His thinking was firmly grounded in concrete issues facing Bengali society, India and 'Asia.' His early interest in instituting a template for national education in India and pedagogical issues generally saw him establishing schools and at least nine research institutes in Calcutta, including the 'Bengali Institute of Sociology,' 'Bengali Asia Academy,' 'Bengali Dante Society' and 'Bengali Institute of American Culture.' He trained and supervised the research of innumerable post-graduate students; he emphasized here the importance of mastering knowledge from a 'world perspective' in addition to the value of learning at least one European language other than English and the mother tongue. Sarkar was fully aware that institutional and infrastructural changes were necessary before any intellectual shifts could occur in the various social science disciplines in India. He was at the forefront of instituting curriculum and disciplinary reform in tertiary institutions, introducing changes with the intention of producing a generation of Indian social scientists with a global outlook and cosmopolitanism, but also a firm awareness of Indian problematics.

Sarkar's Methodology: Hindu Positivism and the Critique of 'Orientalism'

In *PHS*, Sarkar argues for the basic universalism of the human species, despite the recognition of 'pluralities' at individual and national levels. This work is an early critique of Indological and Orientalist thinking, pre-dating by decades, Said's *Orientalism*.[26] Stolte and Fischer-Tine suggest that Sarkar produced, in effect, 'post-Orientalist knowledge of the Orient.'[27] In the very first chapter Sarkar demolishes what he deems

---

[25] Ghoshal, *Sarkarism: The Ideas*, 2.

[26] Edward W. Said, *Orientalism*, (New York: Vintage, 1979).

[27] Stolte and Fischer-Tine, *Imagining Asia in India*, 89.

to be the problematic and fallacious assumptions of Euro-American theorizing before presenting alternative arguments based on his own research. In Sarkar's firm critique[28] of Comte, only the category 'positive' is accepted. He did not subscribe to the evolutionary tone of Comte's theorizing. Sarkar rejected Comte's thesis of the evolution of the human mind through theological, metaphysical and positive stages (with science and the latest, dominant phase). For him positivism meant an 'association of scholarly brains, exact knowledge, experience or experiment, generalization, specialization and science as the antithesis of religion.'[29]

In his essay 'Asiatic Positivism' Sarkar elaborates further, 'If the term (Positivism) be applied to any inculcation of humanitarian principles or social duties and the like, every religion is surely positivist and every human being is a positivist,'[30] rejecting in effect the positivist (scientific)-non-positivist dualism. In *Futurism*, Sarkar reiterates his call for 'revolt against Orientalists.'[31] One core objective in the *PHS*, for Sarkar, was to demonstrate that 'positivism, materialism and activism were also inherent in the Hindu tradition.'[32] His historical researches on India were focused on highlighting the materialist, secular and rational bases of Hindu and Indian traditions. At the same time, Sarkar did not propose that India should embrace a *Hindu* path (rooted in mysticism or metaphysics) to development. Rather, he posited that the only way ahead for modern India was to 'rise to the challenge of economic development through industrialization.'[33] Neither did he advocate a narrow-minded empiricism. Instead Sarkar

---

[28] See: Sarkar, *Villages and Towns*, 1941. Sarkar is critical of Marx, Weber, Durkheim and Freud and finds them guilty of 'monistic determinism' in their theorizing of economic and social change. According to Tisdale, for Sarkar 'Marx is charged with economic determinism, Durkheim with 'societarianism,' Weber with fallacious typology, Freud with 'sexological determinism' and others with faults of a similar monomaniacal nature' (1942, 517); Bhattacharya, *Indian Sociology*, 1990.

[29] Sarkar, *Positive Hindu Society*,1.

[30] Sarkar, *Chinese Religion Through Hindu*, 73.

[31] Sarkar, *The Futurism*.

[32] Beteille, Society and Politics in India: Essays in a Comparative Perspective, (Athlone Press: London, 1991) 206. See Uberoi and Sundar 2008.

[33] See Dutt 1939, Beteille, *Society and Politics*, 206.

saw himself as both pragmatic and pluralist with a methodological commitment to positivism:

> It is beyond any doubt that I lay stress on empiricism and positivism. But I always used to pay due respect to transcendentalism and spiritualism. I am a double-edged sword, a pluralist indeed.

Sarkar thus makes space for both the spiritual and material in Indian and Euro-American traditions, not being drawn into debates over the primacy of one over the other. He sees both as constitutive of universal human experience. Sarkar's twinning of 'Hindu' and 'Positivism' is radical and counterintuitive, given the firm contemporary approach to 'Hindu' as a category embedded in religious discourse.

Sarkar was a radical figure in many ways and lived by the maxim that India (and Indian intellectuals) must engage what he designated 'Eur-American' culture and civilization by approaching these as objects of study and through mastering European languages. This was in itself a radical idea for the times, and in some ways ironically even more so today. He made a call for constructing 'Eur-America' as a subject of study *by Indian social scientists*; the call being that Asians can and should theorize Eur-America. Contemporary students of social science have noted the geo-politics of global academia and its division of labour, with the non-West defined as providers of empirical material which the West then theorizes. Sarkar was well ahead of the game in crafting Eur-American cultures as objects of study for Asian social scientists. He established institutions for the study of Eur-American arts, language, literature, philosophy and culture in India itself and influenced scores of students and colleagues to conduct research in these areas.[34] Sarkar led from the front by critically engaging Western scholarship on/about Asia and offered critical commentaries on these

---

[34] Chaudhury notes Sarkar's ambition that: 'Indians should establish Societies, Academies or Institutes with the objective of carrying on researches into the diverse countries of the modern world' (1940) 56).

to Indian audiences in Bengali and Hindi.[35] In the spirit of disseminating knowledge about Eur-America, Sarkar meticulously produced reports of each and every country he visited. These were published in weekly and monthly periodicals and newspapers[36] in Calcutta, in Bengali and English, and were also translated into Hindi and published in the newspaper *Aj*.[37] For example, he produced two texts on China: In *Chinese Religion Through Hindu Eyes: A Study in the Tendencies of Asiatic Mentality*[38] and *The A, B, C of Chinese Civilisation*[39] (1925). The first two chapters of the former were read before the North China branch of the Royal Asiatic Society in 1915. In the Introduction to Sarkar's text, Wu Ting Fang notes:

> We often have visitors coming to China from Europe and America for various missions; some for scientific research ... It is the first time, if I am not mistaken, that a gentleman from India has come to China for such a purpose. Professor Benoy Kumar Sarkar is now on a visit to China to study the religion, literature and social institutions of the people, and the result of his earnest and laborious research extending over several months in seen in the following pages. Whether the reader will follow him and

---

[35] Sarkar published numerous essays in Calcutta Review (CR) on sociological figures and subjects. Examples include: 'French thought from Fenelan to Bougle' (CR, May 1934); 'Tonnies and the New Sociology' (CR, November 1935); 'The Paretain circulation of Elites examined' (CR January 1936); 'India's affinities with Eur-America in Sorokin's Sociology (CR, April 1936); 'Formal Sociology' as interpreted by Leopold von Weise (CR, August 1937); 'Hindu Sensatism and Ideationalism in Sorokin's *Social and Cultural Dynamics*'; 'Neo-idealism in Hocking's *Man and the State*' (CR, December 1938); 'A short-coming of the Hegel-Marxian Dialectic' (CR, February 1939); 'Pareto's *Mind and Society*' (CR, April 1939) and 'Mannheim's Sociology of Knowledge' (CR, April 1939).

[36] Chaudhury notes 'From 1914 to 1925, then, no man or woman could open a Bengali monthly or weekly without encountering something of Sarkar's *Varttaman Jagat* ... The monthly and weekly magazines were then, as they are even now, the most important medium of extra-school or extra-University higher culture in Bengal ... This means that the entire reading public of Bengal, the whole of Bengali intelligentsia, female as well forces)' (1940) 49.

[37] Chaudhary notes: 'From 1921 to 1925 Sarkar's writings were being published every week in Hindi in Shivprasad Gupta's daily *Aj* (Today) under the caption *Hamari Oropki Chitthi* (Our European Letter)' (1940, 54).

[38] Sarkar 1916.

[39] See Giuseppe 1994, China Sabhyatar 'A, A, Ka, Kha, "The A, B, C, of Chinese Civilization"' (1923).

agree with all his views expressed in this book it must be conceded that he
has not hastily come to his conclusions without personal study. The mass
of facts collected by him and his views expressed thereon should afford the
students of Sociology and Comparative Religion much food for thought
and deserve their impartial consideration.[40]

Sarkar's narrative about Chinese religion was based on firsthand observations
in contrast to other regnant European secondhand accounts of the same,
including that of Max Weber. Within the context of teaching classical
sociological theory, teaching Sarkar's text on Chinese religion alongside
Max Weber's text *The Religion of China* would reveal fascinating comparative insights. Coincidentally, both the texts were first published at the same
time. Sarkar's interest in China, Japan and Persia was reflective of his broader
pan-Asian project, in which he saw 'a collective battle of Asians against the
political and intellectual dominance of the West or as he called it "Euro-
America".'[41] The logic of broader Asian co-operation for Sarkar amounted
to a 'war against colonialism in politics and against *orientalism* in science.'[42]
    Throughout, Sarkar's work is evidence of what would be called today,
critique of Orientalism and Eurocentrism assumptions in social science
theorizing of the time Immanuel Wallerstein's signature piece,
'Eurocentrism and Its Avatars: The Dilemmas of Social Science,'[43] lists
'at least five ways in which social science has been said to be Eurocentric.'
The following extract from Sarkar, penned in 1916, bears an uncanny
resemblance to Wallerstein's (and before him Edward Said's) nuanced
and robust criticism of Eurocentric social science scholarship:

The progress of the nineteenth century and the sixteen years of the
twentieth in discoveries and inventions is a unique phenomenon in the
history of six millenniums. *But Eur-America, which is mainly responsible for
this, and Asia, which has contributed almost nothing to it, had been equally
'primitive' or 'pre-scientific' and pre-'industrial down to nearly the end of the*

[40] Wu Ting Fang, 'Introduction', Sarkar 1916, 17.
[41] Stolte and Fischer-Tine, 88.
[42] Sarkar, *The Futurism*, 1922, iv.
[43] Wallerstein, *Eurocentrism and Its Avatars*, 199.

eighteenth century, if judged by the standard of to-day. Neither politically nor culturally was there East or West till then. It is the subordination of the East to the West in recent times both in politics and culture that has inspired the bombastic jingo fallacy: 'East is East and West is West.' ... *The 'superior races' of those times (c. A.C. 600–1600) were the Islamites and Buddhist-Hindu Tartars of Asia.*[44]

Sarkar challenged the core assumptions of Orientalist discourse: he rejected the discourse of difference between East and West; the assumption superiority of Western races and cultures; the uniqueness of European experience; the denial of history to Eastern nations and; the idea of their 'splendid isolation.' With respect to India, he challenged the 'spiritualistic/materialistic' binary, and therefore Indological readings and interpretations of India as predominantly mystical and spiritual and unconcerned with the secular and the worldly domains. Here, his views stood directly opposed to that of Max Weber, and he also countered eighteenth- and nineteenth-century thinkers, many of whom (including J S Mill, Harriet Martineau and Karl Marx) had internalized without questioning Orientalist imaginaries of India. In the following statement from Sarkar, there is an obvious but interestingly *unstated critique* of Weber's ideas carried in *The Protestant Ethic*[45] and his works in the Comparative Sociology of Religion:

The new ideas, aspirations, movements, etc. engendered by the steam-and-machine age are revolutionary not only to Asians but also to Eur-Americans. The economic, political, military, social and domestic polities of the West prior to the epoch-making triumphs of human intellect did not differ, except superficially and in a few trifling incidents, from the

---

[44] Sarkar 1914, 16.

[45] Weber's search for the origins of and the emergence of modern, rational, industrial capitalism in seventeeth century Western Europe – defined as a unique historical phenomenon and the non-appearance/failure of the same in India and China – due to the absence of the requisite 'spirit of capitalism' in these civilizational contexts are carried in his texts: *The Protestant Ethic and the Spirit of capitalism* (1904/1905, first English translation in 1930) and *Hinduismus und Buddhism* (1916) and *Konfuzianismus und Taoismus* (1915) mis-translated in English respectively as *The Religion of India: The Sociology of Hinduism and Buddhism* (first translated in 1958) and *The Religion of China: Confucianism and Taoism* (first translated in 1951).

contemporary institutions obtaining in Asia. *The institutions and ideals, the achievements and experiments, the motives and inspirations, the theories and hypotheses, the fads and hobbies prevailing today in England, German, France and America should not consequently be regarded by unbiased investigators of facts as anything (i) peculiarly occidental or (ii) non-oriental or (iii) unsuited to oriental 'genius' or (iv) antagonistic to the 'spirit' of the Orient or (v) materialistic. Scientifically speaking, all these are to be honestly known (i) as modern, constituting one of the phases of the world's evolution, and (ii) and spiritual to the same extent and in the same sense as anything in previous epochs of human culture since the Pharaonic and Vedic ages.* These can therefore, be availed of and assimilated to, any system of human polity according to the stage and requirements of its growth (e.g., as has been done by Japan without practically changing any of her old-Asian institutions, ideals, prejudices and superstitions.[46] (emphasis added)

Through historical research, Sarkar argued for similarities between India and Europe vis-à-vis scientific, material and technological developments prior to the eighteenth century. In so doing, he challenged the definition of India as predominantly mystical and spiritual society, in contrast to the 'West' which was defined as material, scientific and industrial. In the *PHS* and his other writings on Hinduism, Sarkar was committed to demonstrating the material, secular basis of Hindu society. Sarkar refuted the assumption of fundamental and irreconcilable differences between Asia and Europe – a view that was pervasive in popular thinking, political and international relations discourses as well as in much of social science scholarship of the time, both Indian and European. In the preface to Sarkar's *PHS*, Dr. Lalit M. Basu notes:

When the first edition of the first volume was published my father as editor of the *Sacred books of the Hindus Series* used to say: 'One side of India was presented by Max Muller in his writings, *India; What can it teach US? Chips from a German Workshop* etc., and especially through the *Sacred Books of the East Series*. This was the subjective, the idealistic and the metaphysical or the mystical side. The other side of Indian culture, – the materialistic, the

---

[46] Sarkar, *The Positive Background of Hindu Sociology*, 1937, 17.

secular, the worldly the objective side has been presented by Professor Sarkar. To understand the Hindu mind and Indian civilization scholars will have to devote attention to both sides.'[47]

Sarkar provided alternative and contrary readings of India, which were at odds with current opinion, which had been fortified through the works of Max Muller, Rudyard Kipling, Max Weber, Rabindranath Tagore, Swami Vivekananda and Sri Aurobindo, to name a few intellectuals.[48] These premises were debunked as myths and rejected by Sarkar as offering an analytical frame for explaining India's 'backwardness' and Europe's 'progress.' Sarkar located the reasons for India's underdevelopment elsewhere – in the domination, control and hegemony given in India's colonial experiences and their debilitating effects on her material advancement. This discourse was supported by his arguments about the 'equality' and 'unity' of the human civilization. These counter-arguments were politically powerful within the hegemonic logic of imperialism. It also challenged Eurocentric and Orientalist theorizing about East and West and in particular economic and material differences between these cultures/civilizations – carried in the writings of nineteenth-century founders of Sociology. Speaking of his present as the 'age of modernism,' Sarkar notes:

The present is the age of Pullman cars, electric lifts, bachelor apartments, long distance phones, Zeppelins, and the 'new woman'. In their Oriental studies the Eur-American scholars seem to assume that these have been the inseparable features of the Western world all through the ages. Had they been really conscious that some of these were not known to their grandfathers, and others even to their fathers, they could easily resist the temptation of finding some essential distinction between Occidental and Oriental 'ideals.' Most of the emphasis laid on the influence of latitude, altitude, temperature, and 'general aspects of nature' on civilization and

[47] Sarkar *The Positive Background of Hindu Sociology*, 1937, 9.
[48] Beteille suggests that Sarkar was 'somewhat more sympathetic to Marx and Engels' (1991, p 206). Sarkar translated their *The Origin of the Family, Private Property and the State* into Bengali in 1924.

Weltanschauung could then be automatically condemned as unhistorical.[49]

In a short piece entitled 'Demand for a new logic,' Sarkar argues forcefully against the Orientalist discourse of difference and the assumed 'superiority' of Western race:

> Neither historically nor philosophically does the Asiatic mentality differ from the Eur-American. It is only after the brilliant successes of a fraction of mankind subsequent to the Industrial Revolution of the last century that *the alleged difference between the two mentalities has been first stated and since then grossly exaggerated.* At the present day science is being vitiated by pseudo-scientific theories or fancies regarding race, religion and culture. Such theories were unknown to the world down to the second or third decade of the nineteenth century'[50] (emphasis added).

He further challenged the view that India stood outside history as it was assumed in a great deal of nineteenth-century theorizing about Eastern societies. He undertook the project of demonstrating India's interactions and inter-connectedness with other regions and civilizations through history:

> India was never shunted off from the main track of humanity's progress, but has always grown in contact with, by giving to and taking from, – the moving currents of the world's life and thought. India had no epoch of 'splendid isolation' but, like every other country, had her values tested by the universal standard of merit measurement.[51]

Sarkar was unorthodox, revolutionary and challenged conventional wisdom about everything, often providing his own original theorizing on the subject. An early statement about Sarkar, carried in a 1917 issue of

---

[49] Sarkar, *The Futurism.*
[50] Sarkar, *The Hindusthanee Student,* February, II(5) 5.
[51] Sarkar, *The Positive Background of Hindu Sociology,* 17.

The Hindusthanee Student, already recognized the distinct flavour of Sarkar's scholarship on Indian society and religion:

> *His interpretation of Hindu History and Civilisation is based on what in modern science is called the 'historical method'. He therefore differs from those writers, Hindu or foreign, who have based their estimate of India and its people on a priori considerations, i.e., on abstract ideas or ideals without reference to actual facts and movements evolved in the country through the ages.* On the other hand, he differs also from those thinkers and scholars, whose interest in India is merely archaeological and antiquarian, i.e., who look upon Hindhustan as only as a land of anthropological curios or as the land of human fossils which have no part to play in the achievements of the main world. *Professor Sarkar studies the facts of universal history in the light of comparative chronology . . .* [52] (emphasis added)

Sarkar produced the document 'Postulates of Young India' in Japan during his 1916 visit to the country. This article carried his arguments about the unity of the human species, his theories of historical change and his explanations for the economic and material differences between East and West, evident by the nineteenth century. The idea of the unity of the human civilization is further stated categorically in here:

> Humanity is fundamentally one, in psychology, logic, ethics, aesthetics and metaphysics, (i) in spite of physical and physiognomic varieties, and (ii) in spite of age-long historic prejudices. [53]

In *Futurism* Sarkar offered a scathing critique of colonial policies and the ideological import of this for Euro-American theorizing about the East. Sarkar's massive 12 volumes of *Varttaman Jagat, Futurism and PP* present his political theories and advanced the idea of *vishwa-shakti* (world forces) which can be interpreted as global and historical economic, social, cultural and political processes. In a 1912 essay, 'Science

---

[52] Editorial piece entitled 'Hindu Sociologist in America.' *The Hindusthanee Student,* 3 (6–7) (March-April 1917), 8.

[53] Sarkar, *The Positive Background.*,14.

of History and the Hope of Mankind,' Sarkar notes that the path taken by individual nations is inevitably shaped by broader forces operating internationally:

> It is impossible that a national should be able to acquire or preserve freedom or prestige solely on the strength of its own resources in national wealth and character... every people has to settle its policy and course of action by detailed study of the disposition of the world forces and the situation of the political centre of gravity at the time.[54]

In contemporary language, Sarkar highlighted the inevitable role of global politics and world history in mediating individual nation's aspirations for sovereignty and independence. This has been recognized as Sarkar's brand of internationalism.

Sarkar's Political Sociology

Sarkar's social and political thought are complex. He was a pioneer in calling for an objective analysis of political institutions, values and ideologies[55] and highlighting the secular nature of politics. While Sarkar's political writings were limited in being elitist, Bandhopadhyaya notes in a highly generous and commendatory tone:

> For despite his shortcoming(s) he can certainly claim to be a pioneer and path-breaker in some fields of political research in India. He is perhaps the first political scientist who analysed objectively diverse political institutions, ideologies, concepts and theories. In the course of this analysis he showed politics to be an absolutely secular phenomenon, and revealed crude political realities in Machiavellian style. In this sense he liberated Indian politics from a metaphysical bondage and sought to create an awareness among people of India about the hard task of nation-building

---

[54] Sarkar cited in Ghoshal, Sarkarism: *The Idea*, 30.
[55] Bandhopadhyay, *The Political ideas of Benoy*, 1982.

that lay ahead. He taught the Indians to look at politics with a clear, purposeful, realistic and pragmatic vision.[56]

Sarkar pioneered an empirical and secular approach to the modern state as well as the recognition that this was man-made. His political theorizing was premised on this following view of the state:

> ...a voluntary association, an artificial corporation, an institution consciously created or manufactured like the Standard Oil Co. of New York or the University of Oxford.[57]

He observed that the 'the state may come and the state may go, but the people go on for ever and may live on to create new partnerships or states according to the needs of the hour.'[58]

Andre Beteille has observed that Sarkar's projects were numerous and wide-ranging. Having 'too much on his plate' also produced 'lack of focus, clarity and consistency in his works' (1991, 206). In the *PP* Sarkar proposed the categories of 'demo-despotocracy,' 'neo-socialism,' 'neo-capitalism,' 'neo-democracy' for theorizing political systems globally and historically. Tisdale notes that Sarkar 'has a proclivity for making words – "plannification," "uptodatization," "epichofication," "groupification," "despotocracy," "albinocracy", to name only a few.'[59] While Sarkar does elaborate some of this terminology, others remain fuzzy. Sarkar assumed a prophetic and predictive stance in *PP*, speculating on the kind of world economy and political system that could be expected between 1944 and 1960. A review of the book published in the *Journal of Philosophy* in 1942 pronounced the following judgement on the book: 'Simply as a catalogue of ideas on the world's ills this series of books should prove a valuable addition to the library of students of post-war reconstruction.' At the first Indian Political Science Conference in Benares in December 1938, Sarkar

---

[56] Bandhopadhyaya, *The Political ideas of Benoy*, 161.
[57] Cited in Ghoshal, *Sarkarism: The Ideas*, 30.
[58] Cited in Ghoshal, *Sarkarism: The Ideas*, 31.
[59] Tisdale, review of *Villages and Towns*, 518.

presented a paper entitled 'Demo-Despotocracy and Freedom.'[60] Here Sarkar offers his conceptualization of 'democracy' and 'despotocracy':

> Democracy is as stern, as eternal and as universal and ubiquitous a reality in societal organizations as despotocracy. The two polarities constitute a moral unit in the *Zwischenmenschliche Beziehungen und Gebilden* (inter-human relations and forms), to use an expression from von Wiese, of all denominations.[61]

Sarkar did not see these two as mutually exclusive categories but rather saw them as co-existing and as supplementing each other. He saw them not as 'absolute terms' but as 'conditional, conditioned, limited and relative.'[62] For Sarkar, the notion of freedom was central to the conceptualization of these categories. Democracy did not signal absence of despotic tendencies, neither did a despotocracy mean the absolute end of freedom. His comparison of real totalitarian and democratic states is instructive. He observes:

> In spite of his traditional British ideology Chamberlain is a despotocrat. In spite of his Nazi philosophy Hitler is a democrat. Chamberlain knows how to ignore the British Parliament when he wills it. The British Cabinet is indeed an organ of despotocracy. Hitler has deliberately abolished *Parlamentarismus*. But he knows how to serve *vox populi* and obey the popular will...The Leviathan has not been thoroughly swept off the British constitution. Nor is the contract social, individual liberty, entirely silenced in the totalitarian *Staatsrason* of the Nazis.[63]

Sarkar presents these categories as 'ideal types' and heuristic devices for theorizing actual, empirical realities of democratic and totalitarian states. Conceptually too, he preserves space both for freedom under conditions of despotism and for domination and oppression under democratic

---

[60] Also see Chaudhury 1990; Ghoshal, *Sarkarism: The Ideas*, 35.

[61] Cited in Ghoshal, *Sarkarism: The Ideas*, 35.

[62] Cited in Ghoshal, *Sarkarism: The Ideas*35.

[63] Cited in Ghoshal, *Sarkarism: The Ideas*, 35–6.

conditions. Bringing Sarkar into conversation with the French political thinkers Alexis de Tocqueville (especially his dichotomy of liberal/despotic democracy and the notion of the 'tyranny of the majority' in liberal democracies) and Harriet Martineau (her discussion of political participation, liberty and democracy) is productive. According to Bandhopadhyaya, Sarkar's 'demo-despotocracy' is a term that describes 'the basic character of a state in different countries irrespective of the differences in their socio-economic structure. While it exposes the despotic features of the formally democratic states marked by the presence of representative institutions and multiple political parties, it also emphasizes the democratic features of the formally despotic states dominated by a single political party.'[64] On the other hand, he suggests that Sarkar's 'new-democracy' 'reflects a basic trend in world politics. It is based on the belief in the growth of and expansion of freedom and democracy throughout the world . . . The term also signifies that modern totalitarian dictatorial regimes are more and more realising the significance of freedom and initiative of the masses as a creative force in politics.'[65] Manjapra offers a concrete instance of how Sarkar used the concept of 'despo-democracy':

> Sarkar coined his phrase 'despo-democracy' in 1938 in order to explain how his beneficent and therapeutic rule of an Indian strongman over his *jati (people, caste, or volk)*, would lead to a rewriting of the world map and could win world recognition for Bengalis. Sarkar spoke of *jati*, but it was not a Hindu (Aryan) nationalism that he invoked – as was the case for the Hindu Mahasabha or the Savarkar group – but a Greater Bengali ethnic nationalism. It included Hindus and Muslims. Sarkar's fascism was based on Hindu-Muslim unity within the cultural category of Bengaliness. And it is no wonder that Sarkar's great archetypal hero was Subhas Chandra Bose, who in 1941 began his campaign to both unify Hindus and Muslims and to destroy the British empire through close collaboration with Nazi and Axis powers.[66]

---

[64] Bandopadhyaya 1984, 138.

[65] Bandopadhyaya 1984, 138–139.

[66] Manjapra, *Age of Entanglement; German*, 209.

A critical reading of Sarkar's notion of 'despo-democracy' is necessary given this curious confluence of the need for fascism and authoritarianism coupled with a valorization of cultural pluralism in his political thought – with clear influences from German political philosophy. The term 'fascism'[67] has been associated with Sarkar for his praise for Hitler and his 'virtual silence'[68] on anti-semitism which Bhattacharya rightly describes as 'inexplicable and disconcerting.'[69] Andrew Sartori observes:

> By 1934, Sarkar was declaring the Hitler state to be the culmination of a quest for the kind of dynamic national self-empowerment that Bengal and India desperately needed, and Hitler himself 'the greatest if Germany's teachers and inspirers since Fichte' as the product of 'the moral idealism of a Vivekananda multiplied by the iron strenuousness of a Bismarck.'[70]

Zachariah notes that Sarkar has been read as 'a hero and ideologue of the Bengal Swadeshi movement, whose indigenous forms of sociology made him a desirable intellectual.' He also suggest that his theorizing has been compromised by his 'open support for Nazi ideas of social engineering.'[71] Manjapra speaks of Sarkar's 'pro-Nazi sentiment... filtered through the language of scholarly internationalism'[72] and argues that not only did Sarkar praise Nazism 'as a form of benevolent dictatorship,'[73] but suggested that this would lead to the end of colonial subjugation for Indians. Sarkar was a nationalist and a liberal and firmly believed in freedom from colonial rule. He staunchly supported socialist and communist thought and yet argued that Hitler's model of the German state was both workable and desirable for India – a view that marked his political sociology with ambivalence. The charge of Eurocentrism cannot be levelled at Sarkar's ideas; if anything he might

---

[67] Manjapra, *Age of Entanglement; German,* 209.

[68] Bhattacharya, *Indian Sociology: The Role of Benoy Kumar Sarkar,* 88.

[69] Bhattacharya, *Indian Sociology: The Role of Benoy Kumar Sarkar,* 88.

[70] Sartori, *Beyond Culture-Contact And Colonial Discourse: 'Germanism',* 83.

[71] Zachariah, *Transfers, Formations, Transformations,* 180

[72] Manjapra, *Age of Entanglement,* 209.

[73] Manjapra, *Age of Entanglement,* 209.

be accused of being a 'nativist', albeit a rather sophisticated one. Sarkar's ideas are limited in being sympathetic to dictatorship, even if it is in the interest of ending 'colonial subjugation.' The critical analytic lens must turn on Eurocentrism as well as on fascism and other forms of repression in gauging contributions to production of knowledge.

Theory of Progress: Creative Disequilibrium and Freedom

While Sarkar's works are infused with a strong historical perspective, he was not an historical determinist. Sarkar's concept of 'creative disequilibrium' was an original contribution to debates about the source of historical change and direction of human progress. While he acknowledged the role of history (and the past) in shaping the future, he also held open the possibility of forces independent of past events and processes in shaping history, thereby highlighting the role of chance, accidents and unpredictable events.[74] In this, he assumed a different position from Bankimchandra, Sorokin, Spengler, Marx and Hegel. He avoided a stage theory of change and saw the 'disequilibrium' (between the forces of 'good' and 'evil') as creative, in constructively moving humanity towards an improved, more perfect state, and as the basis for change. Unlike Bankimchandra's view, he held 'that history-less groups and classes have often, by sheer energism and self-determination, succeeded in changing the face of the world.'[75] Sarkar articulated his theory of progress thus:

> In every social pattern of today as of yesterday,- in the rural areas as well as the urban,-it is not the 'haves' but the 'have-nots' who create culture or civilization, i.e., the 'as-ifs,' fictions, ideals in progress. The 'haves' represent the status quo, the 'have-nots' embody the creative disequilibrium that challenges the status quo. In the 'haves' the world sees the fatigue of

[74] Mukherjee, *Benoy Kumar Sarkar-A study,* (1942).
[75] Sarkar, *Political Philosophies Since 1905,* 112.

age and the inertia of tradition. The 'have-nots,' on the contrary, exhibit the creativities of youth and the dynamics of adventure.... It is the triumph of the have-nots over the haves that constitutes progress in every region or race as well as in every epoch.[76]

Sarkar addressed Marx's, Tonnies', Spengler's and Sorokin's analyses of how historical change occurred. He acknowledged that they were right to note the role of 'antithesis' (conflicts, tensions) in producing change but he departed in not considering these as the dominant or determining factor. Sarkar viewed progress as 'a condition of perpetual unrest and eternal conflict between what is and what is not . . . It is "indefinite and indeterminate," eternally evolving.'[77] Although he admitted similarities between his theory of change and the Marxian-Hegelian notion of the 'dialectic,' he also registered the distinction of his own theorizing:

In the Hegelian dialectic there is an *alleged synthesis* which comprises both thesis and antithesis. This synthesis becomes later a thesis and is confronted with a new antithesis. In the doctrine of creative disequilibrium *the synthesis is more apparent than real.* It is nothing more than a phase of the eternal conflicts between the thesis and the antithesis.[78] (emphasis added)

Thus Sarkar did not operate with a vision of a perfect utopia. He did not imagine an ideal society, free of blemishes, waiting for humanity at the end of history. Chaudhury phrases this stance well:

Neither directly not indirectly has Sarkar ever declared his faith in a progress that leaves no room for evil. The totalitarian annihilation of misery, misfortune, poverty, disease, vice, sin or other forms of evil is not to be found in Sarkar's conception of progress. His progress is an eternal struggle between what happens for the time being to be called good and what happens at the same time to be called evil. Each and every

---

[76] Sarkar, *Villages and Towns*, 647.

[77] Sarkar cited in Tisdale, review of *Villages and Towns*, 517.

[78] Sarkar, *Villages and Towns*, 522.

condition in inter-human relations or even in the individual psyche is according to him a state of discontent, disharmony, disequilibrium and so forth.[79]

Sarkar argued that it was precisely the various kinds of societal imperfections (in structure and function) and thus disequilibrium which provided the dynamic for change. The best Sarkar could hope for was that in being aware of the 'shortcomings,' 'we may always be on the alert to remove them and attempt everyday to be something new and great or rather *somewhat less imperfect, less defective*'[80] (emphasis mine). In a 1942 review of *VT*, Hope Tisdale commended Sarkar's theory of progress which did not speak of an absolute move from good to evil/wrong to right or vice versa: 'In many ways, it makes an engaging theory of progress. Certainly, it eliminated the objectionable elements of Spengler and Sorokin, who both, though using different approaches and methods, arrive at the same conclusion, namely that decadence characterizes the modern era.'[81] Sarkar was critical of Marxists and socialists who could imagine a golden age, a perfect society through the capitalist revolution. Neither could he place his faith in modernity to deliver individuals from suffering and poverty.

In the Preface of the 1941 text *VT*, Sarkar explains the objective of the book thus: 'In this study villages and towns have been used as pegs in which to hang the topics relating to sociation... The fundamental theme is the social relations, reconstruction or remakings that constitute progress.' He further describes the book as 'a study in the processes and forms of societal transformation and progress.' Sarkar's assertion in the book that there are no differences between villages and towns in terms of the patterns or processes of sociation is open to critique.[82] The only distinction he admitted is what he denotes as 'quantity':

---

[79] Chaudhury 1940, 37.

[80] Sarkar's prayer/speech at the 'International Parliament of Religions' held in Calcutta on 8 March 1937, cited in Ghoshal, *Sarkarism: The Ideas*, 1 9–10.

[81] Tisdale, review of *Villages and Towns*, 517.

[82] An obvious comparison is with F Tonnies' account of Gemeinschaft and Gessellschaft modes of sociality in rural and urban settings.

They differ but in the number of inhabitants and density of the population per square mile.[83]

We notice that the distinctions between patterns, – whatever be the name – consist fundamentally more in the quantity and magnitude than in the nature or quality of social processes.[84]

He did not romanticize or glorify village life as idyllic, lamenting its passing and dilution, arguing instead that, 'In the last analysis it is the annihilation of the villages that is the aim and objective of the rural reconstruction ideology.'[85] In a related vein, he challenged the patterns of social differentiation in Spengler's urban-rural dichotomy. He also rejected, in this discourse, the romanticized (non-political and soulful) image of the village community and the more negative portrayal of the average city-dweller. He writes, 'The milk of human kindness does not flow more frequently in the interactions of the village "community" than those in the town "society."'[86] An early review of the book by Dwight Anderson of Cornell University finds the book lacking in 'concrete evidence upon which to base an empirical analysis of his topic by inductive generalizations.' He concedes, although, that Sarkar 'recognized that sociology is concerned with the analysis of the behavior of patterns of groups.'[87] Ironically this is absent in Sarkar's text. Anderson also makes the important point that Sarkar recognizes the difference between Sociology as 'the analysis of sociations' and 'applied sociology.'

Sarkar's political and sociological theorizing are embedded in a conception of rugged individualism, human agency and activism – and which supported his theory of historical change. Invoking Marx's language, Sarkar too conceived of individuals as history-making agents. In this context, positioning Marx's theory of human nature alongside Sarkar's view of individuals as creative, inventive, moral and rational

---

[83] Sarkar, *Villages and Towns*, 16.

[84] Sarkar, *Villages and Towns*, 491.

[85] Sarkar, *Villages and Towns*, 492.

[86] Sarkar, *The Positive Background*, (1914, 1921)

[87] Dwight Sanderson, *American Sociological Review*, Vol. 7, No. 3 (Jun., 1942), 459.

beings who desired to be self-autonomous and self-determining is instructive:

> It is the eternal privilege of creative, inventive or world-making intelligence to establish new standards of moral and spiritual judgment new measures of social justice, rational good, human welfare and world progress.[88]

While he was a firm advocate for the rights of the less privileged groups in society such as the lower classes and lower castes of Hindus, Muslims and tribals. He argued that literacy and formal education were recent, modern phenomena, and that illiteracy could not be correlated with lack of intellect, morality or culture. His socialism viewed the natural intelligence and practical experience of illiterate members of the community as 'valuable intellectual assets.'[89] In Sarkar's words:

> Political suffrage should have nothing to do with literacy. The illiterate has a right to political life and privileges simply because of the sheer fact that as a normal human being he has factually demonstrated his intellectual strength and moral civic sense. The rights of the illiterate ought to constitute a social psychology the foundation of a new democracy. A universal suffrage independent of all considerations as to school going, ability to read and write or other tests should be the very first postulates of social economics. It is orientations like these that democracy needs today if it is to function as a living faith.[90]

Sarkar acknowledged different modalities of human inequality even as he argued for equality amongst races, classes and nations and supported individual right to be free. Interestingly, Sarkar argued for the pursuit of individual freedom as an end in itself rather than a means to an end. He says:

---

[88] Sarkar, *Villages and Town*, 536.
[89] See Madan 2011, Cited in Mukherjee, *Social Thoughts of Benoy Kumar*, 55.
[90] Sarkar, *Dominion India in World Perspectives*, 168.

I am not ready to accept at random the authority of the family, group, party, nation, state etc., over the individual. Usually and generally, sub-ordination (of the individual) to the group amounts to slavery. In my theory of freedom the Individual is fully autonomous. So I can hardly and only at times, stand for encroachment or curtailment of Individuality and Personality. But the occasion for that rarely arises. If anybody can prove with sufficient evidence that the integrity of a nation, state and society is really threatened by enemy action, then only shall I allow the state, nation, government and law to be supreme over the Individual. In this respect I am anti-Hegel and pro-Kant.[91]

In a realist and pragmatic (but problematic) mode Sarkar accepted inequality as a universal given:

Man is not equal by nature. The absence of equality is patent in every human enterprise, in every human theatre of action, in every human organization. Rosseausque equality, the equality of the French revolution is a myth. The inequalities are physical, intellectual, moral, economic and social. The sooner these inequalities are accepted, as first postulates, the better for human welfare.[92]

Yet Sarkar could speak of 'creative individualism' with his conception of humans as dynamic creators and innovators. He says:

Human psyche or rather personality is essentially a dynamic entity, ever on the go; and by nature it is a differentiating organism, -carrying within itself the mechanism of a transformer.[93]

The mixture of the rational and the irrational, the logical and the illogical is an integral part of the human psyche. Herein is to be found the eternal duplicity of man, as Pascal maintained.[94]

---

[91] Sarkar, *Dominion India in World Perspectives*, 169.

[92] Sarkar, *Villages and Towns as Social Patterns*, 573.

[93] Sarkar, 1(2), (1928).

[94] Sarkar in a speech at the International Parliament of Religions, Calcutta 1937. Cited in Ghoshal, *Sarkarism: The Idea*, 5.

Sarkar admired the sense of activism and dynamism in Vivekananda's ideas. Vivekananda had urged his fellow countrymen to adopt the stance of 'world conquest,' to recognize the might of individual capacity, ideas that Sarkar had affinities with. With his capitalist frame of mind, in his vision of futurism and optimism, he argued that for India to progress (and become modern) she must embrace science and technology, rationality and materiality given that it was *precisely the lack of achievements* in these areas (due to colonialism, exploitation and oppression) that had rendered Asia (and India) backward and non-progressive. Furthermore, Sarkar had ambition for India to become an 'engineering nation.' But he did not propose a peculiarly Indian capitalism for India. He argued that European capitalism could be transposed onto the Indian landscape. In *The Futurism*, he rejects the romantic and idyllic visions of Eastern cultures by stating categorically the way forward for Asia:

> The people of Asia have no choice before them but to accept all the new *vidyas* and *kalas*, sciences, arts, mechanisms and institutions of Eur-America from the steam-engine to radioactivity...The only problem before the East is to try by all means to catch up to the West at the Japanese rate of advance and establish once more the foundations of equality and reciprocal respect that governed the relations between Asia and Europe in ancient and medieval times.[95]

Absent from Sarkar is the vision of *alternative non-European paths* to development and social historical change. In *Futurism* Sarkar declares:

> Economic determinism, like the law of gravitation, does not know latitude and longitude. If during all the epochs of world-culture previous to the advent of the steam-engine East and West have run parallel in agricultural methods, serfdom, cottage industry, guilds of artisans, usury, local markets and so forth, together with the legal system and social *Weltanschauung* adapted to such 'primitive' or mediaeval industrial organization, it is but natural that 'modernism' will also manifest itself in almost identical manner in Asia and Eur-America. The logic of human evolution is inexorable.

---

[95] Sarkar, *The Futurism*, 333.

While Sarkar did desire this kind of economic development as a strategy, he was nonetheless aware that formal rationalization processes (in the vein of Weber's theorizing) and political systems (historically and in his present) did restrict individual liberty and freedoms. Yet he also saw the value in industrialization and economic planning. In this, his views were akin to those of Harriet Martineau and Jose Rizal for whom the East could and should become like the West by following the same path.

Concluding Thoughts

Even a decade or so ago, Sarkar was less known internationally and referenced within a narrower range of scholarly fields. Today, Sarkar's ideas are invoked in deliberations in the fields of intellectual history, Indian art and artists, cultural representations, Germanism, Nazism and Fascism and post-colonial Sociology. His name now surfaces in unexpected discourses – a visibility made possible by recent substantial analytical and critical commentaries on his ideas.[96]

Looking ahead how can Sarkar meaningfully be invoked in contemporary social science scholarship? Admittedly, to some extent Sarkar is now encapsulated in alternative and counter-mainstream social science discourses as a social thinker and theorist whose ideas are akin to the concerns of contemporary post-colonial thinkers.[97] Satadru Sen astutely observes that 'Sarkar matters not because his scholarship has stood the test of time: much of it is dated. That, of course, is where its value lies.'[98] He is a perfect candidate (in alternative, counter-Eurocentric and counter-Orientalist discourses) for the title of a social thinker whose ideas and activities were not confined to Indian shores, and whose ideas are/were modern, universal and relevant. Despite Sarkar's credentials and achievements, his students and supporters note that he remains a marginal

---

[96] Sen 2015, Goswami 2013, Sartori 2010, Zachariah 2011, Feuchter et al. 2011, Garfield and Nalini Bhushan 2011, Fischer-Tiné and Stolte 2012, Manjapra 2014.

[97] Manu Goswami, *From Swadeshi to Swaraj: Nation, Economy*, 2013.

[98] Satardu Sen's, *Benoy Kumar Sarkar*, 2.

figure amongst contemporary social scientists. Sarkar's vast and encyclo-paedic scholarship and his unorthodox and revolutionary thought have been neglected by generations of sociologists in India. Strikingly he has limited presence in Indian scholarship about efforts to 'indigenize' Sociology. These latter debates have been in existence in Indian circles for several decades. But it is curious that these efforts not stumbled upon Sarkar's name and ideas and rendered him more visible to Indian sociologists by locating his contributions historically and institutionally in Indian academic circles. It is as important to theorize this neglect and to ask what this says about Indian social science traditions and their historiography.

Sarkar should be re-read and re-positioned as a pioneering thinker who was confronting late nineteenth-century modernity and making sense of this complex phenomenon. On the basis of the evidence presented here, Sarkar can be approached meaningfully as an inter-locutor who critically engaged the ideas and theories of modernity presented by those who would later be crowned the founding fathers of Sociology. Ironically though, the mainstream historical narrative of the discipline has little or no memory of this figure. As a social scientist, Sarkar operated with a cosmopolitan, trans-Asian frame of reference and recognized unifying forces in the space labelled 'Asia' despite the diversity and complexity within, more so than in the present, where a fragmented view of Asia prevails. Writing at the turn of the twentieth century, from a non-Western locale, but deeply and critically engaged with social science concepts, theories, issues and problematics current in the 'West' (where social science disciplines were institutionalized) mark Sarkar's pioneering status as a social thinker and a theorist of modernity. He is conspicuous as an early critic of European theorizing about Asia, in general, and India, in particular, and offers alternative readings of the same. Presenting Sarkar here as a sociologist, the argument is that while he was emplaced in the intellectual milieu of his times, he was also a thinker well ahead of his time. His hazy presence in contemporary social science narratives (Indian and international) despite the tenor and weight of his scholarly work renders him an intriguing figure from the perspective of intellec-tual history and as a theorist of modernity.

References

Bandhopadhyaya, B. *The Political Ideas of Benoy Kumar Sarkar.* Calcutta: K.P. Bagchi & Company, 1984.

Behn, Wolfgang. 'Benoy Kumar Sarkar: 1887–1949'. Vols. 3 (N–Z). In *Concise Biographical Companion To Index Islamicus, 1665–1980: An International Who's Who In Islamic Studies From Its Beginnings Down To The Twentieth Century,* edited by Behn Wolfgang. Leiden; Boston: Brill, 2004.

Bernard, J.S., and L.L. Bernard. 'Leaders of Social Thought'. *Social Forces* 15 (3) (1937): 428–434.

Bhattacharyya, Swapan Kumar. *Indian Sociology: The Role of Benoy Kumar Sarkar.* Burdwan: University of Burdwan, 1990.

Bhushan Nalini, and L. Garfield Jay., eds. *Indian Philosophy in English: From Renaissance to Independence.* Oxford: Oxford University Press, 2011.

Chaudhury, N. N. *Pragmatism and Pioneering in Benoy Sarkar's Sociology and Economics.* Calcutta: Chuckervertty, Chatterjee, 1940.

Chaudhary, N.N. *Pragmatism and Pioneering in Benoy Sarkar's Sociology and Economics.* Calcutta: Chuckervertty Chatterjee & Company Limited, 1990.

Dass, B., ed. *The Social and Economic Ideas of Benoy Sarkar.* Calcutta: Chuckervertty Chatterjee & Co, 1939.

Dutt, S.C. *Fundamental Problems and Leading Ideas in the Works of Prof. Benoy Kumar Sarkar.* Calcutta: Ray, 1932.

Dutt, S.C. *Conflicting Tendencies in Indian Economic Thought – Sarkarism in Economics.* Calcutta: Chuckervertty Chatterjee & Co, 1939.

Feuchter, Jörg. et al., ed. *Cultural Transfers in Dispute: Representations in Asia, Europe and the Arab World Since the Middle Ages.* Frankfurt: Campus Verlag, 2011.

Fischer-Tiné, Harald, and Carolien Stolte. 'Imagining Asia in India: Nationalism and Internationalism (ca. 1905–1940)'. *Comparative Studies in Society and History* 54 (1) (2012): 65–92.

Frykenberg, R.E. 'Benoy Kumar Sarkar, 1897–1949: Political Rishi of Twentieth Century Bengal.' In *Explorations in the History of South Asia: Essays in Honour of Dietmar Rothermund,* edited by Tilman Frasch, Hermann Kulke Jürgen Lütt, and Georg Berkemer, 197–217. New Delhi: Manohar, 2001.

Ghosal, S.K. *Sarkarism: The Ideas and Ideals of Benoy Sarkar on Man and His Conquests.* Calcutta: Chuckervertty Chatterjee & Co, 1939.

Giuseppe, Flora. *Benoy Kumar Sarkar and Italy: Culture, Politics, and Economic Ideology*. Italy: Italian Embassy Cultural Centre, 1994.

Goswami, Manu. 'Provincialising Sociology: The Case of a Premature Postcolonial Sociologist'. In *Postcolonial Sociology*, edited by Go Julian, 145–176. Bingley: Emerald Group Publishing Limited, 2013.

Madan, T.N. 'Radhakamal Mukerjee and His Contemporaries: Founding Fathers of Sociology in India'. *Sociological Bulletin* 60 (1) (2011): 18–44.

Manjapra, Kris. *Age of Entanglement; German and Indian Intellectuals Across Empire*. Cambridge: Harvard Historical Studies, 2014.

Mukherjee, H. *Benoy Kumar Sarkar-A study*. Calcutta: Shiksha-Tirtha Karyalaya, 1953.

Mukherjee, H. 'Social Thoughts of Benoy Kumar Sarkar'. *Journal of Indian Anthropological Society* 30 (1995): 51–58.

Mukhopadhyaya, A.K. 'Benoy Kumar Sarkar: The Theoretical Foundation of Indian Capitalism' In *The Bengali Intellectual Tradition from Rammohun Ray to Dhirendranath Sen*, edited by A.K. Mukhopadhyay, 212–234. Calcutta: K.P Bagchi and Company, 1979.

Sarkar, Benoy Kumar. *The Positive Background of Hindu Sociology* (Part 1). Allahabad: Pânini Office, OCLC, 1914.

Sarkar, Benoy Kumar. *Chinese Religion Through Hindu Eyes: a study in the tendencies of Asiatic mentality*. Shanghai: Commercial Press, 1916.

Sarkar, Benoy Kumar. *The Positive Background of Hindu Sociology* (Part 2, with appendices by Brajendranáth Seal). Allahabad: Sudhindra Natha Vasu, OCLC, 1921.

Sarkar, Benoy Kumar. *The futurism of young Asia, and other essays on the relations between the East and the West*. Berlin: J. Springer. 1922.

Sarkar, Benoy Kumar. *Political Philosophies Since 1905* (Vol. 1). Lahore, 1941.

Sarkar, Benoy Kumar. *Villages and Towns as Social Patterns*. Calcutta, 1941a.

Sartori, Andrew. 'Beyond Culture-Contact and Colonial Discourse: "Germanism"' In *An Intellectual History for India*, edited by Shruti Kapila and C.A. Bayly, 68–84. New Delhi: Cambridge University Press, 2010.

Sen, Satadru. 'Benoy Kumar Sarkar and Japan.' *Economic and Political Weekly* 48 (2013): 45–46.

Sen, Satadru. *Benoy Kumar Sarkar: Restoring the Nation to the World*. New York, London: Routledge, 2015.

'The Nationalist Sociology of Benoy Kumar Sarkar'. In *Anthropology in the East: Founders of Indian Sociology and Anthropology*, edited by Satish Deshpande, Uberoi, Patricia, and Nandini Sundar, Calcutta: Seagull, 2008.

Zachariah, Benjamin. 'Transfers, Formations, Transformations? Some Programmatic Notes on Fascism in India.' In *Cultural Transfers in Dispute: Representations in Asia, Europe and the Arab World Since the Middle Ages*, edited by Jörg Feuchter, et al, 167–192, 2011.

Epilogue

Syed Farid Alatas and Vineeta Sinha

The Meaning of Alternative Sociologies

This book has presented an alternative account of sociological theory. We have attempted to work in the tradition of autonomous social science. This is defined as a tradition which raises problem, creates concepts and creatively applies theories in an independent manner and without being dominated intellectually by another tradition.[1] Consciously working within the tradition of autonomous social science would lead to the development of alternative sociologies. Alatas had defined alternative discourses as those

> which are informed by local/regional historical experiences and cultural practices in Asia in the same way that the Western social sciences are. Being alternative requires the turn to philosophies, epistemologies, histories, and the arts other than those of the Western tradition. These are all to be considered as potential sources of social science theories and concepts,

---

[1] Syed Hussein Alatas, 'The Development of an Autonomous Social Science Tradition in Asia: Problems and Prospects'. *Asian Journal of Social Science*, 30, 1 (2002), 150–157, 151.

© The Author(s) 2017
S.F. Alatas, V. Sinha, *Sociological Theory Beyond the Canon*,
DOI 10.1057/978-1-137-41134-1_12

which would decrease academic dependence on the world social science powers. Therefore, it becomes clear that the emergence and augmentation of alternative discourses is identical to the process of universalizing and internationalizing the social sciences. It should also be clear that alternative discourses refer to good social science because they are more conscious of the relevance of the surroundings and the problems stemming from the discursive wielding of power by the social sciences – and with the need for the development of new ideas. Alternative is being defined as that which is relevant to its surroundings – is creative, non-imitative and original, non-essentialist, counter-Eurocentric, autonomous from the state, and autonomous from other national or transnational groupings.[2]

Eurocentrism and Androcentrism remain persistent biases in the teaching of the social sciences despite decades of acknowledgement of these orientations. A brief glance at the course outlines and textbooks used for the teaching of various disciplines such as sociology, anthropology, geography, political science and others in many universities around the world will reveal a number of characteristics of Eurocentrism and Androcentrism. Americans, Europeans and men are generally presented as the originators of ideas, theories and concepts and it is Western concepts that dominate in the discussions. Americans, Europeans and men are the ones who theorize. If at all women and non-Europeans appear in the teaching materials, they are usually objects of study of Western male theorists. They are rarely featured as knowing subjects, that is, as sources of theories and ideas. For example, social theory texts generally give accounts of American and European originators of sociology, almost all of whom are male. The impression given is that there were no women and non-European progenitors of originators of social theory during the formative period of Western social theory in the nineteenth century.

What we have done in the preceding chapters is to both read Western and male writers in a non-Eurocentric and non-androcentric way as well as present the social thought of non-European and women thinkers. We use the term 'autonomous' rather than 'independent.' This is because we

---

[2] Syed Farid Alatas, *Alternative Discourses in Asian Social Science: Responses to Eurocentrism* (Delhi: Sage, 2006), 82.

do not call for the delinking from the Western social sciences or from Western institutions. Rather, we call for a creative dialogue between the Western and various non-Western traditions, and for a greater consciousness of various biases in the teaching and learning of the social sciences, such as Eurocentrism and Androcentrism. For this to take place, non-Western and female voices need to be taken seriously. What Connell said about theories that originate from the South also applies to female theorists. Connell says that she 'takes them seriously as theory – as texts to learn *from*, not just *about*.'[3] We wish to be border thinkers in order that we can think *with* Ibn Khaldun, Marx and Ramabai, and not just think with Marx and *about* Ibn Khaldun and Ramabai. As noted by Mignolo, 'border thinkers have an epistemic potential that territorial and imperial thinkers have lost.'[4]

Cross-Border Interactions, Conversations and Applications

One interesting point to note about broadening the sphere of social theory by bringing in non-Western and female founders and pioneers of social thought is interactions between them, or rather, their ideas. That there would not have been such interactions owing to their belonging to different cultural and social universes seems to be the dominant expectation. But, there are in fact several examples of such interactions.

One has to do with possible borrowing from Ibn Khaldun by Marx and Engels. Engels seems to have recognized the Khaldunian cycle in one of his writings, which is worth quoting in full:

> Islam is a religion adapted to Orientals, especially Arabs, i.e., on one hand to townsmen engaged in trade and industry, on the other to nomadic Bedouins. Therein lies, however, the embryo of a periodically recurring

---

[3] Raewyn Connell, *Southern Theory: The global dynamics of knowledge in social science*, Crows Nest: Allen & Unwin, 2007, viii.

[4] Walter Mignolo, 'Spirit Out of Bounds Returns to the East: The Closing of the Social Sciences and the Opening of Independent Thoughts'. *Current Sociology*, 62, 2 (2014), 584–602, 593.

collision. The townspeople grow rich, luxurious and lax in the observation of the 'law'. The Bedouins, poor and hence of strict morals, contemplate with envy and covetousness these riches and pleasures. Then they unite under a prophet, a Mahdi, to chastise the apostates and restore the observation of the ritual and the true faith and to appropriate in recompense the treasures of the renegades. In a hundred years they are naturally in the same position as the renegades were: a new purge of the faith is required, a new Mahdi arises and the game starts again from the beginning. That is what happened from the conquest campaigns of the African Almoravids and the Almohads in Spain to the last Mahdi of Khartoum who so successfully thwarted the English. It happened in the same way or similarly with the risings in Persia and other Mohammedan countries. All these movements are clothed in religion but they have their source in economic causes; and yet, even when they are victorious, they allow the old economic conditions to persist untouched. So the old situation remains unchanged and the collision recurs periodically.[5]

While Engels makes no reference to Ibn Khaldun, it is quite likely that both he and Marx were aware of Ibn Khaldun's works.[6] What Engels described above is very similar to what Ibn Khaldun discusses in his theory. This can be taken as a description of Asiatic societies much like the case of India where the tribes were 'successive intruders who founded their empires on the passive basin of that unresisting and unchanging society.'[7] The periodic rise and fall of dynasties through successive tribal conquests left the basic structure of the Asiatic mode of production unchanged.

Cross-border interactions and conversations are in and of themselves interesting and fascinating. The fact of these interactions, however, also point to the possibility of creative applications of theory that draw from diverse traditions. In the chapter on Ibn Khaldun we had referred to

[5] Frederick Engels, 'On the History of Early Christianity'. In Karl Marx and Frederick Engels, *On Religion*, (Moscow: Progress Publishers, 1975), 276.

[6] See G. -H. Bousquet, 'Marx et Engels se-sont ils interesses aux questions islamiques?' *Studia Islamica*, 30 (1969), 119–30, 123–5.

[7] Karl Marx, 'The Future Results of British Rule in India,' in Karl Marx & Frederick Engels, *On Colonialism* (Moscow: Progress Publishers, 1974), 81–87, 81.

Gellner's merging of Ibn Khaldun's cyclical theory of dynastic succession with Hume pendulum swing theory of religiosity. Alatas has applied Ibn Khaldun's theory of state formation to a number of historical cases. In these applications, it was necessary to bring in Marxist and Weberian concepts in order to strengthen the Khaldunian approach. While Ibn Khaldun's theory provides an explanation for the rise and decline of the state by focusing on the dynamic interaction between social solidarity and state efficacy, his work lacks a conceptualization of the economic system. For this reason it was deemed necessary to bring in Marx's concept of the mode of production and Weber's concept of the pre-bendal feudalism. These were integrated into a Khaldunian theoretical framework that was applied to specific historical cases of state formation in North Africa and West Asia.[8] Such applications, based on creative merging of diverse traditions, make for a more cosmopolitan sociology.

Some Closing Thoughts

As all students of sociology know, there is a body of writings recognized as the sociological canon and a 'must read' list of theorists. This is typically formed through drawing up a catalogue of individuals whose ideas and writings are deemed to be classic works for the discipline. Why is it that even today someone like Martineau (and numerous others like her) continues to hover on the margins despite ample knowledge of her various accomplishments and contributions? I am led to ask these following questions: What are the criteria by which the discipline recognizes social thinkers and theorists? This attention to selection standards assumes paramount importance when 'new' candidates are considered. How does this select list of acceptable theorists get generated? We all know of 'non-sociologists' from Tocqueville to Marx to Freud to Mead to Foucault, who have been appropriated as sociologists and granted honorary entry into the discipline's canon. Many of the

---

[8] Syed Farid Alatas, *Applying Ibn Khaldun: The Recovery of a Lost Tradition in Sociology* (London: Routledge, 2014).

fore-mentioned figures were working in a context that pre-dates the formalization of sociology were thus not trained as sociologists and neither did they see themselves as such. Yet on the basis of interpretation of their works, and abstraction of sociological thought from the corpus of their writings, they have been claimed as 'one of our own' by future generations of sociologists.

We argue that introducing women thinkers like Martineau and Ramabai, together with Marx, Weber, Durkheim, and Jose Rizal, Ibn Khaldun and Benoy Kumar Sarkar as examples of social thinkers, located in diverse sociocultural and political settings and who grappled with the experience and impact of modernity is a critical step.[9] This rethinking has had important consequences for our own education as sociologists, in revisiting the foundations of our discipline, in taking us back to a set of basic questions, which assume even more significance for me in the present.

This experience of trying to include Rizal, Martineau and Sarkar in the course on social thought and social theory has been invaluable in making us think explicitly about the logic, rationale and historical process by which the sociological canon is constructed and how it notes and marks some individuals as social thinkers but not others. Amongst practicing sociologists, this subject has remained part of the discipline's condensed knowledge pool for too long and consequently received scant overt attention. Some sociologists have, however, been transparent about their selection criteria for recognizing sociology's pioneering figures. Here we make a case for the need to reflect on criteria-in-use and to consider others that may be more relevant and broader in scope rather than unreflexively accept those that are steeped in specific and unique historical and cultural experiences, and which are then universally applied.

Fundamental revisions in the canon of any discipline require what Kuhn calls paradigmatic shifts, rooted in the very rethinking of the discipline in question. Our intention in highlighting the presence of a

[9] Syed Farid Alatas & Vineeta Sinha, 'Teaching Classical Sociological Theory in Singapore: The Context of Eurocentrism', *Teaching Sociology*, 29, 3 (2001), 316–331.

sociological canon is less about wishing it away, and more about pushing its boundaries. Having acknowledged and demonstrated marginalization of various non-Western and women thinkers within the historiography and practice of sociology does not necessarily lead to passivity and inertia. Although a canon exists, it is possible in practice, particularly in the realm of university teaching to question it and to raise critical issues for debate. Admittedly, a range of structural constraints can derail individual agency. There is no room in our argument for the suggestion that all sociologists must now include Rizal or Martineau in their teaching. This call would be as oppressive and dogmatic as their omission has been so far. We cite select examples of social thinkers who have been marginalized, neglected and forgotten, but who have subsequently been recovered and are now being read. The consequence of these two great biases in the discipline of sociology is that it is generally American, British, French and German males who are seen to be the originators of theories and ideas. Many social thinkers from Asian and African societies who lived and wrote during the same period as Marx, Weber and Durkheim are either only mentioned in passing in writings of the history of sociology or totally ignored.

For different reasons, other such unknown figures may be more appealing to other sociologists. The larger argument we wish to make is in the recognition that the tapestry of contributions to social thought and theorizing is enormous and multifaceted, emanating from multiple sites and via a variety of different actors. Our aim is to expand the playing field rather than restrict it, and I thus stand with Hill when he says that 'Our discipline grows stronger from inclusion and dialogue, not from exclusion and silence'[10] (2002: 191). Furthermore, we do have reservations about generating yet another 'must read' list of thinkers. The concern here is more about opening the door to a serious consideration of a larger pool of potential contributors to sociological theorizing *in addition* to existing names. There are no doubt numerous others like Martineau, Rizal, Sarkar, men and women, located in different societal contexts – European and non-European – and time frames whose

---

[10] Hill (2002), 191.

contributions and insights for sociological theorizing have for too long gone unnoticed in narrating a history of the discipline. It is time this lack of attention was problematized and *acted upon* by its practitioners.

Reference

Hill, Michael R. 'Empiricism and reason in Harriet Martineau's Sociology.' In *Martineau, How to observe morals and manners*, ed. Harriet Martineau, xv–lx. New Bruniswick: Rutgers University Press, 2002.

Bibliography

Abdesselem, Ahmed. *Ibn Khaldun et ses Lecteurs*. Paris: Presses Universitaires de France, 1983.

Abrahamian, Ervand. 'Oriental Despotism: The Case of Qajar Iran'. *International Journal of Middle East Studies* 5 (1974): 3–31.

Akat, Asaf Savas. 'Proposal for a Radical Reinterpretation of the Asiatic Versus the European Social Formation'. In *The Civilizational Project: The Visions of the Orient*, edited by Anouar Abdel Malek, 69–79. Mexico City: El Colegio de Mexico, 1981.

Al, Jörg Feuchter et al., eds. *Cultural Transfers in Dispute: Representations in Asia, Europe and the Arab World Since the Middle Ages*. Frankfurt: Campus Verlag, 2011.

Al-Tabari. *Tarikh al-Rusul wa-l-Muluk*. Edited by M.J. de Goeje (et al.). Leiden: Brill, 1879–1901.

Alatas, Syed Farid. 'Ibn Khaldun and the Ottoman Modes of Production,' *Arab Historical Review for Ottoman Studies* 1–2 (1990): 45–63.

Alatas, Syed Farid. 'A Khaldunian Perspective on the Dynamics of Asiatic Societies'. *Comparative Civilizations Review* 29 (1993): 29–51.

Alatas, Syed Farid. *Alternative Discourses in Asian Social Science: Responses to Eurocentrism*. New Delhi: Sage Publications, 2006.

Alatas, Syed Farid. *Applying Ibn Khaldun: The Recovery of a Lost Tradition in Sociology*. London: Routledge, 2014.

© The Author(s) 2017
S.F. Alatas, V. Sinha, *Sociological Theory Beyond the Canon*,
DOI 10.1057/978-1-137-41134-1

Alatas, Syed Farid and Vineeta Sinha. 'Teaching Classical Sociological Theory in Singapore: The Context of Eurocentrism'. *Teaching Sociology* 29, no. 3 (2001): 316–331.

Alatas, Syed Hussein. 'Objectivity and the Writing of History'. *Progressive Islam* 1, no. 2 (1954): 2–4.

Alatas, Syed Hussein. 'The Weber Thesis and South-East Asia'. In *Modernization and Social Change: Studies in Modernization, Religion, Social Change and Development in South-East Asia*, edited by Alatas Syed Hussein, 1–20. Sydney: Angus & Robertson, 1972.

Alatas, Syed Hussein. *The Myth of the Lazy Native: A Study of the Image of the Malays, Filipinos and Javanese from the 16th to the 20th Century and its Function in the Ideology of Colonial Capitalism*. London: Frank Cass, 1977.

Alatas, Syed Hussein. 'The Development of an Autonomous Social Science Tradition in Asia: Problems and Prospects'. *Asian Journal of Social Science* 30, no. 1 (2002), 150–157.

Alavi, Hamza. 'The State in Post-Colonial Societies: Pakistan and Bangladesh'. *New Left Review* 74 (1972): 59–81.

Alavi, Hamza. 'State and Class Under Peripheral Capitalism'. In *Introduction to the Sociology of 'Developing Societies'*, edited by Hamza Alavi and Teodor Shanin. London: Macmillan Education Ltd., 1982.

Alexander, J., ed. *Durkheimian Sociology: Cultural Studies*. Cambridge: Cambridge University Press, 1990.

Alpert, H. 'Emile Durkheim: A Perspective and Appreciation'. *American Sociological Review* 24, no. 4 (1959): 462–465.

Andreski, Stanislav. *Max Weber's Insights and Errors*. London: Routledge, 2013.

Armstrong, Amatullah. *Sufi Terminology (Al-Qamus Al-Sufi): The Mystical Language of Islam*. Kuala Lumpur: A.S. Noordeen, 1995.

Aron, Raymond. *Main Currents in Sociological Thought*, Vols. 1& 2. New York: Anchor Books, 1970.

Avineri, Shlomo. Introduction to *Karl Marx on Colonialism and Modernization*, 1–28. Edited by Shlomo Avineri. New York: Doubleday, 1968.

Azmeh, Aziz El. 'The Muqaddima and Kitab Al'Ibar: Perspectives from a Common Formula'. *The Maghreb Review* 4, no. 1 (1979): 17–20.

Balci, Ramazan. *A Short Biography of Bediuzzaman Said Nursi: Wonder of the Age*. Clifton, NJ: Tughra Books, 2011.

Baly, Monica E. and H.C.G. Matthew. 'Nightingale, Florence (1820–1910)'. In *Oxford Dictionary of National Biography* (online edition). Oxford; New York: OUP, 2004.

Banaji, Jairus. *Theory as History: Essays on Modes of Production and Exploitation.* Chicago: Haymarket Books, 2011.

Bandhopadhyaya, B. *The Political ideas of Benoy Kumar Sarkar.* Calcutta: K.P. Bagchi & Company, 1984.

Banerjee, Parthasarathi. 1998. 'The Disciplinary Triplet of "Social Sciences": An Indian Response'. *Review (Fernand Braudel Center)* 21 (3) – 'The States, the Markets, and the Societies: Separate Logics or a Single Domain? Part One': 253–326.

Bannerji, Himani. 'Projects of Hegemony: Towards a Critique of Subaltern Studies' "Resolution of the Women's Question"'. *Economic and Political Weekly* 35, no. 11 (2000): 902–920.

Bapat, Ram. 'Pandita Ramabai: Faith and Reason in the Shadow of the East and West'. In *Representing Hinduism: the construction of religious traditions and national identity,* edited by Vasudha Dalmia and Heinrich von Stietencron, 224–252. New Delhi; Thousand Oaks, CA: Sage Publications, 1995.

Barnes, B. *The Critical Elements of Social Theory.* Pricneton University Press, 1995/2014.

Barnes, Harry Elmer, ed. *An Introduction to History of Sociology.* Chicago: University of Chicago Express, 1948.

Becker, Howard and Harry Elmer Barnes. *Social Thought from Lore to Science,* Vols. 1, 2 and 3 (Third edition). New York: Dover Publications, 1961.

Behn, Wolfgang. 'Benoy Kumar Sarkar: 1887–1949'. Vols. 3 (N–Z). In *Concise Biographical Companion to Index Islamicus, 1665–1980: An International Who's Who in Islamic Studies From its Beginnings Down to the Twentieth Century,* edited by Wolfgang Behn. Leiden; Boston: Brill, 2004.

Bendix, Reinhard. *Max Weber: An Intellectual Potrait.* Berkeley & Los Angeles: University of California Press, 1977.

Bernard, J.S. and Bernard, L.L. 'Leaders of Social Thought'. *Social Forces* 15, no. 3 (1937): 428–434.

Bhattacharyya, Swapan Kumar. *Indian Sociology: The Role of Benoy Kumar Sarkar.* Burdwan: University of Burdwan, 1990.

Bhushan, Nalini, and Jay L. Garfield. *Indian Philosophy in English: From Renaissance to Independence.* Oxford: Oxford University Press, 2011.

Bishop, William J. 'Florence Nightingale's Letters'. *The American Journal of Nursing* 57, no. 5 (1957): 607–609.

Black, A. *Guilds and Civil Society in European Political Thought from the Twelfth Century to Present.* Cambridge, UK: Cambridge University Press, 1984.

Blumentritt, Ferdinand. 'Prologue'. In *Historical Events of the Philippine Islands by Dr Antonio de Morga*, edited by Antonio De Morga, (Published in Mexico in 1609), recently brought to light and annotated by Jose Rizal, preceded by a prologue by Dr Ferdinand Blumentritt, *Writings of Jose Rizal Volume VI*. Manila: National Historical Institute, 1890/1962, viii–xxiii.

Blumhofer, Edith. 'Consuming Fire: Pandita Ramabai and the Global Pentecostal Impulse'. In *Interpreting Contemporary Christianity: Global Processes and Local Identities*, edited by Ogbu U. Kalu and Alaine Low. Grand Rapids, Mich.: William B. Eerdmans Pub. Co, 2008.

Bonoan, Raul J. *The Rizal-Pastells Correspondence*. Quezon City: Ateneo de Manila Press, 1994.

Borochov, Ber Dov. 'Eretz Yisrael in Our Program and Tactics'. Address delivered to the Third Conference of the Russian Poale Zion, Kiev, September 1917.

Bostridge, Mark. *Florence Nightingale: The Woman and Her Legend*. London: Viking, 2008.

Bottomore, Tom. *A Dictionary of Marxists Thought*, 178. Cambridge, MA: Harvard University Press, 1983.

Bousque, G.H.T. 'Marx et Engels se-sont ils interesses aux questions islamiques?' *Studia Islamica* 30 (1969): 119–130.

Boyd, Nancy. *Three Victorian Women Who Changed Their World: Josephine Butler Octavia Hill, Florence Nightingale*. Oxford: Oxford University Press, OUP, 1982.

Brandford, V. 'Durkheim: A brief memoir'. *The Sociological Review*, 10, no. 2 (1918): 77–82.

Bruscino, Thomas A. *A Nation Forged in War: How World War II Taught Americans to Get Along*. Knoxville: University of Tenessee Press, 2010.

Bulliet, Richard. 'Islamo-Christian Civilization'. *Institute for Social Policy and Understanding, Policy Brief*, December 2012. Accessed at http://www.ispu.org/pdfs/ISPU_Brief_IslamoChristianCiv_1212.pdf.

Bulliet, Richard W. *The Case for Islamo-Christian Civilization*. New York: Columbia University, 2004.

Burger, Thomas. *Max Weber's Theory of Concept Formation: History, Laws and Ideal Types*. Durham: Duke University Press, 1976.

Burton, Antoinette. 'Colonial Encounters in Late-Victorian England: Pandita Ramabai at Cheltenham and Wantage 1883–6'. *Feminist Review* 49 (1995): 29–49.

Burton, Antoinette. 'Restless Desire: Pandita Ramabai at Cheltenham and Wantage, 1883–86'. In *At the Heart of the Empire: Indians and the Colonial Encounter in Late-Victorian Britain*. Berkeley: University of California Press, 1997.

Caiden, Gerald E. 'Excessive Bureaucratization: The J-Curve Theory of Bureaucracy and Max Weber Through the Looking Glass'. In *Handbook of Bureaucracy*, edited by Ali Farazman, 29–40. New York: Marcel Dekker, 1994.

Calabria, Michael and Janet A. Macrae. *Suggestions for Thought by Florence Nightingale; Selections and Commentaries*. Phil: University of Pennsylvania Press, 1994.

Cânan, İbrahim. 'The Companions of the Prophet (PBUH) in Bediuzzaman's Works'. In Proceedings of the Third International Symposium on Bediuzzaman Said Nursi – The Reconstruction of Islamic Thought in the Twentieth Century and Bediuzzaman Said Nursi, Istanbul, 24–26 September 1995, Istanbul: Sözler, 1997.

Carré, Olivier. 'Ethique et politique chez Ibn Khaldûn, juriste musulman: Actualité de sa typologie des systèmes politique'. *L'Annee sociologique* 30 (1979–80): 109–127.

Carré, Olivier. 'A Propos de Vues Neo-Khalduniennnes sur Quelques Systemes Politiques Arabes Actuels'. *Arabica* 35, no. 3 (1988): 368–387.

Case, Jay Riley. *An Unpredictable Gospel*. New York: Oxford University Press, 2012.

Catton, W. 'Emile who and the Division of what?'. *Sociological Perspectives* 28, no. 3 (1985): 251–280.

Celarent, Barbara. Review of The High Caste Hindu Woman by; Pandita Ramabai's America: Conditions of Life in the United States (United Stateschi Lokasthiti ani Pravasvritta), edited by Pandita Ramabai Sarasvati, Kshitija Gomez, Philip C. Engblom, and Robert E. Frykenberg. *American Journal of Sociology* 117, no. 1 (2011): 353–360.

Chakravarti, Uma. 'The Myth of "Patriots" and "Traitors": Pandita Ramabai, Brahmanical Patriarchy and Militant Hindu Nationalism'. In *Embodied Violence: Communalising Women's Sexuality in South Asia*, edited by Kumari Jayawardena and Malathi de Alwis, 190–239. London: Zed Books, 1996.

Chakravarti, Uma. *Rewriting History: The Life and Times of Pandita Ramabai*. New Delhi: Kali for Women in association with the Book Review Literary Trust, 1998.

Chakravarti, Uma. 'Wifehood, Widowhood, and Adultery: Female Sexuality, Surveillance, and the State in Eighteenth-Century Maharashtra'. In *Of Property and Propriety: The Role of Gender and Class in Imperialism and Nationalism*, edited by Himani Bannerji, Shahrzad Mojab and Judith Whitehead. Toronto: University of Toronto Press, 2001.

Chapman, Maria Weston. 'An Autobiographical Memoir'. In *Memorials of Harriet Martineau*, 562–573. Boston: James R. Osgood, 1877a.

Chapman, Maria Weston. *Harriet Martineau's Autobiography*. Vol. 2, in *Memorials of Harriet Martineau*. Boston: James R. Osgood, 1877b.

Chapman, Maria Weston. 'Letter'. In *An Epitome of the Positive Philosophy and Religion: Explanatory of the Society of Humanity in the City of New York and Together with the Constitution and Regulations of that Society: To Which is Added an Important Letter of Harriet Martineau in Regard to Her Religious Convictions*, edited by Harriet Martineau, 40–50. New York: The Society of Humanity, 1877c.

Chaudhary, N.N. *Pragmatism and Pioneering in Benoy Sarkar's Sociology and Economics*. Calcutta: Chuckervertty Chatterjee & Company Limited, 1990.

Cheddadi, Abdesselam. 'Le Systeme du Pouvoir en Islam d'apres Ibn Khaldun'. *Annales. Économies, Sociétés, Civilisations* 3–4 (1980): 534–550.

Clementina, Butler. *Pandita Ramabai Sarasvati: Peioener in the Movement for the Education of the Child-Widow of India*. New York: Fleming H. Revell Company, 1922.

Collins, Patricia Hill. *Black Feminist Thought: Knowledge, Consciousness and the Politics of Empowerment*. Boston: Unwin Hyman, 1990.

Comte, Auguste. 'Cours de philosophie positive (Vol. 6). Paris: Bachelier, 1830–42'. In *The Positive Philosophy of Auguste Comte*, translated by Harriet Martineau. New York: William Gowans, 1853.

Conlon, Frank. 'Review of Pandita Ramabai Saraswati, By Padmini Sengupta'. *Pacific Affairs* 44, no. 4 (1971/72): 632–633.

Connell, Raewyn. *Southern Theory: The Global Dynamics of Knowledge in Social Science*. Crows Nest: Allen & Unwin, 2007.

Constantino, Renato. 'Our Task: To Make Rizal Obsolete'. *This Week* 14(24), June 14, 1959

Coser, Lewis A. *Masters of Sociological Thought: Ideas in Historical and Social Context*. New York: Harcourt Brace Jovanovich, 1971.

Coser, Lewis A. *Masters of Sociological Thought*. New York: Harcout Brace, 1977.

Costa, Horacio de la, S.J., ed. *The Trial of Rizal: W. E. Retana's Transcription of the Official Spanish Documents*. Manila: Ateneo de Manila Press, 1961.

Cowan, Bainard. 'Walter Benjamin's Theory of Allegory'. *New German Critique* 22 (1981): 109–122.

Cunningham, C. 'Finding a Role for Durkheim in Contemporary Moral Theory'. In *Philosophy of Education Yearbook*, 328–330, 2002.

Dasgupta, Samir, ed. *The Changing Face of Globalization*. New Delhi: Sage, 2004.

Dass, B., ed. *The Social and Economic Ideas of Benoy Sarkar*. Calcutta: Chuckervertty Chatterjee & Co, 1939.

David, Deidra. *Intellectual Women and Victorian Patriarchy: Harriet Martineau, Elizabeth Barrett Browning, George Eliot*. New York: Cornell University Press, 1987.

De Sacy, Baron Antoine Isaac Silvestre. 'Extraits de Prolégomènes d'Ebn Khaldoun'. In *Relation de l'Egypt, par Abd-Allatif, médecin arabe de Bagdad*, translated by Baron Antoine Isaac Silvestre de Sacy: 509–524 & 558–564 (Arabic text) (Paris, 1810).

Deegan, Mary Jo. 'Women in Sociology, 1890–1930'. *Journal of the History of Sociology* 1 (Fall, 1978): 11–34.

Deegan, Mary Jo. 'Transcending a Patriarchal Past: Teaching the History of Early Women Sociologists'. *Teaching Sociology* 16 (1988): 141–159.

Deegan, Mary Jo. *Women in Sociology: A Bio-Bibliographical Sourcebook*. New York: Greenwood, 1991.

Denisoff, R. Serge. *Theories and Paradigms in Contemporary Sociology*. Itasca: F. E. Peacock, 1974.

Dharwadker, Vinay. 'English in India and Indian Literature in English: The Early History, 1579–1834'. *Comparative Literature Studies* 39, no. 2 (2002): 93–119.

Dietrich, R. 'On Durkheim's Explanation of Division of Labor'. *American Journal of Sociology* 88, no. 3 (1982): 579–589.

Domhoff, William. 'State and Ruling Class in Corporate America'. *Insurgent Sociologist* 4 (1974): 3–16.

Dossey, Barbara Montgomery. *Florence Nightingale: Mystic, Visionary, Healer*. Springhouse, PA: Springhouse Corp, 2000.

Dryjanska, Anna. 'Harriet Martineau: The forerunner of cultural studies.' In *Advancing Gender Reserch from the Nineteenth to the Twenty-First Centuries*, edited by Marcia Texler Segal and Vasilikie Demos. Bingley, UK: Emaradl Group Publishing Limited, pp 63–77, 2008.

Dryjanska, Anna. 'Harriet Martineau and the idea of liberty'. *Sociological Origins* 5, no. 2 (2008a): 9–10, 46.

Dube, S.C. 'India'. In *Social Sciences in Asia and the Pacific*, edited by UNESCO, 229–248. Paris: UNESCO, 1984.

Durkheim, Emile. *The Division of Labour in Society*. New York: Free Press, 1933.

Durkheim, Emile. *Suicide: A Study in Sociology*. Translated by J.A. Glencoe. Illinios: The Free Press, 1951.

Durkheim, Emile. *Suicide: A Study in Sociology*. New York: Routledge & Kegan Paul, 1952.

Durkheim, Emile. *Sociology and Philosophy*. Edited by D. Pocock. London: Cohen and West, 1953.

Durkheim, Emile. *Moral Education: A Study in the Theory and Application of the Sociology of Education*. Translated by Everett K. Wilson and Herman Schnurer. New York: Free Press of Glencoe, 1961.

Durkheim, Emile. *The Rules of Sociological Method*. New York: Free Press, 1982a.

Durkheim, Emile. *The Rules of Sociological Method and Selected Texts on Sociology and Its Method*. Translated by S.L.W.D. Halls. New York: The Free Press, 1895/1982b.

Durkheim, Emile. *The Division of Labour in the Society*. Translated by W. Halls. New York: The Free Press, 1984.

Durkheim, Emile. *The Elementary Forms of the Religious Life*. Translated by K. Fields. New York: Free Press, 1995.

Durkheim, Emilie and George Simpson. *Suicide: A Study in Sociology*. New York: Simon & Schuster, 2010 (1951)

Dutt, S.C. *Fundamental Problems and Leading Ideas in the Works of Prof. Benoy Kumar Sarkar*. Calcutta: Ray, 1932.

Dutt, S.C. *Conflicting Tendencies In Indian Economic Thought – Sarkarism in Economics*. Calcutta: Chuckervertty Chatterjee & Co, 1939.

Dyer, Helen S. *Pandita Ramabai. The Story of Her Life*. London: Morgan & Scott, 1900.

Ebied, R.Y. and M.J.L. Young. 'New Light on the Origin of the Term "Baccalaureate"'. *Islamic Quarterly* 18, no. 1–2 (1974): 3–7.

Emirbayer, M. 'Useful Durkheim'. *Sociological Theory* 14, no. 2 (1996): 109–130.

Emirbayer, M., ed. *Emile Durkheim: Sociologist of Modernity*. New York: Wiley Blackwell, 2003.

Enan, Muhammad Abdullah. *Ibn Khaldun: His Life and Work*. Lahore: Muhammad Ashraf, 1941.

Engels, Frederick. 'Speech at the Graveside of Karl Marx'. In *Marx and Engels through the Eyes of their Contemporaries*. Moscow: Progress Publishers, 1972.

Engels, Frederick. 'On the History of Early Christianity'. In *On Religion*, authored by Karl Marx and Frederick Engels. Moscow: Progress Publishers, 1975.

Engels, Frederick. 'Letters on Historical Materialism'. In *The Marx-Engels Reader*, edited by Robert C. Tucker, 760–768. London & New York: W. W. Norton & Co., 1978.

Farmer, Mary E. 'The Positivist Movement and the Development of English Sociology'. *Sociological Review* (1967): 5–20.

Fischer-Tiné, Harald and Stolte Carolien. 'Imagining Asia in India: Nationalism and Internationalism (ca. 1905–1940)'. *Comparative Studies in Society and History* 54, no. 1 (2012): 65–92.

Fish, S.J. *Defending the Durkheimian Tradition: Religion, Emotion and Morality*. Aldershot: Ashgate, 2005.

Flint, Robert. *History of the Philosophy of History in France, Belgium, and Switzerland*. France: C. Scribner's sons, 1893.

Foley, Sean. 'Muslims and Social Change in the Atlantic Basin'. *Journal of World History* 20, no. 3 (2009): 377–398.

Forbes, Geraldine. *Women in Modern India*. Cambridge: Cambridge University Press, 1996.

Frykenberg, R.E. 'Benoy Kumar Sarkar, 1897–1949: Political Rishi of Twentieth Century Bengal'. In *Explorations in the History of South Asia: Essays in Honour of Dietmar Rothermund*, edited by Tilman Frasch, Hermann Kulke, and Jürgen Lütt Georg Berkemer, 197–217. New Delhi: Manohar, 2001.

Fuller, Mary Lucia Bierce. *The Triumph of an Indian Widow: The Life of Pandita Ramabai* (Third edition). Havertown, Penn: American Council of the Ramabai Mukti Mission, 1939.

Ganachari, Aravind., ed. 'Dilemma of a Christian Convert: Pandita Ramabai's Confrontation with Apologists – Hindu and Christian'. In *Nationalism and social reform in a colonial situation*. Delhi: Kalpaz Publications, 2005.

Gane, M. 'A Fresh Look at Durkheim's Sociological Method'. In *Debating Durkheim*, edited by P.a. Martins, 66–85. New York and London: Routledge, 1994.

Gasset, José Ortega y. 'Abenjaldún nos revela el secreto'. *Revista del Instituto Egipcio de Estudios Islámicos en Madrid* 19 (1976–8): 95–114. Originally published in *El Espectador* 7 (1934): 9–53.

Gellner, Ernest. *Muslim Society*. Cambridge: Cambridge University Press, 1981.

Ghosh, Suniti Kumar. 'Marx on India'. *Monthly Review* 35 (1984): 39–53.

Ghoshal, S.K. *Sarkarism: The Ideas and Ideals of Benoy Sarkar on Man and His Conquests*. Calcutta: Chuckervertty Chatterjee & Co, 1939.

Gianfranco, P. *Durkheim*. Oxford: Oxford University Press, 2000.

Giddens, A. 'The Constitution of Society'. In *The Giddens Reader*, edited by Philip Cassell, 88. MacMillan Press, 1984.

Giuseppe, Flora. *Benoy Kumar Sarkar and Italy: Culture, Politics, and Economic Ideology*. Italy: Italian Embassy Cultural Centre, 1994.

Godlove, F.T., ed. *Teaching Durkheim*. Oxford: Oxford University Press, 2005.

Goswami, Manu. 'From Swadeshi to Swaraj: Nation, Economy, Territory in Colonial South Asia, 1870 to 1907'. *Comparative Studies in Society and History* 40, no. 4 (1998): 609–636.

Goswami, Manu. 'Provincialising Sociology: The Case of a premature post-colonial Sociologist'. In *Postcolonial Sociology*, edited by Julian Go, 145–176. Bingley: Emerald Group Publishing Limited, 2013.

Gourlay, Jharna. *Florence Nightingale and the Health of the Raj*. Aldershot, Hants, England; Burlington, VT: Ashgate, 2003.

Grewal, Inderpal. *Home and Harem: Nation, Gender, Empire, and the Cultures of Travel*. London: Leicester University Press, 1996.

Grint, Keith. 'Nursing the Media: Social Leadership in the Crimean and English Hospitals'. In *The Arts of Leadership*. New York: OUP, 2000.

Guerrero, León Ma. *The First Filipino: A Biography of José Rizal*. Manila: National Historical Institute, 1991.

Guerrero, N. and John Schumacher. *Reform and Revolution*. Manila: Asia Publishing House, 1998.

Guillaume, Alfred. 'Philosophy and Theology'. In *The Legacy of Islam*, edited by Sir Thomas Arnold and Alfred Guillaume, 239–283. London: Oxford University Press, 1931.

Gumplowicz, Ludwig. *Soziologische Essays: Soziologie und Politik*. Innsbruck: Universitats-Verlag Wagner, 1899/1928a.

Gumplowicz, Ludwig. *The Outlines of Sociology*. Translated by Frederick W. Moore. Philadelphia: American Academy of Political and Social Science, 1899/1928b.

Gutierrez, Gustavo. *A Theology of Liberation.* Maryknoll, New York: Orbis Books, 1973.

Harms, J. 'Reason and Social Change in Durkheim's Thought: The Changing Relationship between Individual and Society'. *Pacific Sociological Review* 24, no. 4 (1981): 393–410.

Harriss, John. 'The Great Tradition Globalizes: Reflections on Two Studies of "The Industrial Leaders" of Madras'. *Modern Asian Studies* 37, no. 2 (2003): 327–362.

Harrison, Fredrick. 'Introduction (Vol. 1)'. In *The Positive Philosophy of Auguste Comte*, edited by Harriet Martineau, v–xix. London: G. Bell, 1895.

Hassett, Constance W. 'Siblings and Anti-Slavery: The Literary and Political Relations of Harriet Martineau, James Martineau and Maria Weston Chapman'. *Signs* 21 (Winter 1996).

Hedlund, Roger E., Sebastian Kim and Rajkumar Boaz Johnson, eds. *Indian & Christian: The Life and Legacy of Pandita Ramabai.* Delhi: ISPCK, 2011.

Hill, Michael R. 'Harriet Martineau's Novels and the Sociology of Class, Race, and Gender'. *The Association for Humanist Sociology.* Typescript, 1987.

Hill, Michael R. *'Empiricism and Reason in Harriet Martineau's Sociology'.* Vols. xv–lx. In *How to Observe Morals and Manners*, edited by Harriet Martineau. News Brunswick, New Jersey: Transaction Books, 1989.

Hill, Michael R. 'Harriet Martineau'. In *Women in Sociology: A Bio-Bibliographical Sourcebook*, edited by Mary Jo Deegan, 289–297. New York: Greenwood, 1991.

Hill, Michael R. 'Martineau in Current Introductory Textbooks: An Empirical Survey'. *The Harriet Martineau Sociological Society Newsletter*, no. 4 (Spring 1998): 4–5.

Hill, Michael R. 'Empiricism and Reason in Harriet Martineau's Sociology.' In Harriet Martineau, *How to Observe Morals and Manners, xv–ix.* New Brunswick: Rutgers University Press, 2002.

Hill, Michael R. and Susan Hoecker-Drysdale, eds. *Harriet Martineau: Theoretical and Methodological Perspectives.* London: Routledge, 2003.

Hindess, Barry and Paul Q. Hirst. *Pre-Capitalist Modes of Production.* London: Routledge & Kegan Paul, 1975.

Hirsch, Paul. P. C.-G. 'A Durkheimian Approach to Globalization'. In *The Oxford Handbook of Sociology and Organization Studies: Classical Foundations*, edited by P. Adler. New York: Oxford University Press, 2009.

Hirschman, Charles. 'The Making of Race in Colonial Malaya: Political Economy and Racial Ideology'. *Sociological Forum* 1, no. 2 (1986): 330–361.

Hitti, Philip K. *History of the Arabs*. Houndmills: Macmillan, 1970.

Hoecker-Drysdale, Susan. *Harriet Martineau: First Woman Sociologist*. Oxford: Berg, 1992.

Hoecker-Drysdale, Susan. 'The Enigma of Harriet Martineau's Letters on Science'. *Women's Writing* 2, no. 2 (1995): 155–165.

Hoecker-Drysdale, Susan. 'Harriet Martineau'. In *The Blackwell Companion to Major Social Theories*, edited by George Ritzer, 53–80. Malden: Blackwell, 2000.

Hoecker-Drysdale, Susan and Micheal R. Hill, eds. *Harriet Martineau: Theoretical Methodlogical Perspective*. London: Routledge, 2002.

Holton, Sandra. 'Feminine Authority and Social Order: Florence Nightingale's Conception of Nursing and Health Care'. *Social Analysis: The International Journal of Social and Cultural Practice* 15 (1984): 59–72.

Hume, David. *The Natural History of Religion*. Oxford: Clarendon Press, 1976.

Hunter, Shelagh. *Harriet Martineau: The Poetics of Moralism*. Aldershot, England: Scolar Press, 1995.

Ichikawa, Chieko. 'Writing as Female National and Imperial Responsibility: Florence Nightingale's Scheme for Social and Cultural Reforms in England and India'. *Victorian Literature and Culture* 39, no. 1 (2011): 87–105.

Idriz, Mesut. 'From a Local Tradition to a Universal practice: *Ijazah* as a Muslim Educational Tradition'. *Asian Journal of Social Science* 35, no. 1 (2007).: 84–110.

Imam Al-Hafidh, Jalal al-Din al-Suyuti. *Tarikh al- Khulafa'*. Cairo: Dar a-Fajr l-l-Turath. 1420/1999.

Izzat, 'Abd al-'Aziz. *Etude comparée d'Ibn Khaldun et Durkheim*. Cairo: Al-Maktabat Al-Anglo Al-Misriyyah, 1952.

Jafri, S.H.M. *The Origins and Early Development of Shi'a Islam*. Beirut: Libraire du Liban, 1990.

Jones, S.S. *Durkheim Reconsidered*. Cambridge: Polity Press, 2001.

Jones, Gareth Stedman. *Karl Marx: Greatness and Illusion*. Cambridge, MA: Belknap Press, 2016.

Kalberg, Stephen. 'Max Weber's Types of Rationality: Cornerstones for the Analysis of Rationalization Processes in History'. *American Journal of Sociology* 85, no. 5 (1980): 1145–1179.

Kandal, Terry R. *The Woman Question in Classical Sociological Theory*. Miami: Florida International University Press, 1988.

Kapila, Shruti, and C.A. Bayly, eds. *An Intellectual History for India*. New Delhi: Cambridge Universirty Press, 2010.

Karim, A. K. Nazmul. 'Bangladesh'. In *Social Sciences in Asia and the Pacific*, edited by UNESCO, Paris: UNESCO, 1984: 79–92.

Karpat, Kemal. 'Nursi'. In *Encyclopaedia of Islam* (Second Edition), edited by P. Bearman, Th. Bianquis, C.E. Bosworth, E. van Donzel and W.P. Heinrichs. Brill Online, 2015.

Käsler, Dirk. *Max Weber: An Introuction to His Life and Work*. Cambridge: Polity Press, 1988.

Kaufman-Osborn. T. 'Emile Durkheim and the Science of Corporatism'. *Political Theory* 14, no. 4 (1986): 638–659.

Kelly, Heather. *Florence Nightingale's Autobiographical Notes: A Critical Edition of BL Add. 45844 (England)*. Ontario: Wilfrid Laurier University, 1998.

Khaldoun, Ibn. *Ibn Khaldun: The Muqadimmah – An Introduction of History*. Vols. 1, 2 & 3. Translated by Franz Rosenthal. London: Routledge & Kegan Paul, 1967.

Khaldoun, Ibn. *Histoire des Berbères et des dynasties musulmanes de l'Afrique septentrionale*, Vols. 1, 2 & 3. Translated by Baron de Slane. Paris: Libraire Orientaliste Paul Geuthner, 1982.

Khaldoun, Ibn. *Autobiographie: Al-Sirat Al-Dhatiyyah aw Ibn Khaldun wa Rihlatuhu Gharban wa Sharqan*, ouvrage présenté, traduit et annoté par Abdesselam Cheddadi. Témara: Maison des Arts, des Sciences et des Lettres, 2006.

Kineka, Francis E. *The Dissidence of Dissent: The Monthly Repository, 1806–1838*. Chapel Hill: University of North Carolina Press, 1944.

King, Donald and David Sylvester, eds. *The Eastern Carpet in the Western World, From the 15th to the 17th century*. London: Arts Council of Great Britain, 1983.

Kosambi, Meera. 'Women, Emancipation and Equality: Pandita Ramabai's Contribution to Women's Cause'. *Economic and Political Weekly* 23, no. 44 (1988): 38–49.

Kosambi, Meera. 'Indian Response to Christianity, Church and Colonialism: Case of Pandita Ramabai'. *Economic and Political Weekly* 27, no. 43/44 (1992): WS61-WS63+WS65-WS71.

Kosambi, Meera. 'The Meeting of the Twain: The Cultural Confrontation of Three Women in Nineteenth Century Maharashtra'. *Indian Journal of Gender Studies* 1, no. 1 (1994): 1–22.

Kosambi, Meera. 'Anandibai Joshee: Retrieving a Fragmented Feminist Image'. *Economic and Political Weekly* 31, no. 49 (1996): 3189–3197.

Kosambi, Meera. Pandita Ramabai Through Her Own Words: Selected Works. New Delhi: Oxford University Press, 2000.

Kosambi, Meera. 'Returning the American Gaze: Pandita Ramabai's "The Peoples of the United States, 1889"'. *Meridians* 2, no. 2 (2002): 188–212.

Kosambi, Meera. 'Motherhood in the EastWest Encounter: Pandita Ramabai's Negotiation of "Daughterhood" and "Motherhood" '. *Feminist Review* 65 (Summer), (2000): 49–67.

Kosambi, Meera. *Returning the American Gaze; Pandita Ramabai's The People of the United States*. New Delhi: Permanent Black, 2003.

Kremer, Alfred von. 'Ibn Chaldun und seine Kulturgeschichte der Islamischen Reiche'. *Sitzunsberichte der Kaiserlichen Akademie der Wissenschaften*. Vienna: *Philosoph.-histor. Klasse* (Vienna) 93, 1979

Kyi, Khin Maung. 'Burma'. In *Social Sciences in Asia and the Pacific*, edited by UNESCO, Paris: UNESCO, 1984: 93–141.

LaCapra, D. *Emile Durkheim: Sociologist and Philosopher*. Cornell: Cornell University Press,1972.

Lacoste, Yves. *Ibn Khaldun: The Birth of History and the Past of the Third World*. London: Verso, 1984.

Lafargue, Paul. 'Reminisences of Marx'. In *Marx and Engels through the Eyes of their Contemporaries*. Moscow: Progress Publishers, 1972.

Landau J. 'Nasir al-Din Tusi and Poetic Imagination in the Arabic and Persian Philosophic Tradition'. In *Metaphor and Imagery in Persian Poetry*, edited by Ali Asghar Seyed-Gohrab, 15–66. Leiden: Brill, 2012.

Laubach, Frank. *Rizal: Man and Martyr*. Manila: Community Publishers, 1936.

Lefebvre, Henri. The Sociology of Marx. New York: Columbia University Press, 1982.

Lehmann, J.M. *Deconstructing Durkheim: A Post-post Structuralist Critique*. London: Routledge, 1993.

Lemert, C. *Durkheim's Ghosts: Cultural Logics and Social Things*. Cambridge: Cambridge University Press, 2006.

Lengermann, Patricia, and Jill Niebrugger-Brantley. 'Early Women Sociologists'. In *Classical Sociology*, edited by George Ritzer, 294–328. New York: McGraw-Hill, 1996.

Lengermann, Patricia, and Jill Niebrugger-Brantley. *The Women Founders: Sociology and Social Theory, 1830–1930*. New York: McGraw-Hill, 1998.

Lewis A. Coser, Charles Kadushin and Walter W. Powell. *The Culture and Commerce of Publishing*. New York: Basic Books, 1982.

Lukács, Georg. *History and Class Consciousness: Studies in Marxist Dialectics*. Cambridge: MIT Press, 1971.

Lukes, S. *Emile Durkheim, His Life and Work; A Historical and Critical Study*. Standford: Standford University press, 1973.

Lukes, S. 'Alienation and Anomie'. In *Emile Durkheim: Critical Assessments*, Vol. II, edited by P. Hamilton, 77–97. London: Routledge, 1990.

Lynch, G. *The Sacred in the Modern World*. Oxford: Oxford University Press, 2012.

MacNicol, Nicol. *Pandita Ramabai: The Story of Her life*. Calcutta: Association Press, 1926.

Macnicol, Nicol and Vishal Mangalwadi. *What Liberates A Woman? The Story of Pandita Ramabai: A Builder of Modern India* (1926; reprint). New Delhi: Nivedit Good Books, 1996.

Madan, T.N. 'Radhakamal Mukerjee and His Contemporaries: Founding Fathers of Sociology in India'. *Sociological Bulletin* 60, no. 1 (2011): 18–44.

Madelung, Wilferd. *The Succession to Muhammad: A Study of the Early Caliphate*. Cambridge: Cambridge University Press, 1997.

Majul, Cesar Adib. 'Rizal in the 21st Century: The Relevance of His Ideas and Texts'. *Public Policy* 3, no. 1 (1999): 1–21.

Majul, Cesar Adib. 'Rizal's Noli and Fili: Their Relevance to the Coming Millenium'. In *Centennial Lecture Series: Memories, Visions and Scholarship and Other Essays*, edited by Gemino Abad (et al.), 55–75. Quezon City: UP Center for Integrative and Development Studies, 2001.

Mak, Geertje and Berteke Waaldijk. 'Gender, history, and the politics of Florence Nightingale'. In *Doing Gender in Media, Art and Culture*, edited by Rosemarie Buikema and Iris Van Der Tuin. New York: Routledge, 2009.

Manjapra, Kris. *Age of Entanglement; German and Indian Intellectuals Across Empire*. Cambridge: Harvard Historical Studies, 2014.

Mannheim, Karl. *Ideology and Utopia: An Introduction to the Sociology of Knowledge*. London: Routledge and Kegan Paul, 1936.

March, Artemis. 'Female invisibility and in Androcentric Sociological Theory'. *Insurgent Sociologist* XI, no. 2 (1982): 99–107.

Mardin, Şerif. *Religion and Social Change in Modern Turkey: The Case of Bediuzzaman Said Nursi*. Albany: SUNY Press, 1989.

Martindale, D. *The Nature and Types of Sociological Theory*. Boston: Houghton-MiiSin, 1960.

Martineau, Harriet. *Traditions of Palestine*. London: Longman, Rees, Orme, Brown and Green, 1830.

Martineau, Harriet. 'Essay on the Proper Use of the Prospective Faculty'. Vol. 1. In *Miscellanies*, edited by Harriet Martineau, 224–230. Boston: Hilliard, Gray and Company, 1836a.

Martineau, Harriet. *On the Duty of Studying Political Economy*, Vol. 1, in *Miscellanies* translated by Harriet Martineau, 272–287. Boston: Hilliard, Gray and Company, 1836b.

Martineau, Harriet. *Retrospect of Western Travel*. London: Saunders and Otley, 1838.

Martineau, Harriet. *Eastern Life, Present and Past*. Philadelphia: Lea and Blanchard, 1848.

Martineau, Harriet. *British Rule in India*. London: Smith, Elder, 1857.

Martineau, Harriet. 'What is "Social Science"'? Vol. 31. *The Spectator*, 11–20, 1858.

Martineau, Harriet, ed. *The Positive Philosophy of Auguste Comte*. London: Kegan Paul, Trench, Troebner, 1868.

Martineau, Harriet, ed. *The Positive Philosophy of Auguste Comte*. New York: AMS Press, 1893.

Martineau, Harriet. 'Harriet Martineau's America'. In *Society in America*, edited by S.M. Lipset, 4–42. New Brunswick, NJ: Transaction, 1981.

Marx, Karl. 'Entwürfe einer Antwort auf den Brief von V. I. Sassulitsch'. In *Werke*, edited by Karl Marx and Friedrich Engels, Band 19, 384–406. Berlin: Dietz Verlag, 1962.

Marx, Karl. *The Economic and Philosophic Manuscripts of 1844*. New York: International Publishers, 1964.

Marx, Karl. *Precapitalist Economic Formations*. New York: International Publishers, 1965.

Marx, Karl. *Capital: A Critique of Political Economy (Vol. 1) – A Critical Analysis of Capitalist Production*. New York: International Publishers, 1967a.

Marx, Karl. *Capital: A Critique of Political Economy (Vol. 3) – The Process of Capitalist Production as a Whole* New York: International Publishers, 1967b.

Marx, Karl. *Capital* (Vol. 3). London: Lawrence & Wishart, 1970a.

Marx, Karl. *A Contribution to the Critique of Political Economy*. Moscow: Progress Publishers, 1970b.

Marx, Karl and Frederick Engels. *On Colonialism*. Moscow: Progress Publishers, 1972.

Marx, Karl. *Grundrisse: Introduction to the Critique of Political Economy*. New York: Vintage Books, 1973a.

Marx, Karl and Frederick Engels. *Manifesto of the Communist Party*. Peking: Foreign Languages Press, 1973b.

Marx, Karl. 'The British Rule in India'. In *On Colonialism*, edited by Karl Marx and Frederick Engels, 35–41. Moscow: Progress Publishers, 1974a.

Marx, Karl. 'India'. In *On Colonialism*, edited by Karl Marx and Frederick Engels, 77–80. Moscow: Progress Publishers, 1974b.

Marx, Karl. 'The Future Results of the British Rule in India'. In *On Colonialism*, edited by Karl Marx and Frederick Engels, 81–87. Moscow: Progress Publishers, 1974c.

Marx, Karl and Frederick Engels. *The First Indian War of Independence, 1857–1859*. Moscow: Progress Publisher, 1975.

Marx, Karl. *The German Ideology*. New York: International Publishers, 1978.

Marx, Karl and Frederick Engels. *Selected Letters: The Personal Correspondence, 1844–1877*. Boston: Little Brown, 1981.

Marx, Karl. *The 18th Brumaire of Louis Bonaparte*. New York: International Publishers, 1963.

Maunier, René. 'Les idées économiques d'un philosophe arabe au XIVe siècle'. *Revue d'histoire économique et sociale* 6 (1912): 409–419.

McDonald, Lynn. *The Early Origins of the Social Sciences*. Montreal: McGill-Queens University Press, 1993.

McDonald, Lynn. *The Women Founders of the Social Sciences*. Ottawa, Canada: Carleton University Press, 1994.

McDonald, Lynn. *The Women Founders of the Social Sciences*. Montreal: McGill-Queen's UniversityPress, 1996.

McDonald, Lynn. *Women Theorists on Society and Politics*. Waterloo, On: Wilfrid Laurier University Press, 1998a.

McDonald, Lynn. 'Classical Social Theory with the Women Founders Included'. In *Reclaiming the sociological classics*, edited by Charles Camic. Malden, MA: Blackwell Publishers, 1998b.

McDonald, Lynn, eds. *Collected Works of Florence Nightingale* [16-volume project]. Waterloo, Ontario: Wilfrid Laurier University Press, 2001 (to present).

McDonald, Lynn, ed. *Florence Nightingale on Public Health Care*. Waterloo, Ont.: Wilfrid Laurier University Press, 2004.

McDonald, Lynn. 'The Nightingale-Martineau Collaboration: Differences of Philosophy and Religion'. *Sociological Origins* 3, no. 2 (2005): 79–80 & 120.

McDonald, Lynn. 'Florence Nightingale as a Social Reformer'. History Today 56, no. 1 (2006). http://www.historytoday.com/lynn-mcdonald/florence-nightingalesocial-reformer. Retrieved 25 Sep 2013.

McGee, Gary B. 'Latter Rain Falling in the East: Early-Twentieth-Century Pentecostalism in India and the Debate over Speaking in Tongues'. Church History 68, no. 3 (1999): 648–665.

McGirr, Lisa. *Suburban Warriors: The Origins of the New American Right*. Princeton: Princeton University Press, 2002.

McKinnon, Andrew M. 'Elective Affinities of the Protestant Ethic: Weber and the Chemistry of Capitalism'. *Sociological Theory* 28, no. 1 (2010): 108–126.

McLellan, David. *Karl Marx*. Harmondsworth: Penguin, 1978.

Mehring, Franz. *Karl Marx: The Story of His Life*. London: George Allen & Unwin, 1936.

Merad, Ali. 'L'Autobiographie d'Ibn Khaldun'. *IBLA (Institut des Belles Lettres Arabes)* 19, no. 1 (1956): 53–64.

Merton, R. 'Durkheim's Divison of Labour in Society'. *American Journal of Sociology* 40, no. 3 (1934): 318–328.

Merton, R. 'Social Structure and Anomie'. *American Sociological Review* 3, no. 5 (1938): 672–682.

Mestrovic, S.G., ed. 'Durkheim's Concept of Anomie Considered as a "Total" Social Fact'. *The British Journal of Sociology* 38, no. 4 (1987): 567–583.

Mestrovic, S.G. 'Anomie and the Unleashing of the Will'. In *Emile Durkheim and the Reformation of Sociology*. New Jersey: Rowman & Littlefield, 1988.

Michaud, Gerard. 'Caste, Confession et Societe en Syrie: Ibn Khaldoun au Chevet du `Progressisme Arabe'. *Peuples Mediterraneens* 16 (1981): 119–130.

Michie, Jonathan. *The Reader's Guide to the Social Sciences*. Vol. 1. London: New York: Routledge, 2001.

Miliband, R. 'Marx and the State'. In *Socialist Register*, edited by R. Miliband and J. Saville. London: Merlin Press, 1965.

Mills, John. *Carpets in Paintings*. London: National Gallery, 1983.

Mitter, Partha. *The Triumph of Modernism: India's Artists and the Avant-garde, 1922–1947*. London: Reaktion Books, 2007.

Molainville, Barthélemy D'Herbelot de. 'Khaledoun'. In *Bibliotheque Orientale*. Paris, 1697.

Montagne, Robert. *The Berbers: Their Social and Political Organisation*. London: Frank Cass, 1931.

Mukherjee, H. *Benoy Kumar Sarkar-A study*. Calcutta: Shiksha-Tirtha Karyalaya, 1953.

Mukherjee, H. 'Social Thoughts of Benoy Kumar Sarkar'. *Journal of Indian Anthropological Society* 30 (1995): 51–58.

Mukhopadhyaya, A.K. 'Benoy Kumar Sarkar: The Theoretical Foundation of Indian Capitalism'. In *The Bengali Intellectual Tradition from Rammohun Ray to Dhirendranath Sen*, edited by A.K. Mukhopadhyay, 212–234. Calcutta: K.P Bagchi and Company, 1979.

Muslim, Sahih. *Kitab al-Fada'il al-Sahabah* (The Book Pertaining to the Merits of the Companions (Allah Be Pleased With Them) of the Holy Prophet (ص). Accessed at http://www.usc.edu/org/cmje/religious-texts/hadith/mus lim/031-smt.php.

Niebrugge-Brantley Jill and Patricia Lengermann. 'Early Women Sociologists'. In *Classical Sociology*, edited by George Ritzer, 294–328. New York: MacGraw-HIll, 1996.

Niebrugge-Brantley Jill and Patricia Lengermann. *The Women Founders: Sociology and Social Theory 1830–1930*. New York: McGraw-Hill, 1998.

Niebrugge-Brantley Jill and Patricia Lengermann. 'Early Women Sociologists'. In *Classical Sociology*, edited by George Ritzer. New York: McGraw-Hill, 2000.

Niebrugge-Brantley Jill and Patricia Lengermann. 'Back to the Future: Settlement Sociology'. *The American Sociologist* 33, no. 3 (2002): 5–20.

Niebrugge-Brantley, J. and P. Madoo Lengermann. 'Early Women Sociologists and Classical Sociological Theories: 1830–1990'. In *Classical Sociological Theory*, edited by G. Ritz and D. Goodman, 271–300. London: McGraw-Hill, 2004.

Nightingale, Florence. 'Florence Nightingale's Letter of Advice to Bellevue'. *The American Journal of Nursing* 11, no. 5 (1911): 361–363.

Nisbet, Robert. 'Tocquville's Ideal Types'. In *Reconsidering Tocquvelli's Democracy in America*, edited by S. Abraham Eisentadt. New Brunswick, NJ: Rutgers University Press, 1988.

Nisbet, Tom Bottomore and Robert Nisbet, eds. *A History of Sociological Analysis*. London: Heinemann, 1978.

Nursi, Bediuzzaman Said. *The Rays Collection*. Istanbul: Sözler, 1998.

Nursi, Bediuzzaman Said. *Al-Mathanawi al-'Arabi al-Nuri*. Istanbul: Sözler, 1999.

Nursi, Bediuzzaman Said. 'Seeds of Reality'. In Bediuzzaman Said Nursi, *Letters -1928–1932*, 541–554. Istanbul: Sozler, 2001a.

364   **Bibliography**

Nursi, Bediuzzaman Said. *The Damascus Sermon*. Istanbul: Sözler, 2001b.

Nursi, Bediuzzaman Said. *Al-Maktubat*. Istanbul: Sözler, 2003.

Nursi, Bediuzzaman Said. *The Flashes Collection*, From the Risale-I Nur Collection 3. Istanbul: Sözler, 2004a.

Nursi, Bediuzzaman Said. *The Words: On the Nature and Purpose of Man, Life, and All Things*. Istanbul: Sözler, 2004b.

Nursi, Bediuzzaman Said. *Al-Khutbah al-Shamiyyah (The Damascus Sermon)*. Istanbul: Sözler, 2007.

Ocampo, Ambeth. R. 'Rizal's Morga and Views of Philippine History'. *Philippine Studies* 46 (1998): 184–214.

O'Leary, De Lacy. *Arabic Thought and Its Place in History* (revised edition). London: Kegan Paul, 1939.

Oppenheimer, Franz. *System der Soziologie*. Jena: G. Fischer, 1922–1935 (Volume 4).

Orazem, Claudia. *Political Economy and Fiction in the Early Works of Harriet Martineau*. Frankfurt am Main: Peter Lang, 1999.

Ozdemir, Ibrahim. 'Nursi, Said (1877–1960)'. In *The Encyclopedia of Religion and Nature Vol. 1*, edited by Bron Taylor, 1214–1216. London: Thoemmes, 2005.

Ozdemir, Ibrahim. 'Said Nursi and J.P. Sartre: Existence and Man – A Study of the Views of Said Nursi and J.P. Sartre'. 2009. Accessed at http://iozdemirr.blogspot.com/2009/12/said-nursi-and-j-p-sartre.html.

Papadopoulo, Alexandre. *Islam and Muslim Art*. New York: Harry N. Abrams, 1979.

Parsons, T. *The Structure of Social Action* (Vol. III). Glencoe: Free Press, 1937.

Pearce, F. *The Radical Durkheim*. Canada: Canadian Scholar's Press, 2001.

Penner, Louise. *Victorian Medicine and Social Reform: Florence Nightingale among the Novelists (Nineteenth Century Major Lives and Letters)*. Richmond, Texas: Palgrave Macmillan, 2010.

Pickering, M. 'A New Look at Auguste Comte'. In *Reclaiming the Sociological Classics*, edited by C. Camic. Malden: Blackwell Publishers, 1998.

Pickering, W., ed. *Durkheim Today*. New York: Berghahn Books, 2002.

Pickering, M. 'Auguste Comte'. In *The Wiley-Blackwell Companion to Major Social Theorists*, edited by G.R. Stepnisky. Malden: Wiley Blackwell, 2011.

Pickering, W.S.F and H. Martins, eds. *Debating Durkheim*. London; New York: Routledge, 1994.

Pinchanick, Valerie K. *Harriet Martineau: The Woman and Her Work, 1802–1876*. Ann Arbor: University of Michigan Press, 1990.

Pirenne, Henri. *Economy and Social History of Medieval Europe*. New York: Harvest, 1937.

Pirenne, Henri. *A History of Europe*, Vols.1 & 2. Garden City, NY: Double Day Anchor Books, 1956.

Pirenne, Henri. *Medieval Cities, Their Origins and Revival of Trade*, 57 & 76. Princeton: Princeton University Press, 1969.

Poggi, Gianfranco. *The Development of the Modern State*. Stanford, CA: Stanford University Press, 1978.

Poggi, Gianfranco. *Weber: A Short Introduction*. Cambridge: Polity Press, 2006.

Poulantzas, Nicos. *Political Power and Social Classes*. London: New Left Books, 1973.

Pugh, Evelyn L. 'Florence Nightingale and J.S. Mill Debate Women's Rights'. *Journal of British Studies* 21, no. 2 (1982): 118–138.

Pugh, Martin. *The March of the Women: A Revisionist Analysis of the Campaign for Women's Suffrage, 1866–1914*. Oxford: OUP, 2002.

Purgstall, Joseph Freiherr von Hammer 'Extraits d'Ibn Khaledoun'. *Fundgruben des Orients* 6 (1818): 301–307; 362–364.

Purgstall, Joseph Freiherr von Hammer. 'Notice sur l'Introduction a la connaissance de l'histoire, Celebre Ouvrage arabe d'Ibn Khaldoun'. *Journal asiatique* (Paris), 1 ser. 1 (1822): 267–278; Iv, 158–161.

Qummi, Shaykh 'Abbas'. In *Mafatih al-Jinan (The Keys of Paradise)*. Qom: Ansariyan, 2001.

Rabi, Ibrahim Abu. 'Introduction' to *Islam in Modern Turkey: an Intellectual Biography of Bediuzzaman Said Nursi* edited by Sükran Vahide, xiii–xvi. Albany: SUNY Press, 2005.

Ramabai, Pandita. *Stree Dharma Neeti (Morals for women)*, written in Poona, India, June 1882.

Ramabai, Pandita. *'An Autobiographical Account'* (written in England, and reproduced in 1979 as *My Story*., with an introdcution by Shamsundar Manohar Adhav, published by the Christian Institute for Study of Religion and Society, Bangalore), September 1883a.

Ramabai, Pandita. *The Cry of the Indian Woman*. Letter to Sir BartleFrere Saheb Bahadoor, written in England, June 1883b

Ramabai, Pandita. Indian Religion Cheltenham Ladies. College Magazine, No. XIII, Spring 1886.

Ramabai, Pandita. *The High-Caste Hindu Woman*. Philadelphia: J. B. Rodgers Printing Co., 1887.

Ramabai, Pandita. *United Stateschi Lokasthiti ani Pravasavritta*. Bombay: Nirnayasagar Press, 1889.

Ramabai, Pandita. *Famine Experiences*. Kedgaon: Ramabai Mukti Mission, 1897.

Ramabai, Pandita. *To the friends of Mukti School and Mission*. Kedgaon: Ramabai Mukti Mission, 1900.

Ramabai, Pandita. *A Short History of Kripa Sadan*. Kedgaon: Ramabai Mukti Mission, 1903.

Ramabai, Pandita. *A Testimony* of Our Inexhaustible Treasure. Kedgaon: Ramabai Mukti Mission, 1907.

Ramabai, Pandita. *The Word-Seed*. Kedgaon: Ramabai Mukti Mission, 1908.

Ramabai, Pandita. *Marathi Version of the Entire Bible: The Old Testament*. Kedgaon: Ramabai Mukti Mission, 1922.

Ramabai, Pandita. *Marathi Version of the Bible: The New Testament*. Kedgaon: Ramabai Mukti Mission, 1924.

Ramabai, Pandita. *The Peoples of the United States*. Translated and edited by Meera Kosambi. *Bloomington* Indiana University Press, 2003.

Ramanna, Mridula. 'Florence Nightingale and Bombay Presidency'. *Social Scientist* 30, no. 9/10 (2002): 31–46.

Rana, Ratna S.J.B. 'Nepal'. In *Social Sciences in Asia and the Pacific*, edited by UNESCO. 354–373. Paris: UNESCO, 1984.

Reinharz, Shulamit. 'Teaching the History of Women in Sociology: Or Dorothy Swaine Thomas, Wasn't She the Woman Married to William I?'. *The American Sociologist* 20, no. 1 (1989): 87–94.

Reinharz, Shumalit *Feminist Methods in Social Research*. New York: Oxford University Press, 1992.

Reinharz, Shumalit. 'A Contextualised Chronology of Women's Sociological Work'. In *Women's Studies Program*, edited by Shumalit Reinharz. Waltham, MA: Brandeis University, 1993.

Riedesal, Paul L. 'Who Was Harriet Martineau'. *Journal of the History of Sociology* 3 (Spring–Summer 1981): 63–80.

Ritzer, George. *Sociological Theory*. New York: Alfred A Knopf, 1983a.

Ritzer, George. 'The "McDonaldization" of Society'. *Journal of American Culture* 6, no. 1 (1983b): 100–107.

Ritzer, George. *Classical Sociological Theory*. New York: McGraw Hill, 1996.

Ritzer, George and Douglas J Goodman, eds. *Sociological Theory* (6th edition). Boston: McGraw Hill, 2003.

Rizal, José. *One Hundred Letters of José Rizal to his Parents, Brother, Sisters, Relatives*. Manila: Philippine National Historical Society, 1959.

Rizal, José. *The Lost Eden* (Noli me Tangere). Translated by Leon Ma. Guerrro. New York: W. W. Norton & Co., 1961.

Rizal, José. 'To the Filipnos'. In *Historical Events of the Philippine Islands*, edited by Dr Antonio de Morga, Published in Mexico in 1609, recently brought to light and annotated by Jose Rizal, preceded by a prologue by Dr Ferdinand Blumentritt, Writings of Jose Rizal (Vol. VI). Manila: National Historical Institute, 1890/1962.

Rizal, José. 'Filipino Farmers'. In *Political and Historical Writings*, 19–22. Manila: National Historical Institute, 1963a.

Rizal, José. 'The Indolence of the Filipino'. In *Political and Historical Writings*, 111–139. Manila: National Historical Institute, 1963b.

Rizal, José. 'Message to the Young Women of Malolos'. In *Political and Historical Writings*, 12–18. Manila: National Historical Institute, 1963c.

Rizal, José. 'The Truth for All'. In *Political and Historical Writings*, 31–38. Manila: National Historical Institute, 1963d.

Rizal, José. *Dr. José Rizal's Mi Último Adiós in Foreign and Local Translations*. Manila: National Historical Institute, 1989.

Rizal, José. 'The First Letter of Rizal'. In *The Rizal-Pastells Correspondence*, edited by Raul J. Bonoan, 121–125. Quezon City: Ateneo de Manila Press, 1994.

Robinson, Catherine A. *Tradition and Liberation: The Hindu Tradition in the Indian Women's Movement*. New York: St. Martin's Press, 1999.

Roma Chatterji, 'The Nationalist Sociology of Benoy Kumar Sarkar'. In *Anthropology in the East: Founders of Indian Sociology and Anthropology*, edited by Satish Deshpande and Patricia Uberoi Nandini Sundar. Calcutta: Seagull, 2008.

Rosenthal, Franz. 'Ibn Khaldun's Life'. In *Ibn Khaldun: The Muqadimmah – An Introduction of History*, Vol. 1, 2 & 3. Translated by Franz Rosenthal, xxvii–lxvii. London: Routledge & Kegan Paul, 1967.

Rossi, Alice S. 'The First Woman Sociologist: Harriet Martineau (1802–1876)'. In *The Feminist Papers: From Adams to de Beauvoir*, 118–124. New York: Bantam Books, 1973.

Roussillon, Alain. 'La représentation de l'identité par les discours fondateurs de la sociologie Turque et Egyptienne: Ziya Gökalp et 'Ali Abd Al-Wahid Wafi'. In *Modernisation et mobilisation sociale II, Egypte-Turquie*, 31–65. Cairo: Dossier du CEDEJ, 1992.

Sanders, Valerie. *Reason Over Passion: Harriet Martineau and the Victorian Novel*. New York: St. Martin's Press, 1986.

Sanders, Valerie and Gaby Weiner, eds. *Harriet Martineau and the Birth of Disciplines*. London: Routledge, 2016.

Sarkar, Benoy Kumar. *Chinese Religion Through Hindu Eyes: A Study in the Tendencies of Asiatic Mentality (With An Introduction By Wu Ting-Fang)*. Shanghai: Commercial Press, 1916a.

Sarkar, Benoy Kumar. *Love in Hindu Literature*. New: Award Publishing House, 1916b.

Sarkar, Benoy Kumar. *Hindu Achievements in Exact Science A Study in the History of Scientific Development*. New York: Longmans, Green and Co., 1918.

Sarkar, Benoy Kumar. *The Positive Background Of Hindu Sociology*. Allahabad: Panini Office, 1914 & 1921 (published in 2 parts).

Sarkar, Benoy Kumar. *The Futurism of Young Asia, and Other Essays on the Relations Between the East and the West*. Leipzig: Markert & Petters, 1922.

Sarkar, Benoy Kumar. *The Sociology of Indian: Socialism and Feminism*. Calcutta: Calcutta University Press, 1936.

Sarkar, Benoy Kumar. *The Politics of Boundaries and Tendencies in International Relations: Analysis of Post-War World Forces*. Calcutta: N. M. Ray Chowdhury & Co., 1938.

Sarkar, Benoy Kumar. *The Political Institutions and Theories of the Hindus: A Study in Comparative Politics*. Calcutta: Chuckervertty Chatterjee & Company Limited, 1939.

Sarkar, Benoy Kumar. *Villages and Towns as Social Patterns*. Calcutta: Chuckervertty Chatterjee & Company Limited, 1941.

Sarkar, Benoy Kumar. *Political Philosophies Since 1905* (Vol. 1). Lahore: Creative India, 1942.

Sarkar, Benoy Kumar. *India in America: The Diary of Professor Benoy Sarkar's Travels and Lectures in the U.S.A*. Michigan: Craft Press, March 7–June 22, 1949a.

Sarkar, Indira. *Social Thought in Bengal, 1757–1947: A Bibliography of Bengali Men and Women of Letters*. Calcutta: Calcutta Oriental Book Agency, 1949b.

Sarkar, Indira. *My Life With Prof. Benoy Kumar Sarkar*. Translated by Indira Palit from German. Calcutta: Prabhat Press, 1977.

Sarkar, Benoy Kumar. *An Encyclopaedic Survey of the Political Philosophies Since 1905*. Delhi: Sri Satguru Publications, 1986.

Sarkar, Benoy Kumar. *Folk elements in Hindu culture*. New Delhi: Cosmo Publications, 1987.

Sarkar, Benoy Kumar. *The Bliss of a Moment*. Reprint. Kessinger Publishing, 2006.

Sarkar, Benoy Kumar. *The Science of History and the Hope of Mankind.* [reprint]. BiblioLife, 2009

Sartori, Andrew. 'Beyond Culture-Contact And Colonial Discourse: "Germanism"'. In *An Intellectual History for India*, edited by Shruti Kapila and C.A. Bayly, 68–84. New Delhi: Cambridge University Press, 2010.

Scharff, R.C. *Comte After Positivism.* Cambridge; New York: Cambridge University Press, 1995.

Sengupta, Padmini S. *Pandita Ramabai Saraswati: Her Life and Work.* Bombay: Asia Publishing House, 1970.

Shah,A.B., ed. *The Letters and Correspondence of Pandita Ramabai.* Bombay: Maharashtra State Board for Literature and Culture, 1977.

Shah, A.B. 'Pandita Ramabai: A Rebel in Religion'. In *Religion and Society in India*, edited by A.B. Shah. Bombay: Somaiya, 1981.

Shaw, Stanford K. and Ezel Kural Shaw. *History of the Ottoman Empire, Vol. II – Reform, Revolution, and Republic: The Rise of Modern Turkey 1808–1975.* Cambridge: Cambridge University Press, 1977.

Showalter, Elaine. 'Florence Nightingale's Feminist Complaint: Women, Religion, and "Suggestions for Thought"'. *Signs* 6, no. 3 (1981): 395–412.

Sichrovsky, Harry. *Ferdinand Blumentritt: An Austrian Life for the Philippines: The Story of José Rizal's Closest Friend and Companion.* Manila: National Historical Institute, 1987.

Simon, Heinrich. *Ibn Khaldun's Science of Human Culture.* Lahore: SH. Muhammad Ashraf, 1978.

Simpsons, E.D. *Division of Labour.* New York: Macmillan, 1933.

Singer, Milton. *When a Great Tradition Modernizes. An Anthropological Approach to Indian Civilization.* Chicago and London: The University of Chicago Press, 1972.

Sinha, Vineeta. 'Reconceptualising the Social Sciences in Non-Western Settings: Challenges and Dilemmas'. *Southeast Asian Journal of Social Science* 25, no. 1 (1997): 167–182.

Sinha, Vineeta and Syed Farid Alatas. 'Teaching Classical Sociological Theory in Singapore: The Context of Eurocentrism'. *Teaching Sociology* 29, no. 3 (2001a): 316–331.

Sinha, Vineeta. 'Decentering Social Sciences in Practise through Individual Acts and Choices'. *Current Sociology* 51, no. 1 (2003): 7–26.

Sinha, Vineeta. 'Sarkar, Benoy Kumar (1887–1949)'. In *Blackwell Encyclopedia of Sociology*, edited by George Ritzer. Malden: Blackwell Publishing, 2006.

Smith, Fances T. 'Florence Nightingale: Early Feminist'. *The American Journal of Nursing* 81, no. 5 (1981): 1020–1024.

Smith, Dorothy E. *The Everyday World as Problematic: A Feminist Sociology*. Boston: Northeastern University Press, 1987.

Smith, Christian. *The Emergence of Liberation Theology: Radical Religion and Social Movement Theory*. Chicago: University of Chicago Press, 1991.

South Asian American Digital Archive (SAADA). http://www.saadigitalarchive. org/entity/benoy-kumar-sarkar.

Spellberg, Denise A. 'Could a Muslim be President? An Eighteenth Century Constitutional Debate'. *Eighteenth Century Studies* 39, no. 4 (2006): 485–506.

Spender, Dale. 'Harriet Martineau'. In *Women of Ideas and What Men Have Done to Them*, edited by Dale Spender, 125–135. London: Routledge & Kegn Paul, 1982.

Sperber, Jonathan. *Karl Marx: A Nineteenth-Century Life*. New York: W. W. Norton, 2013.

Spickard, J.V. 'Tribes and Cities: Towards and Islamic Sociology of Religion'. *Social Compass* 48, no.1 (2001): 103–116.

Strachey, Lytton. *Eminent Victorians: Cardinal Manning, Florence Nightingale, Dr. Arnold, General Gordon*. London: Chatto & Windus, 1928a.

Strachey, Ray. *'The Cause': A Short History of the Women's Movement in Great Britain*. London: G. Bell & Sons Ltd, 1928b.

Sunar, Lutfi. *Marx and Weber on Oriental Societies: In the Shadow of Western Modernity*. Surrey: Ashgate, 2014.

Symonds, Richard. *Far Above Rubies; The Women Uncommemorated by the Church of England*. Herefordshire: Fowler Wright Books, 1993.

Symonds, Richard. 'Ramabai, Pandita Mary Saraswati (1858–1922)'. In *Oxford Dictionary of National Biography*. Oxford: Oxford University Press, 2004.

Szacki, J. *History of Sociological Thought*. Westport: Greenwood Press, 1979.

Talbi, M. 'Ibn Khaldūn'. In *The Encyclopaedia of Islam (vol. iii)*, 835–831. Leiden: Brill, 1971.

Talbi, M. *Ibn Haldun et l'histoire*. Tunis: MTD, 1973.

Terry, James L. 'Bringing Women . . . A Modest Proposal'. *Teaching Sociology* 10, no. 2 (1983): 251–261.

Tharu, Susie and K. Lalita, eds. *Women Writing in India, 600 B.C to the Present*, vols. 1 & 2. New Delhi: Oxford University Press, 1995.

The Koran. Translated by George Sales, 5th edition. Philadelphia: J.W. Moore, 1856.

Thomas, C.Y. *The Rise of the Authoritarian State in Peripheral Societies*. New York & London: Monthly ReviewPress, 1984.

Thomas Michel, S.J. 'Grappling with Modern Civilization: Said Nursi's Interpretive Key'. In *Said Nursi's Views on Muslim-Christian Understanding*, edited by Thomas. F. Michel, 79–108. Istanbul: Sözler, 2005.

Timasheff, S.N. *Sociological Theory: Its Nature and Growth*. New York: Random House, 1967.

Tiryakian, E. 'Montesquieu's Contribution to the Rise of Social Science (1892)'. In *Montesquieu and Rousseau: Forerunners of Sociology*, (R. Manheim, Trans., Vol. 9). Ann Arbor: The University of Michigan Press, 1960.

Tiryakian, E. 'Revisiting Sociology's First Classic: The Division of Labour in Society and its Actuality'. *Sociological Forum* 9, no. 1 (1994a): 3–16.

Tiryakian, E. 'Revisiting Sociology's First Classic: *The Division of Labour in Society* and its Actuality'. *Sociological Forum* 19, no. 1 (1994b): 3–15.

Torr, D., ed. *The Correspondence of Marx and Engels*New York: International Publishers, 1942.

Truzzi, Marcello. 'Definition and Dimensions of the Occult: Towards a Sociological Perspective'. *Journal of Popular Culture* 5 (1971): 635/7–646/18

Turner, Bryan S. 'Avineri's View of Marx's Theory of Colonialism: Israel'. *Science and Society* 40, no. 4 (1976): 385–409.

Turner, Bryan S. *Marx and the End of Orientalism*. London: George Allen & Unwin, 1978.

Vahide, Şükran. *Islam in Modern Turkey: an Intellectual Biography of Bediuzzaman Said Nursi*. edited and with an introduction by Ibrahim M. Abu-Rabi. Albany: SUNY Press, 2005.

Vahide, Şükran. 'Proof of the Resurrection of the Dead: Said Nursi's Approach'. In *Theodicy and Justice in Modern Islamic Thought: The Case of Said Nursi*, edited by Ibrahim M. Abu-Rabi', 41–52. Surrey: Ashgate, 2010.

Valdez, Maria Stella S. *Doctor Jose Rizal and the Writing of His Story*. Manila: Rex Bookstore, 2007.

Vallee, Gerard, ed. *Florence Nightingale on Social Change in India*. Wifrid Laurier University Press, 2007.

Vicinus, Martha. '"Tactful Organising and Executive Power": Biographies of Florence Nightingale for Girls'. In *Telling Lives in Science: Essays on Scientific Biography*, edited by Michael Shortland and Richard Yeo. New York: CUP, 1996.

Viswanathan, Gauri. 'Silencing Heresy'. In *Outside the Fold: Conversion, Modernity, and Belief*. Princeton: Princeton University Press, 1998.

Wafi, Wahid. 'Ali 'Abd al. *Al-falsafah al-ijtima'iyyah li Ibn Khaldun wa Aujust Kumt*. Cairo, 1951.

Wafi, Wahid. 'Ibn Khaldūn, awwal mu'assis li 'ilm al-ijtimā''. In *A'mal Mahrajan Ibn Khaldun* (Proceedings of the Ibn Khaldun Symposium), 63–78. Cairo: National Centre for Social and Criminological Research, 1962.

Webb, R.K. *Harriet Martineau: A Radical Victorian*. London: Heinemann, 1960.

Weber, Alfred, *History of Philosophy*. New York: Charles Scribner's Son, 1925.

Weber, Max. 'Science as a Vocation'. In Max Weber, *From Max Weber: Essays on Sociology*. Translated and edited by H.H. Gerth and C. Wright Mills, 129–146. New York: Oxford University Press, 1946a.

Weber, Max. *From Max Weber: Essays in Sociology*. Translated and edited by H. H. Gerth and C. Wright Mills. New York: Oxford University Press, 1946b.

Weber, Max. 'The Social Psychology of the World Religions'. In *From Max Weber: Essays on Sociology*, translated and edited by H.H. Gerth and C. Wright Mills, 267–301. New York: Oxford University Press, 1946c.

Weber, Max. *The Methodology of the Social Sciences*. Translated and edited by Shils, Edward A. Shils and Henry A. Finch. New York: Free Press, 1949.

Weber, Max. *The Religion of China: Confucianism and Taoism*. New York: The Free Press, 1951.

Weber, Max. *Ancient Judaism*. Translated and edited by Hans H. Gerth and Don Martindale. New York: The Free Press, 1952.

Weber, Max. *The Religion of India: The Sociology of Hinduism and Buddhism*. Translated and edited by Hans H. Gerth and Don Martindale. New York: The Free Press, 1958a.

Weber, Max. *The Protestant Ethic and the Spirit of Capitalism*. Translated by Talcott Parsons. New York: Charles Scribner's Sons, 1958b.

Weber, Max. *The Religion of India: The Sociology of Hinduism and Buddhism*. Translated and edited by Hans Gerth and Don Martindale. New York: The Free Press, 1958c.

Weber, Marianne. *Max Weber: A Biography*. Translated from the German and edited by Harry Zohn. New York: Wiley, 1975.

Weber, Max. *Economy and Society: An Outline of Interpretive Sociology*. Vols.1 & 2, edited by G. Roth, and C. Wittich. Berkeley, Los Angeles & London: University of California Press, 1978.

Weber, Max. *General Economic History*. Translated by Frank Knight. New Brunswick & London: Transaction Books, 1981.

Weiner, Gaby. *Introduction* (Vol. 1). In *Harriet Martineau's Autobiography*, edited by H. Martineau, 1–20. London: Virago press, 1983.

Whimster, Sam, ed. *The Essential Weber: A Reader*. London: Routledge, 2004.

Whittaker, Elvi Waik and Virginia L. Olesen. 'Why Florence Nightingale?' *The American Journal of Nursing* 67, no. 11 (1967): 2338–2341.

Wikipedia. 'Islamic Art'. http://en.wikipedia.org/wiki/Islamic_art#Rugs_and_carpets. 2017. Accessed on January 19, 2014.

Williams, Keith. 'Reappraising Florence Nightingale'. *BMJ: British Medical Journal* 337, no. 7684 (2008): 1461–1463.

Woodham Smith, Cecil. *Florence Nightingale*. London: Constable,1951.

Wilson, T.A., ed. *Reappraising Durkheim for the Study and Teaching of Religion Today*. Boston: Brill, 2002.

Wolf, Eric. *Europe and the People Without History*. Berkeley: University of California Press, 1982.

Yang, C.K. 'Introduction'. In *The Religion of China: Confucianism and Taoism*, edited by Max Weber, xiii–xliii. New York: The Free Press, 1951.

Yates, Gayle G., ed. *Harriet Martineau on Women*. New Brunswick, NJ: Rutgers University Press, 1985.

Zachariah, Benjamin. 'Transfers, Formations, Transformations? Some Programmatic Notes on Fascism in India'. In *Cultural Transfers in Dispute: Representations in Asia, Europe and the Arab World Since the Middle Ages*, edited by Jörg Feuchter et al, 167–192, 2011.

Zaide, S. 'Historiography in the Spanish Period'. In *Philippine Encyclopedia of the Social Sciences*, 4–19. Quezon City: Philippine Social Science Council, 1993.

Zaleznik, Abraham. 'A Change Agent: Florence Nightingale and Medical Reform'. In *Hedgehogs and Foxes: Character, Leadership and Command in Organizations*. New York: Palgrave Macmillan, 2008.

Zeitlin, I.M. *Ideology and the Development of Sociological Theory* (Sixth edition). Upper Saddle River: Prentice Hall, 1997.

Ziemann, W. and M. Lanzendorfer. 'The State in Peripheral Societies'. In *Socialist Register*, 143–177. London: Merlin Press, 1977.

Index

© The Author(s) 2017
S.F. Alatas, V. Sinha, *Sociological Theory Beyond the Canon*,
DOI 10.1057/978-1-137-41134-1

Letters of Florence Nightingale
(Monteiro), 273
*Letters on the Laws of Man's Nature
and Development* (Martineau
and Atkinson), 82
Liberal democracy of
America, 100–101
Liberty, Martineau on, 105–106
Lipset, S. M., 88
Lobbying process, 72
Locke, John, 230
London Statistical Society, 270
Lord-vassal relationship, 52
*A Lost Commander: Florence
Nightingale* (Andrews), 273

M

Macionis, Linda M., 191
MacNicol, Nicol, 241
MacRae, Janet A., 278–279
Madras entrepreneurs, 128
Maghreb, 26
Maharashtra, India, 238
Majul, 168
Malay, 130, 169, 218
Malda, India, 303
Malpas, Phyllis, 284–285
Malthus, Thomas, 80, 86
Mana-yi harfi, 210, 233–234
Mana-yi ismi, 210, 233
'A Manchester Strike'
(Martineau), 88
Manifesto of the Communist Party
(Marx and Engels), 68
Manjapra, 322–323, 331
Manners
Martineau on, 88–93

Mannheim, Karl, 7, 105, 312
Manorama, 238
Manu's Code of Laws, 255
Marathi, 238, 240,
249, 259
Marinids, 26, 38
Marks, Stephen, 191
Marriage
Nightingale on, 280–290
The Marriage of the Virgin, 229
Martineau, Harriet
on American society, 97–103
compromised feminism, 93–97
Comte and, 91
deafness, 79, 99
Durkheim and, 87, 91, 104
early life, 79–81
on education, 83–86
fiction as social
commentary, 86–88
on freedom, 103–106
on happiness, 103–106
health problems, 90
on observation, 89–90
political economy tales, 83–84,
86
positivism, 80, 82, 92
science of morals and
manners, 88–93
sociological theories, 81–85
travels, 88, 98–99
Unitarianism, 80
works, 80–81
writing, 79–80, 93, 97
Yates on, 93
Marxism, 58, 60–61, 71, 75
Marxists, 75, 326
Marxist theories, 172

See also Hindu women
Woodham-Smith, Cecil, 271,
280–281
'The Word Seed' (Ramabai), 241
World War I, 172,
226
Wundt, William, 172
Wu Ting Fang, 312–313

Printed by Printforce, the Netherlands